Outlawry, Governance, and Law in Medieval England

AMERICAN UNIVERSITY STUDIES

SERIES IX
HISTORY

Vol. 206

PETER LANG
New York · Washington, D.C./Baltimore · Bern
Frankfurt am Main · Berlin · Brussels · Vienna · Oxford

MELISSA SARTORE

Outlaawry, Governance, and Law in Medieval England

PETER LANG
New York · Washington, D.C./Baltimore · Bern
Frankfurt am Main · Berlin · Brussels · Vienna · Oxford

Library of Congress Cataloging-in-Publication Data

Sartore, Melissa, author.
Outlawry, governance, and law in medieval England / Melissa Sartore.
pages cm. — (American University Studies IX : History; volume 206)
Includes bibliographical references and index.
1. Exile (Punishment)—England—History. 2. Outlaws—England—
History. 3. Common law—England—History. 4. Great Britain—
History—1066–1687. 5. Law, Medieval. I. Title.
KD7885.E95S37 345.42009'02—dc23 2013032454
ISBN 978-1-4331-2357-3 (hardcover)
ISBN 978-1-4539-1218-8 (e-book)
ISSN 0740-0462

Bibliographic information published by **Die Deutsche Nationalbibliothek**.
Die Deutsche Nationalbibliothek lists this publication in the "Deutsche
Nationalbibliografie"; detailed bibliographic data is available
on the Internet at http://dnb.d-nb.de/.

29 Broadway, 18th floor, New York, NY 10006
www.peterlang.com

Table of Contents

Chapter 1: Outlaws, outlawry, and the complexities of language and practice 7

Chapter 2: Outlawry, exile, and banishment in Anglo-Saxon England 19

Chapter 3: Outlawry, exile, and imprisonment in Norman and Anglo-Norman governance and law 41

Chapter 4: Outlawry, kingship and legal reform during the reign of Henry II 77

Chapter 5: Outlawry, abjuration, and imprisonment up to the personal rule of Henry III 105

Chapter 6: Henry III and the customs, laws, and politics of outlawry and imprisonment during the thirteenth century 137

Chapter 7: Edwardian legislation, the end of the eyre, and the position of outlawry at the end of the thirteenth century 177

Chapter 8: Reassessing outlawry in governance and law in medieval England 211

Index 229

Bibliography 235

Chapter 1: Outlaws, outlawry, and the complexities of language and practice

According to the tenth-century laws of King Edmund (939-946 AD), "if any one shed a Christian man's blood, let him not come into the king's presence…ere he go to penance." Failure of the *manslaga* (or "man-slayer") to atone and make amends could result not only in exclusion from the presence of the king, but perhaps even in exile and outlawry, or pilgrimage and excommunication, thus making the act of homicide an event that resulted in exclusion from one's relationship with King and God alike.[1] Centuries later, during the judicial eyre of 1286, a suspected killer was brought before royal justices at Cambridgeshire and refused to place himself upon the country for judgment. As a result, he was thrown into prison, forced to endure the harsh prison *forte et dure* until pleading to the charges against him. Prison *forte et dure*, or "hard and strong imprisonment" was a form of imprisonment in which wrong-doers were physically laden with heavy fetters and given few provisions to survive.[2] Coercive imprisonment was made possible by the widespread expansion of prisons and gaols since the earlier reforms of Henry II, indicative of the trend by which legal processes geared toward exclusion and exile had given way to processes geared toward incarceration, coercion, and containment.

How did actions against wrongdoers in Anglo-Saxon England such as exile, banishment, and outlawry, transition to the widespread use of gaols and prisons in the administration of the English common law in the late thirteenth century? The processes of exclusion, namely outlawry, defined as the action of declaring a person to be outside the protection of the law; exile and banishment, or enforced removal from the land according to an edict or sentence; and abjuration

---

1 I Edmund 3, II Edmund 4, 6; *Die Gesetze der Angelsachsen*, ed. F. Liebermann, vols 1-3, Halle, 1903-1916, vol. 1: 184-190; P. Wormald, *The Making of English Law: King Alfred to the Twelfth Century, Volume I: Legislation and its Limits* (Oxford, UK: Blackwell Publishers Ltd., 1999), 312, 324-325.

2 London, The National Archives, JUST 1/92, m. 12 (1286); H.R.T. Summerson, "The Early Development of *Peine Forte et Dure*," *Law, Litigants, and the Legal Profession: Papers Presented to the Fourth British Legal History Conference at the University of Birmingham 10-13 July 1979*, eds E. W. Ives & A. H. Manchester. Royal Historical Society Studies in History series vol. 36, (London, UK: Humanities Press, 1983), 116-125; T.FT. Plucknett, *Concise History of the Common Law*, 2nd edn. (Rochester, NY: Lawyers Cooperative Publishing Co., 1936), 118-119.

of the realm (or a town), an oath to leave an area forever, were soon supplanted and supplemented with various forms of imprisonment, the condition of being kept in captivity or confinement and forcible deprived of personal liberty. This work explores the movement from outlawry, exile, and banishment to the emergent use of imprisonment in medieval England.

From the late tenth through the thirteenth centuries outlawry held an essential place within political and legal practices in medieval England. Contrary to the dominant narrative which sees the rise of imprisonment as a progressive response to the older modes of outlawry and exile, this project argues that the older exclusionary processes actually facilitated the transition to systems of authority, law, and order grounded in the use of imprisonment. Outlawry and exile were such strong, effective processes resistant to control by royal authority that the Crown was forced to adapt and innovate in response, specifically with the use of imprisonment.

Problems and Perspectives of Outlawry

Outlawry, exile, and banishment have long histories dating back to ancient times, and vary in duration and social context.[3] Outlawry, banishment, and exile were methods of controlling order and governance exercised in England from the Anglo-Saxon period to the eighteenth century. These mechanisms were used by judicial authorities as tools of legal and social regulation as well as instruments of political control.

Outlawry in England has been considered the alternative judicial procedure for systems lacking a centralized police force and imprisonment facilities and is identified as weak, a representation of legal and governmental failure unable to control society and bring about justice. T.F.T. Plucknett states "the dreadful penalty of outlawry was originally the last resort of criminal law."[4] According to Pollock and Maitland, outlawry was "the last weapon of ancient law" and a sign of weak law. Pollock and Maitland argue that the earliest form or the "old law"

---

3 Laura Narpran, "Introduction," *Exile in the Middle Ages, Selected Proceedings from the International Medieval Congress, University of Leeds, 8-11 July 2002*, eds L. Napran and E. van Houts. (International Medieval Research, Vol. 13). Turnhout: Brepols, 2002: 1-9. Asceticism, a self-imposed form of religious exile, was important with respect to the development of monasticism, and excommunication, a denunciation by the Church, are two forms of exclusion which will not be discussed in-depth here.

4 T.F.T. Plucknett, *A Concise History of the Common Law*. 5th edn. (London, UK: Butterworth & Co. (Publishers) Ltd., 1956), 385.

of outlawry (that was based in community involvement) was characterized by arbitrariness, but the practice as a whole was the root of many "pure" and "afflictive" punishments, such as the death penalty, and imprisonment, (which has been argued were emendations of elements of outlawry.)[5] An outlaw forfeited all life, limb, lands, and goods, but as law and kingship grew stronger, the fate of many criminals fell under the king's discretion and they were subjected to banishment, abjuration, or forfeiture.[6] Maurice Keen echoes this sentiment, stating that the sentence of outlawry "implied an admission of weakness on the part of the law itself. You have defied us, the Law said to Outlawry, therefore we will disown you." [7]

Outlawry existed alongside other methods of punishment, namely, banishment, exile, abjuration, and imprisonment. Outlawry, banishment and exile were consistently used, although their forms varied and transitioned, and collectively they represent the political and judicial methods of exclusion. There is, however, great difficulty in definition and dissemination of the individual practices. Pollock and Maitland argue that true exile was not known in medieval English law. Rather, a criminal could flee to a church and plead sanctuary and was then allowed to abjure the realm. Other criminals were allowed to abjure the realm without the sanctuary element, and there are also some accounts of a man abjuring a town. When an individual pled sanctuary, he or she was given the option to go to trial or abjure. If he abjured, he "hurried dressed in pilgrim's guise to the port that was assigned to him, and left England, being bound by his oath never to return. His lands escheated; his chattels were forfeited, and if he came back his fate was that of an outlaw."[8]

Scholarship on the history of exile, however limited, offers many of the insights into the politics of exclusion and the social, judicial, and cultural role of exiles. Events of exile and ostracism as an institution in Ancient Greece reveal how ancient Greeks perceived their historical past as well as their relationship to their present and future:

> Through the institution of ostracism, not only did the Athenians define themselves in relation to the past history of exile by linking political power with control over deci-

5 F. Pollock and F.W. Maitland, *The History of English Law Before the Time of Edward I.* vols 1-2. 2nd edn (Washington D.C.: Lawyers" Literary Club, 1959), vol. 2: 461.

6 Pollock and Maitland, *History of English Law*, vol. 2: 451; 461; 464-467.

7 Pollock and Maitland, *History of English Law*, vol. 1: 49; M.H. Keen, *The Outlaws of Medieval Legend* (London, UK: Routledge and Kegan Paul, Ltd., 1987), 9-10.

8 Pollock and Maitland, *History of English Law*, vol. 2: 518 and 590.

> sions of exile, but they also marked themselves off from that prior history in both ideology and practice by using the power of expulsion with moderation.[9]

The conceptual boundaries created by exile and ostracism helped to create and reinforce culture and identity within Ancient Greek society, an idea applicable to the role of exile and outlawry in England in the Middle Ages. Similarly,

> ...decisions about who is included or excluded from a community are always bound up with political power and that, in some sense, political power is the power to determine who shall and shall not be a member of a community.[10]

The struggle to control society in terms of law and politics from the tenth through the thirteenth century in England is a key component to the overall concept of authority explored here. In *The Politics of Exile in Renaissance Italy*, Catherine Shaw surveys the role of exiles within and among the political communities and regional states of fifteenth century Italy, revealing the "persistent political fragmentation...survival of local particularism...and the disunity of political elites" that characterized a society in which political exiles were common.[11] Exiles played an important role in politics and society and were of great concern to both the governments that banished them and the leaders of the lands to which they fled, demonstrated by efforts by the former to control where an exile was allowed to flee and active use of exiles against their regional rivals by the latter. The emphasis on the existence and importance of exiles in society as demonstrations of political efficacy and local strength found here are again pertinent to investigations of exclusionary practices in England.

Outlawry in Medieval England: Origins, Terminology, and Application

The origins of outlawry as a practice in England are unknown but it has been argued that the practice was introduced by the Danes who invaded northern England in the ninth and tenth centuries. According to Scandinavian and Icelandic

---

9 S. Forsdyke, *Exile, Ostracism, and Democracy: The Politics of Expulsion in Ancient Greece*. (Princeton, NJ and Oxford, UK: Princeton UP, 2005), 5.

10 Forsdyke, 8.

11 Catherine Shaw, *Politics of Exile in Renaissance Italy* (Cambridge, UK: Cambridge UP, 2000), 238. Her assertion that the number of political exiles was on the rise in Italy during the second half of the fifteenth century counters the notion that the emerging balance of power among Italian states resulted in a decline in exiles proposed by Randolph Starn in *Contrary Commonwealth: The Theme of Exile in Medieval and Renaissance Italy* (Berkeley and Los Angeles, CA: University of California Press, 1982).

sagas, outlawry provided a means to justifiably kill an offender while remaining within the confines of customary law. Obtaining a proclamation of outlawry was one way by which the revenge impulses of a feuding culture found validation in law and society.[12] Outlawry could be punishment in and of itself, specifically in instances that involved "public and serious harm."[13]

In pre-Conquest England, outlawry was often indistinguishable from exile and banishment. Their respective uses often depended on the context and form of any particular historical texts. Outlawry has been described as a more local, smaller scale equivalent to the banishments performed by royal authorities.[14] Outlawry required forfeiture of goods to the king and liability to be killed with impunity. An outlaw was stripped of any property and was essentially a "friend-less" and "lawless" man. He had no more rights than a hunted animal and was said, in a colorful turn of phrase, to wear the "wolf's head," supposedly because the original price for the life of an outlaw was identical to that of a wolf.[15]

With increased use and royal interest, outlawry became more administrative in nature. By the thirteenth century, the distinctions between outlawry, exile, and banishment were clear in matters of law and politics. Outlawry as a legal process was used to compel people to stand trial and as an alternative to pecuniary payment as well as in response to serious crime and wrongdoing. If an outlaw

12 W.I. Miller, "In Defense of Revenge" in *Medieval Crime and Social Control*, eds B.A. Hanawalt and D. Wallace. Medieval Cultures vol. 16. (Minneapolis, MN: University of Minnesota Press, 1999): 70-89, at 79; See also W.I. Miller, *Bloodtaking and Peacemaking: Feud, Law and Society in Saga Iceland* (Chicago, IL: University of Chicago Press, 1990), 238-239.

13 C. Calisse, *A History of Italian Criminal Law*, Continental Legal History Series, vol. 8, (1928), 301.

14 E. van Houts, " L"Exile dans l"Espace Anglo-Normand," in *La Normandie et l"Angleterre au Moyen Age, 4-7 Octobre 2001 Colloque Cerisy-la Salle*, ed. V. Gazeau (Turnhout, Belgium: Brepols, 2003): 116-127. In her discussion of Anglo-Norman exile, Van Houts claims that eleventh and twelfth century exile in the Anglo-Norman realm was used to provide time and space and allow for the parties to calm down and reconsider the matter. E. van Houts, "The Vocabulary of Exile and Outlawry in the North Sea Area around the First Millenium," in *Exile in the Middle Ages*, eds. L. Napran and E. van Houts (Turnhout, Brepols, 2004): 13-28. Van Houts discusses the similarities between Scandinavian, Norman and Anglo-Saxon terminology for exile and outlawry. To illustrate the complexities of terminology, see T.S. Jones, "The Outlawry of Earl Godwin" in *Medieval Outlaws: Ten Tales in Modern English*, ed.T.H. Ohlgren. (Stroud, Gloucesteshire, UK: Sutton Publishing, 1998): 1-11 at 3 where Jones does not even attempt to distinguish between outlawry, exile, and banishment as they appear in Bede and the Anglo-Saxon Chronicles.

15 Keen, *Medieval Outlaws*, 9.

was brought back into the law, he was reborn; he acquired new rights but did not have the ability to assert any of the rights he had prior to being an outlaw. [16] Because of the changes within the process of outlawry and its expanded use, many men were outlawed without proof of guilt or intentional contumacy and "there was therefore great need for royal writs inlawing an outlaw."[17]

A practice so common and engrained in English society deserves close study, but outlawry is conspicuous in its absence from discussions of the formation of English common law. Doris Stenton rightly points out that every criminal roll of the thirteenth century contains many references to outlawry. H.R.T. Summerson, for instance, argues that outlawry was "the logical development of a system of law enforcement which employed exclusion to prevent crime…[and] at least until the end of the thirteenth century…outlawry could be regarded as a genuine and adequate punishment for felony."[18]

From the late Anglo-Saxon period to the end of the thirteenth century, legal prescriptions and motivations for outlawry vary. Legal documents provide insight into the intent of and relationship between authoritative powers and criminals in England from the turn of the first millennium through the thirteenth century. The discussions of outlawry and exile in narrative sources reveal just how complex and multifaceted these two sanctions actually were in medieval England. By the end of the thirteenth century, outlawry as the action of declaring an individual to be outside of the law had become a formalized legal process as part of formal English law. [19]

In addition to a survey of outlawry and exile in medieval England, this work assesses the relationship between these practices and other tools of punishment and governance, namely imprisonment and, at times, abjuration of the realm. [20] Imprisonment was used in various contexts during the Middle Ages, the aims of

---

16 Pollock and Maitland, *History of English Law*, vol. 2: 449; 476-477.

17 Pollock and Maitland, *History of English Law*, vol. 2: 580-581.

18 H.R.T. Summerson, "The Structure of Law Enforcement in Thirteenth Century England," *The American Journal of Legal History*, vol. 23, no. 4 (Oct., 1979): 313-327, at 314.

19 Pollock and Maitland, *History of English Law*, vol. 2: 518 and 590.

20 J.G. Bellamy, *Crime and Public Authority in the Later Middle Ages*, pg. 180. For social theories on punishment, see M. Foucault, *Discipline and Punish: The Birth of the Prison*, trans A. Sheridan. (New York: Vintage Books, 1977); D. Garland, "Sociological Perspectives on Punishment" in *Crime and Justice*, vol. 14 (1991): 115-165; N. Elias, *On Civilization, Power, and Knowledge: Selected Writings,* eds S. Mennell and J. Goudsblom. (Chicago, IL: University of Chicago Press, 1998); P. Spierenurg, *The Spectacle of Suffering: Executions and the evolution of repression: from a preindustrial metropolis to the European experience* (Cambridge, UK: Cambridge UP, 1984).

which were intended to preserve the social order.[21] The Roman law principle that imprisonment was meant for custodial purposes influenced the application of imprisonment, as did Canon law, which prescribed imprisonment as a corrective and rehabilitative punishment.

Historically, prisoners were held in monasteries, Episcopal churches, and private venues as circumstances and availability dictated. Imprisonment can be found in the ancient world, used under the Roman Empire mostly for shorter periods of detention, for minor offences and safe keeping of offenders.[22] In late antiquity, Justinian's *Code* and *Digest*, scripture and the "Acts of the Christian Martyrs" formed the secular, religious, and moral foundation for understandings of imprisonment, however during the early medieval period, imprisonment appears in so-called barbarian law codes as well as narrative sources. On the whole, prisons were not frequently used by Lombards or Franks, but were relatively more common among the Goths due to their increased proximity and assimilation with Rome and its legal traditions.[23] Roman law dictated imprisonment for custodial purposes, and the assertions put forth by Roman jurist Ulpian's that prisons were to be temporary and custodial rather than punitive was influential in the emerging study of law in the thirteenth century. Bracton himself restates this principle.[24] Canon law, however, prescribed imprisonment as a corrective and rehabilitative punishment, and likewise used exile, excommunication, and pilgrimage as part of its penitential discipline.[25]

Scholars have tended to identify modes of disciplinary imprisonment with the Early Modern, not the medieval era. The classic account is Michel Foucault's *Discipline and Punish: The Birth of the Prison*, in which he states that

---

21 C. L. von Bar, *History of Continental Criminal Law*, Continental Legal History Series, vol. 6: 35, accessed at HeinOnline; E. Peters, "Prison before the Prison" in *Oxford History of the Prison: the Practice of Punishment in Western Society*, eds N. Morris and D. J. Rothman, (New York, NY: Oxford UP, 1995): 13-23.

22 C. L. von Bar, *History of Continental Criminal Law*, vol. 6:35; Peters, "Prison," 13-19.

23 Peters, "Prison," 20-23.

24 Ulpian, *Digest of Justinian*, 48.19.8.9; Bracton, *De legibus et consuetudinibus Angliæ*, ed. Travers Twiss. vols 1-6 (London, UK: Longman & Co., 1878-1883), vol. 2: 155; G. Geltner, *The Medieval Prison: A Social History* (Princeton, NJ: Princeton UP, 2008), 44-56. Ulpian states that "[g]overnors are in the habit of condemning men to be kept in prison or that they might be kept in chains, but they ought not do this; for punishments of this type are forbidden. Prison ought to be employed for confining men, not punishing them." Peters, "Prison," 39; T. Oakley, *English Penitential Discipline and Anglo-Saxon Law in Their Joint Influence* (New York, NY: Columbia UP, 1923); *Medieval Handbooks of Penance*, trans. J. McNeill and H.M. Garner, (New York, NY: Columbia UP, 1990).

25 Peters, "Prison," 39.

"the emergence of the prison marks the institutionalization of the power to punish."[26] In his assessment of organization of the power to punish in the eighteenth century, he identifies imprisonment within monarchical law as a punishment that is "ceremonial of sovereignty; it uses the ritual marks of vengeance that it applies to the body of the condemned man; and it deploys before the eyes of the spectators an effect of terror as immense as it is discontinuous, irregular and always above its own laws, the physical presence of the sovereign and of his power."[27]

Was imprisonment in England in the central Middle Ages nothing more than ritualized monarchical and feudal sovereignty, as indicated by Foucault, or did it contain socially maintained ideas of deterrence and correction as well? By the end of the thirteenth century, imprisonment had become more prominent in administrative and legal practices in England, a phenomenon that reflected the shifting authoritative framework. Investigation into this historical transformation opens an understanding into the changing organization of power in medieval England. An examination of outlawry, its variations, and relationship with the increased use of imprisonment makes clear that the social system was changing from one of exclusion to one based on the confinement of offenders who were brought into a closer relationship with the law by a strengthened governmental authority. This resulted in new perceptions of social space and judicial authority. The details and transformations of exclusionary practices within the English legal tradition reveal much about legal power and political concerns, as well as conceptions and modes of providing justice.

The seminal work on imprisonment in medieval England is that of Ralph Pugh. His assessment focuses on post-Conquest England and he argues that imprisonment was not widely used in England until after the end of the twelfth century. According to Pugh, imprisonment emerged as early as the days of Alfred and there were more than likely prisons found in private jurisdictions, but "in a primitive society there is a strong temptation to enforce a line of conduct on a defaulter by pledges or payments rather than detaining the body."[28] Jean

26 M. Foucault, *Discipline and Punish: The Birth of the Prison*, trans. A. Sheridan. (New York, NY: Vintage Books, 1977), 130.

27 Foucault, 130.

28 R. Pugh, *Imprisonment in Medieval England*, (Cambridge, UK: Cambridge UP, 1968), 2; Pugh briefly discusses punitive imprisonment (often associated with a fine), custodial imprisonment (intended to result in a trial), and coercive imprisonment (which is not found in legal texts until Henry II), but concerns himself little with imprisonment as a whole prior to the mid-twelfth century. Perhaps this is due to the sources Pugh uses, relying heavily on legal documents and secondary works, the former of which becomes

Dunbabin's work on captivity and imprisonment from the turn of the millennium to the start of the fourteenth century does not explicitly discuss England, she finds no need due to the work of Pugh, but Dunbabin does argue, however, that as the confidence in the efficacy of human justice grew, the need for imprisonment developed. The correlation between serious crime and imprisonment is not always complete, as wealth and patronage protected some individuals and not others. To Dunbabin there is no real logic in the use of imprisonment, as debtors, hostages, and prisoners of war were often held in the same conditions as political or felonious prisoners.[29]

John Gillingham has come closest to an in-depth assessment of imprisonment and its uses in the late eleventh and twelfth centuries in England.[30] He attributes changes in punishments for rebels, specifically from death to the use of imprisonment, to the increasingly aristocratic sense of honor and chivalry found in England following the Norman Conquest of 1066.[31] Even scholars investigating the thirteenth century are hesitant to ascribe any overwhelming importance to the use of imprisonment. Trevor Dean reminds his readers that "most offenders paid money fines, and were subject to neither physical punishment nor incarceration," and J.G. Bellamy claims that the public and exclusive nature of medieval punishment probably account for "why a term of imprisonment, although it was inflicted more and more as time went by, was not the predominant penalty for law-breaking but used only when circumstances would permit no other type."[32] These accounts imply that imprisonment in medieval England was as much a method of "last resort" as outlawry, thus adding necessity to the study of the relationship between the two practices.

The chronological structure of this work begins in Anglo-Saxon England. Chapter two assesses outlawry, exile, and banishment prior to the end of Anglo-

---

increasingly available from the mid-twelfth century forward. For a brief discussion of imprisonment and English Common Law, see Peters, "Prison before the prison," 31-33.

29 J. Dunbabin, *Captivity and Imprisonment in Medieval Europe, 1000-1300*. (2002).

30 J. Gillingham, "The Introduction of Chivalry into England," in *Law and Government in Medieval England and Normandy: Essays in honour of Sir James Holt*, eds. G. Garnett and J. Hudson (Cambridge, UK: Cambridge UP, 1992): 31-55.

31 Gillingham, "Chivalry," 51, 54. Gillingham argues that social rank played a role in the treatment of a rebel, as a noble was more likely to be spared and death was more likely for a low-born man. He also claims that contemporary sources and their interpretations of imprisonment are best read as commentaries on the chivalrous merits of the captors. For more on the chivalry in post-conquest England, see M. Strickland, *War and Chivalry: The Conduct and Perception of War in England and Normandy, 1066-1217* (Cambridge, UK: Cambridge UP, 1994).

32 T. Dean, *Crime in Medieval Europe 1200-1550* (London, UK: Pearson Education, Ltd., 2001), 119-120; Bellamy, *Crime and Public Order*, 180.

Saxon period. In pre-Conquest England, outlawry and exile functioned as fundamental mechanisms of social order. They were effective, powerful legal and political tools based in custom. Royal efforts to maintain peace and to end feuding behavior resulted in legislative efforts to control, influence, and enforce aspects of outlawry and exile. The complexities of law, governance, and order are apparent from the start, as there is rarely a discernible difference between outlawry, exile, and banishment. This phenomenon continues through the eleventh and twelfth centuries, as distinctions slowly emerge.

Chapter three moves to the post-Conquest period of English history as well as examines outlawry and exile in pre-Conquest Normandy. The circumstances which caused Norman kings of England to combine their Continental practices with those of the Anglo-Saxons are explored. The Normans used exile against their political enemies as well as encouraged the legal practice of outlawry. The Norman presence in England also brought about the increased use of imprisonment, often at the discretion of the king, and led to changes in governance in Anglo-Norman England.

Chapter four assesses the impact of Henry II's legal reforms during the twelfth century and how these reforms contributed to shifts in England's social, political, and governmental structures. This chapter focuses on the competition for authority over the power to punish and control that arose between Church and Crown as well as on the royal use of assizes, writs, and itinerant justices to centralize the administration of justice. Twelfth-century reforms in England adapted outlawry and abjuration of the realm, to meet royal needs as the interests of the Crown in local events increased. These reforms also comprehensively incorporated confinement and captivity into matters of law, society, and governance.

Chapter five examines transformations in modes of punishment and governance during late twelfth and early thirteenth centuries. During the reign of King Richard, coroners were introduced as royal officials that were responsible for documenting outlaws in England. During the reign of King John, the king's exploitation of power through the use of outlawry and imprisonment resulted in limitations placed upon royal jurisdiction and authority. The struggle between King John and the English Baronage led to the creation of Magna Carta, which restricted the power of the Crown, in part by delineating between outlaw and exile as tools of legal and political order. By the middle of the thirteenth century, those distinctions between outlawry and exile were firmly in place.

Sources from the period of the personal rule of Henry III, the subject of chapter six, provide a wealth of information about the administration of justice in the thirteenth century. Records from judicial eyres reveal the ubiquitous nature of outlawry in England and political disputes between the King and the

English Barons demonstrate continued and unsuccessful royal attempts to use and harness the power of outlawry for its own purpose. As a result of this failure, imprisonment became increasingly relied upon to function as a tool of governance and authority.

Legal action during the reign of King Edward, and the administrative and judicial reforms associated with his rule, are focused upon in chapter seven. During the last decades of the thirteenth century, Edward I's legislation fundamentally altered the function and efficacy of criminal law in England. The marked impulse to legal codification, increased bureaucracy and efforts at administrative uniformity impacted the administration of criminal law and punishment in late medieval England. By looking at Edwardian legislation in the context of plea records and chancery documents, it becomes possible to understand the increasing role imprisonment played in English law and society by the end of the thirteenth century.

Chapter eight summarizes the conclusions of the work as a whole, as by the end of the thirteenth century and into the early decades of the fourteenth century, the relationship between outlawry and imprisonment was very different than it had been three centuries earlier. This was the result of the changing role of royal authority in England and the development of the English Common Law. Outlawry and imprisonment interacted in matters of law but the latter had become much more common in legal processes and legislation. Imprisonment had become the tool by which authorities could compel, punish, and threaten wrongdoers without customary or traditional interference. Outlawry withstood royal attempts to seize its power and position in law and society with such fortitude that by the end of the thirteenth century, imprisonment was a mechanism that had been used to replace and circumvent its practice and processes in the English Common Law.

Chapter 2: Outlawry, Exile, and Banishment in Anglo-Saxon England

Exile and outlawry defined the social, political, and legal boundaries of Anglo-Saxon world.[33] They were organizing principles of the Anglo-Saxon social order, instruments of the complex system of friendship, peace, feud, and revenge. As such, they were crucial means for the exercise power and authority.[34] To be without friends or to be expelled from one's kinship group was the harshest sanction an individual faced in Anglo-Saxon society.[35]

---

33 Pollock and Maitland, *History of English Law*, vol. 1: 30-43; H.R. Lyon, *The Governance of Anglo-Saxon England, 500-1087* (London, UK: Edward Arnold Publishers, Ltd., 1984), 41-50; J. Campbell, *The Anglo-Saxons* (Ithaca, NY: Cornell UP, 1982), 56; 98-99; P. Hyams, *Rancor and Reconciliation In Medieval England* (Ithaca, NY: Cornell UP, 2003), 71ff.

34 Hyams, *Rancor and Reconciliation*, 14; Pollock and Maitland, *History of English Law*, vol. 1: 46-47. In a contrasting view of the feud in Anglo-Saxon society, Peter Sawyer suggests that the emphasis on blood-feuding and kin-group solidarity that characterizes much historical work on early medieval Europe is exaggerated and a misleading over-simplification. See his "The Bloodfeud in fact and fiction," *Tradition og historie-skrivning: Kilderne til Nordens aeldstae historie*, Acta Jutlandica LXIII: 2, Humanistisk Serie 61 (Aarhus Universitetsforlag, 1987): 27-38.

35 The key source for this period is the *Anglo-Saxon Chronicle* (*ASC*), trans. A. Savage (London, UK: Gramercy, 1995). Supplementary information is taken from later chroniclers, composed with a look back at the Anglo-Saxon period and heavily based on the work of Bede, the Anglo-Saxon Chronicle, and other sources. These include William of Malmesbury, *Chronicle of the Kings of England*, Books 1 and 2, trans. J.A. Giles, 1904; Henry of Huntington, *The Chronicle of Henry Huntington: The History of the English*, trans. T. Forester, 1853; Henry, Archdeacon of Huntington, *Historia Anglorum, The History of the English People*. ed. and trans. D. Greenway (Oxford, UK: Clarendon Press, 1996); and John of Worcester, *The Chronicle of John of Worcester*, eds R.R. Darlington and P. McGurk, trans. J. Bray and P. McGurk, (Oxford, UK: Clarendon Press, 1995). The later narratives reflect contemporary attitudes regarding outlawry and exile, as well as the writers" belief of their importance in telling the story of the earliest English kings and their political and social customs and practices. Therefore, these works contains numerous tales of exile, banishment, and outlawry, which indicates both the existence and understanding of these practices in later centuries. See also E. Van Houts, "Historical Writing" in *A Companion to the Anglo-Norman World*, eds C. Harper-Bill and E. Van Houts (Woodbridge, Suffolk: The Boydell Press, 2003), 118; E. van Houts, " L"Exile dans l"Espace Anglo-Normand," in *La Normandie et l"Angleterre au Moyen Age*, 118-119; Hyams, *Rancor and Reconciliation*, 27-28; Pollock and Maitland, *History of English Law*, vol. 1: 44-46. Friends were identified and maintained as part of net-

Anglo-Saxon Social Order and Governance – Exile and Banishment

Most accounts of exile and banishment in Anglo-Saxon sources refer to enemies who have been cast out of England in efforts to gain or to maintain political control of a territory or over a people. [36] Similarly, communities sometimes cast out one ruler in exchange for another.[37] Political feuding involved kings and rulers

---

works of support within the feuding culture. Friends stood surety for one another, joined in the pursuit of enemies and wrongdoers; and helped negotiate and advise on marriages, peace settlements, and possessions.

36 *ASC*, year 755. Cynewulf cast King Sigebryht of Wessex out of his kingdom in 755. Cynewulf was a distant kinsman of Sigebryht and acted with the support of the councilmen of Wessex, as Sigebryht was said to be guilty of "unjust actions." Furthermore, Cynewulf wanted to seize control of Wessex and needed to remove Sigebryht to do so. While in flight, Sigebryht killed his most loyal alderman before being driven west to modern-day Hamptonshire, where he lived out his days in exile. In exile, Sigebryht was murdered by one of the retainers of the alderman Sigebryht had killed. Revenge for the death of the alderman brought about an end for Sigebryht just as revenge for driving Sigebryht resulted in the death of Cynewulf. Some three decades after Sigebryht was exiled, his kinsman Cyneheard killed Cynewulf in an act that was both feudal vengeance and a politically motivated killing. *ASC*, year 784; Hyams, *Rancor and Reconciliation*, 3-11, 23-24, 75-78; See also G. Halsall, "Violence and Society: an introductory survey," in *Violence and Society in the Early Medieval West*, ed. G. Halsall (Woodbridge, Suffolk, UK: The Boydell Press, 1998): 1-45; P. Hyams, "Feud and State in Late Anglo-Saxon England," *The Journal of British Studies*, vol. 40, no. 1 (Jan., 2001): 1-43, at 6-7, who follows S. D. White, "Kinship and Lordship in Early Medieval England: The Story of Sigeberht, Cynewulf, and Cyneheard," *Traditio* vol. 50 (1989): 1-18 retelling of the tale at 1-4; B. Yorke, *Wessex in the Early Middle Ages* (London, UK: Cassell Publishers Ltd., 1995), 91-92. Cyneheard had tried to convince the men in Cynewulf's retinue to rebel against their lord but his efforts failed. The loyalty and allegiance of the men to Cynewulf prevented them from taking the "money and land" promised by Cyneheard in exchange for their treachery.

37 *ASC*, year 790; Wm. of Malmesbury, 44-45, 67-68. According to the note provided by translator Giles, his nobles deposed Osred because of a conspiracy in 790. He returned to Northumbria two years later after being persuaded by some local chiefs to return, but was deserted when he arrived. He was then made a prisoner and killed by order of Ethelred; See also Henry of Huntington's accounts in Forester, 141; Greenway, 260-263 and Symeon of Durham, *Libellus de Exordio atque Procursu Istius, hoc est Dunhelmensis Ecclesie* (hereafter *LE*) ed. and trans. D. Rollason in *Tract on the Origins and Process of this Church of Durham*. (Oxford, UK: Clarendon Press, 2000), 82-87, Book 2.4; 90-91, Book 2.5; Symeon of Durham, *History of the Kings*, 451; 455. Symeon states that King Eardulf was driven out in 806; Symeon of Durham, *LE*, 98-99, Book 2.6; Symeon of Durham, *History of the Kings*, 492.

sending their rivals into exile, usurping power though banishment and exclusion. Struggles for power often resulted in the exile of rivals in Anglo-Saxon England.[38] Penda, the seventh century King of Mercia, was notorious for killing or banishing his rivals.[39] In Northumbria in the early seventh century, King Edwin killed or banished all of his rivals in order to acquire power, but did this only after returning to the region from a period of exile in East Anglia.[40] In 790, King Osred was exiled from Northumbria. He returned in 794, and was captured and killed.[41]

Although accounts of kings involved in exile are commonplace in the *Anglo-Saxon Chronicle*, this type of "feud must often have driven lesser men into exile as well."[42] Outlawry, exile, and banishment as instruments of the feud reveal how ongoing struggles for social order played out. Whether used in a local dispute or in a conflict for royal power, exclusion was tied to kin-based loyalties

---

38 In Sussex c. 686-694, Caedwalla was driven into exile after "exciting the animosity of the princes of his country" but he later returned and drove his rivals from power. Caedwalla took a whole military force into exile with him, which he used to regain the throne and control the land. Cuthred, king of Kent, and Wiglaf, ruler of Mercia, were forced into exile after being defeated by King Egbert, who ruled Wessex from 802 to 839. The kings of Mercia practiced the same exclusionary practices when exercising and acquiring political power. In the early Anglo-Saxon period, King Oswald, who had been in exile in Scotland for a time, returned to Mercia and received Bishop Aidan in an effort to advance the spread of Christianity. For eighth century references, see *ASC*, years 722, 725, 774, 778, 790, and 794; during the ninth century, the *ASC* recounts that King Eardwulf of Northumbria was driven out of his kingdom in 806 and Ceolwulf was driven from Mercia in 823.

39 *ASC*, years 645 and 658; D.P. Kirby, *The Earliest Kings of England* (London, UK: Unwin Hyman, 1991), 48, 51, 57-58; Sawyer, 39. According to the Anglo-Saxon Chronicle, King Penda of Mercia drove Cenwalh, King of Wessex from 642 to 672, from his kingdom in 645. The entry from 658 explains that Penda drove Cenwalh into a three-year exile and seized his kingdom for having forsaken his sister. Kirby identifies Cenwalh as the king of the Gewisse, whom Bede considers identical to the West Saxons of his own time; Wm. of Malmesbury, 70, 87, 89; Forester, 99, 101-102; Greenway, 190-195.

40 F. Stenton, *Anglo-Saxon England* (Oxford, UK: Clarendon Press, 1943), 65-66, 113-116; Campbell, *The Anglo-Saxons*, 45; Wm. of Malmesbury, 44-45.

41 *ASC*, year 790; year 794; In 778, Æthelred of Northumbria was driven out by Alfwold, who was killed and succeeded by Osred in 788, see *ASC*, year 774; year 778; Hyams, *Rancor and Reconciliation*, 77. From c. 750 to 796, Northumbria had eight different kings from three different families. In Wessex during the reign of Ine, Ealdbriht the atheling was exiled, and was later killed in battle between Ine and the South Saxons, with whom the atheling had taken refuge. See *ASC*, years 722, 725.

42 Campbell, *The Anglo-Saxons*, 56.

and illustrates how casting out a malefactor was both an appropriate response to a perceived wrong and a mechanism to facilitate royal succession.[43]

Anglo-Saxon Social Order and Law - Outlawry

Legal evidence from the seventh century reveals that the emergence of written law coincided with efforts to reinforce social custom and maintain order. [44] Through the course of the eighth, ninth, and tenth centuries, Anglo-Saxon legislation demonstrated an increased royal interest in maintaining social order. These laws also reveal how royal power inserted itself into matters of punishment and local accountability with more frequency and more efficiency.

A key way that kings influenced justice was through the exercise of mercy. According to the legislation of Edmund, a slayer could be returned to the peace of the king after the appropriate ecclesiastical penance and compensation of the offended kindred were carried out.[45] As punishments became more severe, particularly those in the laws of Æthelstan and Edgar, the power to pardon or to mitigate became increasingly important. Edgar‘s code stated that "if the law is

---

43 Exile in the Anglo-Saxon world was also associated with the Church, Christian punishment, and penitential discipline. Similarly, political rulers could also force churchmen from office and territory. See Oakley, *English Penitential Discipline and Anglo-Saxon Law in their Joint Influence*, 49-50; Bede, *Ecclesiastical History of the English People*, trans and eds L. Sherley-Price and D.H. Farmer (London, UK: Penguin Books, 1990), 3.27-28, 194-196; Campbell, *The Anglo-Saxons*, 88-89; Hyams, *Rancor and Reconciliation*, 19.

44 The complex relationship between oral tradition and the written word makes it difficult to know the intricacies of the administration of law in early Anglo-Saxon England. The laws of Æthelbert (d. 603) were observations of Kentish legal customs, and the laws of his successors, Hlothere and Eadric (c. 685) and Wihtred (695), were in the same vein. The latter collections filled in customary gaps and, on occasion, included new and reactive law to meet specific needs. Ine of Wessex's laws (c. 690) similarly addressed social tensions while more actively taking steps to resolve disputes, making "law in response to individual cases." See James Campbell, ed. *The Anglo-Saxons* (Ithaca, NY: Cornell UP, 1982), 240-246; Kirby, *The Earliest Kings of England*, 1-29; Loyn, *The Governance*, 3-29; P. Wormald, "*Inter cetera bona genti suae*: Law-making and peace-keeping in the earliest English kingdoms," in *La Giustizia nell"alto Medioevo* (Secoli V-Viii),7-13 Aprile 1994, tomo secondo (Spoleto: Presso la sede del centro, 1995): 963-993, at 965, 974-977, 982-986; P. Wormald, *The Making of English Law: King Alfred to the Twelfth Century, Volume I: Legislation and its Limits*. (Oxford, UK: Blackwell Publishers Ltd., 1999), 93-108.

45 II Em 4, 6.

too severe, he [the criminal] is then to apply to the king for alleviation."[46] Stress was placed upon the king's discretion and expanding prerogative as well as his overall authority over certain matters, which indicates other avenues by which the crown was attempting to influence and control the administration of law.

Anglo-Saxon legislation, particularly that of Æthelstan, showed increasing interest in the administration of justice in the shires, hundreds, and tithings, as well as how royal law was to be carried out in each.[47] The *gemot*, an Anglo-Saxon court or assembly, was held in each hundred in England every four weeks and each member of the community was required to attend.[48] Failure to attend when summoned three consecutive times resulted in a fine payable to the king for disobedience. If the man did not appear and pay the fine, then the suspect's tithingman was sent to bring the man to the court, take his possessions, and swear surety for him. If tithingmen failed to do so, he was then subject to a fine for disobedience as well.[49] After a fourth failure to appear in court, a suspect was required to forfeit his possessions and was considered to be an outlaw unless allowed by the king to remain in the land.[50] According to the laws of Æthelstan, resistance or failure to find pledges by a suspect could result in imprisonment or death, and if an offender fled or escaped custody, pursuit through vendetta and vengeance was prohibited. Acts of vengeance were met with the "hostility of the King and all of his friends" if carried out. If anyone harbored the fugitive, he automatically forfeited his wergeld (man-price) unless he could clear himself by oath that he did not know the man was a fugitive. The custody and pursuit of the offender-fugitive was left to the king's reeve within the shire,

---

46 III Eg 2.1.

47 "The Hundred Ordinance (939-about 961)," in *Select charters and other illustrations of English constitutional history from the earliest times to the reign of Edward the Firstn* ed. W. Stubbs (Oxford, Clarendon Press, 1913), 68-71; The exact date of this ordinance is unknown and has been associated with the reigns of both Edgar and Edmund. For tithings, *borh*, and other aspects of accountability as it relates to the later use of frankpledge, see W.A. Morris, *The Frankpledge System* (Cambridge, MA: Harvard UP, 1910), 8ff.

48 S. Reynolds, *Kingdoms and Communities in Western Europe, 900-1300* (New York, NY: Oxford UP, 1997), 24; Lyon, *Governance*, 141.

49 Ew IIIV. Freemen were placed in groups of ten, or tithings. These tithings were responsible for the behavior of all members as well as the group as a whole, and were fundamental to royal efforts to maintain local order through community-based accountability. To swear surety was to vouch on behalf of one's tithingman.

50 "The Hundred Ordinance (939-about 961)," no. 3.1.

as he was king's man in the localities charged with local responsibility for policing community membership.[51]

One other instrument of local justice that received royal attention was the hue and cry. The hue and cry was raised following a crime and necessitated that all individuals within the community assist in pursuit of a fleeing suspect. Royal interest in the customary hue and cry in Anglo-Saxon England was first clearly demonstrated in Æthelred's laws, with his assertion of rights over certain types of sanctuary seekers.[52] Sanctuary-seekers, as one segment of fugitives, sought the physical and spiritual protection of the Church. They exemplified the public nature of action against crime as well as the private vengeance that was involved. All fugitives were likely pursued, some were lucky enough to reach sanctuary, while others remained at large following the publicity of the hue and cry.[53] This left such men as exiles from their communities, outlaws from the protection of their kindreds, and subject to death if found. On the whole, early Anglo-Saxon legislation required local communities to police community behavior and maintain social order. Kings attempted strengthen their control and power in England by placing themselves within established practices of inclusion and exclusion.

Exile, Banishment, and Outlawry in Ninth and Tenth Century England

Within the expanding corpus of written law, exile, banishment, and outlawry as tools of legal and social order were common. The laws of King Alfred (849-899) placed the king as lord to all and asserted his right to regulate the system of dispute resolution based in private action. Alfred's laws declared that harboring exiles was a wrong against the king, thus more than simply a treasonous act against one's lord. Harboring an exile or outlaw resulted in forfeiture of life and

51 II As 20.7-8; H.R. Loyn, *The Making of the English Nation from the Anglo-Saxons to Edward I* (London, UK: Thames and Hudson, 1991), 68-72; Loyn, *Governance*, 45-53; Stenton, *Anglo-Saxon England*, 289-298; Campbell, ed., *The Anglo-Saxons*, 180; Morris, *The Medieval Sheriff to 1307* (Manchester, UK: Manchester UP, 1927), 1-39; Stenton, *The Anglo-Saxons*, 289-298. The wergild was the sum of money or "man-price" attributed to individuals in society based on social rank.

52 VIII Atr 1.1; Hyams, *Rancor and Reconciliation*, 92-98; Williams, *Æthelred*, 124-125.

53 An analogy between the shame and guilt associated with the exclusion and severed social ties of excommunication and those associated with outlawry and exile is found in Voloda, *Excommunication in the Middle Ages*, 191.

property or in an appropriate payment to the crown.[54] On the whole, the laws of Alfred attempted to break the predominance of private settlement in England in favor of royal control over disputes.

When the Vikings began raiding and settling in England from the late eighth century, struggles for power, control, and order intensified at all levels of society.[55] The mid-tenth century laws of Edward and Guthrum, for example, regulated behaviors that could incite violent feud actions between and among Danes and Englishmen.[56] These laws relied heavily upon outlawry to maintain social order. An individual could be outlawed for withholding a tithe payment or committing homicide, and "wizards or sorcerers, perjurers or they who secretly compass death, or vile polluted, notorious prostitutes" were to be banished.[57] Outlawry and banishment were coterminous and their inclusion in legal proclamations was meant to address both societal obligations and criminal behavior. The severity of banishment is demonstrated by a certain Leofa, who returned unexpectedly to Northumbria in 944 after six years of banishment for thievery. He was slaughtered upon his return to England.[58]

---

54 Af. 4: Attenborough, 2-3; Kirby, 30-47; 124-128; See P. Wormald, *The Making of English Law*; for information on the relationship between manuscripts and law, see Wormald, 162-263, for Alfred's laws as legal text, see Wormald, 264-286; Hyams, *Rancor and Reconciliation*, 4, 78-87, 98-101. References to legal texts are from Liebermann, unless otherwise indicated. Anglo-Saxon justice was administered on the local level in the court of the hundred. The king's reeve participated and intervened in these courts when necessary and guided customary law, but never dictated rule or procedure. For more, see Stenton, *Anglo-Saxon England*, 295-296. In addition to the provisions on exile and outlawry, Alfred's laws briefly make reference to imprisonment, but on the whole, confinement and captivity served very little purpose in Anglo-Saxon society. See R. Pugh, *Imprisonment in Medieval England* (Cambridge, UK: Cambridge UP, 1968), 1-4.

55 Diplomatic relations between Anglo-Saxon kings and Scandinavian leaders also resulted in the taking and exchanging of hostages and prisoners of war. See *ASC*, year 874; year 878; year 893; year 914; years 1012-1013; 160, year 1014; year 1016, among others. These activities were intended to facilitate peace, or at the very least, impart some level of conciliation. The *Anglo-Saxon Chronicle* is rife with accounts of hostage-taking and hostage-exchanges between Anglo-Saxons and Vikings during the ninth, tenth and eleventh centuries. Hostage-taking and hostage-exchange as surety-ship were elements of the peace between English and Danes; peace and friendship were closely tied to feud, and by extension, to exile.

56 Wormald, *Making of English Law*, 285-290; 389-391; Attenborough, 97; The exact dates of the promulgation of these laws and the specific kings of England and Denmark who ratified them remains unclear.

57 E Gu. 11.

58 This story comes from the twelfth-century chronicler William of Malmesbury, 143.

In the laws of Æthelstan (c. 925-939), a lordless man was considered to be outside of the protection of the law unless his kin secured residence and lordship for him. If this was not done, the man was considered to be a fugitive, an outlaw. While in a state of outlawry, the lordless man was assumed a thief and could be killed with impunity. Any individual who harbored the lordless man had to make payment to the king for doing so.[59] An outlaw was a dead man if caught and any person who helped him was punished by mandate of the king.

Outlawry as a form of punishment continued to earn royal attention and began to take on a different legislative tone. In the laws of Æthelstan,

> ...if anyone is so rich or belongs to so powerful a kindred, that he cannot be restrained from crime or from protecting and harbouring criminals, he is to be led out of his native district with his wife and children, and all his goods, to any part of the kingdom which the king chooses, be he noble or commoner, whoever he may be—with the provision that he shall never return to his native district. And henceforth, let him never be encountered by anyone in that district; otherwise he shall be treated as a thief caught in the act...and if anyone harbours him, or sends to him any of his men, he shall be liable to the confiscation of all his property.[60]

The notion of removing serious wrongdoers from the community at the behest of the king was innovative. The individual in question not only represented a danger to his kindred, community, and the whole Anglo-Saxon system of peace and friendship, but also served as a threat to royal law and order. Oaths and suretyship were no longer enough to allow such a man to remain among his kindred. Similarly, the man's kin and possessions were displaced at the pleasure of the king. Although this was not a formal declaration of outlawry, as the king did not have legal authority to take such action, this provision represented a blending of royal prerogative and local custom. Crimes such as failure to pay a fine or practicing witchcraft had long resulted in exclusion from local communities and offenders were considered outlaws, a sentence pronounced by the county court. Outlawry was always proclaimed in the county courts and nowhere else, but now the king was an active agent in social relationships on the local and familial level. This was a new aspect of royal authority inserted into written law.

Æthelstan's law may have intended to remove powerful yet troublesome landholders from their lands so that the king could strengthen his own position. Regardless of intent, it clearly illustrates the relationship between power and exclusion while marking the first royal attempt at intervention into matters of local politics and society with such force. Outlawry as the local, territorial

---

59 II As 2.1-2; Attenborough, 112-113; Stenton, *Anglo-Saxon England*, 347-351; Wormald, *Making of English Law*, 290-308.

60 IV As 3.

equivalent to the use of exile and banishment by rulers and kings, was identical in principle to the political exclusion practiced on a royal scale.[61] Law was not yet national in any sense, but this provision links local, immediate, kin-based, and often feud-driven action with attempts by kings to use law to exclude. Certainly, kings, clerics, and lords all had the authority to expel in certain contexts, and kingdoms, communities, and jurisdictions lacked clear definition, but proclamations of outlawry and the like were coercive and punitive tools of local power which royal law sought to use and harness.[62]

The laws of Edmund (939-946) pioneered royal efforts against the feud by imposing punishments for participation in personal vendetta, violation of king's peace, and refusal to pay appropriate compensation for theft.[63] Sweeping actions against individuals engaged in acts that violated the king's peace resulted in exclusion as the ultimate punishment. The king's law incorporated feuding behaviors into offenses classified as a breach of the king's peace.[64] Home invasion and all types of killing became offenses against the king, and such offenders were banned from the "king's company, and eventually from God's."[65] As more offenses fell under the king's peace, royal law had an increased role in excluding malefactors from society. In these instances, both forfeiture of property and outlawry were common, although it should be noted that these two punishments did not always go hand-in hand.[66]

The trend of royal law to incorporate private actions under its jurisdiction continued under Kings Æthelred and Cnut.[67] The inception of *botless* offenses

---

61 E. van Houts, "L"Exile dans l"Espace Anglo-Normand," in *La Normandie et l"Angleterre au Moyen Age,* 118-119.

62 Pollock and Maitland, *History of English Law*, vol. 1: 32-43; Lyon, *Governance*, 47-50.

63 Hyams, *Rancor and Reconciliation*, 82; Campbell, *The Anglo-Saxons*, 168-181; Wormald, *Making of English Law*, 308-312.

64 N. Hurnard, *The King's Pardon for Homicide to 1307* (Oxford, UK: Clarendon Press, 1969), 2-5; Campbell, *The Anglo-Saxons*, 176; Hyams, *Rancor and Reconciliation*, 82-85.

65 Wormald, *Making of English Law*, 312; II Em 1, 4, 6.

66 II Em 1; 6; I Eg 1; 3; 6; III Eg 7. ed. and trans. A. J. Robertson, *Laws of the Kings of England from Edmund to Henry I* (Cambridge, UP, 1925. [New York, AMS Press, 1974]). For more details, see Robertson, 47-51; Wormald, *Making of English Law*, 308-345 and J. Goebel, *Felony and Misdemeanor: A Study in the History of Criminal Law* (Philadelphia, PA: University of Pennsylvania Press, 1976), 238. Under the earliest Anglo-Saxon kings, "the sanctions against property that eventually take the form of chattel forfeiture and escheat [were] independent penalties."

67 *ASC*, year 975. Following the death of King Edgar in 975, his son Edward became king and ruled for three years. Upon Edward's accession to the throne, the powerful Northumbrian earl Oslac, a loyal subject of Edgar, was exiled from England. Edward's short

under Æthelred, "wrongs so serious that redress may no longer be taken by private agreement with the wronged," probably lies in the hands of Wulfstan, Archbishop of York, homilist and legislative advisor to both kings Æthelred and Cnut.[68] The laws of Æthelred, promulgated throughout his reign from 978-1016, contained a shift in the administration of justice with the creation of *botless* or unamendable offenses, the penalty for which could not be commuted to a financial payment. These offenses included housebreaking, arson, and treason.[69] This allowed for royal jurisdiction as well as claims and any monies associated with these matters to go directly to the king, removing them from remedy by recompense and the whole feud process.

Still more *botless* offenses appeared during Cnut's reign, and banishment, exile, and outlawry repeatedly occurred as punitive responses to both secular and ecclesiastical offenses. A thief who failed to clear himself through surety forfeited his wergeld to the king and was declared an outlaw. Similarly, if an accused thief escaped through the alleged assistance of his lord, the lord must

---

reign ended in 978 and Æthelred Unraed became king. A. Williams, *Æthelred the Unready: The Ill-Counselled King* (London, UK: Hambledon and London, 2003), 22; S. Keynes, "Æthelred II (c. 966x8–1016)", *Oxford Dictionary of National Biography*, Oxford UP, 2004; S. Keynes, ""Crime and Punishment in the Reign of King Æthelred the Unready," in *People and Places in Northern Europe, 500-1600. Essays in Honor of Peter Hayes Sawyer*, eds by I. Wood and N. Lund. (Woodbridge, Suffolk, UK: The Boydell Press, 1991): 67-82. Keynes assesses law and order during Æthelred's reign in terms of royal control over the administration of justice. His "top-down" approach of law biases many of his claims, but his assertion that law and order under Æthelred was similar to that of tenth-century kings seems strong. Æthelred Unraed is a pun meaning "Noble council, No council" but has earned him the moniker "Unready". The Old English word "unraed" is translated "ill-advised" or "ill-counseled" and does not indicate that he was unready to be king, but rather that he was without proper council and advice during his reign, or that he failed to take the advise of his council.

68 Hyams, *Rancor and Reconciliation*, 84-85; Wormald, *Making of English Law*, 320-345; Williams, *Æthelred*, 84-89, 125; D. Whitelock, "Wulfstan and the Laws of Cnut," *The English Historical Review*, vol. 63, no. 249 (Oct., 1948): 433-452; D. Whitelock, "Wulfstan's authorship of Cnut's laws," *The English Historical Review*, vol. 70, no. 274 (Jan., 1955): 72-85; M.K. Lawson, "Archbishop Wulfstan and the Homiletic Element in the Laws of Æthelred and Cnut," *The English Historical Review*, vol. 107, no. 424 (Jul., 1992): 565-586; D. Whitelock, "Archbishop Wulfstan, Homilist and Statesman," *Transactions of the Royal Historical Society*, Fourth Series, vol. 24, (1942): 25-45; P. Wormald, "Wulfstan (d. 1023)", *Oxford Dictionary of National Biography*, Oxford UP, 2004; Wormald, *Making of English Law*, 330-345, 352-366 450-465; Campbell, ed. *The Anglo-Saxons*, 207; D. Berthrum, *The Homilies of Wulfstan* (Oxford, UK: Clarendon Press, 1957).

69 Pollock and Maitland, *History of English Law*, vol. 1: 465.

clear himself through surety or forfeit his possessions and be outlawed as well.[70] Here, an outlaw was to be treated as such by the whole nation.[71]

Through the use of law, Anglo-Saxon kings were claiming an idealized form of sovereign authority. For the king to have physical control over the whole of the kingdom was not possible and many serious disputes were likely reconciled outside of the royal influence or even royal knowledge. By the turn of the millennium, however, the king's justice was accessible to all in spite of fact that the crown did not necessarily have direct authority over or knowledge of every crime or dispute. Royal interests did not compete outright with those of lords, nor did the kings intend to remove the rights of private individuals in the feud and reconciliation processes. The king's mercy and emphasis on royal law in the localities were methods by which the crown came to exhibit more control over exclusion in law and politics. The king could pardon or mitigate punishments, most often death sentences, but this did not eliminate a wrongdoer's obligations to the kindred of the afflicted.[72] In this context, exile and outlawry were ubiquitous in the legislation of the Anglo-Saxon kings but did not lose their customary functions in political and social interactions.

Exile, Outlawry, Banishment, and Power in Anglo-Scandinavian England

In the eleventh century, kings of Wessex made gains against Viking settlers in the north and repeatedly exiled Danish rulers from Northumbria.[73] In 1002, King Æthelred extended a tribute, the *danegeld*, to the Viking invaders so that they

---

70 I Atr 1.9a-14.

71 I Atr 1.9a; III Atr 10; VIII Atr 26; 42; Campbell, *The Anglo-Saxons*, 199-201. Criminous priests were deprived of office, banished, and sent on pilgrimage as defined by the Pope. Individuals who harbored an excommunicate beyond a designated length of time were subject to loss of life and property. This property, however, would then be given to the "deputies of Christ, who shall be the defenders and upholders of the Christian religious and royal authority as long as God shall permit."

72 Recent scholarship has suggested that in matters of homicide, the obligations of a wrongdoer to the kin of the slain man may have been limited to a *wergild* payment. Jurasinski argues that compensation may have been used as part of royal efforts to quell violence and feuding behaviors. See S. Jurasinski, "*Reddatur Parentibus*: The Vengeance of the Family in Cnut's Homicide Legislation," *Law and History Review*, vol. 20, no. 1 (Spring, 2002): 157-180.

73 For example, see *ASC*, year 927; Wm. of Malmesbury, 131-133; 141; John of Worcester, vol. 2: 386-387; Stenton, *Anglo-Saxon England*, 352-354.

"desist from their mischief."[74] The *danegeld* was a failure. The Danes continued to attack and demanded ever-larger sums from the English. The resurgence of Viking attacks in the late tenth and early eleventh centuries contributed to the difficulties of two culturally different groups living on the island of Britain and soon led to a treaty between King Æthelred and the Danes. One of the provisions that discussed the treatment of killers brought increased detail to the outlawry process:

> And if their men slay eight of us, they shall be treated as outlaws by them and by us, and shall not be allowed to settle the matter by any payment of compensation.[75]

The ethnic distinctions with in this provision shed light upon social tensions and how order was maintained. In order to encourage peace, specific numbers of men slain were now beyond recompense. The expanding reach of outlawry as a tool of authority reveals that outlawry was a punishment applicable to Danes and Englishmen alike, and that an outlaw to one population was an outlaw to both. In order to maintain order, social control, and public security, an outlaw was an outlaw across the land.

The political situation for Anglo-Saxon kings was tenuous during the eleventh century. King Æthelred was forced into exile in 1013, during which time Swein and the Danes controlled England.[76] When Swein died in 1014, the Viking fleet chose his son, Cnut, to be their king. The English Witan (king's council), however, sent for Æthelred, who in turn sent his son Edward to secure full loyalty from the kingdom before returning to rule England. According to the *Anglo-Saxon Chronicle*, an agreement was made between Æthelred and the English people, as "full friendship was established and…every Danish king they proclaimed [to be] an outlaw for ever from England."[77] But the English people

---

74 *ASC*, year 1002; One of Æthelred's aldermen, Leofsy made peace with the Danish fleet in 1002, but while on that mission for the king, he killed the king's steward, Eafy. Leofsy was then banished from England. See Keynes, "Crime and Punishment in the Reign of Æthelred," 79-80.

75 II Atr 7.1.

76 Williams, *Æthelred*, 118-122; Stenton, *Anglo-Saxon England*, 379-380, 382; R. Fletcher, *Bloodfeud: Murder and Revenge in Anglo-Saxon England* (Oxford, UK: Oxford UP, 2003), 79-81. He fled to the Isle of Wight and later joined his wife Emma and their two sons, Edward and Arthur, in Normandy. Æthelred had accepted the service of Thorkell the Tall, a mercenary soldier who had fought for Swein and inflicted much damage upon the north of England. Thorkell's alliance with Æthelred was the justification for Swein's invasion in 1013. Thorkell later switched back to ally himself with Cnut in 1014.

77 *ASC*, year 1014; Williams, *Æthelred*, 123-124; Stenton, *Anglo-Saxon England*, 381; Loyn, *Governance*, 96-100.

failed to effectively exclude the Danes and following the deaths of Æthelred and his son, Edmund, in 1016, the whole of England submitted to Cnut as their king.[78]

England was now united under Danish rule. Narrative accounts of the early years of Cnut‘s reign (1017-1035) reveal the use of exile and banishment against men who threatened the king's authority. Upon becoming King of England in 1017, Cnut banished his rival to the throne, Edwy the Etheling, and in 1020, he ordered that Ethelward, a powerful alderman in England at the time, be outlawed.[79] In addition to exiling powerful English magnates, Cnut killed several English aldermen and their kin. However, his actions against political enemies were not reserved for English natives. In 1021, Cnut ordered the outlawry of Thorkell, to whom he had given authority over East Anglia, and he later drove out Eric, Earl of Northumbria, whom he had appointed in 1017.[80] Political exclusion was a fundamental part of Danish kingship in England just as it had been to their Anglo-Saxon predecessors.

That the Danish kings of England used exile and outlawry as the Anglo-Saxon rulers had done is not surprising. In fact, exile and outlawry were as much a part of the Scandinavian social order as they were among Anglo-Saxons. Both peoples engaged in the feud. The coexistence of Danes and Saxons had been established through treaties and *danegeld* payments was meant to maintain peace and friendship and prevent acts of vengeance and violence.[81] King Cnut

---

78 Stenton, *Anglo-Saxon England*, 384-387; Williams, *Æthelred*, 131-150. Æthelred was restored to the throne in 1014 and was engaged in war with Cnut and the Danes until his death in 1016. Æthelred was succeeded by his son Edmund, who along with many other powerful English earls, continued to fight the Viking forces. Edmund died in November 1016.

79 *ASC*, years 1017 and 1020; Stenton, *Anglo-Saxon England*, 409.

80 *ASC*, year 1021; Wm. Of Malmesbury, 196-197; See also Symeon of Durham, *History of the Kings*, 526-527; John of Worcester, vol. 2: 506-507; Forester, 196; Greenway, 362-363; *Anglo-Saxon Chronicle*, year 1021; Stenton, *Anglo-Saxon England*, 392-396; Campbell, ed. *The Anglo-Saxons*, 208-209. See also "Memoriale Fratis Walteri de Covenetria" or *The Historical Collections of Walter of Coventry*, ed. Wm. Stubbs, vols 1-2. *In Rerum Britannicarum Medii Aevi Scriptores or Chronicles and Memorials of Great Britain and Ireland during the Middle Ages* (Rolls Series) vol. 58, parts 1 and 2 (London, UK: Her Majesty's Stationary Office, 1872); Kraus Reprint Ltd., 1968), vol. 1: 47. Cnut later reconciled with Thorkell and sent him to govern Denmark in his name, most likely because Thorkell was too powerful for Cnut to have as an enemy. See *ASC*, year 1023.

81 For some discussion of Scandinavian feuding practices, see C.J. Clover, "Regardless of Sex: Men, Women, and Power in Early Northern Europe," *Speculum*, vol. 68, no. 2 (Apr., 1993): 363-387; W.I. Miller, "Choosing the Avenger: Some Aspects of the

was just as concerned with peace and order in England as the Anglo-Saxon kings had been, and in 1020, proclaimed that all individuals not living in accordance with religious and secular law would be driven out of the kingdom.[82] This banishment was to be carried out regardless of social rank or ethnic origin.[83]

The laws of Cnut, more comprehensive than any of their precursors, exhibit royal interest in the maintenance of order by reinforcing long-standing legal and social practices.[84] Cnut's laws not only emphasized custom but also implemented measures to prevent unjust actions by officials and abuses of law. Cnut's laws stressed the importance of local courts and local officials, and required that no matter should be brought before him without having been heard in the appropriate hundred and shire courts.[85] Corresponding with the king's concern and respect for local justice, outlawry (*utlaga*) received specific attention:

> If anyone does a deed of an outlaw (a deed which legally involves outlawry), the king alone shall have the power to grant him security...and whoever feeds or harbours a fugitive shall pay five pounds to the king, unless he clear himself by a declaration that he did not know that he was a fugitive.[86]
>
> And therefore if anyone maintains or harbours an outlawed man, he shall make amends in accordance with the established law.[87]
>
> [If a lord fails to clear himself from the accusation of assisting a thief] the king shall take the wergild and the thief shall be treated as an outlaw by all the nation.[88]

Bloodfeud in Medieval Iceland and England," *Law and History Review*, vol. 1, no. 2 (Autumn, 1983): 159-204; and generally W. I. Miller, *Bloodtaking and peacemaking: feud, law, and society in Saga Iceland* (Chicago, IL: University of Chicago Press, 1990).

82 Wormald, *Making of English Law*, 354-355 and Table 5.4, 356-360; The influence of Wulfstan upon legal texts and law itself during the reign of Cnut are seen in the homiletic characteristics that stress political loyalty and living a Christian life based in prayer. See also D. Whitelock, "Wulfstan and the Laws of Cnut,"; D. Whitelock, "Wulfstan's authorship of Cnut's laws,"; M.K. Lawson, "Archbishop Wulfstan and the Homiletic Element in the Laws of Æthelred and Cnut,"; D. Whitelock, "Archbishop Wulfstan, Homilist and Statesman,"; P. Wormald, "Wulfstan (d. 1023)", *Oxford Dictionary of National Biography*; Wormald, *Making of English Law*, 330-345, 352-366, 450-465; D. Berthrum, *The Homilies of Wulfstan*; M.K. Lawson, *Cnut: The Danes in England in the Early Eleventh Century* (London and New York: Longman Group Ltd., 1993), 61-63, 204-210.

83 Cnut, 1020, 10; Wormald, *Making of English Law*, 345-366; Stenton, *Anglo-Saxon England*, 402-406.

84 Robertson, 137-139, at 138; Wormald, *The Making of English Law*, 349-366.

85 II Cn 17.

86 II Cn 13.

87 II Cn 15a.

> [Lords are responsible for all men within their households]...and if [a man within that household] is accused and escapes the lord shall pay the wergild to the king...if the lord is accused of advising to escape, he shall clear himself...and if he fails to clear himself he shall pay his own wergild to the king and the man shall be an outlaw towards the king.[89]
>
> Concerning men in holy orders: if a minister of the altar commits homicide or perpetrates any other crime he shall be deprived of his ecclesiastical office and banished, and shall travel as a pilgrim as far as the Pope appoints for him, and zealously make amends...and unless he begins to make amends both to God and men within 30 days, he shall be outlawed.[90]

Furthermore, wizards, sorcerers, and prostitutes were to be driven from the land and murderers, perjurers, and those who injure clergymen and adulterers were to make amends or leave the kingdom.[91]

Cnut‘s laws showed increased reliance upon outlawry as a legal custom in England. Harsher penalties and efforts to use the process more effectively were put into place, but Cnut‘s innovations changed the king’s relationship with outlawry as a tool of legal and social control. The implications for outlawry as it stood in 1035 were actually quite remarkable. The laws of Cnut articulated a timeframe for which men of the church who were criminals were to come to justice. After this period of time expired, the individual was outlawed. Under Æthelred, criminous priests were deprived of office, banished, and sent on pilgrimage as defined by the Pope, but there were no details included as to when amends were to be made. Cnut‘s laws, most likely at the hand of Wulfstan, tightened up this process.

The laws of Cnut also placed the power to bring an outlaw back into peace solely in the hands of the king. Æthelstan‘s and Edgar‘s laws had stressed the importance of royal discretion in handling unfair punishments and unjust laws, but now the king had exclusive power over pardon and mercy. Cnut‘s laws also added to those of Æthelred, which proclaimed that an outlaw in one area was to be considered an outlaw throughout the nation. Under Cnut, anyone who harbored said outlaw was subject to a fine payable to the king. This brought another aspect of outlawry under direct royal authority. The right to outlaw was still held by counties, but now outlawry had “acquired character as a royal process...when

---

88 II Cn 30.9.

89 II Cn 31a.

90 II Cn 41.

91 I Cn 4a; 6; *Handbooks of Medieval Penance*, 387.

the procedural prerogative is assured by the king's fine of £5 which harborers of outlaws must pay."[92]

Prior to this, outlawry in England had been more of a regional activity than a practice carried out on a countrywide level. Outlawry was a local or district process but, according to Julius Goebels, Cnut's legislation was necessary to make outlawry operative throughout the land. Regional outlawry regarded the peacelessness of the man involved in a feud as merely a legal and social matter pertaining to the kindred of the injured party rather than to the community at large. Cnut, however, declared outlawry to be the right of the crown, a punishment that could be proclaimed by the king.

While outlawry may have become fixed as a legal procedure in Cnut's day, it would be an over-statement to call it a royal process. That Cnut was able to create a form of national outlawry is doubtful given the difficulties in controlling the whole kingdom of England and the king by no means had the authority to proclaim outlawry in all aspects of law and order. The king could outlaw and banish malefactors under certain circumstances and his efforts to garner the strength of exclusion echo those of his predecessors. Outlawry and the like had had an immense amount of social force behind it during preceding centuries, a strength so great that kings from Alfred to Æthelred had attempted to manipulate the means and ends of exclusionary practices.[93] Outlawry as a process had always had the support of royal law and attempts to harness its power were underway well before Cnut's reign. For centuries, Anglo-Saxon kings sought to gain power and authority by influencing and controlling exclusion, as the latter was fundamental in maintaining social order. To control and use exclusion, vis-à-vis outlawry, was to have an immense amount of power in Anglo-Saxon England and Cnut's legislation brought new elements of outlawry under the authority of the king.[94]

Outlawry, Exile, and Authority under the last of the Anglo-Saxon Kings

Just before Edward (later called the Confessor) became King of England in 1042, he returned to his homeland after spending decades as an exile in Normandy. He had been taken to the Continent as a child in 1013 and was fearful to

92 J. Goebel, *Felony and Misdemeanor: A Study in the History of Criminal Law* (Philadelphia, PA: University of Pennsylvania Press, 1976), 418-421, at 421.

93 Goebel, 16, 57, 420-421.

94 Goebel, 421-423; 374, 378.

return after the death of his father Æthelred in 1016. He remained in Normandy during the reigns of Cnut (1016-1035), Harold Harefoot (1035-1039), and Harthacnut (1039-1042), making one failed attempt to visit his mother in England in 1036.[95] His mother Emma, Æthelred‘s widow, had married Cnut in 1017 and when Edward and his brother Alfred visited England, they were treated so severely that Edward was forced to return to Normandy that same year. His brother Alfred, however, was captured by the Earl of Wessex Godwin and placed into prison. Godwin and his men 'seized him [Alfred] and put him in close confinement, dispersed some of his companions, put some in chains" and then tortured and extracted fines from them. [96] While in captivity, Alfred was blinded and he later died as a result of the brutality of his injuries.

The situation was very different for Edward in 1042, and "all folk received Edward as king, as was his natural right."[97] He was crowned on April 3, 1043 and reigned until 1066, during which time individuals who resisted Edward‘s kingship "were carefully marked, and afterwards driven out of England."[98] Edward removed threats to his authority, nothing new for a King of England, and summoned Normans who had assisted him during his own period of exile to serve in governmental and religious positions. One such man was Robert of Jumièges, whom Edward appointed Archbishop of Canterbury.[99] Chronicle information recounts that Edward the Confessor exiled Cnut‘s sister and her sons in 1044, banished Osgod Clapa in 1046, and outlawed Earl Alfgar twice, once in 1055 and again in 1058. Politically, it was advantageous for Edward to remove Cnut‘s relatives from England, and Osgod Clapa had been a powerful Danish landholder under Cnut as well. Alfgar, Earl of East Anglia, was accused of being a traitor in 1055 and was outlawed at a royal council in March of that year.

---

95 F. Barlow, *Edward the Confessor* (Berkeley and Los Angeles, CA: University of California Press, 1970), 3-53; F. Barlow, *The Godwins: The Rise and Fall of a Noble Dynasty* (London, UK: Pearson Education Ltd., 2002), 27-33.

96 John of Worcester, vol. 2: 522-525; Symeon of Durham, *History of the Kings*, 529; Walter of Coventry, *Memoriale*, vol. 1: 63; Barlow, *The Godwins*, 30-31; Stenton, *Anglo-Saxon England*, 414-415.

97 *ASC*, year 1042. According to the Anglo-Saxon Chronicle entry for 1041, Edward returned to the court of his half-brother Harthacnut that year.

98 William of Malmesbury, 196, 206, 216-217; *ASC*, year 1043. William of Malmesbury is the source quoted here. The Anglo-Saxon Chronicle of course mentions the accession of Edward, as do Henry of Huntington's writings, although their accounts are more abbreviated than that of Malmesbury.

99 Barlow, *Edward the Confessor*, 61-65.

Alfgar was reinstated to his position in East Anglia later that same year, only to be accused of treason and outlawed again in 1058.[100]

The best-known uses of outlawry, exile, and banishment as tools of political and social control during the reign of Edward the Confessor, however, involved the king's treatment of the members of the powerful Godwin family.[101] Earl Godwin, from whom the family derived its name, had risen to prominence and wealth during the reign of King Cnut. His origins are obscure, but in 1018 he became Earl of Wessex and the following year he married Gytha, the king's sister-in-law. This placed him within the inner circle of the king and in a position of importance and influence in Danish England.[102] Earl Godwin served Cnut faithfully and reaped the benefits. According to The *Vita Aedwardi Regis*, Godwin was made *bajulus*, a position of comparable to later office of justiciar, sometime during Cnut's reign.[103] Godwin's influence extended through the reigns of Cnut's sons Harold Harefoot and Harthacnut, and in 1042, his position as Earl of Wessex allowed him to exploit the needs of the returning Edward. Between 1042 and 1051, Godwin cozied up to Edward, even securing the marriage of his daughter, Edith, to the King in 1045. Soon after his coronation, Edward made Godwin's two oldest sons, Swein and Harold, the earls of Herefordshire

---

100 *ASC*, year 1055; year 1058; Symeon of Durham, *History of the Kings*, 532; 538; 540; Lawson, *Cnut*, 163; Barlow, *Edward the Confessor*, 74-75, 99-100, 193, 208-209; Barlow, *The Godwins*, 53. Alfgar's first outlawry may have been at the urging of the influential Godwins, who were engaged in a feud with Alfgar's family. Alfgar's second round as an outlaw seems to have been associated with charges of treasonable correspondence with Gruffydd of Wales. Alfgar returned to England in 1058 by force with the assistance of Gruffydd.

101 F. Barlow, *The Godwins*; "The Outlawry of Earl Godwin from the *Vita Aedwardi Regis*," by T.S. Jones in *Medieval Outlaws: Ten Tales in Modern English*, ed. T. H. Ohlgren (Stroud, Gloucestershire, UK: Sutton Publishing, 1998): 1-11; E. John, "Edward the Confessor and the Norman Succession," *The English Historical Review*, vol. 94, no. 371 (Apr., 1979): 241-267; Stenton, *Anglo-Saxon England*, 442, 545-561. From the reign of Edward the Confessor, the legend of the exile of Hereward the Wake, "the first of the English outlaws," emerges. There is little known about the specifics of Hereward's banishment, but his historicity is proven. See M. Keen, *Outlaws of Medieval Legend*, 9-39; "The Deeds of Hereward," by Michael Swanton in Ohlgren, *Medieval Outlaws*, 28-99.

102 Barlow, *Godwins*, 17-25.

103 *Vita Aedwardi Confessoris or The Life of King Edward who rests at Westminster*, ed. F. Barlow 2nd edn (Oxford, UK: Clarendon Press, 1992), 6-11.

and East Anglia, respectively. This placed a vast amount of wealth, land, and power into the hands of the Godwin clan.[104]

Despite a seemingly good relationship, Edward soon came to resent Godwin‘s power, and as the latter's influence grew, the King took steps to suppress it.[105] Edward used exclusion repeatedly in his efforts. The first chapter in the exile and outlawry of the Godwin clan involved the eldest son of Earl Godwin, Swein. Swein was outlawed in the late 1040s for several acts against the king, the aristocracy, and the church. [106] Swein returned to England in 1050 and was "declared no longer an outlaw," but he and his family remained under the watchful eye of the king.[107]

In 1051, a conflict between King Edward and Earl Godwin resulted in Godwin and his sons being expelled from England.[108] They were subsequently outlawed and the crown confiscated their lands.[109] Edith, Godwin‘s daughter and Edward‘s wife, was sent to a monastery and their marriage was likely annulled.[110] The outlawed Godwins spent the next year ravaging the coast of southern England, garnering support for their cause. In 1052, after repeated appeals to the King and the English nobility, Godwin received "full friendship, full earldom, and all that he had before; and also to all the men that were with

---

104 Barlow, *Edward the Confessor*, 178; Barlow, *Godwins*, 27-37; E. John, "Edward the Confessor and the Norman Succession." *English Historical Review*, vol. 94, no. 371 (Apr., 1979): 241-267, at 248-249. The *Anglo-Saxon Chronicle* reports that Edward and Edith were married in 1044.

105 Barlow, *Godwins*, 34-37, 74-75; John, "Edward the Confessor," 252-253. There must have been some animosity remaining from the role Godwin played in the death of Edward‘s brother, Arthur, in 1036, as well.

106 *ASC*, year 1049; William of Malmesbury, 214-223; Barlow, *Edward the Confessor*, 90-91; Stenton, *Anglo-Saxon England*, 423-424. Swein allegedly seduced or raped Edgifu, the abbess of Leominster, in 1049. He was also said to have killed his cousin, Earl Beorn, who was in command of a royal warship off of the south of England. When Edward heard of this, he had Swein declared to be "a man without honor". According to Stenton, this treatment of a criminal "is a remarkable indication of the extent to which English society under a native king was still governed by Scandinavian habit of mind in regard to matters of honor."

107 *ASC,* years 1046, 1049-1050; Barlow, *Edward the Confessor*, 99-103; Barlow, *Godwins*, 35, 38-39; See also of Coventry, *Memoriale*, vol. 1: 66.

108 Barlow, *Godwins*, 40-42; *ASC*, year 1051. Sources vary in accounts of what the men quarreled over, whether it was the appointment of Robert of Jumièges to the archbishopric of Canterbury or the treatment of the king's kinsman Eustace of Boulogne during a visit to England. According to *ASC* (E) Archbishop Robert was declared an outlaw due to his responsibility "for the disagreement between Earl Godwine and the king,"

109 Barlow, *Godwins*, 40-44.

110 John, "Edward the Confessor," 248-249.

him."[111] Edward had outlawed his political enemies in an attempt to quell their influence in England but ultimately it was this influence and support from the English aristocracy that facilitated the return of their land and power.[112]

This was not the last trouble for the Godwins, however. In 1055, King Edward appointed Tostig, another of Godwin's sons, Earl of Northumbria. A group of Yorkshire thegns, disgruntled by Tostig's strong and seemingly harsh governance, ousted the earl in 1065. They declared Tostig to be an outlaw, and chose Morcar, the younger brother of Edwin, Earl of Mercia, to be their new earl. The group appealed to the king to depose and exile Tostig, a demand to which Edward had no choice but to acquiesce in late 1065.[113] Tostig fled to Flanders but would return to menace his brother Harold in 1066 with the Norwegian king Harald Hardrada.[114]

The reign of Edward, followed by the short rule of Harold Godwinson in 1066, marks the end of Anglo-Saxon kingship in England. There were no legal codes promulgated during Edward's reign, although the twelfth-century document called the *Leges Eadwardi Confessoris* claimed to record the *laga Eadwardi*, or the laws that had been in force while he was king.[115] The *Vita Aedwardi Regis* stated that Edward "abolished bad laws and with the help of his wise counselors enacted good ones," but according to Barlow, there is no direct evidence that Edward was a lawgiver or particularly interested in the exercise of justice.[116] Harold Godwinson was too concerned with fighting off invaders, par-

---

111 *ASC,* year 1052; John of Worcester, vol. 2: 566-573; Barlow, *Godwins*, 44-49; *Vita*, 36-47.

112 One additional component to Edward's dealings with the Godwin family is also discussed by William of Malmesbury, as Godwin's son Wulnod had been given as a hostage by Godwin to Edward. Wulnod was sent to Normandy by Edward and held in captivity there, but was sent back to England by William the Conqueror where he died in confinement at Salisbury. See William of Malmesbury, 222.

113 *Vita Aedwardi Confessoris*, 74-85; *ASC*, year 1065; Barlow, *Godwins*, 83-89; Fletcher, *Bloodfeud*, 149-162; Stenton, *Anglo-Saxon England*, 570-571.

114 Tostig died at the Battle of Stamford Bridge on 25 September 1066.

115 Barlow, *Edward the Confessor*, 178; B.R. O"Brien, *God's Peace and King's Peace: The Laws of Edward the Confessor* (Philadelphia, PA: University of Pennsylvania Press, 1999), 3; 31-36; Wormald, *Making of English Law*, 128.

116 *Vita Aedwardi Confessoris*, 20-21; Barlow, *Edward the Confessor*, 178; O"Brien, *God's Peace*, 3, 31-44; *LEC*, Prologue, found in O"Brien, 159; Pollock and Maitland, *History of English Law*, vol. 1: 95-110; Chibnall, *The Normans*, 53-54. The prologue of the *Leges Eadwardi Confessoris* purports to contain the laws of the realm prior to the Norman Conquest. It was allegedly compiled at a council called by William the Conqueror in 1070 where "wise men and learned in their law" were called together from throughout the realm. O"Brien argues on page 44 that the laws represent "with few exceptions

ticularly Harald Hardrada and Tostig in the north and William of Normandy in the south, to have time for much else.

Observations: Exclusion and Social Order in Anglo-Saxon England

During the Anglo-Saxon period, banishment, exile, and outlawry were tools of kings, feuding families and political rivals. These methods of exclusion were fundamental instruments of maintaining social and political control order. Kings drove out adversaries; powerful lords removed "unjust" rulers; nobles cast out men who offended them; kinsmen drove members of rival families into exile; and fugitive suspects and escaped prisoners were outlawed. Outlaws and exiles were isolated and languished without any kind of social or physical protection. Exclusion may not have been permanent, but it was at all times feared.

From the earliest codification of Anglo-Saxon law, governmental concern for the control, or the very least, limit of, feuding behaviors were present. By the laws of Alfred, Æthelstan and, Cnut, kings attempted to regulate elements of banishment, exile, and outlawry. Kings incorporated exclusion into the developing body of written law and matters of governance. Rulers and "law-makers" were not interested in limiting the exclusion, but rather endorsed, used, and sought to control it. Rulers were not only interested in securing their own positions by driving out their enemies, but also wanted to maintain peace throughout England by ridding the kingdom of individuals who threatened to disrupt the social order. The crown used, influenced, and strengthened the mechanisms of power and justice that were available to it and that were already in place in Anglo-Saxon society.

Outlawry and exile were flexible and amendable as part of the feuding process, and were subject to the rules of compensation, retribution, and community that governed Anglo-Saxon society. By enforcing financial punishments for harboring exiles, the crown deterred individuals from assisting wrongdoers and by expelling thieves who failed to find sureties, kings drove social malefactors out of the realm. Both of these actions exhibit the growing royal and legal interest in exclusion on a local level. Narratives and legal documentation alike attest to the practice, place, and use of outlawry, exile and banishment in society and the role they played in the maintenance of social control in Anglo-Saxon England.

---

some of what must have been, or was supposed to be, in force during, roughly speaking, the century following the Norman Conquest."

Chapter 3: Exile, Outlawry, and Imprisonment in Norman and Anglo-Norman Governance and Law

Practices of exclusion were affected by Norman centralization in late eleventh-century England, as post-Conquest Norman rule brought new characteristics to exile, banishment, and outlawry. To the Normans, many of the customary practices of law and order in England threatened to weaken the authority enjoyed by the dukes of Normandy, now also kings of England. Simultaneously, there was an increased use of imprisonment once the Normans arrived in England. Although imprisonment remained a minimal part of Anglo-Norman society, its presence represented the earliest stages of a shift in methods used to maintain law and order.

Law and Practice in Tenth and Eleventh Century Normandy

Dukes of Normandy retained the right to outlaw public enemies from their Scandinavian ancestors.[117] The power to exile in Normandy was a component of

117 F. Barlow, *The Feudal Kingdom of England: 1042-1216*, 4th edn (London and New York: Longman, 1988), 105; E. van Houts, "The Vocabulary of Exile and Outlawry in the North Sea Area around the First Millennium," 13-28. The similarities between Scandinavian, Norman and Anglo-Saxon terminology for exile and outlawry create some confusion and uncertainty at times but also remind us that political and legal practices were very much intertwined and often indistinguishable. For more on Scandinavian outlawry, see "Outlawry" under the entry "Crime and Punishment" on page 116 of *Medieval Scandinavia: An Encyclopedia* ed. P. Pulsiano and K. Wolf (New York, NY: Garland, 1993) and W.I. Miller, *Bloodtaking and peacemaking: feud, law, and society in Saga Iceland,* (1990). Bates acknowledges that the power to exile was a right imported by the Norman Scandinavian ancestors, while pointing out that many other ducal rights, such as control of fortifications, were Carolingian holdovers. The *Consuetudines et Iusticie* lists the powers held by the duke of Normandy in the eleventh century and were compiled c. 1091 by William II. See Bates, *Normandy Before 1066* (Essex, UK: Longman Group Ltd., 1982), 162-163 and C.H. Haskins, "The Norman "*Consuetudines et Iusticie*" of William the Conqueror," *The English Historical Review*, vol. 23, no. 91 (Jul., 1908): 502-508. Haskins provides the Latin text of the *Consuetudines* on pages 506-508.

ducal authority, and the duke retained the right to make law and to dispense justice. Exile, in practice, could be an authoritative act carried out by anyone holding property in the duchy, as it was tied to land tenure and possessions rather than a formal legal process.[118]

Along with the right to control castle-building, the right of exile was a method by which the duke exercised direct power over the aristocracy.[119] Exile in Normandy was meant to be temporary and often resulted in reconciliation and restitution after a period of time. Due to the paucity of early Norman source material, we rely on chroniclers such as Dudo of St. Quentin, William of Jumièges and Orderic Vitalis for accounts of early Norman historical events, including instances of exile, banishment, and outlawry employed as mechanisms of political, social, and legal power. [120] Charter evidence and later legal documentation reminds us that eleventh-century Norman justice was based upon complex rela-

---

118 The "*Consuetudines et Iusticie*" in Haskins, *Norman Institutions*, 277-284; E. Johnson, "The Process of Norman Exile into Southern Italy," in *Exile in the Middle Ages: Selected Proceedings from the International Medieval Congress, University of Leeds, 8-11 July 2002*, eds L. Napran and E. van Houts, vol. 13 (Turnhout, Brepols: 2002): 29-38, at 31, 35; D. Douglas, *William the Conqueror: The Norman Impact Upon England* (*WC)* (Los Angeles and Berkeley, CA: University of California Press, 1964), 133, 150-152, asserts that as the power of the ducal court strengthened in the period before the Conquest, William had a growing influence on the rights of his vassals.

119 D. Bates, *Normandy before 1066,* 163-167. According to Bates, the use of exile as in Normandy is "informative with regard to the limits to which political punishment could normally be taken," but no duke "employed it as a means to break men or to attempt a radical amendment to the social structure." For a general assessment, see also Pollock and Maitland's *The History of English Law*, vol. 1, chap. 3, "Norman Law."

120 For more on both the mythical and historical origins of Normandy, see Bates, *Normandy Before 1066*, 2-44; R.A. Brown, *The Normans* (New York, NY: St. Martin's Press, 1984), 5, 11-17; J. Dunbabin, *France in the Making: 843-1180.* 2nd edn (Oxford, UK: Oxford UP, 2000), 66-67, 78-84; R. McKitterick, *The Frankish Kingdoms Under the Carolingians, 751-987* (Harlow, Essex, UK: Longman Group Ltd., 1983), 236-257. Dudo of St. Quentin. *History of the Normans.* trans. E. Christiansen (Woodbridge, Suffolk: The Boydell Press, 1998); See also N. Webber, *The Evolution of the Norman Identity, 911-1054* (Woodbridge, Suffolk: The Boydell Press, 2005), 13-14.; M. Chibnall, *The Normans* (Oxford, UK: Blackwell Publishers Ltd., 2000), 16-17. D. Crouch, *The Normans: The History of a Dynasty* (London, UK: Hambledon and London, 2002), 1-8; Dunbabin, *The Making of France,* 60. For more on historical writing in Normandy in the tenth through the twelfth centuries, see M. Chibnall, *The World of Orderic Vitalis* (Oxford, UK: Clarendon Press, 1984), 175-180.

tionships among lords and vassals, and was intertwined with land, oath, obligation, service, and protection.[121]

Dukes of Normandy, Power, Exclusion – and Imprisonment

Exclusion was an activity of ducal power. When Richard the Fearless, son of William Longsword and grandson of Rollo, took possession of Normandy in 947, he faced the challenge of securing loyalty and payments from his subjects. Richard had been a captive of the French King Louis IV during his childhood, and in his absence, Ralph Torta had taken the highest position of authority in Normandy. Once Richard returned to Normandy, Ralph was angry, resentful, and hostile to the Duke. As a result, rumors circulated that Richard was going to expel Ralph from the duchy, and in a preemptive move, Ralph fled from Rouen. Ralph hoped to placate the young duke by abandoning his holdings in Rouen, but was unsuccessful. According to Dudo, Richard was not willing to forgive Ralph's audacity and required that Rolf depart "from our boundaries under sentence of banishment, [or] he will very speedily incur the doom he has deserved."[122]

Political expulsion of this sort was commonly used in Normandy in the tenth and eleventh centuries. In 1027, when William the Conqueror's father Robert became Duke of Normandy, he drove out disloyal subjects, including his uncle, the Archbishop of Rouen. Duke Robert had grown suspicious of the Archbishop, who fled to the court of the French king, but soon recalled his uncle once he realized that he had received advice from counselors who wished to cause a dispute between the two men.[123] Orderic Vitalis tells us about Osmund Drengot,

121 Pollock and Maitland, *History of English Law*, vol. 1: 64-78; C. H. Haskins, "Normandy under William the Conqueror," *The American Historical Review*, vol. 14, no. 3 (Apr., 1909): 453-476, at 455-458, 462. *Tres Ancien Coutumier* was the oldest Norman law book, dating to the late twelfth century. See vol. 1, *Le très ancien coutumier de Normandie* of Ernest-Joseph Tardiff's *Coutumiers de Normandie* (Rouen: E. Cagniard, 1881-1903).

122 Dudo, 122-123; Crouch, *The Normans*, 15-16.

123 *Gesta Normannorum Ducum of William of Jumièges, Orderic Vitalis, and Robert of Torigni, Volume II, Books V-VIII.* (*GND*) ed. and trans. E.M.C. Van Houts (Oxford, UK: Clarendon Press, 1995), 46-49. The title of "duke" or "*dux*" was not commonly used until after 1066, but it was Richard II who first gave himself that distinction in 1006. See Bates, *Normandy Before 1066*, 148-149. Robert later expelled Hugh, bishop

who during the same period fled from Normandy and ended up in Apulia in order to avoid the wrath of Duke Robert.[124] The conciliatory and temporary nature of exclusion is clear, as exile was not only a tool of ducal power but was also a self-imposed means of escape from the wrath of a powerful lord.

Accounts of the actions of Duke William II in Normandy are replete with uses of exile and banishment as means to gain political control over the duchy.[125] William became duke as a child after the death of his father, and fell victim to the machinations of a greedy regent. When he came of age, he used both military and personal strength to rule effectively and control the Norman aristocracy. William exiled rebel *vicecomites* such as Thurstan Goz, William Werlenc, William Busac, and William of Arques, and placed Guy of Burgundy under house arrest.[126] As he consolidated his power in the early 1060s, William expelled some of his highest nobles. Ralf of Tosny, Hugh of Grandmesnil, Arnold d''Courville, and Abbot Robert of Saint-Evroul were all driven from the duchy so that William could rule without interference from powerful nobility.[127] William's use of exile and banishment was indicative of the nature of Norman exile on the whole, as these high nobles were only out of Normandy for a short time

---

of Bayeux, when he attempted to stage a rebellion, and subsequently took over the stronghold at Bayeux. See *GND*, 52-53.

124 Orderic Vitalis, *The Ecclesiastical History of Orderic Vitalis (Historia Ecclesiastica)*. ed. and trans. M. Chibnall. vols 1-6 (Oxford, UK: Clarendon Press, 1969-1980), vol. 2: 56-57. For information on Orderic's writing influences, see Chibnall, *World of Orderic Vitalis*, 177-180; Orderic mentions the library collection at St-Evroult and other works that influenced him throughout his work, including vol. 2: 48-51. See also M. Chibnall, "Charter and Chronicle: The Use of Archive Sources by Norman Historians" in *Church and Government in the Middle Ages: Essays Presented to C. R. Cheney on his 70th Birthday*, eds C. N. L. Brooke et al. (Cambridge, UK: Cambridge UP, 1976); E. Van Houts, "Historical Writing" in *A Companion to the Anglo-Norman World*, eds C. Harper-Bill and E. Van Houts (Woodbridge, Suffolk: The Boydell Press, 2003): 118. Orderic wrote about historical as well as contemporary events in England and Normandy. He was born in England and later sent to Normandy by his father, where he became a monk at the monastery of St-Evroul and produced his ecclesiastical writings. For more information on Orderic's own past, see vol. 2: 262-263; 3: 6-8; 4: 550-557; Chibnall, *World of Orderic*, 3; 8-9; 14; 221-224.

125 *GND,* 8-11.

126 D. Douglas, *WC,* 31-80; M. Bennett, "Violence in eleventh-century Normandy: feud, warfare and politics," in *Violence and Society in the Early Medieval West*, ed. G. Halsall (Woodbridge, Suffolk, UK: The Boydell Press, 1998): 126-140.

127 *GND*, 100-105; 126-129; 120-123; Chibnall, *The Normans*, 30-31; Douglas, *WC*, 66, 92-95, 138; Bates, *Normandy Before 1066*, 166-167; Orderic Vitalis, vol. 2: 79 note 3; 90-91, 94-99, 104-105, 108-109, 112-115, 132-135. Abbot Robert went to the church of St. Eufemia in Italy, where he became a monk.

and were allowed to return to the duchy after making some sort of retribution. Arnold d'"Courville, for instance, took refuge a short distance south of the Norman border and was allowed to return to Normandy after three years. Hugh of Grandmesnil and Ralf of Tosny later fought with William at the Battle of Hastings, indicating that they spent a relatively short time outside of the duke's favor.[128]

The duke's right to exile was essential to his authority but it also served as an exercise in diplomacy. Norman dukes relied upon the use of exile to maintain order and temporarily remove an enemy. This allowed for recompense and forgiveness and generally proved successful. Dukes were able to demonstrate their power as well as receive the necessary recognition and obedience of their exiled subjects once they allowed them to return. Returning exiles necessarily paid homage to their duke and the duke used this arrangement to strengthen his lordship.[129]

In addition to exclusion, Norman dukes used imprisonment to influence men and display authority. Captivity in Normandy was often associated with kinship and feud behavior and nobles, family members, and men of high social standing were frequently cast into prison. Contention for authority in ducal Normandy created a great amount of distrust among men and there was a need to reaffirm loyalty and kinship ties. This resulted in the use of imprisonment by dukes to compel oaths and homage. Kinship was maintained through social obligations and imprisonment was a common means to enforce proper behavior within this construct.[130] For example, Duke Richard II (d. 1026) imprisoned his brother William in the early eleventh century because William would not swear an oath of fidelity to him. The duke then kept his brother in the tower at Rouen for five years for his contempt.[131] Duke Richard III faced a similar problem and imprisoned his brother Robert after the latter rebelled against him in1026 or 1027.[132]

---

128 Orderic Vitalis, vol. 2: 90-91; Bates, *Normandy Before 1066,* 166-167.

129 Bates, *Normandy before 1066*, 166-168.

130 For more on the distrust among Norman dukes and their families, see E. Searle, *Predatory Kinship and the Creation of Norman Power, 840-1066* (Los Angeles and Berkeley, CA: University of California Press, 1988), 246-247. Searle assesses kinship and the use of marriage alliances in the development of Norman ducal authority.

131 *GND,* 8-11. Duke Richard II also killed and exiled William's men who continued to rebel against him. William later escaped, begged for forgiveness, was accepted back into Richard's good graces and given the county of Eu.

132 *GND*, 44-45. Richard III was only duke from 23 August 1026 until his death on 6 August 6 1027.

Robert was subsequently kept in confinement until he paid homage to the duke.[133]

Imprisonment in early Norman history also involved outsiders to the duchy, often powerful men whom the duke wished to control. In 1064, Harold Godwinson, earl of Wessex, traveled to the continent, supposedly on his way to Normandy to reaffirm that Duke William II was the heir to the English throne.[134] En route, Harold was blown off course and landed in Ponthieu. He was captured by Count Guy of Abbeville and held in prison until Duke William II appealed to Guy and paid Harold's ransom. Harold, now in a position of subservience to the Duke, embarked upon a military campaign into Brittany with William and later swore on holy relics that William would be the next king of England.[135]

This exercise in imprisonment, oath-swearing, and fidelity brings us to an important crossroads in the exercise of power in the eleventh century. Duke William secured Harold's release from Guy's prison and therefore, the Earl owed William some sort of homage. Harold fought alongside William in the Duke's campaign in Brittany, but this did not secure his release from captivity and subsequent return to England. William continued to hold Harold captive until he was able to secure a promise from him about the throne of England. According to the Bayeux Tapestry, Harold swore on holy relics that William the Conqueror would be the next king of England.[136] Once Harold returned to England and after the death of Edward the Confessor in 1065, Harold Godwinson became king. William believed that Harold had gone back upon the promises he had made and used the events of Harold's captivity in his justification of the invasion of England and seizure of the throne. This action was fundamental to the justification of William of Normandy's invasion of England in 1066.

The use of imprisonment demonstrated an immense amount of social and political strength held by the duke, and whether or not Harold was coerced while held by William, the latter saw Harold's oath as binding. In the interest of his

133 Haskins, *Norman Institutions*, 28-30.

134 According to sources, Edward the Confessor had made the initial promise of accession to William in 1051.

135 *GND*, 158-161; William of Poitiers, *Gesta Guillelmi*, ed. and trans. R.H.C. Davis and M. Chibnall, (Oxford, UK: Clarendon Press, 1998), 68-77, 120-121; Eadmer, *Historia Novorum in Anglia or Eadmer's History of Recent Events in England*, trans. G. Bosanquet, (London, UK: The Cresset Press, 1964), 5-9; Douglas, *WC*, 175-180; Crouch, 82-85. Sources indicate that Harold was either on a mission to retrieve hostages from Normandy or was acting as an agent of Edward the Confessor to promise Duke William the throne of England.

136 Lucien Musset, *The Bayeux Tapestry*, trans. Richard Rex (Woodbridge, Suffolk, UK: Boydell Press, 2005), 138-151.

own power and authority, William confined men to exercise his authority. To compel an enemy or wrongdoer by using confinement was unknown in Anglo-Saxon England but coercive and authoritative imprisonment traveled across the English Channel with Norman invaders in 1066. Imprisonment, first as an instrument of political power and later as a mechanism of law, slowly influenced the social order in England. Exclusion was the means by which wrongdoers and enemies were dealt with in Anglo-Saxon England and the dukes of Normandy had not shied away from using exile and exclusion when it came to his politics and law. Exile and banishment were temporary methods by which a malefactor would be compelled to leave an area for a time, after which he could buy his way back into favor and pay homage to the duke. Exile and imprisonment were cooperative in Normandy, as they were both used by the Duke in order to maintain power and authority. Once William became King of England, and as the Anglo-Norman realm materialized, these two conceptually opposite practices functioned in very similar ways in England.

Banishment, Outlawry, and Imprisonment following the Norman Conquest of 1066

Regardless of promises made prior to the death of Edward the Confessor, William invaded England and met Harold on the battlefield at Hastings. Harold was killed on 14 October 1066 and England fell under Norman rule.[137] Social order and political stability were of foremost concern to the new Norman kings.[138] Within this context, the use of outlawry, exile, and banishment on both sides of the English Channel became linked under the authority of a single ruler. Just as outlawry and exile could be permanent and linked to animosity and revenge in Anglo-Saxon England, so too could the practices be used to provide necessary time and space for disputing parties to calm down and reconsider the matter as

---

137 *ASC,* year 1066, William of Poitiers, *Gesta Guillelmi,* 128-151; Douglas, *WC,* 198-202; Lewis Thorpe, *The Bayeux tapestry and the Norman invasion: with an introduction and a translation from the contemporary account of William of Poitiers* (London, UK: The Folio Society, 1973); John Langdon-Davies, *1066: a collection of contemporary documents* (London, UK: Cape, 1966); M.K. Lawson, *Battle of Hastings 1066* (Stroud, UK: Tempus, 2002).

138 Douglas, *WC*, 204-264; The Normans brought "Norman law" with them in 1066, which according to Pollock and Maitland, was feudal, unwritten, and was influenced by both Scandinavian and French traditions and customs: *History of English Law*, vol. 1: 64-78.

had been common in Normandy.[139] These forms of exclusion also served as components in legal processes, leading to the suspension of procedural rights and confiscation of property as punishment.[140] In theory, some form of outlawry or exile could result from every misdeed or perceived wrong in the Anglo-Norman realm.

Norman kings of England asserted their royal right to control the outlawry procedure in England, just as they had controlled legal processes, exclusion, and feud behavior in Normandy.[141] Cnut had claimed outlawry to be the right of the Crown during his reign and aspects of the outlawry process had been brought under closer royal scrutiny. Likewise, after the Normans arrived in England, the crown endorsed exclusionary customs and attempted to use outlawry against fugitive criminals and social malefactors. The difficulty in this, however, was that the legal pronouncement of outlawry did not fall under direct royal authority in England. It was a formal right held by the county court. Nominally, all courts in England were conducted under the authority of the King, but the limits and realities of royal intent, power, and strength at the local level become clear upon closer inspection of the use of outlawry.[142]

Outlawry as it existed in Anglo-Saxon England when the Normans arrived in 1066, resembled the Norman practice of *forisbannitio*, a Carolingian form of outlawry that deprived a criminal of all procedural and property rights. [143] An English outlaw did not explicitly lose all property rights, however, and English kings did not maintain the same control over the declaration and enforcement of

---

139 E. van Houts, "L"exil dans l"espace Anglo-Normand," in *La Normandie et l"Angleterre au Moyen Age*, 116-127.

140 Goebel, *Felony and Misdemeanor*, 9, 16, 18, 57, 110. In *Felony and Misdemeanor*, outlawry and its role in judgment, authority, and the definition of crime in English law is assessed in terms of the peace theory. Goebel sets out to disprove the "peace theory" but his insights about outlawry are helpful regardless of the validity of the peace theory. Under a Germanic "peace theory," outlawry was what Goebel termed "relative outlawry" in that a peaceless man was involved in a feud and was an outlaw to the kin of the injured party rather than to community at large. Under Salic Law, outlawry was a process which included suspension of rights through the imposition of exile, loss of status, internment, banishment, and/or confiscation, and under the Carolingians, "qualified outlawry" was closely connected to economic sanctions in general.

141 Goebel, *Felony and Misdemeanor,* 418-419; Douglas, *WC*, 148-153, 305-310.

142 Goebel, *Felony and Misdemeanor,* 420-422.

143 Goebel, *Felony and Misdemeanor*, 308-315; 385-399. The Norman dukes controlled the right of exile and outlawry with respect to the Peace of God and the Truce of God movements on the continent. In Carolingian law, the "forisbannitio" had his procedural rights suspended, just as an outlaw would, but he also forfeited all property. For more, see Goebel, *Felony and Misdemeanor,* 110-113.

outlawry as did their Norman counterparts. A Norman duke had the exclusive right to outlaw and exile within his duchy, and while outlawry in England had increasingly received attention and intervention by the Crown, particularly by Æthelstan and Cnut, it remained a legal action based in local shire courts. William the Conqueror and his successors now found themselves in a position of power where many of the rights they held in Normandy did not apply in England. This warranted further clarifications on exclusionary processes in their newly obtained lands.

The blending of Anglo-Saxon and Norman customary practices resulted in a new form of outlawry. Anglo-Norman law continued to assert royal authority in exclusionary practices and aimed to redefine what offenses could result in outlawry and exile. Whatever the situation at the time of the invasion in 1066, the author of twelfth-century *Leis Willelme* thought that exile could be permanent in certain circumstances and made sure these situations were included within written law. In the *Leis Willelme*, if one man poisoned another, he was to be killed or sent into permanent exile. Permanent exclusion was a departure from Norman justice, but was consistent with Anglo-Saxon practice. The *Leis Willelme* stated that any accused man who failed to appear before the royal court three times was to be seized, deprived of property and placed outside the protection of both his lord and any legal processes.[144] Because a lord was responsible for his subjects and servants, he was considered an accessory in the flight of anyone in his service. In this event, the lord could clear himself of involvement with the oaths of five men or could pay compensation to the king. If the lord did neither, he was outlawed.[145] Outlawry was appropriate for men who failed to appear before the law, for men who could not or did not make amends for wrongdoing, and for men who failed to fulfill social obligations. This was consistent with Anglo-Saxon practice, but in a departure from pre-Conquest law, outlaws in England now lost all rights and property in accordance with Norman *forisbannitio*.

The Anglo-Norman form of outlawry was still not under direct royal authority. Outlawry continued to be a component of local law in the shires and hundreds of Anglo-Norman England. There was a disconnect between local justice and order as the responsibility of kin groups and communities, and the administration of royal law in the localities under the authority of the sheriff. To bridge this divide, William placed trusted men into sheriff positions to exact justice on his behalf. Just as Cnut had done before him, William encouraged local

144 Wormald, *Making of English Law*, 407-409; Robertson, 226-227; Pollock and Maitland, *History of English Law*, vol. 1: 98.

145 Leis Wl 36; Leis Wl 47; Leis Wl 52. The *Leis* were likely promulgated within a half century after William's death in 1087.

justice and required that all legal matters be heard in hundred and county courts before being brought to the direct attention of the king. As a result, matters of criminal justice remained largely in the hands of county courts.[146] In these courts, the sheriff was responsible for the capture of suspects, pursuit of outlaws, and at times, he acted as judge. The sheriff during the Anglo-Saxon period had functioned on behalf of the local earl or alderman, and under the Normans, he increasingly became an agent of the king, placed into his position by royal authority for an unspecified amount of time.[147]

Under the early Norman kings, the position of sheriff became one of power and wealth, and the sheriff enjoyed "great freedom of action…[as] a personal adherent of the king…he combined the prestige of a local magnate and the status of a trusted official."[148] The role of the Anglo-Norman sheriff in local matters of justice and within the county courts brought together customary practices and royal prerogative and law. As a subject of the crown, the sheriff soon acquired the authority to hear pleas concerning the king and his kingdom in local courts.[149] A sheriff could be instructed by royal writ to bring local cases to the attention of the king or to serve as judge on his behalf. The Anglo-Norman sheriff could, at times, pronounce outlawry in the county court. Furthermore, the sheriff's place in the county was that of an overseer of frankpledge, a close relative to the Anglo-Saxon practices of tithings and *borh*, and was an administrator of social accountability. The Anglo-Norman sheriff took tours of the shires in

---

146 Douglas, *WC*, 305-310; Pollock and Maitland, *History of English Law*, vol. 1: 304; Hyams, *Rancor and Reconciliation*, 147; Plucknett, *Concise History*, 392-393; M. H. Kerr, "Angevin Reform of the Appeal of Felony," *Law and History Review*, vol. 13, no. 2 (Autumn, 1995): 351-391, at 352. Anglo-Norman kings introduced appeals of felony into law. Appeals of felony included serious crimes such as homicide, robbery, theft, rape, mayhem and breach of peace which were considered pleas of the crown. The existence of crimes which fell under special interest of the Crown extended back to the Anglo-Saxon period and following the Conquest, many of those offenses became felonies.

147 Morris, *Medieval Sheriff*, 24-26; 41-46; W.A. Morris, *The Early English County Court: An Historical Treatise with Illustrative Documents*. University of California Publications in History, vol. 14. eds H.E. Bolton et al. (Berkeley, CA: University of California Press, 1926), 89-240. The sheriff maintained fiscal, military, and judicial responsibilities. For more details of the role of the early sheriff, see generally Morris, chapters 1 and 2.

148 Morris, *Medieval Sheriff*, 50; Douglas, *WC*, 305-310. For similarities between the Norman *vicecomites* and the Anglo-Norman sheriff, see Morris, chapter 3.

149 Morris, *Medieval Sheriff*, 50; Douglas, *WC*, 305-310.

England to account for the sureties and pledges of all community members.[150] Royal law was concerned with local law and order and, within the confines of social custom, used the sheriff to influence community action. The sheriff bridged the gap between community and crown and represented the obligations and limitations of both.

William needed to affirm his political authority throughout the whole of England. Exile and outlawry were identical in principle in the Anglo-Norman world, and while kings failed to hold complete control over outlawry as a local practice, they could still exile their enemies and rivals on a larger, political scale. King William exiled secular rebels and traitors, but also used imprisonment as a new element of royal authority, when dealing with his enemies in England. The *Anglo-Saxon Chronicle* recounts the deeds and treatment of rebels such as of Æthelwine, Hereward, Edwin, Morcar, Odo, and Waltheof, all of whom were either imprisoned or banished, or perhaps underwent both.[151] The blending of punitive inclusion and exclusion marks a change in how rivalry and disorder were dealt with in England.

Soon after his coronation on Christmas day 1066, William left England and returned to Normandy. In his absence, William left William Fitz Osbern and Odo of Bayeux as his vice-regents. According to *The Ecclesiastical History of Orderic Vitalis*, Fitz Osbern and Odo plundered and ravaged England so severely that the people fled in voluntary exile to escape.[152] This harsh treatment contributed to the social unrest in England and led to rebellions against Norman rule. In 1069, Bishop Æthelwine of Durham, thought to be a conspirator against the king, was captured at Ely, and placed in prison until his death. Æthelwine had been a monk at Peterborough and active in the tenth-century monastic reform in England prior to becoming bishop at Durham in 1056. He was received

---

150 Morris, *Medieval Sheriff*, 56-58; Morris, *The Early English County Court*, 112-113, 121-122; 143-146; Morris, *The Frankpledge System*, 35ff; R.C. van Caenegem, *Royal Writs in England from the Conquest to Glanville*, A Selden Society Publication (London, UK: Bernard Quaritch, 1959), 88, 201-202. Frankpledge did not function proportionately in all counties, particularly eleventh century northern and border shires. Just as Norman kings of England placed trusted men into shrieval positions in order to control localities, William placed loyal supporters into the ecclesiastical positions in England. During the Anglo-Saxon period, bishops such as Dunstan in the tenth century had been subjected to periods of exile, but during the reign of William I, imprisonment was used to constrain men of the Church thought to be a threat to royal political power and authority.

151 Hereward and the like rebelled against William as King of England, and more complete (and perhaps embellished) versions of their actions are found in the works of later chroniclers.

152 Orderic Vitalis, vol. 2: 202-203.

by William I in 1068 and served as an ambassador to the Scots on behalf of the King, but after the destruction of the church at Durham in 1070, Æthelwine's allegiance changed. According to Simeon, Æthelwine fled England with church treasures while the *Anglo-Saxon Chronicle* reports that Æthelwine was outlawed in 1070 by the King and later joined the resistance efforts against the Normans led by Hereward at Ely. [153]

In 1071, Earl Morcar of Ely rebelled against the king with his brother Edwin and others, and as a result, King William "flung [Morcar] into fetters without any open charge, and kept him in prison to the end of his days."[154] Edwin supposedly died avenging his brother and his men were later exiled, even after bringing Edwin's head to the King and begging for forgiveness.[155] Other rebels such as Agelric and Waltheof were also placed into confinement for their rebellious deeds.[156] In the earldom of Norwich, Ralph of Gael was forced give up his land and go into exile after his garrison made peace with the king and for his recalcitrance, however Earl Roger of Hereford was condemned to perpetual imprisonment.[157]

The contemporaneous use of imprisonment and exile by William the Conqueror reminds us that these two practices in the maintenance of public order were closely connected in political and legal spheres. According to Pollock and Maitland, the Anglo-Saxon punishment for treason was beheading and deprivation of property to his progeny while Norman law stated that traitors were to forfeit property and be imprisoned.[158] The use of imprisonment by William was in line with Norman law, but captivity under William the Conqueror was not limited to holding one's enemies in one location. At times, William took his prison-

---

153 Symeon of Durham, 170-173, Book III.9; 192-195, Book III.17; *ASC*, 1070; "DURHAM: Bishops", *Fasti Ecclesiae Anglicanae 1066-1300: volume 2: Monastic cathedrals (northern and southern provinces), ed.* Diana E. Greenway, (1971), 29-32. URL: http://british-history.ac.uk/report.aspx?compid=33859. Date accessed: 18 May 2012; David Rollason, "Æthelwine (*d.* in or after 1071)", *Oxford Dictionary of National Biography*, Oxford University Press, May 2011 [http://www.oxforddnb.com/view/article/95139, accessed 21 May 2012].

154 Orderic Vitalis, vol. 2: 256-261. According to the Anglo-Saxon Chronicle, Edwin and Morcar both swore loyalty to William at London in 1066 and then accompanied him to Normandy in 1067 as part of his personal entourage. See *ASC*, 1067; Symeon of Durham, *History of the Kings*, 557; Walter of Coventry, *Memoriale*, 1: 88; Barlow, *WC*, 206.

155 Orderic Vitalis, vol. 2: 256-261.

156 Symeon of Durham, *History of the Kings*, 555-558; Hyams, *Rancor and Reconciliation*, 125-128.

157 Orderic Vitalis, vol. 2: 316-319.

158 Pollock and Maitland, *History of English Law*, vol. 1: 51-52.

ers with him back to Normandy, namely the former Archbishop of Canterbury Stigand, rebels Earls Edwin, Morcar and Waltheof, and the only remaining blood-relative of Edward the Confessor, Edgar the Ætheling. All of these men represented how tenuous William's position was in England and were threats to his authority and rule. This form of imprisonment was one of personal proximity, as William kept his enemies close to him, within his authoritative sphere where he could very literally keep an eye on individuals that posed a threat to him.[159]

Orderic repeatedly mentions William's actions against the "rebellious inhabitants" of England:

> ...threw some into prison, disinherited others or drove them into exile and dispersed them far from the shores of their native land.[160]

His power and authority were dependent upon ridding himself of enemies by whatever means necessary. William would appoint men of his choosing as local officials, giving them land to hold as a vassal to him.[161] The Domesday Survey tells us that the King acquired and allocated land in various ways. In Kent, the king imposed land forfeiture upon anyone who received an outlaw. In both Worcestershire and Shropshire, willful breakage of the king's peace could result in outlawry, after which any land possessed by the offender was forfeited to the king.[162] The Domesday Survey records the new possessors of these forfeited lands, such as Godric in Suffolk who possessed the outlaw Eadric's former holdings, and Hugh De" Hourain, who held land taken from William D"Auberville while the latter was held as a prisoner of the king. De" Hourain was said to hold his lands illegally, however, because William D"Auberville had never been disseized of his lands.[163] This makes clear the important social and legal distinctions between an outlaw and a prisoner. Outlaws forfeited property but prisoners did not. The harsh nature and widespread implications of outlawry remained

159 *ASC*, years 1066-1075; *ASC*, year 1082. William's treatment of the English after the Conquest has been described by all, medieval and modern alike, as brutal. According to the Chronicle, he "killed those who could not flee" and "ravaged and laid waste to the shire and all that was in it." See Chibnall, *The Normans*, 48.

160 Orderic Vitalis, vol. 2: 222-223; 264-265; 3: 214-217.

161 Douglas, *WC*, 207-244.

162 R. Fleming, *Domesday Book and the law: Society and legal custom in early medieval England* (Cambridge, UK: Cambridge UP, 1998), no. 887; Pollock and Maitland, *History of English Law*, vol. 2: 457.

163 Fleming, *Domesday*, no. 2897, no. 3047.

influential in the maintenance of social order while imprisonment was taking hold as a minor, less punitive, form of punishment.

The Domesday Survey also records the redistributed lands of Hereward, a banished nobleman from Lincolnshire. Hereward, who returned to England from his period of exile shortly after the Conquest, takes on legendary status in Anglo-Norman England. Hereward had been exiled during the reign of Edward the Confessor but returned to England after his family lands were confiscated and his brother was killed. Hereward joined in the rebellion against William the Conqueror, and was said to have wandered around England, an outlaw stirring up opposition against the Normans. Hereward fought with the Danish in the siege of Ely in 1070, but was captured and placed into prison. He was later released and made peace with the King, but his fate remains wrapped in legend.[164] Depending on the account of his deeds, Hereward returned to his lands to live out his days in peace or suffered a brutal death in a later act of vengeance.[165] Regardless of how he met his end, Hereward came to represent the heroic outlaw who stood up to "the infliction by arbitrary power of unfamiliar laws upon an unwilling people."[166] According to the *Gesta Herewardi* tradition, he fought for his land and what was his, and the unjust Norman power and law manifest itself in the use of imprisonment against Hereward.[167] Hereward's imprisonment was foreign to the Anglo-Saxon sense of justice and order and its use represents the new methods being used by Anglo-Norman rulers. Hereward as an Anglo-Saxon hero in later legend and literary genres represents the eleventh century sentiments on contemporary events as well as the place of an outlaw with respect to justice and society.[168]

Exile, outlawry, and imprisonment were increasingly linked in political matters of Anglo-Norman kings. The treatment of Odo of Bayeux provides a good example of the causes and results of these practices. Odo had been appointed to the bishopric at Bayeux in 1049, where he functioned in a spiritual capacity as well as patron to his residence in the diocese. In 1066, Odo accompanied his brother William on the Norman Invasion of England. The exact role Odo played

164 Swanton, "Introduction: The Deeds of Hereward," 28-30; Keen, *Outlaws*, 11-14; J. Hayward, "Hereward the Outlaw," *Journal of Medieval History* vol. 14 (1988): 293-304.

165 Swanton, "The Deeds of Hereward," 89-99; Keen, *Outlaws*, 21-22.

166 Keen, *Outlaws*, 209-210; 20-22.

167 Swanton, "The Deeds of Hereward," 67-89. In legend, Hereward was portrayed as strong, smart, and rebellious in the face of royal authority, continuously on the run and always evading capture by royal authorities, leading the last of the active resistance against an invading population.

168 Keen, *Outlaws*, 31-38.

in the invasion is much debated, specifically concerning his contributions to the Norman effort and his actions during the battle. Odo was to protect and defend south-eastern England and pacify the area around Canterbury. During the fifteen years he was in England, Odo continued to fulfill his duties in Bayeux, making extended visits to the continent in 1074, 1077, 1080 and 1082. Odo benefited financially as a result of the Norman Conquest, obtaining the most wealth within England of any Norman, excluding William himself and three months after his coronation, William returned to Normandy, leaving Odo and William fitz Osbern to serve as vice-regents in his absence.[169]

By 1082, the king's half-brother, Odo, Bishop of Bayeux and Earl of Kent, reached a position of extreme wealth, power, and dominance in England. During 1082, however, Odo fell from his position and out of favor with William, as indicated by the brief passage from the *Anglo-Saxon Chronicle*.[170] Odo had set his sights on seizing a position associated with the Papacy in Rome and had been gathering troops in anticipation of his journey. The Holy See was weakened by the Investiture Controversy of the late eleventh and early twelfth centuries and seemed appealingly vulnerable to the Bishop.[171] King William, who was in

---

169 For more on William Fitz Osbern, see Douglas, *WC*, table 8 and C. W. Hollister, "Greater Domesday Tenants-in-Chief," in *Domesday Studies. Papers read at the Novocentenary Conference of the Royal Historical Society and the Institute of British Geographers*, Winchester, 1986, ed. J.C. Holt, xix, 347(Woodbridge, Suffolk: Boydell & Brewer, 1987): 219-248 at 220, 242. For Odo, see Douglas, *WC*, 207, 212; William of Poitiers, *Gesta Guillelmi,* 164-165; D. Bates, "The Character and career of Odo Bishop of Bayeux (1049/50-1097)," *Speculum*, vol. 50, no. 1 (1975): 1-20 at 12, 15.

170 Douglas, *WC*, 207, 212; William of Poitiers, *Gesta Guillelmi*, 164-165, D. Bates, "Odo," 12, 15.

171 Orderic Vitalis, vol. 2: Book 7, 38-45; Bates, "Odo," 15. Davis speculates that Odo may have been gathering troops to "intervene in the wars of Emperor and Pope and procure from Gregory VII a reward in the shape of spiritual or secular promotion." The Investiture Controversy of the late eleventh century was the catalyst for combat, however, as war between Henry IV and Gregory VII broke out in late 1075, when Gregory outlawed lay investiture. Their conflict led to each man claiming to depose the other, Henry's excommunication, the recognitions of a respective anti-pope and anti-king, and the military occupation of Rome by Henry IV in 1084. In late 1084, Gregory was rescued by a Norman named Robert Guiscard, a native of Coutances (Cotetin) and the first duke of Apulia, but a Roman uprising against Norman looters drove the Norman force and Gregory to Salerno, where he died on 25 May 1085. In the end, Gregory VII had lost the support of most European monarchs as well as many of his cardinals. Supplemental information on this subject is from D. Douglas's *The Norman Achievement: 1050-1100*, 112, and John Julius Norwich's *The Normans in Sicily* (London: Penguin Books Ltd., 1992), 243-244.

Normandy when he heard of Odo's actions, immediately set out for England to stop his ambitious half-brother. William sought to arrest Odo on grounds that his preparations were a threat to peace in his kingdom. The King confronted Odo on the Isle of Wight, where Odo was based, and ordered his arrest. Because of Odo's position as bishop, William's subordinates refused to take him into custody.[172] The King was forced to seize Odo himself, reportedly stating that he condemned "neither a clerk nor a bishop, but arrested my earl, whom I have made viceroy in my kingdom, desiring to hear an account of the stewardship entrusted to him."[173] William was careful to assert his right to punish Odo as his secular lord. William was not in the position to antagonize the English Church and needed to emphasize that he was not usurping ecclesiastical authority.[174] Odo was not punished as a bishop, but rather as an earl.

William sent Odo back to Normandy, where he spent the next five years in prison. His imprisonment at the hands of his brother, lord, and King echoes earlier Norman uses of imprisonment as a mechanism of controlling problematic kinsmen. There is no indication that Odo was going to be released by William, but he was freed by the dying King in 1087. Odo's release was granted after Robert of Mortain, brother to both men, begged William for mercy.[175] The deathbed speech of William the Conqueror provided in Orderic's history recounts how the king exercised acts of mercy as well as used exile and imprisonment alike against his enemies. When William was struggling to acquire and maintain authority in Normandy, he exiled men, often for a just short time, in order to exact an oath of loyalty and to receive some financial recompense. His use of imprisonment in England was of similar fashion. When William opened his prisons and released prisoners in England and Normandy alike before his death, he required that all those who were freed swear an oath of the realm "to preserve the peace in England and Normandy in every way, and to resist ene-

---

172 Orderic Vitalis, vol. 4: Book 7, 40-41.

173 Orderic Vitalis, vol. 4: Book 7, 42-43; F. Stenton, *Anglo-Saxon England*, 616; Symeon of Durham, *History of the Kings*, 566; Walter of Coventry, *Memoriale*, vol. 1: 96; G. E. Slocombe, *Sons of the Conqueror: Robert Curthose, William Rufus, Henry Beauclerc and the grandson, Stephen* (London, UK: Hutchinson & Co. Publishers, Ltd., 1970), 26. Many historians credit Lanfranc with advising William to distinguish Odo's roles as Earl and Bishop during the arrest.

174 For more on ecclesiastical jurisdiction in England on both sides of the Norman Conquest, see F. Barlow, *The English Church, 1000-1066, A History of the Later Anglo-Saxon Church* (London, UK and New York, NY: Longman, 1979), 255-276 and *The English Church, 1066-1154* (New York, NY: Longman, 1979), 145-176.

175 Orderic Vitalis, vol. 4: Book 7, 98-101; Slocombe, *Sons of the Conqueror,* 26-28.

mies of the peace stalwartly with all their might."[176] This act of clemency was intended to demonstrate how the King was a fair and generous ruler, performing merciful deeds of forgiveness in his final hours.[177] It also demonstrates how similar confinement and exclusion could be in use, purpose, and end result.

Law, Politics, and the Conqueror's Sons

William Rufus promulgated no formal laws during his reign that are extant, but narrative sources indicate that legal and social practices were consistent with those of his father.[178] William Rufus placed his political rivals and rebels into confinement and often transported his prisoners back and forth across the English Channel. This was a seemingly Norman phenomenon and reflected concerns about controlling individuals perceived to be a threat to one's power. William the Conqueror had kept his prisoners close to him, William Rufus did the same. Rufus had been in Normandy at the time of his father's death in 1087, but quickly traveled to England with the recently freed prisoners Morcar and Wulfnoth. When he arrived in England, however, Rufus placed them back into captivity at Winchester.[179]

The political climate in England was tenuous for William Rufus, and throughout his reign, Rufus imprisoned rebels such as Robert of Mowbray, and banished others, such as Roger of Lacy and Hugh of Salisbury in 1095.[180] These

176 Orderic Vitalis, vol. 4: Book 7, 97-99.

177 A. Gransden, *Historical Writing in England, Volume 1, c. 550 to c. 1307* (London, UK: Routledge & Kegan Paul, 1974), 152-165.

178 Although Eadmer reports in his *Historia Novella* that Rufus had some sort of legislative document sealed during a period of illness in 1093, no document remains. Eadmer, *Historia Novella in Anglia et opuscula duo de vita Sancti Anselmi et quibusdam miraculis ejus*, ed. M. Rule. Rolls Series. *Rerum Britannicarum Medii Aevi Scriptores*, vol. 81. (London, UK: Longman & Co., 1884), 30-31; Pollock and Maitland, *History of English Law*, vol. 1: 94-95. This was purported to free captives, forgive debts, and maintain secular and ecclesiastical law. According to Eadmer, after the king recovered from his illness, he revoked the document, stating that "those who had been set free were to be imprisoned again...old debts, which had already been cancelled, were exacted again in full; pleas of the crown and criminal suits were revived in the ancient form and heard and examined by men who cared more for the subversion of justice than for its maintenance and defense, more for the oppression of the poor and the exaction of money than for the suppression of crime."

179 Symeon of Durham, *History of the Kings*, 568.

180 Orderic Vitalis, vol. 4: Book 7, 50-51; Book 8, 278-285; *ASC*, year 1095; Crouch, *The Normans*, 148-149; Slocombe, *Sons of the Conqueror*, 38-41; Symeon of Durham, *History of the Kings*, 577; Walter of Coventry, *Memoriale*, vol. 1: 112-113. According to

events took place without public trials because, according to Orderic, William Rufus was careful in his punishment of traitors, wanting to avoid any retribution in Normandy and prevent further unrest in England.[181] In the autumn of 1087, King William II restored his uncle Odo to the earldom of Kent. Odo may have reclaimed his land in England in 1088, but he was unable to regain his prominence. Odo was also taken on as an advisor by the new duke of Normandy, William the Conqueror's oldest son, Robert.[182] He soon plotted against William Rufus with other Norman earls, including his brother Robert of Mortain, the Earl of Cornwall, Roger of Montgomery, the Earl of Shropshire, and Geoffrey of Mowbray, the bishop of Coutances, in the hopes of replacing the king with the Norman duke.[183]

Orderic, Robert of Mowbray, the earl of Northumbria rebelled against William Rufus in 1095 and spent over thirty years in prison as a result. His co-conspirators Roger of Lacy and Hugh of Salisbury were punished with banishment and huge fines, respectively.

181 Orderic Vitalis, vol. 4: Book 8, 284-285; William of Malmesbury, 339-340. William Rufus sought to protect himself from the many conspiracies against him, perpetually imprisoning Robert of Mowbray for example, while mutilating and executing others such as William de Hou and William of Aldrey. According to Malmesbury, William of Hou was "deprived of his sight, and his manhood" and William de Aldrey was sentenced to be hanged.

182 Orderic Vitalis, vol. 4: Book 7, 114-119; Barlow, *William Rufus* (Los Angeles and Berkeley, CA: University of California Press, 1983), 68-69; Bates, "Odo", 17. Bates states "no attempt seems to have been made to deprive Odo of his bishopric." William's oldest son Robert became Duke of Normandy rather than King of England because the dukedom was William's primary genealogical possession. This is why William's son, called William Rufus, became King of England upon his father's death in 1087.

183 Orderic Vitalis, vol. 4: Book 8, 120-127; Freeman, *WR*, 24, 27; Barlow, *William Rufus*, 71; Freeman, *A Short History of the Norman Conquest of England*, 131-132; Crouch, *The Normans*, 132-135; Slocombe, *Sons of the Conqueror*, 28-32; Symeon, 24-23, vol 4: 8, note 37 states that Bishop William of Saint-Calais, who had been banished in 1088, joined in the rebellion. According to Hollister, Robert of Mortain and Roger of Montgomery received their holdings in England shortly after the Norman Conquest in 1066 as a result of their contributions to William the Conqueror's campaign. Hollister also speculates on page 229 that Geoffrey "evidently owed his enrichment to his intimate friendship and devoted administrative service to the Conqueror." On page 25, Freeman offers another possible motivation, "that to men who held lands in both countries it would be a gain to have only one lord instead of two…it was held that, if England had again a king of her own, though it were a king of the Conqueror's house, the work of the Conquest would be undone…if they have two lords, there will be no hope of pleasing both; faithfulness to the one will only lead to vengeance on the part of the other."

Odo's rebellion began in late 1087 or early 1088 with the pillaging of Kent. William Rufus responded by staging a six-week assault on Odo's stronghold at Pevensey. Odo's garrison surrendered in June 1088 and Odo was captured and taken to Rochester. Once at Rochester, a garrison of troops loyal to Odo captured Rufus's men and the king established a blockade of the town in response. War continued through the summer of 1088, and negotiations between Rufus and the dissenters began in late June or early July. The King allowed "the rebels a semi-honourable discharge," the terms of which were as follows:

> …that the lives and limbs of the garrison should be safe, that they should come forth from the castle with their arms and horses. But they must leave the realm; they must give up all hope of keeping their lands and honours in England, as long at least as King William lived.[184]

Odo responded to Rufus's decision by asking that the rebels not have to endure the ceremonial trumpet blast, signaling their defeat, as they left the castle. Rufus refused and Odo and his companions then surrendered, left England as exiles, and were deprived of all English rights and possessions.[185]

Odo had rebelled twice and failed. His exile was humiliating and left him without land and prestige in England. Cast out from England and no longer Earl of Kent, Odo still maintained his bishopric of Bayeux. He returned to Normandy in 1088 where he placed himself in the court of Robert Curthose, eldest son of William the Conqueror and the Duke of Normandy. Many barons involved in the insurrection led by Odo, such as Geoffrey of Coutances, were later pardoned by William Rufus, but Odo never received a pardon or regained the favor of the King.[186]

---

184 Orderic Vitalis, vol. 4: Book 8, 130-135.

185 Orderic Vitalis, vol. 4: Book 8, 132-135; E. Freeman, *The Reign of William Rufus and the Accession of Henry the First, Vol. 1*, (*WR*) 3rd edn (Oxford, UK: Clarendon Press, 1922), 86-87; Barlow, *William Rufus*, 81; Slocombe, *Sons of the Conqueror*, 30-32; Walter of Coventry, *Memoriale,* vol. 1: 100; Whitelock, *The Anglo-Saxon Chronicle*, 167-168, "E"; Bates, "Odo," 18; Hyams, *Rancor and Reconciliation*, 129-130; Symeon of Durham, Book IV.8 mentions that the bishop of Durham, William of Saint-Calais's was exiled in 1108, but is biased as he does not include the fact that he was banished and fled to Normandy as a part of Odo's revolt. William of Calais was later restored to Durham by William Rufus.

186 Orderic Vitalis, 4: Book 8, 146-155; Symeon of Durham, *History of the Kings*, 568-570; Bates, "Odo," 18-19; Freeman, *WR*, 87; Hyams, *Rancor and Reconciliation*, 129-130. Although the uprising in southeastern England was now quelled, other rebellions in the west continued. The specifics are not particularly important to this work, but Barlow states on page 96 that "the turbulence of 1088 was followed by a year of peace in Eng-

Just like Odo, William of Calais, bishop of Durham, was unable to escape the ire of Rufus. Calais had been on the side of the king in 1088, but when called by Rufus to fight, Calais deserted the king, fled, and took refuge at Durham. As a result, Rufus prosecuted the bishop of Durham for infidelity and perjury in 1088. Rufus sought to prosecute Calais as a feudal baron rather than as a bishop, just as his father had done against Odo, but Calais refused to recognize the authority of the king to do so. Despite Calais's offer to accept judgment by a canonical court, the king saw his refusal to plead in his court as grounds for condemning the bishop to forfeiture of land and exile. According to the *Regesta regum Anglo-Normannorum*, William of Calais was outlawed in March of 1088. Calais did appear before the royal court in November 1088, but never recognized its authority to pass judgment upon him. Rather, he appealed to Rome for a canonical trial. Ultimately, William of Calais forfeited his fief of Durham Castle and was allowed to leave England from Southampton, the port of his choosing, with the intended destination of Rome. Calais went as far as Normandy where he remained until he received pardon from the king in 1091.[187]

As a disobedient vassal, William of Calais was outlawed; as a churchman, he refused to accept secular authority. Jurisdictional disputes between the king and clergy continued during William Rufus's reign and in 1097, the King forced Anselm, Archbishop of Canterbury, from the kingdom. Just as William of Calais had done, Anselm refused to accept that his primary loyalty was to king rather than to God. Once Anselm left England, he spent four years in exile and only

---

land," suggesting that the revolts were put down in a relatively easy manner by Rufus and his men by the end of 1088. Odo accompanied Duke Robert into Maine in 1088 and 1094, as well as on a campaign against William Rufus in 1089. A war between Rufus and Robert erupted in 1090 as a result of the Norman aggressions, which led to a short-lived English invasion of eastern Normandy. Negotiations followed, and Rufus pardoned the Norman aggressors, although the king "persisted in excluding Odo of Bayeux from the benefits of the amnesty."

187 *Regesta regum anglo-normannorum,* 1066-1154, vols 1-3 ed. with introductions, notes and indexes by H. W. C. Davis, with the assistance of R. J. Whitwell, B. Litt. (Oxford, UK: Clarendon Press, 1913-69), William II, no. 305; H.S. Offler, ed., *"De Iniusta Vexacione Willelmi Episcopi Primi per Willelmum Regem Filium Willemi Magni Regis"* in *Chronology, Conquest and Conflict in Medieval England, Camden Miscellany XXIV* (Cambridge: Cambridge UP (Camden Society, Fifth Series, vol. 10), 1997), 58-101; H.S. Offler, "*The Tractate de Iniusta Vexacione Villelmi Episcopi Primi,*" *The English Historical Review*, vol. 66, no. 260 (July, 1951): 321-341; Barlow, *The English Church, 1066-1154*, 281-287; Barlow, *William Rufus*, 83ff.; Freeman, *WR*, 1: 89-116. The author of *De Iniusta Vexacione Willelmi Episcopi* is unknown, but the text is also found in the *libellus* contained in the works of Simeon of Durham.

returned to England after Henry I became king in 1100.[188] The case of William of Calais and actions of Anselm were indicative of the conflicts taking place over jurisdiction in England and, as the case of Odo had been, a precursor to conflicts on a much grander scale between church and lay jurisdiction and authority in Anglo-Norman England.[189]

Early Norman kings of England used both exile and imprisonment against troublesome laity and problematic churchmen, and as a result, each practice took on new characteristics. Odo, William of Calais, and Anselm were all men of the church who threatened royal authority and they were all removed from the kingdom by way of exile. Exclusion, however, was intertwined with the use of imprisonment. During the reign of William I, Bishop Æthelwine of Durham had been held in prison but this was done only after the bishop had previously been expelled from the kingdom. Odo was a bishop, a vassal, and a relative to the Norman kings, and he was both imprisoned and banished as an earl, a subject of the English king.

William of Calais and Anselm were men in ecclesiastical positions who were driven from England because the Crown had no other recourse against them. William of Calais was prosecuted as a vassal of the king but refused to recognize William Rufus, and chose to take his case to Rome instead. The king could not imprison a man of the Church without a valid grievance at the risk of inciting the Holy See in Rome. Imprisonment as a coercive and detentive action could not be used without some end, such as a fine or a man answering to formal charges against him. Because the clergy was not answerable to the king, or at least claimed not to be, the king had little recourse when dealing with men of the church. Therefore, the only way that the king could rid himself of churchmen who tested or resisted his authority, but committed no other misdeed, was to remove them from the country completely.

---

188 Wm. of Malmesbury, 338, 344, Henry of Huntington, Forester, 237; Greenway, 444-445; Barlow, *The English Church, 1066-1154*, 287-292; *ASC*, year 1100; William of Malmesbury, *Chronicle of the Kings of England*, 338, 344. Anselm had gone to the continent in 1097 due to disputes over land and personnel with William Rufus. He ultimately ended up at Lyons, but also traveled to Rome, Cluny and Vienne during this period of exile. He was exiled again in 1103 by King Henry I. See Southern, *Anselm and his Biographer*, 160-163; 173-180; Southern, *Saint Anselm*, 278-307.

189 *The Annals of Roger of Hoveden: Comprising the History of England and of other countries of Europe from A.D. 732 to A.D. 1201*, trans. H.T. Riley (London, UK: H.G. Bohn, 1853), vol. 1: 195; see also Hovedon, Roger, *Chronica Magistri Rogeri de Houedene*, ed. W. Stubbs. 4 vols (London, 1868-1871); Barlow, *The English Church, 1066-1154*, 297-302. Anselm‘s conflict with Rufus would be reignited with Henry I, who recalled the prelate, only to banish him in 1103.

Disputes over control, authority, and jurisdiction in Anglo-Norman England were playing out in terms of exile and imprisonment. One other aspect of jurisdiction in England that was taking shape under the early Anglo-Norman kings was that of forest law. Royal concerns with forests in England are attributed to William the Conqueror‘s creation of the New Forest in the decades following the Norman Conquest. It was said that William the Conqueror imposed forest laws for the "great protection of game," and that the punishment for killing hart, boar, or stag was the deprivation of eyesight.[190] Royal forests as an institution in England communicated power to an Anglo-Saxon society under new rule, and what forest law represented was indicative of changes taking place with respect to methods of maintaining law and order.[191] Although, specifics about the administration of forest law under the first two Norman kings remain unclear, the establishment of laws that fell exclusively under the prerogative right of the king exhibit clashes between custom and law in England following the Conquest.[192] Twelfth century chroniclers lament the creation of the New Forest, claiming that the king ruined a flourishing region. These same chroniclers describe William Rufus‘s death in the New Forest in 1100 as a judgment from heaven brought upon the king by the cruel deeds of his father.[193]

---

190 *ASC,* year 1087.

191 For the Norman afforestation of England and royal forests as institutions of power, see generally R. Vollmer, *The English Royal Forests: A Communication in Power and Politics*. Unpublished Ph.D. dissertation. University of California-Berkeley, 2005. She articulates her argument most clearly on pages 72 and 79-80.

192 C.R. Young, "English Royal Forests under the Angevin Kings," *The Journal of British Studies* vol. 12, no. 1 (Nov., 1972): 1-14 at 3; C.R. Young, *The Royal Forests of Medieval England* (Philadelphia, PA: University of Pennsylvania Press, 1979), 7-17. Very little is known about forest law in Normandy as well, although the existence and importance of ducal forests is clearly indicated. See Haskins, *Norman Institutions*, 47-48. Something resembling forest law can be found in the "Constitutions of the Forest" attributed to the reign of Cnut, a forgery believed to reflect practices during the reign of King Henry I.

193 W. Stubbs, *The Constitutional History of England in its Origin and Development*. vols 1-3, 6th edn (Oxford, UK: Clarendon Press, 1903), vol. 1: 402-403; F. Baring, "The Making of the New Forest," *The English Historical Review* vol. 16, no. 63 (July 1901): 427-438 and vol. 27, no. 107 (July 1912): 513-515; F.H.M. Parker, "The Forest Laws and the Death of William Rufus" *The English Historical Review*, vol. 7, no. 105 (Jan. 1912): 26-38 at 27. The extent of the upheaval brought upon the inhabitants of this area is contested, as geographical studies related to the Domesday Survey indicate that large portions of what was considered the Forest were infertile and uninhabitable. See H.C. Darby and E.M.J. Campbell, *The Domesday Geography of South-East England* (Cambridge, UK: Cambridge UP, 1962).

Upon the death of William Rufus in 1100, the new king, Henry I, released all prisoners in England and promulgated an edict annulling the "illegal ordinances of his brother and of Ranulf [Flambard]," the king's chief minister and advisor. Henry threw Ranulf Flambard into prison in the Tower of London. Ranulf escaped from the Tower in February 1101 and fled to Normandy to the court of Duke Robert.[194] Henry had effectively humiliated and neutralized Flambard as an enemy in England, but failed to hold him within the kingdom. However, Flambard was now a fugitive, excluded from England and unable to return.

King Henry I often sent rebels into perpetual exile.[195] In 1102, Henry summoned Robert of Bellême and his two brothers to court to answer charges against them. The loyalty of all three men was in doubt, and once Robert realized he could not clear his name, he fortified his castles in the west of England and planned for war against the King. His efforts failed and he was driven out of England, exiled by the king.[196] Because of Robert's behavior, Henry also exiled his brothers, Roger the Poitevin and Arnulf, and all three men returned to Normandy. According to Orderic Vitalis, the two brothers behaved as cruelly and immorally as Robert, and once the three brothers arrived in Normandy, they resumed their menacing behavior. They were now a thorn in the side of Duke Robert.[197] At one point, Belleme was even captured by Robert and turned over to King Henry.[198] Henry placed Belleme into confinement, but he soon escaped and fled back to Normandy. He returned to ducal favor and later fought with

194 Wm. of Malmesbury, 428-429; Symeon of Durham, *LE*, 270-275, Appendix B.1; Symeon of Durham, *History of the Kings*, 582; Walter of Coventry, *Memoriale*, vol. 1: 119; Forester, 239-241; Greenway, 448-451; "The History of William of Newburgh" in *The Church Historians of England, Vol. IV, Part II*, ed. J. Stevenson. (London, UK: Seeleys, 1851), 406; Barlow, *William Rufus*, 195ff. Ranulf was restored to his position at Durham in 1102. See also Orderic's account, which holds that Ranulf was not restored in 1102; *ASC*, years 1100-1101. See also "Ranulf Flambard" in R. W. Southern's *Medieval Humanism and Other Studies* (Oxford, UK: Basil Blackwell, 1070): 183-205; In chapter eight of *The Tower of London: Its Buildings and Institutions*, ed. John Charlton, (London, UK: Dept. of the Environment, H.M. Stationery Office, 1978), A.C.N. Borg refers to Ranulf Flambard as the first prisoner in the Tower of London.

195 Orderic Vitalis, vol. 6: Book 11, 12-13.

196 *Placita Anglo-Normannica: Law Cases from William I to Richard I – Preserved in Historical Records*, ed. Bigelow, (1881), 83-84.

197 Orderic Vitalis, vol. 6: Book 11, 82-93.

198 Wm. of Malmesbury, 430; 433; J.A. Green, *Henry I: King of England and Duke of Normandy* (Cambridge, UK: Cambridge UP, 2006), 68-72, 124-125.

Duke Robert against Henry I. Belleme was captured by the king in 1112 and imprisoned in Wareham Castle until his death.[199]

Belleme's behavior and fate highlights the difficulty of enforcing punitive exclusion in England. Exiles from England, such as Belleme, Robert of Pontefract and Robert Malet, simply fled to Normandy and sought favor with Duke Robert.[200] Tensions between siblings Henry, king of England, and Robert, duke of Normandy, remained high and war broke out between them in 1104. Their dispute culminated in the battle of Tinchebray in September 1106. At Tinchebray, Henry captured Robert and many of his men, and while "some of them were pardoned by the king's grace to enjoy the freedom for which they begged…others were kept in fetters to the day of their death, as their crimes deserved."[201] Henry sent many of his brother's companions to England "and condemned William of Mortain, Robert of Stuteville, and several others to perpetual imprisonment."[202] Most importantly, he placed his brother, Duke Robert, in prison in England, where he remained in "honorable confinement" until his death in 1134.[203] Henry also ordered the arrest of Duke Robert's son, William Clito, who was captured and exiled by the King in 1119.[204]

---

199 Wm. of Malmesbury, 430; 433; Green, *Henry I*, 68-72, 125-127; *ASC*, year 1112; Orderic Vitalis, vol. 6: Book 11, 98-99; 178-179; Henry of Huntington, Forester, 245; Symeon of Durham, *History of the Kings*, 593; Walter of Coventry, *Memoriale,* vol. 1: 133; Slocombe, *Sons of the Conqueror*, 85.

200 Orderic Vitalis, vol. 6: Book 11, 18-19; 20-25; 30-37; Slocombe, *Sons of the Conqueror*, 85-85; *Placita Anglo-Normannica*, 82-83; Symeon of Durham, *History of the* Kings, 583-584; Crouch, *The Normans*, 174-175.

201 Orderic Vitalis, vol. 6: Book 11, 82-93, see specifically 90-91; Walter of Coventry, *Memoriale,* vol. 1: 124-125; Crouch, *The Normans*, 177-178.

202 Orderic Vitalis, vol. 6: Book 11, 94-95; Henry of Huntington, Forester, 242-243.

203 Orderic Vitalis, vol. 6: Book 11, 162-165, 180-181; Walter of Coventry, *Memoriale,* vol. 1: 124-125; Barlow, *Feudal Kingdom of England*, 176-177. Henry later pardoned many of the individuals who had rebelled against him, including Amaury of Montfort and William Crispin, as well as recalled many exiles that Robert had driven out of Normandy during his time as duke.

204 Orderic Vitalis, vol. 6: Book 12, 236-243, 256-259, 288-289; Green, *Henry I,* 151-156. King Louis of France saw the discontent in the Anglo-Norman sphere as an opportunity to weaken his English counterpart and many prominent Normans were enlisted in his cause, including William Clito, the son of Duke Robert. At the battle of Brémule in 1119, for example, William Clito had aligned himself with the king of France as part of his efforts to get his father out of prison, but was himself captured and exiled. The battle was actually a huge defeat for the French, whose captured knights were kept captive by Henry in different castles in Normandy until an exhaustive ransom was paid. Also in 1119, at the Council of Reims, the two men aired their grievances against one another, and among Loius's complaints were Henry's poor treatments of Duke Robert, Robert of

In terms of political enemies, Henry recognized that it was more practical to imprison a man than it was to risk exile and banishment, as long as the captivity could be maintained. An exile was an unknown, a man who was out of the control of law and order and able to plot, threaten, and build opposition to the king. Henry I was plagued by enemies who were able to obtain refuge and support from his brother in Normandy. In return, Robert of Normandy was able to garner strength for his desire to seize the English throne. It was prudent for Henry to place his opponents, especially his brother, into captivity where they could be controlled and neutralized as a threat.

This idea of control and order is found within the *Leges Henrici Primi (LHP)*, the laws of King Henry I, specifically in efforts to bring aspects of outlawry under royal jurisdiction.[205] Discussion of legal outlawry reflects an emphasis on royal leadership and mercy in the maintenance of law and order. An accused man could not have judgment passed on him while outlawed but rather was entitled to "legal periods of respite and proper freedom to appear and make his defence." [206] Thus, accused criminals were entitled by order of the King to the customary exaction process. Technically, the king could not proclaim a man to be an outlaw, as it was the exclusive right of the county court to do so. The king's endorsement and encouragement of the exaction process not only gave

Bellême, and William Clito, all of whom had either been imprisoned or exiled and were technically vassals of the French king. In 1123-1124, rebellion again broke out against Henry, this time on behalf of William Clito. Waleran, count of Meulan, Amaury of Montfort, and others met to conspire in September 1123, a meeting of which Henry was aware, and the armies of the two sides met in several skirmishes over the coming months. Henry's force overcame the rebels and in mid-1124, the king sent many of the conspirators, including Waleran and Hugh of Montfort, to England to be held in captivity while taking possession of their land. Amaury was captured as well, but was spared by William of Grandcourt, who "out of human compassion he took pity on a man of such great valour, knowing for certain that if he were ever captured he would never, or only with great difficulty, get out of the king's clutches again. He chose therefore rather to desert the king, abandon his own lands, and go into exile than to condemn the noble count to perpetual prison." See Orderic Vitalis, vol. 6: Book 12, 328-337, 346-347, 350-357; Green, *Henry I*, 185-189.

205 *Leges Henrici Primi (LHP)*, ed. and trans. L.J. Downer (Oxford, UK: Clarendon Press, 1972).

206 *LHP*, 108-109, c. 10, 1; 84-85, c. 5, 3; 158-159, c. 47, 1; Robertson, 227-229; Hyams, *Rancor and Reconciliation*, 138, 144; Hurnard, *King's Pardon*, 13-14; Chibnall, *The Normans*, 53-54; Wormald, *The Making of English Law*, 410-414; 465-476; For more on the contents and influences upon the *LHP*, see Downer, "Introduction," 1-78.

him a role therein, but also made him the protector and champion of local justice.[207]

Within the *LHP*, outlawry resulted from secular and ecclesiastical offenses and applied to men and women, Norman and English alike.[208] If a man was negligent in payment of the tithe and killed someone while resisting to pay, he was outlawed and in the name of justice could be pursued by all; if anyone kept and maintained an excommunicate or an outlaw, he lost his life and property or he himself became an outlaw; if a man slayed a minister, he was outlawed in the eyes of God and man and remained as such unless the proper penance and earthly amends were made within thirty days; if a woman married two brothers, she was cast out until her death but could be received back into the church in her final hour; and if anyone disturbed a grave in a "scandalous or criminal fashion," he was declared an outlaw.[209]

As had always been the case, an outlaw had no legal rights, and if he accused another man within the king's protection of any offense, his charges had no effect.[210] A pronouncement of outlawry placed a man in the mercy of the king and any land that an outlaw possessed fell into the king's possession. Failure to appear in county court and subsequent flight resulted in outlawry.[211] Harboring an outlaw was an offense against the crown, and the collective duty held by the community with respect to outlaws was emphasized in Henry's laws:

> It shall be fitting that individual persons above all observe true justice and exercise mercy in respect of evil-doers in such a way that they do not leave unpunished an outlaw or a thief caught in the act, whether French or English, where the miscreant is more than twelve years old and the value of the property concerned is more than eightpence.[212]

---

207 *LHP*, 116-117, c. 13, 1. This is when the source is taken at face value. For more on the author and his possible knowledge of the law and biases in writing this text, see Wormald, *Making of English Law*, 413-414 and Downer's introduction, 37-44.

208 A woman was said to be "waived" rather than "outlawed" but the principles of exclusion apply. Phrases such as "cast out" are still found, specifically when women were the offenders. A woman was said to be "waived" rather than outlawed, as she was technically not within the law and therefore could not be placed outside of it. The legal designation of "outlaw" became more commonplace and, as a result, the distinctions among exile, banishment, and outlawry slowly became more clear.

209 *LHP*, 114-115, c. 11, 14a; 116-117, c. 13, 1; 118-119, c. 13, 10; 208-209, c. 66, 1; 210-211, c. 66, 2b; 224-225, c. 70.17; 260-261, c. 83, 5.

210 *LHP*, 154-155, c. 45, 5.

211 *LHP*, c. 53, 1e.

212 *LHP*, 188-189, c. 59, 20.

Details as to the age of an outlaw or thief as well as the value of property affected added clarity and instruction to the local outlawry process. Royal law was both cooperating with and adding to local judicial practice.

In addition to this emphasis on community action, the role of the sheriff remained key in the administration of justice and within the relationship between courts and communities. Just as his father and brother had done, King Henry I placed men he considered to be loyal in shrieval positions. Rather than appoint barons, however, Henry I used men from his *curia* in the administration of the shires. During the reign of Henry I, the sheriff was also brought under closer scrutiny of the exchequer, now more accountable for monies owed the Crown, and the king occasionally commissioned a justice through writ to hear important pleas of the crown and pleas of the forest.[213] These limits and checks upon the administration of justice in shires and hundreds placed the sheriff in a subjugated position and demonstrated the tools by which the crown was attempting to use to increase its influence upon local power.

On the whole, the principles of exclusion remain strong throughout the *LHP*, as do royal efforts to control them.[214] As a practice grounded very much in custom, outlawry was exercised outside of the direct jurisdiction of the crown and royal law was limited in how it could use and modify the outlawry process. Rather than try to alter or eliminate outlawry, the crown tried to control aspects of the powerful social tool.[215]

---

213 Morris, *Medieval Sheriff*, 72-73, 78-79; 100-104; J. Hudson, *The Formation of the English Common Law: Law and Society in England from the Norman Conquest to Magna Carta* (London, UK: Addison Wesley Longman Ltd., 1996), 31-34. The final step in the decline of the baronial sheriff began as early as William Rufus and involved the implementation of the king's justice in specific pleas. Evidence indicates the earliest years of the eyre system took place during the reign of Henry I.

214 In terms of conceptual clarity, most of the provisions from the *LHP* that refer to exclusion specifically use "outlaw" (*utlaga*).

215 Downer, "Introduction," 7; There was a link between excommunication and outlawry found in the *LHP* that was in no way surprising, as the use of secular law to assist in the enforcement of ecclesiastical sanction had been practiced both England and Normandy prior to the Conquest. For more on ecclesiastical discipline and secular law, see Oakley, *English Penitential Discipline*, 141ff; F. D. Logan. *Excommunication and the Secular Arm in Medieval England: A Study in Legal Procedure From the Thirteenth to the Sixteenth Century* (Toronto, Canada: The Pontifical Institute for Mediaeval Studies, 1968), 13-23 at 21. Imprisonment came to be used as a secular punishment for excommunicates during the late twelfth century, but the origins of this practice remain unclear, as there is no mention of secular punishment for excommunicates in royal writs from the period.

Stephen and the struggle for kingship

Henry I's successor, King Stephen (1135-1154), was plagued by rebellion, political unrest, and competition for royal authority. As a result, the royal involvement in the administration of justice that characterized the reign of Henry I experienced a steady decline. Stephen, who regularly exiled and banished his opposition during his struggle to retain control of England, shifted his focus from legal efficiency and royal power in the localities to his own personal efforts to maintain his position as king.

Although Stephen's reign is generally considered to have been a period of anarchy in England, the events of his tenure brought the use of imprisonment and exile against political enemies into a new phase. Stephen quickly banished powerful political enemies in England upon becoming king. In 1136, he banished Baldwin de Redvers, Count of Anjou, and forced Robert of Bampton to give up his castles and flee to Scotland.[216] Redvers, who had never recognized Stephen as the rightful ruler of England, found favor in Anjou after leaving England. He returned in 1139 to aid in the rebellion against the King and was rewarded for these actions by Empress Matilda in 1141 with the earldom of Devon.[217] Robert of Brampton aligned himself with David, king of the Scots, and invaded England with Scottish forces in 1138.[218] While the northern invasion was taking place, Robert of Gloucester rebelled in the south with other nobles such as Geoffrey Talbot and Gilbert de Lacy. Geoffrey Talbot was captured at Bath and "very closely confined in chains and barely escaped a sentence of condemnation…[because] after fettering his feet very tightly they thrust him into a

216 *Gesta Stephani*, ed. And trans. K.R. Potter (Oxford, UK: Clarendon Press, 1976), 28-31; 42-45; *Historical Works of Gervase of Canterbury, Vol. 1, The Chronicle of the Reigns of Stephen, Henry II, and Richard I.* ed. W. Stubbs. London, UK: Kraus Reprints Ltd., 1965), 95; *William of Newburgh, The History of English Affairs, Book I*, eds P.G. Walsh & M.J. Kennedy (Warminster, UK: Aris & Phillips Ltd., 1988), 54-55, 150; "The History of William of Newburgh" in *The Church Historians of England,* vol. 4, part 2, ed. J. Stevenson (London, UK: Seeleys, 1851), 409.

217 *Gesta Stephani*, 32, n. 2; 42-45; 84-85; William of Newburgh, Book 1, 54-55, 150.

218 *Gesta Stephani*, 54-55. Much of the information on the events of 1138 is missing. See note 1, page 56; Matthew, *King Stephen*, 78-82. The Scottish forces were initially repelled by Stephen's army, but reinvaded after Stephen turned south. English and Scottish forces then met at the Battle of the Standard, where the Scots were defeated.

dungeon under guard."[219] Talbot, who had previously been exiled from England, was now thrown into prison so that he no longer pose a threat to the King.

Stephen was plagued by political troubles and his use of banishment and exile against rivals and enemies came back to haunt him. Many of the men Stephen sent out of the kingdom simply found support elsewhere and joined in other efforts against the king. Not all individuals who represented a threat to peace and order during Stephen's reign were driven out, however, as some were "either deprived them of their lives or put them in chains."[220] In 1139, King Stephen

> ...held his council at Oxford, where he seized bishop Robert of Salisbury, and his nephews, bishop Alexander of London, and chancellor Roger and put them all into prison until they gave up their castles.[221]

The capture of the bishops in 1139 allowed Stephen to physically hold three men who had been of administrative importance during the reign of his predecessor. Stephen needed the support of the bishops and defended their imprisonment much the same way that William the Conqueror had when arresting Bishop Odo in 1082: by arguing that he had arrested the castle holders, not the bishops.[222]

Perhaps Stephen was aware that exiling and banishing his enemies allowed them the opportunity to continue to be a menace to him; or maybe he knew that imprisoning men of the church as vassals was an easier, more controllable option than sending them out of England. The King essentially confined all bishops in England within his kingdom and shut them off from the outside world by forbidding their attendance at the Council of Rheims in 1148. The Archbishop of Canterbury, Theobald, defied the King, escaped from England on a fishing boat, and attended the Council. As a result, Theobald was stripped of his property and banished by the king, unable to return to England. Only after Theobald prevented Stephen from getting excommunicated by Pope Eugenius was he able

---

219 *Gesta Stephani*, 58-59; Matthew, *King Stephen,* 80. Robert was half-brother of Empress Matilda and although he had sworn an oath of fidelity to Stephen in 1136, he switched loyalty to Matilda in early 1138.

220 *Gesta Stephani*, 6-9. The exact identity of Henry's doorkeeper is unknown.

221 *ASC*, year 1137; William of Malmesbury, 495, 499-500; William Newburgh, 410-422; Walter of Coventry, *Memoriale,* vol. 1: 163; Matthew, *King Stephen*, 84-86. Although the Anglo Saxon Chronicle reports these events occurred in 1137, they actually took place in 1139.

222 Orderic Vitalis, vol. 6: Book 8, 532-535; Barlow, *The English Church, 1066-1154*, 303-308.

to return to the King's favor and to England. Theobald was exiled again, however, when he failed to crown Stephen's son, Eustace, in 1152.[223]

Accused traitors, political allies, and family members of powerful nobles alike all faced forms of exclusion and imprisonment as the struggle for political control of England played out during the mid-twelfth century.[224] Through the course of Stephen's reign, captivity and confinement were increasingly used by the men and women vying for power in England.[225] King Stephen himself was imprisoned for a time after he was defeated at the battle of Lincoln in 1141. He surrendered to Robert of Gloucester and was turned over to Empress Matilda, who then placed him in prison at Bristol with other knights from his retinue, and kept there in chains.[226] It was only after Stephen's followers captured and imprisoned Robert of Gloucester at Stockbridge in late 1141 that an agreement was

223 F. Barlow, "Theobald (c.1090–1161)", Oxford Dictionary of National Biography, Oxford UP, 2004 [http://www.oxforddnb.com/view/article/27168]; K.J. Stringer, *The Reign of King Stephen: kingship, warfare, and government in twelfth-century England* (New York, NY: Routledge, 1993), 67-68. Theobald, who had been a moderator for peace since his election to the archbishopric in 1138, had grown increasingly concerned about the authority of the Church within the political climate in England, and by disobeying the King in 1152, he essentially chose to exclude himself from royal favor rather than endure any oppression by the Crown. These actions were direct statements against royal uses of constraint, and influenced the churchmen under his patronage, especially Thomas Becket and John of Salisbury.

224 *Gesta Stephani*, 162-163; 174-177; 186-187; J. Bradbury, *Stephen and Matilda, The Civil War of 1139-53*. Gloucestershire, UK: Alan Sutton Publishing Ltd., 1996), 134-140; Gervase of Canterbury, 128-129; William Newburgh, 415; J.H. Round, *Geoffrey de Mandeville: A Study of the Anarchy* (New York, NY: Burt Franklin, 1982), 201-209.

225 *Gesta Stephani*, 140-143; 146-149; 176-181; Bradbury, *Stephen and Matilda*, 118-125; Matthew, *King Stephen*, 113-115. Although the *Gesta* does not make mention of Stephen being ill during early 1142, it is known that he was sick during the early part of that year, probably a result of his imprisonment. The *Gesta* provides the several accounts and perspectives on the methods of imprisonment used. For example, in 1145, Matilda imprisoned a man named Walter and because "she hated him more unrelentingly than any of her opponents, sometimes cajoled him, mingling endearments with her words, sometimes uttering threats of torture and death if he did not deliver up to her the castle of Malmesbury; but he…could not be weakened…[and] now that her hope was baffled, burnt with one emotion towards the an, that of cruelty, and after fettering him very tightly delivered him to torment in a filthy dungeon…."

226 Orderic Vitalis, vol. 6: Book 13, 539-547; William of Malmesbury, 515-518; *Gesta Stephani*, 112-117; Walter of Coventry, *Memoriale,* vol. 1: 169; Matthew, *King Stephen*, 102-105.

reached for an exchange of the two men and Stephen was released after nine months of captivity.[227]

In addition to the physical removal or confinement of one's enemy, there were elements of humiliation and publicity associated with this form of punishment. The treatment of Robert de Berkeley by Walter, brother of the Earl of Hereford and supporter of Matilda was described in the *Gesta Stephani*:

> …they stripped him of his clothes and exposed him to insult, likewise fettering him very tightly, then put a halter around his neck and hanged him three times before the castle he had in the neighbourhood, the third time loosening the halter and letting him drop to the ground. Threatening him with death in this revolting fashion, or rather most cruelly bringing him to the point of death, if he did not deliver up his castle to the earl, at last they went away unsuccessful, and taking with them the wretched body of the half-dead Roger, because a faint breath of life yet fluttered in his tortured frame, they still kept him to endure the torments of the dungeon.[228]

The use of imprisonment in a military context is not surprising, as prisoners of war were quite common.[229] The publicity of imprisonment is not unique either, as outlaws were known throughout their communities. What is notable, however, is the indulgent description of an instance of imprisonment in the context of a society that was more reliant upon external methods of punishment and order, such as outlawry, exile and banishment. The details about Roger's humiliation and harsh treatment reveal how imprisonment was used but also informs us how serious, painful, and brutal it could be. It is perhaps a bit ironic that imprisonment, a supposed evolved and civilized form of punishment, saw its heightened use in such a cruel manner during a period in English history considered to be one of anarchy.

Forests, Abjuration, Approvers – Exclusion and its other uses in maintaining order

Forest law is instructive as to how punishment, jurisdiction, and authority took shape in medieval English law and society. The royal respect for, or perhaps royal obedience to, the county courts and the use of outlawry is present in the

---

227 *Gesta Stephani*, 132-133; 136-137; William of Malmesbury, 524; William Newburgh, 413-414; Gervase of Canterbury, 113-122; Herman of Tournai, Chapter 16, 33-34; Slocombe, *Sons of the Conqueror*, 175-176. The Earl was captured by William de Warenne, handed over to William of Ypres and placed at Rochester in confinement.

228 *Gesta Stephani*, 190-191; Bradbury, *Stephen and Matilda*, 138-140.

229 *Gesta Stephani*, 192-197; 200-203; Gervase of Canterbury, 130; Bradbury, *Stephen and Matilda*, 136-138.

administration of forest law during the reign of Henry I. In his first charters, Henry "retained the forests" of his father and, although from a slightly later period, the *Course of the Exchequer* tells us that forests in England were exclusively under the royal authority and the will of the king. [230] Forests were outside of the common law and the administration of justice within them fell under the jurisdiction of special laws, customs, and personnel.[231] Evidence indicates that if either a freeman or unfreeman, "by coursing or hunting, shall force a Royal beast, which the English call a staggon, to pant and be out of breath, the freeman shall lose his natural liberty for a year, the other shall lose his liberty for two years, and if he be a bondman, he shall be reckoned for an outlaw, which the English call a friendless man."[232] It is most likely that enforcement of forest laws took place at the county courts and penalties for the violation of forest law include a royal prescription of outlawry.[233]

230 "The Charter of Liberties, 1 Henry I (1100)," *Select charters,* ed. Stubbs, 99-102, c. 10; Fitz Nigel, *Dialogue of the Exchequer*, 59-60; Wormald, *The Making of English Law*, 400-401; Stubbs, *Constitutional History*, vol. 1: 402-403; H.A. Cronne, "The Royal Forest Under Henry I" in *Essays in British and Irish History in Honour of James Eadie Todd.* Eds. H.A. Cronne, T.W. Moody, and D.B. Quinn (London, UK: Frederic Muller Ltd., 1949): 1-23 at 1-3; J. A. Green, *Government of England under Henry I* (Cambridge, UK: Cambridge UP, 1986): 124-128.

231 C. Petit-Dutailis, *Studies and Notes Supplementary to Stubbs" Constitutional History down to the Great Charter* (Manchester, UK: Manchester UP), 166-178. See also *Select Pleas of the Forest,* ed. by G. J. Turner. Publications of the Selden Society, vol. 13. (London, UK: Bernard Quaritch. 1901). Charles Petit-Dutaillis argued that "The Assize of the Forest" from 1184, discussed below, largely reflects forest law as it functioned during the reign of Henry II's grandfather. As mentioned above, the "Constitutions of the Forest" attributed to Cnut were most likely a forgery from the reign of Henry I, but nonetheless reflect early twelfth century practice.

232 "Staffordshire Forest Pleas: Introduction", Staffordshire Historical Collections, ed. Major-General Hon. G. Wrottesley, vol. 5 part 1 (1884), 123-135. URL: http://www.british-history.ac.uk/report.aspx?compid=52372. *Ancient laws and institutes of England : comprising laws enacted under the Anglo-Saxon Kings...with an English translation of the Saxon, the laws called Edward the Confessor's, the laws of William the Conqueror, and those ascribed to Henry the First* : also, *Monumenta ecclesiastica anglicana*, from the seventh to the tenth century : and the ancient Latin version of the Anglo-Saxon laws : with a compendiuous glossary, &c. [s.l.], 1840. 184; P. J. N. Havens, *The Forests of England* (Devon, UK: Robert Hale & Company, 1976), 19-20; N. D. G. James, *A History of English Forestry* (Oxford, UK: Basil Blackwell, 1981), 9-10.

233 Young, "Royal Forests," 3.

An additional method of legal and social exclusion, abjuration of the realm, is found in documentation from the early twelfth century.[234] The *Leges Edwardi Confessoris*, or *Laws of Edward the Confessor,* were a collection of laws attributed to Edward the Confessor written during the reign of either Henry I or Stephen.[235] The earliest references to abjuration of the realm in England dictate that a common thief or robber who "with unexpected luck flees to the church frequently...shall abjure the district [and] not return after what had been stolen had been returned."[236] Pardoned murders and traitors were not allowed to remain in England and were to "swear that they will travel to the sea in the time which the justice set for them and cross it as quickly as they can have ship and wind."[237] Abjuration was closely related to Anglo-Saxon outlawry and was most often associated with fugitives who first fled to a sacred place and then swore an oath to leave a particular area. Under Norman rule, abjuration became a more defined and precise instrument by which a fugitive could achieve sacred status, be allowed to forfeit a trial, and swear to leave a town, a county, or England forever.[238] During the Anglo-Norman period, abjuration became increasingly "national" as opposed to "regional," as abjuration of the realm came to combine the ancient practice of sanctuary-seeking and ecclesiastical intercession with the judicial institution of outlawry.[239]

---

234 B.R. O"Brien, *God's Peace and King's Peace: The Laws of Edward the Confessor (Contains "Leges Edwardi Confessoris" (LEC))* (Philadelphia, PA: University of Pennsylvania Press, 1999), 103-104; Wormald, *The Making of English Law*, 409-411.

235 O"Brien, *God's Peace*, 60-61; *LEC*, 6.1; 6.2a-6.2b; 18; For Maitland's assessment of outlawry in *LEC*, see O"Brien, 129-130; *LEC*, 37-38; *LEC*, 18.1-18.3a; *Leges Edwardi* identified violation of king's justice and failure to obtain sureties as offenses which resulted in outlawry and exile. Anyone convicted of usury was outlawed, as was an individual who sold items but could not attest for their law-worthiness. The power of the king to pardon criminals as well as his mercy over captives was emphasized, although a murderer of a traitor had to swear to leave the kingdom as soon as possible in exchange for the king's mercy. For more on pardons, see chapter one of N. Hurnard, *The King's Pardon for Homicide,* "The Origin of the Medieval Pardoning System," 1-30.

236 *LEC*, 5.1-5.3a.

237 *LEC*, 18.2; A. Reville, "L"Abjuratio Regni, Histoire d"une Institution Anglaise." In *Revue Historique*. ed. Felix Alcan. vol. 50, Septembre-Decembre 1982 (Paris, France: Ancienne Librairie Germer Balliere): 1-42, specifically 3, 5-6; J. C. Cox, *The Sanctuaries and Sanctuary Seekers of Mediaeval England* (London, UK: George Allen & Sons, 1911), 8, 10.

238 Cox, *Sanctuaries and Sanctuary Seekers*, 11.

239 Reville, 14; N. M. Trenholme, *The Right of Sanctuary in England: An Institutional History*. (Columbia, MO: University of Missouri Press, 1903), 23; Cox, *Sanctuaries and Sanctuary Seekers*, 3, 8, 12; O"Brien, *God's Peace*, 65-68.

Abjuration in the context of the *LEC* functioned as both a form of mercy and as a part of punishment. If a pardoned felon was unable to stand to right or find sureties needed to re-establish himself within the peace of the king and law of the kingdom, he was to exile himself from the land. Murderers and traitors, if pardoned by the king, were required to leave England as soon as possible. The power of the king to pardon prisoners had been a long-standing right of kingship from the Anglo-Saxon period, but this type of pardon was not a remittance of punishment or social accountability. It was a royal act in the interest of ensuring peace.[240]

A pardoned criminal was required to stand to right on appeal by the individual he had wronged or said individual's kin, making the use of abjuration in this context a limited extension of royal authority.[241] If an appeal was made but the accused was unable to find sureties, he or she was presumably required to abjure the realm. Evidence points to the use of abjuration during the reign of Henry I with respect to approvers as well. An approver was a man who turned on his associates and accomplices in the commission of a felony by appealing them in court as a means to protecting his own life. If an approver could secure the conviction of his accomplices or of a certain number of men against which he appealed, he was able to avoid death or perpetual imprisonment by being allowed abjuration of the realm. He essentially became a judicial officer, appointed at the privilege of the king to bring appeals into royal courts. The earliest Pipe Roll from 1130 offers some indication that approvers existed in the early twelfth century, but because the next extant exchequer record does not date until the reign of Henry II, the exact time of its inception remains unknown. By 1156, however, approvers were an establish presence in the administration of justice in England.[242]

Observations: Exile, Outlawry, and Imprisonment in Anglo-Norman Politics and Law

From the mid-eleventh to the mid-twelfth century, practices used to maintain social order and exhibit political authority underwent a period of transition in England. Exile, banishment, and outlawry were practiced in matters of law, feud, and power, but were altered by the meeting of English and Norman cus-

240 Hurnard, *King's Pardon*, 14-16; O'Brien, *God's Peace*, 83-85.

241 Hurnard, *King's Pardon*, 16-18.

242 Frederick C. Hamil, "The King's Approvers: A Chapter in the History of English Criminal Law," *Speculum*, vol. 11, no. 2 (April, 1936): 238-258 at 238-240. For the procedure of becoming an approver, see Hamil, 240-241.

toms. The Dukes of Normandy had the power to exile rebellious aristocrats on the continent and brought with them a more temporary, conciliatory version of the practice to England. The permanence of Anglo-Saxon outlawry likewise influenced Norman practices of exclusion.

Given the source material for the Anglo-Norman period and its focus upon the aristocracy, it is difficult to know precisely how law and social order functioned in the localities. Overall, outlawry and exile functioned in England under the Anglo-Norman kings much the same way as it had under their Anglo-Saxon predecessors. The kings of England continued to try to control outlawry and used exile against enemies just as Æthelred and Cnut had done before them. We are told that Norman kings of England consciously endorsed maintaining and returning to the ancient law of the Anglo-Saxons. By the end of the eleventh century, the distinction between outlaw and exile becomes a bit clearer, but the principle of exclusion functioned uniformly no matter what word was used to describe its instance.

Efforts to centralize the administration of justice under William the Conqueror and his successors are seen in the growing relationship between local and royal courts. Royal emphasis on local order stressed the important of royal officials, specifically sheriffs, throughout England. Sheriffs were required to hold shire and hundred courts and attendance by all local men was mandatory. During these bi-annual occurrences, the sheriff was to make sure that all members of the community were in a tithing.[243] The use of the writ as a tool by which to instruct the sheriff also illustrates the royal concern with justice in the shire courts and attempts to control its administration. Given the shire court's exclusivity in pronouncing outlaws, the writ allowed Henry control, albeit a limited amount, within the local courts, while he simultaneously exercised the prerogatory use of exile and banishment when dealing with own enemies. The use of personnel (the sheriff, king's justice, exchequer) to centralize legal processes and writs to enforce his will on localities exhibits the "increasing integration of the county into the royal administration of justice by 1135."[244]

The use of imprisonment in post-Conquest England was more common than it had been in the Anglo-Saxon period. Confinement was a strategic political tool regularly used by Norman dukes. Before he even arrived in England, the Conqueror confined Harold Godwinson as a technique of coercion and negotiation, and the Earl had been compelled to promise Duke William II the crown of

243 Stubbs, *Select Charters*, 103-104; Hudson, *Formation of the English Common Law*, 28; 34; Morris, *The Frankpledge System*, 87.

244 Hudson, *Formation of English Common Law*, 37.

England. Once he was king, William was faced with the difficult task of conquering the large, hostile, and rebellious kingdom. From 1066 forward, the kings of England began to use imprisonment more often as a means to strengthen their respective positions of power. William the Conqueror imprisoned rebels such as Edwin, Waltheof, and Odo; Henry I confined Robert of Belleme and his brother Robert Cuthose; and Stephen held bishops and nobles alike in captivity in attempts to secure his own power. Perhaps this was in part due to the problem of exiles going back and forth from England to Normandy, or later from England to Anjou, politically playing King against Duke or Count or vice versa.

Social order was altered by the Norman Conquest of 1066, but not upended. Exclusion remained a constant and fundamental part of social interaction. Outlawries were pronounced locally and the Crown sought to seize some of the power behind its use for itself. The later Anglo-Saxon kings had done the same thing. Law and justice functioned in much the same way as it had prior to the invasion. There was more of a change, however, in matters of politics and authority. The Norman kings of England were much more inclined to imprison their enemies and rivals. Unlike outlawry and exile in England, imprisonment was not restricted by custom and easier for the new rulers to use. William the Conqueror, William Rufus, and Henry I went so far as to travel back and forth across the English Channel in the interest of keeping them close, confined, and controlled. Bishops, dukes, and the like were placed into prison at times because there was no other option in dealing with them. Henry I captured Robert Curthose in 1106 and his hands were tied as to how to deal with his problematic brother. Henry could not kill Robert, nor could he exile him, and he could not hold him for ransom, so he placed him in perpetual confinement until his death. Imprisonment of all sorts was used during the turbulent reign of Stephen as well. Imprisonment in politics would grow to influence matters of law and social order as a result of the practices of these first Anglo-Norman kings.

Chapter 4: Kingship, Law, and Reform during the reign of Henry II: The impact upon social order and power

The reign of Henry II is characterized by a renewed and reforming concern with law and justice. From 1154 when Henry became king, England ushered in a period of legal history that has been extensively studied and long debated. Maitland and his followers argued that the legal reforms of Henry II were original actions taken by the monarch and his advisors to usher in the system that is now recognized as English Common Law. Challengers to this tradition have argued that law under Henry II simply transformed Anglo-Norman customs, rules, and moral obligations of tenants and lords into a more centralized system and authoritative sovereign state. Centralization of law and power was not the result of the crown enacting a system of governance parallel to that which was already in place, but was rather a byproduct of the Angevin desire to incorporate existing systems into royal processes. Investigation into the so-called ingenuity of the Angevin period has led to controversy over the extent to which legal changes under Henry II were innovations. Many reforms of Henry II's reign are in fact latent in English society all the way back to the Anglo-Saxon period. Research into the processes of common law alongside investigations into the origins of each specific element of the emerging body of law has led to assertions that Angevin reforms combined with Anglo-Saxon and Anglo-Norman traditions formed English Common Law.

Within the context of debates over the efficiency of the Henrician reforms and the foundations of English Common Law, one unexplored avenue of investigation remains: the exclusion of wrongdoers in the administration of the realm.[245] Research into the use of outlawry, exile, and banishment as tools of order and authority reveals much about innovation, continuity, custom, and law during the reign of Henry II. Similarly, the relationship between these practices

245 Pollock and Maitland, *History of English Law*, vol. 1: 137-138; J. G. H. Hudson, "Milsom's legal structure: interpreting twelfth-century law" *Tijdschrift voor Reichtsgeschiedenis* vol. 59 (1991): 47-66; Hyams, *Rancor and Reconciliation*, 155-158; 168-169; Wormald, *Making of English Law*, 15-20; Hudson, *Formation of English Common Law*, 19-23. See also D. M. Stenton, *English Justice between the Norman Conquest and the Great Charter, 1066-1215* (Philadelphia, PA: American Philosophical Society, 1964) and R. C. van Caenegem, *The Birth of the English Common Law* (Cambridge, UK: Cambridge UP, 1973).

and emerging use of imprisonment contributes to the understanding of governance and order in twelfth-century England.

Angevin Reforms: The Church, the Crown, and the Administration of Justice

The struggle between Henry II and Thomas Becket in the latter half of the twelfth century brought disputes over jurisdiction and the power to punish to the forefront of religion and politics in England. At issue was who had the authority to punish criminous clerics and by whose authority those men could leave England. As the Archbishop of Canterbury, Becket punished felonious clerks by degrading their clerical status and requiring that they abjure the realm.[246] It is difficult to know if this practice was widespread in England, but contemporaneous evidence from Normandy indicates that this form of ecclesiastical punishment was common:

> If a clerk be arrested on whatever ground, and the church claims him, he ought to be given up to the church, and should he be convicted of the theft or homicide, he shall be degraded and shall abjure the realm; nor shall he be otherwise punished for that offence. And he must not enter the realm thereafter without the king's license or jus-

246 See accounts of the debate at the Council of Woodstock (1163), the case of Philip"de Brois", and the Council of Westminster (October 1163) in volume 4 of *Materials for the History of Thomas Becket archbishop of Canterbury (canonized by Pope Alexander III., A. D. 1173), Rerum britannicarum medii ævi scriptores; or, Chronicles and memorials of Great Britain and Ireland during the middle ages.* Rolls Series, vols 1-7, eds. J.C. Robertson and J.B. Sheppard (London, UK: Longman, 1875-1885); W.L. Warren, *Henry II* (London, UK: Eyre Methuen, 1973), 447-449, 481, 482, 538-543; F. Barlow, *Thomas Becket* (Berkeley and Los Angeles, CA: University of California Press, 1986), 88-116; P. Chaplais, "Henry II's reissue of the Canons of the Council of Lillebonne at Whitsun 1080 (? 25 February 1162)," *Journal for the Society of Archivists*, vol. 8 (1973): 627-634. William the Conqueror had placed boundaries between secular and religious jurisdiction at Lillebonne in 1080 (see Douglas, *WC*, 331-335 and Haskins, *Norman Institutions,* 30-37, 116, 170-174). These lines were blurred and ecclesiastical jurisdiction expanded under the "weakness" of Stephen's reign. Henry II did not like the way the church "was exercising its jurisdiction…clerks in holy orders who were guilty of secular crimes were punished too leniently by church courts. These could pass quite severe sentences, including flogging and imprisonment. Their awards of pilgrimage, especially to Jerusalem, came close to outlawry and banishment. But they were debarred from ordering the spilling of blood, which included sentences of death and mutilation, as well as, by extension, blinding and branding" (from Barlow, *Becket*, 91).

> tice will be done on him. And if he commit any offence afterwards, the king shall execute justice on him as a layman.[247]

King Henry took issue with the Church's assertion that it had the ability to remove offenders from the kingdom without royal consent. The king claimed that he alone possessed the right of exile and that the church had no authority to impose any form of banishment. Henry further claimed ecclesiastical punishments such as defrocking, banishment, flogging, and imprisonment were not harsh enough for serious criminal offenders.[248]

The boundaries between church and royal jurisdiction were ill-defined in twelfth-century England. During the Anglo-Saxon period, the church and crown had cooperated well when it came to law, order, and the application of penance and punishments. Following the Norman Conquest, however, the relationship between secular and ecclesiastical authority changed and became more fraught. As Duke of Normandy, William the Conqueror asserted his complete authority and jurisdiction over the church in Normandy at the Council of Lillebonne in 1080. This action carried implications for power and authority in England as well.[249] The Norman kings of England saw themselves as having jurisdiction

---

247 A.L. Poole, "Outlawry as a punishment for criminous clerks" in *Historical Essays in Honour of James Tait*, eds J.G. Edwards, V.H. Galbraith, E.F. Jacob. (Manchester, UK, Manchester UP: 1933): 239-246 at 243, from Round, *Calendar of Documents Preserved in France*, no. 1318.

248 Poole, "Outlawry as a punishment for criminous clerks," 239. Poole cites one case mentioned by Henry of Bosham of Becket making a criminous clerk abjure the realm in 1163. See accounts of the debate at the Council of Woodstock (1163), the case of Philip"de Brois", and the Council of Westminster (October 1163) in volume 4 of *Materials for the History of Thomas Becket archbishop of Canterbury*. According to Poole, "there is some evidence to show that during the later years of the twelfth and the first half of the thirteenth centuries, felonious clerks were sometimes degraded from their orders and forced to abjure the realm," but the use of outlawry as a punishment against clerks probably ceased in 1261 when life imprisonment became the punishment for clerks who, if they had been laymen, would have been subject to capital punishment for their crimes. See Poole, "Outlawry as a punishment for criminous clerks," 239, note 4 and "Council of Lambeth," 1261, D, ed. Wilkins, *Concilia Magnae Britanniae et Hiberniae, A Synodo Verolamiensi A.D. CCCXLVI ad Londinensem A.D. [MDCCXVII]. Accedunt constitutiones et alia ad historiam Ecclesiae Anglicanae spectantia,* vols 1-4 (London, UK: R. Gosling, 1737), vol. 1: 755.

249 In 1080, William the Conqueror clarified the relationship between Episcopal and ducal or baronial courts in Normandy in "The Canons of Lillebonne," asserting his right to complete oversight and jurisdiction. Ultimate authority as held by the Duke transferred

over all matters, ecclesiastical and secular alike. In 1154, King Henry believed he possessed full jurisdictional rights, just as his ancestors had, and in 1162, he reissued the canons from Lillibonne. Henry asserted that he was entitled to have a role in the punishments given to criminous clerics, as well as to approve excommunications pronounced by the church.[250] Henry wanted to control individuals leaving England, either by force or by choice, as well as how ecclesiastical punishment was meted out within his realm.

This was the situation when the case of Philip de Broi was brought to the attention of the king in 1163. Philip, a canon at Bedford, had been cleared of a murder charge in an ecclesiastical court, but when a royal justice in eyre sought to reopen the case, the cleric insulted the justice and failed to recognize any secular jurisdiction over his crime. The royal justice then complained to Henry, who became infuriated and threatened the cleric with secular punishment. Becket intervened and it was agreed that Philip would be tried in the archbishop's court for his insults to the royal justice as well as for the homicide. Philip pled guilty to the charges of insulting one of the king's justices but denied the murder. He argued that he should not be tried for the crime again after already having been acquitted. Becket's court accepted his pleas and sentenced Philip to a monetary punishment, a public flogging, and a period of banishment.

Henry was incensed by the leniency of the court's decision, but took great offense at Becket's behavior, which he viewed as deceptive and disloyal.[251] The tensions between the king and the church, issues of disputed jurisdictions, and questions concerning the treatment of criminous clerks led to the councils of Woodstock (July 1163), Westminster (October 1163) and Clarendon (January 1164). The latter culminated in the "Constitutions of Clarendon," a document agreed upon by both the King and the Archbishop in January 1164. The "Constitutions" declared customs and authority held by the church, the king, and the barons in England and were meant put to rest further disputes over such matters.[252] Clause three of the "Constitutions" defined the procedure of dealing with criminous clerks:

---

to England under William as king. Barlow, *English Church, 1066-1154*, 148-154. Similarly, since the reign of William the Conqueror, crown held the right to be consulted before any excommunications took place. See Douglas, *WC*, 331-345.

250 Haskins, *Norman Institution*, 30-35, 37-38, 276-279; Barlow, *Becket*, 90-91; Warren, *Henry II*, 95-96.

251 *English Lawsuits from William I to Richard I*, vol. 2: nos 405-411; "Excerpts, 1163," *Select Charters*, 129; Barlow, *Becket*, 93. The issue at the council of Woodstock was payments of dues to the king, although their exact nature remains unclear.

252 For accounts of these councils, see *Materials for the History of Thomas Becket archbishop of Canterbury,* vols 1 and 2; *"The Constitutions of Clarendon (1164)"* in *Select*

> Clerks cited and accused of any matter shall, when summoned by the king's justice, come before the king's court to answer there concerning matters which shall seem to the king's court to be answerable there, and before the ecclesiastical court for what shall seem to be answerable there, but in such a way that the justice of the king shall send to the court of holy Church to see how the case is there tried. And if the clerk be convicted or shall confess, the Church ought no longer to protect him.[253]

The "Constitutions" reaffirmed that royal consent was needed to excommunicate a baron or royal tenant. It also restricted church personnel from departing England without royal permission and limited church appeals and contact with Rome.[254] All of these provisions reflected royal attempts to control ecclesiastical personnel, their movements to and from England, and their ability to influence the movements of others. In certain circumstances, the church lost the right to punish a cleric for a felony and the crown now found itself in control of aspects of banishment, outlawry, and abjuration of the realm involving clerics. The overall result of the "Constitutions" was a victory for the crown in terms of the acts of exclusion but the conflict with the church had not yet run its course.

Following the council at Clarendon in 1164, Becket continued to antagonize the king, and soon fell out of royal favor. Henry strengthened his resolve to enforce the "Constitutions" and the conflict between the two men became personal

---

charters and other illustrations of English constitutional history: from the earliest times to the reign of Edward the First, ed. Wm. Stubbs (Oxford, UK: Clarendon Press, 1905), 135-140; See also Hudson, *Formation of English Common Law*, 129-130, and Barlow, *English Church, 1066-1154*, 156-158.

253 "*Constitutions of Clarendon*," no. 3; F.W. Maitland, "Henry II and the Criminous Clerks," *The English Historical Review* vol. 7, no. 26 (April 1989): 224-234; C.R. Cheney, "The Punishment of Felonous Clerks" *The English Historical Review* vol. 51, no. 202 (April 1936): 215-236; Barlow, *Thomas Becket*, 101-103. While the exact meaning of this clause has been much debated, it is generally agreed that a serious felon was to answer before the king and plead benefit of the clergy, then to appear before an ecclesiastical court while a representative of the king looked on, after which he would either retain or lose his protection from the church based on conviction or acquittal. A cleric found guilty in a court tribunal was to be degraded to layman status and return to the temporal court of the king. Maitland argues that the clause lays out the following scheme: "accusation and plea in the temporal court; trial, conviction, degradation in the ecclesiastical court; sentence in the temporal court to the layman's punishment." According to Cheney, the clause was actually not practiced in England and that clerks were not handed back over to secular authorities, but because the crown insisted upon a clerk proving his clerical status prior to being tried in ecclesiastical court, it gained "jurisdiction over any clerk who flees from justice or voluntarily abjures the realm."

254 "*Constitutions of Clarendon*," nos 7, 4, 8,; Barlow, *Becket*, 100-105; Warren, *Henry II*, 460-490; Reville, 9.

as well as political. As a result, Becket attempted to flee from England without the king's permission in late 1164, a clear violation of the "Constitutions." He was caught and put on trial at Northampton, not for his attempted flight but rather for financial suits brought against him by the king. Becket was convicted of the charges against him but fled from Northampton, a martyr in his own eyes but a fugitive in Henry's. Becket escaped to Flanders, where he met up with John of Salisbury, who had made preparations in anticipation of Becket's flight from England.[255] Archbishop Becket spent November 1164 to November 1170 in exile, during which time Henry exiled all of Becket's relations and members of his household, as well as their families, from England.[256]

Between 1164 and 1170, a series of negotiations took place between Henry and Becket.[257] The two men reached a compromise and in late November or early December 1170, Becket and the others who had joined him in exile returned to England.[258] After less than a month in England, Becket was murdered at Canterbury on December 29, 1170. He was quickly considered to be a martyr by John of Salisbury, dying in zealous defense of the Church and defiance of royal

255 Barlow, *Thomas Becket*, 108-116; Warren, *Henry II*, 488-492; L. Robertson, "Exile in the Life and Correspondence of John of Salisbury, in *Exile in the Middle Ages*: 181-197; David Luscombe, "Salisbury, John of (late 1110s–1180)", *Oxford Dictionary of National Biography*, Oxford UP, Sept 2004; online edn, May 2006 [http://www.oxforddnb.com/view/article/14849]. Both Becket and Henry had their supporters, as the writers of the period reflect the spectrum of interpretations and perspectives on the incidents of 1163 and 1164.

256 *Historical Works of Gervase of Canterbury, Vol. 1, The Chronicle of the Reigns of Stephen, Henry II, and Richard I*, ed. W. Stubbs. (London, UK: Kraus Reprints Ltd., 1965), 196-201; Barlow, *Thomas Becket*, 116-117, 126-134. Barlow, *Thomas Becket*, 117 gives the following quote regarding exile and Archbishops of England: "It had not been unusual since the death of Lanfranc in 1089 for an English archbishop to go into exile. Anselm had taken leave of William Rufus in 1097 and of Henry I in 1103. Thurstan of York had gone abroad in 1116. In 1148 Stephen had banished both archbishops from England, and in 1152 had driven Theobald out. In all these cases the prelate had been defending the rights of the church, or of his own church, against a "tyrant". In most there had also been personal or political differences between archbishop and king."

257 For a summary of the events between 1164 and 1170, see Barlow, *Thomas Becket*, 117-224.

258 L. Robertson, "Exile in the Life and Correspondence of John of Salisbury, in *Exile in the Middle Ages*: 181-197; Barlow, *Thomas Becket*, 215; but also see generally 117-197; D. Luscombe, "Salisbury, John of (late 1110s–1180)", online edn, May 2006 [http://www.oxforddnb.com/view/article/14849].

authority.[259] A cult of Thomas Becket soon developed and he was canonized in 1173.[260]

Henry's suspected involvement in Becket's murder resulted in an immense outcry and backlash against the King. He received papal censure, made amends to Becket's former fellow exiles, and performed public penance at Avranches in May 1171. One of the conditions of his penance was the abolition of "all customs introduced in his time injurious to the church of his land."[261] The bishops of England were then released from their oaths to abide by the "Constitutions of Clarendon" but the concept of "injurious customs" was so vague that Henry's promises were left open to interpretation. In a letter written shortly after his compromise at Avranches, Henry expressed his belief that there had been few bad practices created during his reign with respect to the Church.[262] Henry justified the continued enforcement of aspects of the "Constitutions" of 1164 by reducing them "to the status of those laws of the realm, comprehended in the king's "earthly honour", which bishops, before their consecration, swore to uphold, 'saving their order"." This meant that bishops in England were still subject to their oaths to the king and to ancient custom which, not only did the king need not gain Church approval to enforce, but that the "Constitutions" were acknowledged as practiced in England long before the reign of Henry II.[263]

The king conceded automatic control over appeals to Rome, but retained the right to know about any plea that was appealed. He had the right to exact a promissory oath from any suspect leaving England that no harm would be brought to him or to the kingdom. In 1175, it was agreed that clerks guilty of forest offenses were subject to royal courts and temporal punishments, cases involving secular lands and the services of clerks were to be heard in feudal

259 Barlow, *Thomas Becket*, 224-250.

260 Barlow, *Thomas Becket*, 264-269.

261 Barlow, *Thomas Becket*, 251-272 at 261; Warren, *Henry II*, 518-534. It is believed that Henry was given private penance by the papal legates at Avranches as well, but the specifics are unknown.

262 Barlow, *Thomas Becket*, 251-272; Warren, *Henry II*, 532-534.

263 Warren, *Henry II*, 532, 469. The phrase "saving their order" had been a qualification placed in clause twelve of the "Constitutions" as part of a compromise between Becket and Henry in 1163 at the Council of Westminster. Becket had argued that when bishops swore "homage and fealty to the lord king as his liege lord for his life and limbs and his earthly honour saving their order," royal customs were included within that "earthly honour". This qualification had originally caused the king to storm out of his meeting with the Archbishop, but now proved to be beneficial to the king. See c. 12, "*Constitutions of Clarendon*".

courts, clerks would not be forced to endure trial by battle, and that the murderers of clerics would receive the most severe royal punishments.[264]

Matters of jurisdiction in England were being clarified and differentiated incrementally, as was the use of exclusion. The dispute between Henry II and Thomas Becket in the 1160s demonstrated the importance of controlling who could leave and enter England and under what circumstances. The King wanted to regulate ecclesiastical contact with Rome as well as the movements of criminous clerks ordered by church courts to leave England. Following the death of Becket, Henry negotiated away some, albeit very little, of the power he had gained over ecclesiastical jurisdiction but the Angevin king's concern with the maintenance of peace, increased royal involvement in the administration of justice, and centralized control over courts, procedures, and personnel within England had remained intact.

Angevin Reforms: Judicial actions and processes and how they related to outlawry

Henry II's reign is characterized by legal reforms, administrative changes, and procedural centralization. Through actions and processes such as writs, juries of presentment, and the questions of inquest, Angevin reformers sought to rid the country of malefactors and exercise royal power over "the local community to coerce its recalcitrant members."[265] Exile, outlawry, and banishment were reshaped by these legal changes and affirmations during the reign of Henry II.

Writs developed during the reign of King Henry II were largely associated with issues of land tenure and services rendered. For example, the "writ of right" allowed for tenants to take a land claim out of the court of their lord and into the county courts, thus providing a royal outlet through which they could proceed.

264 Barlow, *Thomas Becket*, 273. This abandonment of the procedure found in provision three of the "Constitutions" as part of the proposed divorce settlement from Eleanor of Aquitaine that the King negotiated with papal legate Hugh of Pierleone.

265 R. Mortimer, *Angevin England, 1154-1258* (Oxford, UK: Blackwell Publishers, 1994), 55; W.L. Warren, *The Governance of Norman and Angevin England 1086-127* (London, UK: Edward Arnold Ltd., 1987), 106-110; W.L. Warren, *Henry II* 2nd edn (New Haven, CT and London, UK: Yale UP, 2000), 282. On the jury of presentment and its origins in relation to the Assize of Clarendon, see N. Hurnard, "The Jury of Presentment and the Assize of Clarendon" *English Historical Review* vol. 56, no. 223 (July, 1941): 374-410; For a history of the earliest Articles in Eyre, see H.M. Cam, *Studies of the Hundred Rolls: Some Aspects of Thirteenth-Century Administration, Volume VI, Oxford Studies in Social and Legal History*, ed. P. Vinogradoff (Oxford, UK: Clarendon Press, 1921), 9-22.

This served to clearly define seigniorial jurisdiction and involve royal officials, specifically the sheriffs, in local and feudal matters, thus weakening the power the lords throughout England.[266] Writs of "novel disseisin" and "morte d"ancestor" served similar functions, as they allowed for those newly dispossessed of their land to summon the alleged dispossessor to court and, for matters of inheritance, to be brought before royal justices. These actions resulted in more cases heard before the justices in eyre and marked one aspect of the strengthened royal mechanisms of law. Although Angevin writs were not always obeyed, implemented, or successful, they did serve as legal instruments of royal authority and contributed to the routinization of land-pleading during the period of reform.[267]

The eyre emphasized legal accountability and social order and encouraged community members and local officials alike to fulfill their respective duties in the interest of social stability. Barons, sheriffs, and other officials who conducted shire and hundred court proceedings were held accountable by legal standards as well as by the community at large.[268] Tithings were under obligation to hold wrongdoers in custody and were likewise held responsible, and often fined, for suspects that fled or prisoners who escaped. Angevin legal practices brought officials under closer scrutiny of the law and local practice while continuing to require freemen to maintain sureties, participate in the hue and cry, and secure their immediate social surroundings.

In this context, Angevin legal reforms called for royal justices to tour the kingdom to hear pleas of all kinds. Upon visitation of the itinerant justices, juries of presentment, which consisted of representatives from every hundred and village within the county, replied to judicial and financial inquiries.[269] The or-

---

266 J. Biancalana, "For Want of Justice: Legal Reforms of Henry II," *Columbia Law Review* vol. 88, no. 3 (April 1988): 433-536 at 442-466; Van Caenegem, R.C., ed. *Royal Writs in England from the Conquest to Glanvill: Studies in the Early History of the Common Law.* A Selden Society Publication, vol. 77 (London, UK: Bernard Quaritch, 1959), 206-233; Plucknett, *Concise History*, 318-327.

267 Van Caenegem, R.C., ed. *Royal Writs*, 261-324; Biacalana, "For Want of Justice," 466-514; Hudson, *Formation of English Common Law*, 193-204, 218-219; Hyams, *Rancor and Reconciliation*, 152-153; Plucknett, *Concise History*, 318-327. Both Biancalana and Hudson use the word "routinisation" in their discussions of English land law during the Angevin reforms.

268 "Introduction," *Crown Pleas of the Wlitshire Eyre, 1249*, ed. C.A.F. Meekings. (Wiltshire Archaeological and Natural History Society. Devizes, UK: Northumberland Press, 1961), 9.

269 Hudson, *Formation of English Common Law*, 123-126; Morris, *The Frankpledge System*, 91-98. Evidence suggests that the eyre was in place during the reign of King Henry I and that during the tenure of King Stephen, when England descended into a state of

ganization of presentment juries required members of each community to report to the justices in eyre about strangers and known malefactors who threatened peace and order.[270] By the end of the twelfth century, the names submitted by the jurors were given to the sheriff, who in turn was to arrest the alleged offenders and bring them to court.[271] Jurors also reported on offenses committed within their hundred through a list of questions, the answers to which they submitted to the justices in eyre. [272] Often the individuals involved in offenses were not known or had fled. The process of presentment brought all offenses and suspected offenders to a public forum in the interest of protecting peace and order.

This inquest was used as a means to gather information was essentially an extension of the methods by which William the Conqueror had gathered information for the Domesday Survey.[273] Juries of presentment gave royal officials an avenue to find out about crimes and misdeeds in localities without requiring a formal appeal to be brought before the courts. The information presented by the juries could result in *ex officio* prosecutions, as royal officials were able to take action against a criminal in the name of the king.[274] To commit a serious offense was a breach of the "king's peace," and action in the king's name could be exercised during court proceedings by his officials. Royal officials hearing matters in local courts was a strategic and effective way for the Crown to exercise control on the community level.[275]

In the Assize of Clarendon (1166), Angevin reformers extended the reach of royal authority in the pursuit and capture of outlaws and other criminals. Sheriffs acquired the right to enter any land where an accused or suspected person

---

disorder and broken-down royal authority, it fell into disuse. The level of anarchy in the early twelfth century remains debatable, but regardless, the eyre was active during the reign of Henry II. The form and work of the eyre and its relationship with the criminal processes in localities were addressed in Assizes of Clarendon (1166) and Northampton (1176).

270 N. Hurnard, "The Jury of Presentment and the Assize of Clarendon," *English Historical Review* vol. 56, no. 223 (July, 1941): 374-410 at 374-396 discusses juries of presentment prior to 1166, the possible origins of the institution, and historiography on the subject.

271 Hyams, *Rancor and Reconciliation*, 160.

272 Hurnard, "Jury of Presentment," 396-397; Hyams, *Rancor and Reconciliation*, 159-160. The later form of this questionnaire was called the articles in eyre, discussed below.

273 Plucknett, *Concise History*, 106-107.

274 R.C. Van Caenegem, "Public Prosecution of Crime in Twelfth-Century England," in Brooke, et. al, eds *Church and Government in the Middle Ages: Essays presented to C.R. Cheney on his 70th Birthday* (Cambridge, UK: Cambridge UP, 1976), 41-76.

275 Reynolds, *Kingdoms and Communities*, 38-39.

may be present.[276] The Assize of 1166 also stated that an individual who returned to England without permission after having abjured the realm was an outlaw.[277] The Assize states:

> And if any one be taken who has the spoil of his robbery or theft in his possession, if he bear an ill name and have a notoriously bad reputation, and have no warrant, let him not have law. But if he be not suspected on account of what he has in his possession, let him go to the water.
>
> Moreover the lord king wills that those who make their law and are quit thereby, if they have a very bad reputation and are publicly and scandalously decried on the testimony of many lawful men, shall forswear the king's lands, to the effect that within eight days they shall cross the sea unless the wind detain them; and with the first wind which they have thereafter they shall cross the sea, and they shall never return to England unless by the grace of the lord king; and there let them be outlaws, and if they return let them be taken as outlaws.[278]

Individuals of ill-repute were distinguished from other criminals, which by all indications was an extension of pre-Angevin practice. The exclusion of such individuals from law, community, and kingdom had become royally endorsed. The jury held immense power in its presentation of information to the justices and was able to use the presentment process to facilitate local judicial practices. At the same time, the King acquired the lands and possessions of outlaws and retained the right to remit such a punishment. Both king and community were able to cooperate and achieve order.[279] The Assize of Clarendon continues:

---

276 "*Assize of Clarendon*," no. 11 in *Select Charters,* ed. Stubbs, 141-146; Hudson, *Formation of English Common Law*, 130-132; See generally Pollock and Maitland, *History of English Law,* vol. 1, "The Age of Glanville" 136-189 for more on the legal reforms during the reign of king Henry II, 137-139 for discussion of the Assizes of Clarendon and Northampton.

277 "*Assize of Clarendon*," no. 14.

278 "*Assize of Clarendon*," nos 12, 14.

279 Pollock and Maitland, *History of English Law*, vol. 1: 137-144; Hurnard, "The Jury of Presentment and the Assize of Clarendon," 391-392; R. D. Groot, "Jury of Presentment before 1215," *The American Journal of Legal History*. vol. 26, no. 1 (Jan., 1982): 1-24 at 3-4; T.A. Green, "The Jury and the English Law of Homicide, 1200-1600," *Michigan Law Review* vol. 74, no. 3 (Jan. 1976): 413-499. Hurnard discusses the dual system of proof (compurgation and ordeal), its presence before and after 1166, and the relationship between the method of proof and type of offender. Groot discusses "medial adjudication" and jury's influence upon proof, accusation, and finality, and Green looks at jury behavior and its ability to control, manipulate, and impact information within the judicial sphere and the effect this had upon the development of homicide law.

> And if any one, in the presence of lawful men or the hundreds, make confession of robbery, murder, theft, or the reception of those committing them, and should later wish to deny it, let him not have law.[280]
>
> And let all the sheriffs cause a record to be made of all fugitives who have fled from their countries; and let them do this before the county courts and carry the names of those written therein before the judges, when next they come to them, so that these men may be sought throughout England, and their chattels may be seized for the needs of the king.[281]

Misinformation was a punishable offense and false, inaccurate, or inconsistent presentment by the jury resulted in amercement of the jurors. Confession to a criminal act was irrevocable and resulted in outlaw status.

There was also a shift in the exercise of the ordeal during the reign of Henry II, which influenced outlawry, exile and banishment. The custom of allowing a criminal to purge himself through oaths-helpers and iron was now supplemented with the ordeal by water. If an accused criminal failed the ordeal by water, he was to be hanged, mutilated, or banished. By the time of the Assize of Northampton in 1176, even accused criminals who survived the ordeal and were "notoriously suspect of a "base felony" were obliged to leave the realm within forty days."[282] This was an addition to the obliged abjuration of individuals said to be of ill-repute by sworn testimony found in the Assize of Clarendon. Judicial abjuration, found in the Assizes of Clarendon and Northampton, is as follows:

> Moreover, the lord king wills that those who shall be tried by the law and absolved by the law, if they have been of ill repute and openly and disgracefully spoken of by the testimony of many and that of the lawful men, shall abjure the king's lands, so that within eight days they shall cross the sea, unless the wind detains them; and with the first wind they shall have afterwards they shall cross the sea, and they shall not return to England again except by the mercy of the lord king; and both now, and if they return, let them be outlawed; and on their return let them be seized as outlaws.[283]

---

280 "*Assize of Clarendon*," no. 13.

281 "*Assize of Clarendon*," no. 18.

282 Warren, *Henry II*, 281-283, 355; "*Assize of Northampton*," no. 1 in *Select Charters,* ed. Stubbs, 150-153Hudson, *Formation of the English Common Law,* 176-177. Not necessarily an indication of the ineffectiveness of earlier customs surrounding the ordeal, as argued by Warren on page 360 (echoing Maitland), this procedural change of the ordeal as an element of criminal law does however reflect the legal reforms which aimed to deter serious crimes. For more on the ordeal, see generally R. Bartlett, *Trial by Fire and Water: The Medieval Judicial Ordeal* (Oxford, UK: Clarendon Press, 1986), 65-69 for information related to the Assizes of Clarendon and Northampton.

283 "*The Assize of Clarendon*," no. 14.

> ...and if he fail [the ordeal of water], let him lose one foot. And at Northampton it was added for the sake of stern justice that he shall likewise lose his right hand with his foot, and shall abjure the realm and within forty days be banished from the kingdom...if he has been accused [or murder or some other base felony by common report of the county and of lawful knights of the country], although he may have come safely through the ordeal of water, nevertheless let him depart from the realm within forty days, and let him take his chattels with him, saving the rights of his lords, and let him abjure the realm at the mercy of the lord king.[284]

The distinction between individuals of ill-repute and those accused of a lone offense is again found in these provisions, and further indicates the amount of power wielded by the juries as they presented information to the justices. Abjuration was heavily influenced by presenting jurors and the "medial adjudication" of a wrongdoer's guilt, "thus the abjuration system accorded substantial finality to that adjudication, and in fact accorded it greater weight as proof of guilt than was accorded the ordeal."[285] The power to exclude through this form of abjuration was a power held by members of the hundreds and the villages. Jury members were responsible for bringing to the attention of the justices the "ill-repute" of a criminal and ultimately controlled whether a criminal remained in the community, and within England. The judicial process was nominally under royal control, but the practical workings of its procedures remained in the hands of local communities and its members.

In a variant form of abjuration, abjuration of the realm was often a self-imposed exile from the kingdom by a sanctuary seeker. By the late twelfth century, the majority of sanctuary seekers were felons being pursued after the hue and cry had been raised or escapees from nearby prisons. A felonious sanctuary seeker could remain in his place of refuge for forty days before having to either stand trial or abjure the realm.[286] Ecclesiastical abjuration remained in use as well, which was more akin to outlawry pronounced upon an offender-cleric who then presumably had to take an oath of abjuration. In all aspects of abjuration, the impetus was to remove a malefactor from the kingdom and to secure an oath from the wrong-doer that he would leave and never return.

---

284 "*The Assize of Northampton,*" no. 1; T.F.T. Plucknett, *Edward I and Criminal Law*, (Cambridge, UK: Cambridge UP, 1960), 68-70.

285 Groot, "Jury of Presentment before 1215," 22-23.

286 R. F. Hunnisett, *Medieval Coroner* (Cambridge, UK: Cambridge UP, 1961), 37; Cam, *The Hundred and The Hundred Rolls, An Outline of Local Government in Medieval England.* London, UK: Merlin Press Limited, 1963), 130-131. Although I use the masculine throughout, women were able to, and often did, take sanctuary and abjure the realm.

Concerns for removing individuals who threatened law and order are also found in the checks upon outlawry and exile implemented in the Assize of Northampton:

> Item, the justices shall have investigation made, according to the custom of the land, as to those who have left the kingdom; and unless they are willing to return within a stated time and to stand trial in the court of the lord king, they shall then be outlawed; and the names of the outlaws shall be brought to the exchequer at Easter and Michaelmas, and shall thence be sent to the lord king.[287]

Here outlawry was specifically pronounced by the county courts against fugitives who did not return to stand trial before the justices in eyre. This was in contrast to the Assize of Clarendon, in which fugitives" names were simply listed and offenders were to be sought out with the forfeiture of property. The explicit statement that these individuals were to be outlawed reflects the use of outlawry by royal law within the limits that custom provided. Additionally, fugitives were given a specific amount of time during which they are allowed to return, a product of the increasing regularization of legal processes.

The increased centralization of the outlawry process under the nominal authority of the Crown is clear, as is the royal desire to control how outlawry was used in the localities. Not only did the Crown want to control all aspects of outlawry, but it wished to control the exercise of justice in the local courts in such a way that met its best interest. The inclusion of the justices in eyre in the outlawry process in county courts, as well as the requirement that the names and possessions of outlaws be recorded by the king's officials, represented royal attempts to assert control over the local administration of justice. County courts were technically courts of the king but within those courts, outlawry remained an action brought about by criminal appeal or by personal complaint, and was still used as a means to an end in private disputes, wrongs, and misdeeds. The checks put in place by the Crown mark important changes taking place in the spheres of what we could term private and public litigation. They also bear witness to the royal efforts to incorporate existing legal practices into the administration of justice in the twelfth century.

Outlawry as a local infamy, in which individuals were known to be undesirables by those in their immediate surroundings, had transitioned to a process by which the king's official, the sheriff, brought these criminals to the direct atten-

---

287 "*Assize of Northampton*," no. 13; D. Stenton, *Pleas before the Kings or his Justices, 1198-1202, Volume 1: Introduction with Appendixes Containing Essoins 1199-1201, A "King's Roll" of 1200, and Writs of 1199-1200*, ed. for the Selden Society, vol. 67. (London, UK: Bernard Quaritch, 1953), 134-135.

tion of the crown. The sheriff had long been the king's man, at least nominally, in the county, and played an active role in the pronouncement of outlawry in the county court. It was essential to the authority of king and the force of royal law that the sheriff come under closer scrutiny and control. By extension, this allowed for an increased role of the crown in outlawry processes. The "Inquest of the Sheriff" of 1170 investigated sheriffs in England, attempted to reform the position, and brought about the removal of many corrupt officials. Henry removed "evil" sheriffs from office and commissioned the "Inquest" to inquire about the administration in the shires and to assess the conduct and accountability of the sheriffs.[288]

At the same time that sheriffs were being assessed by the crown, their position as the king's official in the counties was gaining importance as a key component to the extension of royal jurisdiction. In addition to collecting revenues and conducting duties in the shires, sheriffs were responsible for guarding prisoners, handling writs, assembling juries, and preparing for the arrival of the itinerant justices. Henry's sheriffs acted with renewed royal authority as well as with local power. As seen in the Assize of Clarendon, the sheriff had the extension of authority to override local custom at times, and could surpass franchise and private jurisdictions and privileges with the help of a jury presentment. The exercise of justice was still in the hands of the localities, but increased royal mechanisms were put into place to facilitate this work.

Angevin Reforms: The use of imprisonment

Many of the actions and legal measures implemented during Henry II's reign facilitated the transition of English law into a more efficient, stable system of jurisprudence, and the administration of justice came under a more centralized royal authority. Traditionally, scholars have argued that this stability was focused in matters of property rather than criminal law, but Angevin reforms brought about new centralization to criminal proceedings as well.[289] This is

288 W.A. Morris, *The Medieval English Sheriff to 1300* (Manchester, UK: Manchester UP and London, UK: Longmans, Green & Co., Ltd., 1927), 57, 111-113, 115-126; W.A. Morris, "The Sheriff and the Administrative System of Henry I," English Historical Review vol. 37, no. 146 (April 1922): 161-172; Warren, *Governance*, 109-110; Hudson, *Formation of English Common Law*, 131-132; Hyams, *Rancor and Reconciliation*, 163-164. See "Inquest of the Sheriffs (1170)," in *Select Charters,* ed. Stubbs, 147-150.

289 For more on English Common law and property law, see R.C. Palmer, "The Origins of Property in England," *Law and History Review*, vol. 3, no. 1 (Spring, 1985): 1-50.

most apparent in the relationship between juries of presentment and the use of imprisonment as a legal tool.

The removal of a malefactor from society and law continued through the late twelfth century. Suspects presented before the justices were subjected to the ordeal, and even if successful, they could still be forced to abjure the realm if deemed a threat to the kingdom. Fugitives and outlaws were publicized at presentments and were to be pursued throughout the kingdom.[290] There was, however, new attention paid to captivity and confinement during the Angevin period. This reflected and acknowledged the need for prisons in the legal, social, and political processes of the late twelfth century. The Assize of Clarendon (1166) called for the establishment of a gaol in every hundred in England:

> And in the several counties where there are no gaols, let such be made in a borough or some castle of the king at the king's expense and from his wood, if one shall be near, or from some neighbouring wood at the oversight of the king's servants, to the end that in them the sheriffs may be able to guard those who shall be arrested by the officials accustomed to do this, or by their servants.[291]

Twelfth century gaols were very much custodial in purpose and function and were used to detain criminals following an arrest and prior to trial rather than as a form of prescriptive punishment. The requirement of their existence in each county reflects the royal response to a local need as well as the implementation of a tool of social order that was not based in custom and could be controlled by the Crown.[292]

Angevin imprisonment, termed "coercive" by Pugh, was in fact highly punitive, public, and met the needs of officials when imposing further penalties.[293] The Crown, by way of the justices in eyre, encouraged the use of gaols and captivity of wrongdoers in the shires by imposing punishments when communities failed at doing so. Failure of a frankpledge group or township to pursue and capture a criminal often resulted in a fine placed upon the appropriate group.[294]

---

290 Hurnard, "Jury of Presentment," 398.

291 "*Assize of Clarendon*," no. 7.

292 Pollock and Maitland, *History of English Law*, vol. 1: 49, 136-138; vol. 2: 516-519; Warren, *Henry II,* 281-283, 354-351; R. B. Pugh, "The King's Prisons before 1250," Transactions of the Royal Historical Society, 5th ser. vol. 5, (1955): 1-22, at 2-4; A. Babington, *The English Bastille: A History of Newgate Gaol and Prison Conditions in Britain 1188-1902* (London, UK: MacDonald and Company, 1971), 3-5.

293 Pugh, *Medieval Imprisonment,* 255-256; R.B. Pugh, "The King's Prisons before 1250," 1-22; Meekings, *Wilsthire Crown Pleas*, 92-93.

294 Morris, *The Frankpledge System*, 93-98.

Closely tied to the procedure of indictment, post-1166 gaols would be cleared by the king and his justices when conducting an eyre. This had previously been done by the sheriffs but "gaol delivery" soon came under the onus of special commissions. Gaol delivery commissions were first appointed on a national scale but by the 1220s they were sent out by the Crown on a regional or county basis, reflecting the increased number and use of gaols throughout England resulting from the Angevin legal actions. Additionally, the expanded use of fines to enforce procedural rules of criminal law during the reign of Henry II corresponded with the emphasis on gaols, as failure to pay could result in temporary imprisonment.[295] In Richard Fitz Nigel's *The Course of the Exchequer*, the debtor who,

> ...not giving satisfaction for the amount of his summons, shall have deserved to be seized, he is handed over to the marshal to be guarded, and when the exchequer of that day is dissolved, the latter shall, if he wish, send him to public gaol; he shall not, however, be chained or thrust into the dungeon, but shall be apart by himself or above the subterraneous gaol. For although he be not solvent, he has not, nevertheless, on this account deserved to be put with the criminals.[296]

Debt in England was viewed as a breach of faith and associated with criminal behavior, but was neither felonious nor worthy of harsher punishments such as death or mutilation. Imprisonment was a form of punishment considered to be appropriate for the offense and was increasingly used during this period.[297]

Similarly, the "Assize of the Forest" of 1184 dictated that any individual who hunted at night anywhere in the kingdom or trapped an animal in the king's forest was subject to the "pain of imprisonment for one year and the payment of a fine or ransom at his [the king's] pleasure."[298] Concerns over forests and the

---

295 Kerr, "Angevin Reform of Felony," 361-364. For what Kerr describes as an "incomplete list" of offenses that could result in fines, see 362-363.

296 "*Dialogus de Scaccario*" or *The Course of the Exchequer* by Richard Fitz Nigel, ed. and trans. C. Johnson. Corrections by F.E.L. Carter and D.E. Greenway (Oxford, UK: Clarendon Press, 1983), lii. The *Dialogus* is considered a "practical treatise" on the treasury and office of the exchequer. For more on Fitz Nigel and the exchequer in the twelfth century, see generally Johnson's "Introduction."

297 See Pugh, *Imprisonment in Medieval England*, 5-8 and R. Ireland, "Theory and Practice within the Medieval English Prison," *The American Journal of Legal History*, vol. 31, no. 1 (Jan., 1987): 56-67.

298 "*Assize of the Forest*," no. 16 in *Select Charters* ed. Stubbs, 156-159; C.R. Young, "English Royal Forests under the Angevin Kings" *The Journal of British Studies* vol. 12, no. 1 (Nov. 1972): 1-14 at 5; James, *Forestry*, 10; Havins, *Forests*, 20-26; C.R. Young, "The Forest Eyre in England during the Thirteenth Century" *The American*

king's right over land and animals therein had long been part of English kingship and Henry II claims to be exacting justice as his grandfather, Henry I, had done.[299] Forest law, although "solely to the will of the king or that of some official specially appointed for this purpose," was separate from Common Law but still enforced by sheriffs and justices in eyre.[300] The side-by-side existence of the two types of law must have overlapped, either intentionally or out of necessity, and they both contain references to outlawry and imprisonment.[301] The king had sole discretion in determining illegalities of the forest as well as punishments for those offenses. Imprisonment, in fact, was prescribed as a punishment for a specific amount of time within forest laws, a rarity in English law. Because imprisonment was not tied to customary processes or laws, it could be used at the prerogative of the king with greater ease than outlawry and exile. As a result, it was increasingly being employed in the administration of justice and governance.

It was more difficult for the Crown to exercise control over felonies and the treatment of felons. The appeal of felony in England was used to prosecute pleas of the Crown, which nominally fell under the jurisdiction of the king, but the process of appeal remained in the hands of individual men.[302] Angevin concerns for serious offenses and efforts to centralize authority led to an expanding list of felonies, but appeals of felony were not automatically under the prevue the king, as private appeals and presentments "took precedence over public prosecution."[303] As a result, the Crown actively sought out men to facilitate bringing felons to the court of the King and encouraged offenders to turn approver. Fitz Nigel discussed some of the intricacies of turning approver, or confessed felons who informed up and appealed their accomplices, and their role in judicial processes.[304]

Journal of Legal History, vol. 18, no. 4 (Oct., 1974), 321-331; C.R. Young, *The Royal Forests of Medieval England* (Philadelphia, PA: University of Pennsylvania Press, 1979), 27-33; E.C. Wright, "Common Law in the Thirteenth-Century English Royal Forest," *Speculum*, vol. 3, no. 2 (April, 1928): 166-191; Pugh, *Medieval Imprisonment*, 20, 23, 130-132, 386; Hudson, *Formation of English Common Law*, 133.

299 *LHP*, 120-121, c. 17,1 and c. 17.2. *ASC*, year 1087 describes the punishment by mutilation prescribed for individuals who violated the king's forest by either "vert" or "venison", as they were subject to blinding.

300 Young, *The Royal Forests of Medieval England,* 22, 27-29; Vollmer, *The English Royal Forest*, 34-37; Havins, *Forests*, 24; Pugh, *Medieval Imprisonment*, 386.

301 Vollmer, *The English Royal Forest*, 41-42; W. L. Warren, *Governance of Norman and Angevin England* (London, UK: Edward Arnold Publishers, Ltd., 1987), 160.

302 Kerr, "Angevin Reform of Felony," 382.

303 Kerr, "Angevin Reform of Felony," 354.

304 "*Dialogus*," 102, 87-88.

> ...when some notorious criminal is apprehended by the King's officers of the peace, crime being so rife, the justices sometimes consent, as an extreme measure to purge the country of criminals, that if such a man confesses and turns King's evidence against his associates, and succeeds in proving by battle a charge against one or more of them, he may escape the death he has deserved, and save his skin by losing his civil rights and abjuring the realm.[305]

In this context, abjuration was a means to escape and salvation, an imposed outlawry taken at the mercy of the king only after bringing other criminals to justice. The use of approvers as agents of the king publicized a greater number of felons while simultaneously fostered royal power by ridding the country of malefactors. Abjuration in this context could be construed as both a punishment and an incentive, and thus, a doubly powerful tool.

Likewise, the role of approvers in the late twelfth century reveals how the Crown began to influence the system of appeal. Juries of presentment were soon used in appeals *de odio et atia*, or "of spite and hate," which gave appellees the opportunity to request royal intervention via the jury to investigate if an appeal was brought maliciously.[306] The use of juries in appeals began to expand and slowly what had been private legal practice became intertwined with public prosecutions. Juries were used to investigate abandoned appeals and appeals that could be continued *ex officio*. With increased royal involvement in appeals came more punitive fines, which in turn, led to the imprisonment of individuals who could not or did not pay.[307]

Angevin Reforms: Assessment

The overall importance of the Angevin Reforms as they relate to outlawry is striking. The "Constitutions of Clarendon of 1164" and the Becket dispute saw the Crown attempting to limit the Church's use of abjuration and outlawry for

305 "*Dialogus*," 87-88, Hamil, "King's Approvers," 238; M. Kerr, "Angevin Reform of the Appeal of Felony," 351-391 at 353; Tables 1-6, 384-391; Hyams, *Rancor and Reconciliation*, 166. If an approver garnered enough convictions, the approver was presumably allowed to abjure the realm, but in order to get to such a position, he had to prove himself against his defendants through trial by battle. See also M.T. Clanchy's "Highway robbery and trial by battle in the Hampshire eyre of 1249" in *Medieval Legal Records: Edited in memory of C.A.F. Meekings*, eds R.F. Hunnisett and J.B. Post (London, UK: Her Majesty's Stationery Office, 1978): 25-61.

306 Kerr, "Angevin Reform of the Appeal of Felony, 370.

307 Kerr, "Angevin Reform of the Appeal of Felony," 370-371, 377-383.

criminous clerics. Henry's insistence that clerics receive his permission before leaving the country reflects the growing concern with physically keeping individuals in the kingdom in order that they be controlled. The dangers of being outside of the country and beyond the control of the King were becoming more and more clear. The "Assize of Clarendon," which ordered that gaols be built in all counties, reflected this same concern by emphasizing captivity and detention of criminals.

The Assize, however, added detail to the outlawry process, emphasizing its use and need. Its successor, the "Assize of Northampton," took outlawry still further by essentially pronouncing it against men of ill-repute who had in fact succeeded at the ordeal by causing them to abjure the realm. The "Inquest of the Sheriffs" sought to remove corrupt officials and control the future sheriff, a key figure in the proclamation of outlawry. The use of the eyre brought about increased accountability of county courts, sheriffs, and their actions, as did juries of presentment, and because the county was the sole place in which outlawry could be proclaimed, these administrative mechanisms increased royal participation and control in local practice.

Legal practice during the reign of Henry II

Tractatus de legibus et consuetudinibus regni Anglie, attributed to Ranulf Glanvill, Justiciar of England from 1180-1189 under king Henry II, attests to the continued presence of outlawry in England, as well as demonstrates that the whole of the practice was long-established and, on the whole, exercised with consistency of custom throughout the kingdom. [308] Glanville reaffirmed the banishment of usurers, who were to forfeit all property to the Crown and be treated as outlaws throughout the realm.[309] With respect to civil pleas, royal attention was paid to outlaws and land holdings. Any land or movables forfeited to the king upon outlawry were held by the king for one year before reverting back to the individual's lord. Anyone who had been…

---

308 *The Treatise on the Laws and Customs of the realm of England commonly called Glanville or Tractatus de legibus et consuetudinibus regni Anglie qui Glanvilla vocatur. Ranulf Glanvill*, ed. and trans. G.D.G. Hall (London, UK: Thomas Nelson and Sons, Ltd. in association with the Selden Society, 1965). For more on the background, plan and debated authorship of this work, see xi-lxx. See also Pollock and Maitland, "The Age of Glanville" in *The History of English Law*, 1: 136-189 at 162-165; J.C. Russell, "Ranulf de Glanvill" *Speculum* vol. 45, no. 1. (Jan., 1970): 69-79; F. West, *The Justiciarship in England 1066-1232* (Cambridge, UK: Cambridge UP, 1966), 54-63.

309 *Glanville*, Book 7.16. The banishment of usurers was found in *LEC*.

> ...duly outlawed and later restored to the peace by royal favour, neither he nor his heirs may on that account recover from their lord any inheritance which he had, except by grace and favour of the lord; for the lord king does not wish, when pardoning wrongdoing and outlawry, to infringe thereby the rights of others.[310]

This indicates that although the royal arm of administration had a vested interest in outlawry and its processes, the crown did not, or could not, infringe upon its local roots and implications. This statement occurs in portions of Glanville related to land possession and, by extension, it can be supposed that Henry II "safeguarded the right of the injured party or relatives of the slain to prosecute" in capital crimes as well. In this way, the King benefited to some financial extent by granting a pardon to an outlaw, but was careful to not disrespect the process or its significance in society.[311]

Failure to appear when summoned, failure to make payment, and the swearing of false oaths were all offenses that could result in imprisonment. Imprisonment was meted out regardless of an individual's role or stage in any legal proceeding. If the "demandant" or plaintiff failed to show up to prosecute his claim, the tenant (defendant) would be sent away.

> If however, the case is not only his but also the lord king's, as in a criminal case for breach of the lord king's peace, then, since he must not prejudice anyone but himself by defaulting in the case and is indeed bound to prosecute it, he shall immediately be put in prison and kept in safe custody until he is willing to prosecute his appeal, and his sureties shall, moreover, be liable to amercement.[312]

If a lord failed to appear after his three chances to essoin, his "essoiners shall be imprisoned and he shall also be attached in person for his contempt of court, and in this way compelled to come to court, where whatever he wishes to say shall be heard."[313] And anyone who failed to make payment on a fine imposed by the king's court, "shall be liable to amercement by the lord king; and he shall be imprisoned until he finds good security for keeping the fine in future, either by performing his undertaking if that is possible or else by making reasonable satisfaction to the other party."[314] Furthermore, even jurors were subject being held captive:

---

310 *Glanville*, Book 7.17. See also Hyams, *Rancor and Reconciliation*, 198 for discussion of the relationship between peace and pardon in this context.

311 Hurnard, *King's Pardon*, 20.

312 *Glanville*, Book 1.31, 21.

313 *Glanville*, Book 3.6. An "essoin" was an excuse tendered by or on behalf of one who is summoned to appear in court to perform suit or answer to an action, by reason of sickness or infirmity, or other allowable cause of absence (Warren, *Henry II*, 634).

314 *Glanville*, Book 8.5

> If the jurors are duly convicted in court of perjury, or confess to it in court, then they shall be deprived of all their chattels and moveable goods which shall pass to the king, by whose great mercy their free tenements are excepted from this forfeiture. They shall, moreover, be cast into prison and kept there for a year at least. In addition they shall lose their law for ever and thus rightly incur the lasting mark of infamy."[315]

Overall, Glanville paid little attention to criminal law, most often deferring to custom and the reforms put into place by the Assizes of Clarendon and Northampton, but he did comment about the relationship between the Crown and the county courts in the final clause of his treatise.[316] Glanville wrote of his "aim…to consider only the king's court," defining theft and other pleas as "belonging to the sheriff, which are heard and determined according to the varying customs of different county courts."[317] He informed his reader, however, that the process concerning criminal pleas could result in the use of imprisonment, as "if no specific accuser appears but the accusation is based on public notoriety, then immediately the accused shall be safely attached, either buy suitable sureties or by imprisonment…."[318] Similarly,

> …if a specific accuser appears, he shall be immediately attached to give security for prosecuting his suit, by sureties if he has any. If he has no sureties, then he is put on a solemn oath, as in all pleas of felony. An oath is deemed sufficient in such cases lest others should be deterred by excessive demands for security from making similar accusations. When the accuser has given security for prosecuting his claim the accused shall, as we said above, be attached by sound and reliable sureties; if he has none, he shall be put in prison.[319]

The accused was freed upon giving surety in all felonies except homicide, and was required to return to court on an assigned day.[320] This coincides with the increased use of fines by Henry II as a means to enforce proper criminal processes, as well as the expanding use of imprisonment in matters of law.

---

315 *Glanville*, Book 2.19.

316 *Glanville*, Book 14, "Criminal Pleas." Hall notes that Glanville does not always stress nor conform to the Assizes of Clarendon and Northampton, particularly with respect to the jury of presentment. See note 1 on page 171, N.D. Hurnard, "The Jury of Presentment and the Assize of Clarendon," 374-410 and the introduction to *Earliest Lincolnshire Assize Rolls A.D. 1202-1209* (Lincoln Record Society, vol. 22 (1926) by D. Stenton as sources for further discussion of the matter.

317 *Glanville*, Book 14.8.

318 *Glanville*, Book 14.1.

319 *Glanville*, Book 14.1.

320 *Glanville*, Book 14.1. Homicides were to remain in prison until their case was heard.

The increased royal influence or interaction with county courts in civil matters is also clear in Glanville's work. Crown extended itself into local matters with the use of two legal processes, tolt and a "writ of pone." Tolt could be initiated as an action to remove litigation from a feudal court into that of the county. This could only be done if an injustice was alleged to be taking place and was only possible through a complaint by the demandant in a case.[321] According to Glanville, the demandant…

> …made his complaint to the sheriff. The sheriff would then send his bailiff and four knights of the county to that court, and the demandant would there prove by oath – his own and that of two men who had heard and understood – that the court was proceeding unjustly. If his proof was good, the case was thereby removed – "lifted" – into the county court.[322]

Tolt removed a matter from feudal or manorial jurisdiction into that of the county, bringing it to the attention of royal sheriffs, coroners, or justices in eyre. Similarly, cases could be removed from the county court into a royal court by way of a "writ of pone."[323] *Pone* was a procedure that was available to either demandant or plaintiff, and would later be used to remove almost any type of case begun by writ from the county courts. Again, the sheriff would exercise the writ and summon the complainant to Westminster on a day assigned, thus terminating action in the county court and placing it in the court of the king.[324] The importance of writs and their effect on the jurisdiction of county courts would continue to have a prominent function in the development of Common Law, in the judicial power of the crown, and development of constraint in its various forms.

The other legal treatise of twelfth century, *The Course of the Exchequer*, provides additional information about the administration of justice in the shires.[325] Richard Fitz Nigel, who held a position at the head of Henry II's treas-

---

321 Pollock and Maitland, *History of English Law*, vol. 2: 666; Plucknett, *Concise History*, 345; R.C. Palmer, *The County Courts of Medieval England, 1150-1135* (Princeton, NJ: Princeton UP, 1982), 144-147.

322 Palmer, *County Courts*, 144-145, citing *Glanville*.

323 Pollock and Maitland, *History of English Law*, vol. 2: 666.

324 *Glanville*, 61; Palmer, *County Courts*, 148-149; Morris, *The Early English County Court, An Historical Treatise with Illustrative Documents*. University of California Publications in History. vol. 14, no. 2 (Berkeley, CA: University of California Press, 1926), 89-230 at 130-131. The origins of *pone* are unknown. For Palmer's discussion of the date of *pone's* first appearance in surviving records, see note 18 on page 148.

325 "*Dialogus*", lii. For more on Fitz Nigel and the office of the exchequer in the twelfth century, see generally Johnson's "Introduction."

ury, writes about revenues due to the crown from the localities and discusses the criteria by which the chattels of outlaws and other felons became the possession of the King and his officials. Chattels of fugitives who either had or had not yet been outlawed went to the King's treasury, those of apprehended felons went to the sheriff, and those of criminals involved in cases appearing before the King went to the Crown.[326] With the implementation of the eyre and the presentation of cases to royal justices, this meant that unless an outlaw was captured, all property of fugitives and outlaws remained in the possession of the King. It was the sheriff's responsibility to record and deliver forfeitures accordingly and any records relating to outlawry kept by the sheriff would be given to the Exchequer.[327] This is another example of how the Crown was becoming increasingly involved in the outlaw process and from the earliest extant Pipe Roll records from the reign of King Henry II, the cattle of fugitives was being recorded as property of the crown.[328]

Pipe Roll documentation from the mid- to late twelfth century reveals an increased accountability involving officials and matters relating to outlaws. The treatment of outlaws, their possessions, and their relationship with royal authority fell under the onus of the sheriff. If an outlaw was pardoned, it was by royal writ addressed to the sheriff. The sheriff was held accountable for any revenues and chattels due to the King by the Exchequer, head of the royal treasury.[329] The sheriff was the guardian of local peace and the custodian of local prisoners, and any mistakes in the processes of outlawry would result in his amercement by the Crown.[330] Pipe Rolls reveal that individuals and communities alike would be amerced for receiving an outlaw, demonstrated by the monetary penalties paid to the crown by Alured from Hampshire in 1167 and by an entire Lincolnshire village in 1168.[331]

---

326 "*Dialogus*," 102.

327 "*Dialogus*," 101-103.

328 *The Great Roll of the Pipe for the Reign of King Henry the Second as part of The Great Rolls of the Exchequer, commonly called The Pipe Rolls, and other documents prior to the year AD 1200.* pub. by the Pipe Roll Society. vol. 7, year 1163 (*PR 10 Henry II*) (London, UK: Wyman and Sons, 1884), 1, 12. Subsequent years of Pipe Rolls reflect the increasing number of fugitive cattle being transferred to the crown, or else an increased documentation of the practice.

329 Morris, *Medieval Sheriff*, 124-135; 146-147; R. L. Poole, *The Exchequer in the Twelfth Century* (Oxford, UK: Clarendon Press, 1912), 171-182. This would change with the development of the position of coroner, see below.

330 Morris, 115-117, 119, 122-124; Gillingham, "Formation," 180-183; Poole, *The Exchequer in the Twelfth Century*, 127-149; 174-180. Gradually many of the judicial duties held by the sheriff were taken over by the justices and the coroner.

331 *PR 13 Henry II*: 182; *PR 14 Henry II*: 75.

During 1165-1166, Pipe Rolls record 27 entries for fugitive's cattle and over nine entries of payments by a pledge for a fugitive. Within a decade, there are numerous lists of fugitives and cattle found within each year of Pipe Roll records, reflecting the increased recognition and documentation by royal authorities regarding the property of outlaws.[332] Villages in Wiltshire in 1167 and in Yorkshire in 1169 were held accountable for the cattle of outlaws detained and disseized there, while vicecomes in Gloucestershire were accountable to the crown for cattle of fugitives and hanged criminals.[333] Nobles and clerks were not exempt from such amercements, as the Earl of Stratford owed money to the Crown for receiving an outlaw in 1169 or 1170 and a bishop in Hampshire owed for the cattle of a detained and concealed outlaw in 1168.[334] And there is one recorded instance of a man, Gilbert son of Walter, paying a fine and having his outlawry remitted by the king. Gilbert paid part of this fine in the twenty-second year of Henry II's reign (1175-1176) and was still paying according to documentation from the following year.[335]

Observations: The Impact of Henry II's Reforms upon methods of outlawry, exile, and imprisonment

The centralization of justice that took place as a result of the Angevin reforms sought to routinize outlawry, exile, and imprisonment as part of legal and administrative processes. The Crown attempted to control the punishments of clerics, specifically their prescribed abjurations and pilgrimages, and generally sought to regulate the comings and goings of religious men to and from England. The "Constitutions of Clarendon" established that Henry's permission was needed by Church personnel to leave the kingdom as well as appeal to Rome and that all excommunications had to be approved by the king. When Becket left England in 1164 without permission, it prompted the wrath of Henry and the king exiled Becket's family members and associates alike. He did this to rid the country of perceived wrongdoers and trouble-makers and to demonstrate his authority. When Becket returned to England from his period of exile and was subsequently killed, Henry was forced to acquiesce and release clerics from their oaths to abide by the "Constitutions," losing much of what he had gained in 1164 as far as control over clerical matters and persons. Henry II acknowledged and accepted the right of the Church to discipline its personnel and was only

332 For an example of a list from Buckinghamshire, see *PR 5 Henry II*: 27.

333 *PR 13 Henry II*: 163; *PR 16 Henry II*: 46; *PR 15 Henry II*: 118.

334 *PR 16 Henry II*: 62; *PR 14 Henry II*: 186.

335 *PR 22 Henry II*: 90; *PR 23 Henry II*: 85.

now to be made aware of clerical offenses, trials, and punishments. The King did maintain the right to consent to the excommunication of his tenants-in-chief and other officials.

In the counties and hundreds of England, the Crown intended to exercise more authority when dealing with criminals, wrongdoers, fugitives, and malefactors of all kinds in the interest of maintaining peace. Attempts were made to control outlawry as a process conducted in local county courts. Supervision and accountability of county sheriffs was essential to royal involvement in outlawry. Furthermore, offenders who had abjured the realm in a local setting but then returned to England were to be outlawed in the name of the king; itinerant justices and the royal exchequer were made aware of men who had been outlawed by the county courts; the coming of the eyre became part of the exigency process, as a meeting of the court in front of royal justices qualified as one failure to appear for a fugitive criminal; and men of ill-repute could be banished or forced to abjure the realm in the interest of maintaining the king's peace.

Royal law was taking shape in the context of a legal and social custom that used local exclusion as a means to the maintenance of order. Nominal royal authority existed throughout England, but the local juries of presentment and county courts held the power to control the information given to the king's officials. They also, and perhaps more importantly, controlled whether or not a criminal could remain in the kingdom or was required to abjure the realm.[336] Men of ill repute were to abjure the realm and it was the jury that held the power to present an individual in such a way that would require he leave the kingdom. The Crown obliged and endorsed the long held rights of the localities to exclude malefactors, or at the very least encouraged the practice to continue, by dictating that men of ill-repute must leave England in both the Assize of Clarendon in 1166 and the Assize of Northampton in 1176. The localities were left content by such pronouncements and in control of who could stay and who was to leave their communities while the Crown was left with the belief that it held the power to enforce such punishment in its name. Pollock and Maitland's assertion that it was at this point in the twelfth century that outlawry ceased to be a punishment and became merely a "process" by which offenders could be compelled to appear fails to grasp the role of outlawry and exclusion in England during the eleventh century.[337]

336 Hyams agrees. On page 156 of *Rancor and Reconciliation*, he offers his impression that although Angevin reforms broadened "access to the king's law… local power equations may in fact have changed rather little." See also 184-186.

337 Pollock and Maitland, *History of English Law*, vol. 2: 458-461.

Henry's reforms offered no widespread replacement of "violent self-help by royal legal processes...but instead [provided] an intermediate step involving a more complex combination of extra-legal violence with vigorous lawsuits."[338] In this context, exile and outlawry increasingly came into contact with and functioned alongside imprisonment. New litigation resulted in new categories of offenders, as well as an increased number of accusers and accused men. The increased presence and use of gaols as part of Henry II's legal agenda reflected a growing concern with offenders and wrongdoers and a means by which the Crown and its royal officials dealt with such individuals. Outlawry remained strong as a process of law and custom, but the Crown needed to visibly flex its authoritative legal muscle and maintain public order. This was accomplished by implementing the use of gaols on a regularized basis. The Crown placed gaols in the hands of its trusted royal officials, thus physically demonstrating its power in dealing with legal matters. Imprisonment was serving a more prominent role in the administration of justice in medieval England.

The immediate impact of Angevin efforts at control and centralization, much less their success, cannot be known. On the whole, legal changes in the late twelfth century brought about continued adaptation and expansion of royal justice, courts, personnel, and administration. Law and politics in the late twelfth and through the thirteenth century would shape and be shaped by the Angevin reforms. Efforts to harness outlawry and the like during the late twelfth century were unsuccessful, but the use of gaols and confinement had been expanded to counter this failure. The struggle between royal authority and local justice, between public order and private vengeance, would continue – a key element of which was the power to exclude or confine malefactors in law, politics, and society.

---

338 R.W. Kaeuper, *War, Justice, and Public Order: England and France in the Later Middle Ages* (Oxford, UK: Clarendon Press, 1988), 142; 153-155.

Chapter 5: The Successors of Henry II: Outlawry, Abjuration, and Imprisonment up to the personal rule of Henry III

Late twelfth and early thirteenth century kings of England built upon the legal and administrative reforms of Henry II. During the reigns of Richard, John, and the early years of Henry III, the use and control of outlawry, abjuration, and imprisonment complimented the ebb and flow of royal authority in England, while the prominence of outlawry in local courts demonstrated the strength of legal custom. The crown continued its efforts to seize the strength of outlawry for own purposes, attempting to bring aspects of exclusion under its control. In many instances, this brought law and politics into the close confines of a gaol setting.

The Reign of King Richard

Immediately upon the death of Henry II in 1189, his widow Queen Eleanor issued the following orders on behalf of King Richard, her eldest son and the new king.

> …all captives should be liberated from prison and confinement…in as much as in her own person, she had learnt by experience that confinement is distasteful to mankind, and that it is a most delightful refreshment to the spirits to be liberated therefrom…all persons who had been outlawed for forest offences should return in peace, acquitted of all previous offences against the forest laws; and further, that all persons who had been taken and detained by the will of the king, or of his justice, and who had not been detained according to the common law of the county or hundred, or on appeal, should be acquitted; and those who were detained by the common law…those, also, who, on appeal had been detained in custody upon any criminal matter, if they could find sureties…were to be set at liberty…those, also, who were outlawed at common law, without appeal, by the justices, were to return to peace…."[339]

339 Hoveden, vol. 2: 112-113; H. G. Richardson, "The Letters and Charters of Eleanor of Aquitaine," *The English Historical Review*, vol. 74, no. 291 (Apr., 1959): 193-213 at 200; A. Weir, *Eleanor of Aquitaine: A Life*, (New York, NY: Ballantine Books, 1999), 48-49; J.T. Appleby, *England Without Richard, 1189-1199* (Ithaca, NY: Cornell UP, 1965), 1-3; Young, *The Royal Forests of Medieval England*, 23. Eleanor of Aquitaine

The combined use of imprisonment and outlawry as instruments of social order is clear from this passage, as are the complexities of the law and politics in late twelfth century England. That kings were using their power to pardon in matters of imprisonment and outlawry alike represented the relationship and power of these two practices. It also adds insight into the royal role in processes and application of each.

According to William of Newburgh, however, the pardons issued by Richard and Eleanor were disastrous, as "those jailpests, by his [Richard's] clemency, went forth from prison to rob, and plunder, more boldly, perhaps than ever."[340] Pardon as a royal act was not always in the best interest of the king's subjects, but the exercises of mercy and authority and what they represented often trumped local concerns. Pardon was a tool that the king could use without legal or customary restrictions and fostered royal power. Richard also recalled many of "those whom the father had banished" during his reign, but banished other individuals whom he, according to Roger de Hoveden, "abhorred."[341]

The criticisms offered by William of Newburgh and Roger de Hoveden offer insight into contemporary perspectives on royal power and punishment. Eleanor was seemingly pious and acted sympathetically to men who had been wronged by Henry II. Her policy, tainted by the tense relationship she had with her husband, did not earn her praise by contemporaries. William of Newburgh, on the contrary, seems to advocate the use of imprisonment and its role in maintaining social order. Roger de Hoveden implies that Richard's use of banishment was motivated by personal animosity rather than political and legal cause. Viewed as abuses of power by contemporary chroniclers, royal interference with imprisonment and banishment outside of legal processes threatened political and social stability.

Richard's recall of his father's enemies and subsequent banishment of his own adversaries highlights the power associated with controlling who could enter and leave England. This was a tension-ridden component of royal authority.

---

had been imprisoned by Henry due to her involvement in the rebellion of their sons in 1173, and kept in confinement at either Winchester or Sarum Castles until his death in 1189. Richard fought with his father throughout the 1180s and attempted to seize the throne of England in 1188 by joining forces with the French king Phillip. For more on Richard, see J. Gillingham, *Richard the Lionheart* (London, UK: Weidenfeld and Nicolson, 1978). Eleanor acted as regent for Richard while he was in Normandy in 1189.

340 "The History of William of Newburgh" in *The Church Historians of England*, vol. 4, part 2, ed. J. Stevenson. London, UK: Seeleys, 1851), 555 (Book 4).

341 Hoveden, vol. 2: 115, 113.

Before going on Crusade in 1189, Richard exacted oaths from his brothers John and Geoffrey that they would remain outside of England for three years during his absence. At the request of his mother, Richard allowed his chancellor, William Longchamp, the discretion as to whether John would be allowed into England prior to Richard's return.[342] Longchamp could determine the length of any such visit, and retained the right to exile John from the land if he saw fit to do so.[343] The rights of King Richard and his key advisors to recall exiles, banish opponents, and dictate the time and circumstances surrounding a period of exile reveals the strength of exclusion as a political tool.

Richard was right to fear what John would do during his absence, and despite Richard's best efforts to remove his ambitious brother from the political sphere in England, John proved to be a menace to royal authority during Richard's reign. John was particularly vexing to Richard's Chancellor, William Longchamp. Longchamp held an immense amount of power while Richard was on Crusade but John was able exploit Longchamp's Norman origins. John garnered baronial support against Longchamp, portraying him as ignorant of English customs and financially extravagant. The allegiance of English nobles against the Chancellor was far-reaching, as one baron loyal to John, allegedly went so far as to form an alliance with the Welsh against the Crown in 1191. No

---

342 Ralph V. Turner, "Longchamp, William de (*d.* 1197)", *Oxford Dictionary of National Biography*, Oxford University Press, 2004; online edn, May 2007 [http://www.oxforddnb.com/view/article/16980, accessed 21 May 2012].

343 "Richard of Devizes" in *Church Historians of England* vol. 5, part 1, ed. J. Stevenson (London, UK: Seeley, 1851), "On the Acts of Richard the First," 252, no. 17; *Cronicon Richardi Divisensis De Tempore Regis Richardi Primi or The Chronicle of Richard of Devizes of the Time of King Richard the First*, ed. J.T. Appleby (London, UK: Thomas Nelson and Sons, Ltd., 1963), 13-14; J. Gillingham, *The Life and Times of Richard I* (London, UK: Weidenfeld and Nicolson, 1973), 166-167. Richard and John shared the same mother, Eleanor of Aquitaine, while Geoffrey was the illegitimate son of Henry and a common Englishwoman. For more on Geoffrey, who was later Archbishop of York, see Appleby, Appendix D. Richard's chancellor was Frenchman William Longchamp, who had long served Richard in Aquitaine and also held custody of the king's seal, was Bishop of Ely and papal legate. His control of the seal allowed him to have control over writs and registers within England, and after the death of William de Mandeville in 1189, he became co-justiciar with Hugh de Puiset as well, whom he later imprisoned. See West, *The Justiciarship of England* and pages 130-132 in W.L. Warren, *The Governance of Norman and Angevin England 1086-1272.*

active rebellion came of Mortimer's actions, but the baron was later exiled by Longchamp, forced to abjure the realm.[344]

William Longchamp's position in England, as well as the security of Richard's kingship, was threatened by Geoffrey, Archbishop of York. Longchamp ordered that the king's half-brother not be allowed to enter England after his three-year sworn exile expired and declared that if Geoffrey somehow got into the kingdom, he was to be placed in prison.[345] Geoffrey did successfully enter England, only to be dragged from a church and arrested by Longchamp's men. This heinous act led to Longchamp's dispossession of all authority and land by an outraged baronage. Longchamp attempted to flee England, but was prohibited from doing so. Longchamp was too much of a political asset and dedicated servant to Richard for John to allow him to escape from England. John needed to keep him in England so that he could not garner support for Richard's cause and threaten John's quest for power. Longchamp was arrested and placed in gaol at Dover, and was later released but only after John had been declared supreme governor of England and given possession of all royal castles. Longchamp fled to Flanders and then to Normandy but returned to England in 1192. He attempted to bribe John into reinstating as Chancellor, but was rebuked and forced to leave England again that same year.[346]

In 1193, Longchamp returned to England briefly to discuss the ransom of King Richard. He then traveled to the courts of Henry VI, the Holy Roman Emperor and Phillip, King of France, to take part in negotiations for the king's re-

344 *Chronica Richardi Divisensis*, 30-31; "Richard of Devizes," 261, no. 37; Appleby, *England Without Richard*, 62; "Roger (II) de Mortimer (d. 1214)" found in "Mortimer, Hugh (II) de (d. 1181?)", by J.F.A. Mason, *Oxford Dictionary of National Biography*, Oxford UP, 2004. Mortimer was forced to leave England, but it is unlikely that he remained out of England for the three-year period described by Richard Devizes. Richard of Devizes is the only chronicler who makes mention of this event.

345 Hoveden, vol. 2: 228; "Richard of Devizes," 264-265, nos 43, 45; *Cronicon Richardi Divisensis*, 41-42.

346 J. Gillingham, *Richard I* (New Haven, CT and London, UK: Yale UP, 1999), 226-229; Ralph V. Turner, "Longchamp, William de (d. 1197)", *Oxford Dictionary of National Biography*, Oxford UP, Sept 2004; online edn, May 2007 [http://www.oxforddnb.com/view/article/16980.] John and his followers launched a large-scale propaganda campaign against Longchamp. Hugh of Nonant, a John-loyalist, described a humiliating scene in which Longchamp attempted to escape England dressed as a woman. According to Hugh, Longchamp attracted the attentions of a lonely fisherman who soon discovered the deception and berated Longchamp on the dock in front of all of his peers.

lease.[347] Longchamp was allowed to come and go from England but only as a diplomat acting on behalf of the German Emperor and King Richard. Richard was released from captivity in 1194 and upon his returned to England he restored Longchamp to the position of Chancellor and granted him royal favor.[348]

The events of Richard's captivity demonstrate the importance of exclusion and captivity in the political sphere. Before he even left England, the King tried to secure assurances from his brothers that they would not threaten his kingdom or his rule. This failed. John and Geoffrey were able to drive the King's Chancellor out of England and effectively take control of the kingdom. William Longchamp, the King's most trusted official, was forced from England by Richard's brothers and was only allowed to enter and leave England on diplomatic missions. Once negotiations for Richard's release from captivity commenced, Longchamp returned to England, but without permanence and any position of authority. Longchamp's exclusion from any position of power in England was not unlike the situation of his King. King Richard's Crusade and subsequent captivity left him ineffective and at the mercy of outside influences, just as Longchamp's exile had rendered him.

Changes in royal personnel and legal procedure

The office of justiciar had developed from the days of William the Conqueror, but through the reign of Henry II its judicial duties were growing and regularizing. Under Henry II, the responsibilities had become clearer, as the justiciars soon took part in the judicial eyre.[349] During the justiciarship of Ranulf de Glan-

347 Hoveden, vol. 2: 225-231; *Cronicon Richardi Divisensis*, 41-54; "Richard of Devizes," 264-267; "William of Newburgh," 577-585; Ralph V. Turner, "Longchamp, William de (d. 1197)", *Oxford Dictionary of National Biography*, Oxford UP, Sept 2004; online edn, May 2007. [http://www.oxforddnb.com/view/article/16980]; Appleby, *England Without Richard*, 70-82, 86, 92-93; *Gesta Regis Henrici*, vol. 2: 209-239ff; Gillingham, *Richard I*, 166-171; F.J. West, *The Justiciarship in England,* 66-74; Gillingham, *Richard I*, 229.

348 Gillingham, *Richard I*, 269-273. Longchamp remained Chancellor until his death in 1196. For Richard's treatment of traitors during his imprisonment, see Roger de Hoveden, vol. 2: 332; "*Memoriale Fratis alteri de Coventria" or The Historical Collections of Walter of Coventry*. Ed. Wm. Stubbs. vols 1-2. In *Rerum Britannicarum Medii Aevi Scriptores or Chronicles and Memorials of Great Britain and Ireland during the Middle Ages* (Rolls Series) vol. 58, parts 1 and 2 (London, UK: Her Majesty's Stationary Office, 1872; Krause Reprints Ltd., 1968), part 2, page 60.

349 West, *Justiciarship in England*, 45-47. For the origins of the office of justiciar, see West, 30 where he summarizes that the needs which led to the creation of the justiciar-

ville (c. 1180), writs of the king and those of the justiciar became equally effective, making this royal official's presence in the counties an even further extension of Crown authority into the localities.[350]

In the last decade of the twelfth century, Hubert Walter served as chief justiciar.[351] Hubert Walter had a heavy hand in administrative and judicial developments in England. This is particularly true with the implementation of county coroners in 1194. The origin of the office of coroner is unclear, and while there is evidence suggesting the existence of an official resembling a coroner in England prior to 1194, no definitive assertion can be made.[352] Coroners first appear in the articles of the eyre from September 1194. During the eyre, a formal method for electing juries was established, as was the set list of questions and duties

---

ship from 1066-1154 as "the need for a regent, the need for a deputy to do justice on the king's behalf, the need for the exploitation of royal resources and their administration," and concludes that prior to the reign of Henry II, temporary solutions to these needs had been tried as circumstances dictated, and as a result, "the justiciar had a number of forerunners, but no lineal ancestors."

350 West, *Justiciarship in England*, 54-63.

351 C.R. Cheney, *Hubert Walter* (London, UK: Thomas Nelson & Sons, Ltd., 1967), 92-93; Gillingham, *Richard I*, 273-282; Robert C. Stacey, "Walter, Hubert (d. 1205)", *Oxford Dictionary of National Biography*, Oxford UP, Sept 2004; online edn, Jan 2008 [http://www.oxforddnb.com/view/article/28633]; Gillingham, *Life and Times of Richard*, 195-197. Hubert Walter was also Archbishop of Canterbury and Papal Legate. He ordered that all of the eyres should conduct their inquiries with the same "articles of the eyre" and at times sat with the judges on circuits in East Anglia, Cambridgeshire, and Huntingtonshire.

352 "Form of Proceeding on the Judicial Visitation, 1194," in *Select Charters* ed. Stubbs, 258-236; R.F. Hunnisett, "The Origins of the Office of Coroner" *Transactions of the Royal Historical Society* 5th series, volume 8 (London, UK: Offices of the Royal Historical Society, 1958), 85-104; R.F. Hunnisett, *The Medieval Coroner*, 108; Morris, *The Early English County Court*, 140; Cheney, *Hubert Walter*, 92-93; West, *Justiciarship in England*, 86-96; Robert C. Stacey, "Walter, Hubert (d. 1205)", *Oxford Dictionary of National Biography*, Oxford UP, Sept 2004; online edn, Jan 2008 [http://www.oxforddnb.com/view/article/28633]; I.L. Langein, "The Jury of Presentment and the Coroner," *Columbia Law Review* vol. 33, no. 8 (Dec., 1933): 1329-1365 argues that the inception of the coroner some thirty years after the Assize of Clarendon changed the effective system of justice created in 1166 to an "ineffective ritual" based in extortion. D.A. Carpenter, however, argues that the implementation of the coroner was tied closely to the reforms of the Exchequer, as reduction in responsibilities of the sheriffs was done in the interest of more efficient revenue collection and enforcement of discipline. See "The Decline of the Curial Sheriff," *English Historical Review* vol. 91, no. 358 (Jan. 1976): 1-32.

meant to guide jury inquiries.[353] According to the 1194 articles, every county was required to elect local knights to serve as keepers of the pleas of the crown. These keepers, later called coroners, were responsible for enrolling pleas of the crown and making sure that the hundred jurors" presentments were accurate.

County coroners were implemented to combat serious crime and local accountability. Coroners inquired into deaths, heard confessions of sanctuary seekers wishing to abjure the realm and those of want-to-be approvers, viewed wounds in appeals of rape, mayhem and wounding, and recorded exactions and outlawries.[354] Although the evidence from the period immediately following the creation of the office of coroner is scant, both sheriffs and coroners were soon required to record appeals and conduct inquests at the county courts. From their inception in the 1190s, coroners began to keep records of appeals of homicide and wounding. They recorded names and chattels of outlaws, as well as abjurations and abjurors, and submitted this information to the Exchequer.[355]

Coroners and sheriffs cooperated in local legal matters, both reported to the Exchequer, and both functioned in the name of the king. The emphasis on local responsibility for law and order was further stressed by Hubert Walter in 1195 when he issued an edict requiring all Englishmen to swear an oath to keep the peace of the king. Men pledged to neither commit crimes nor be outlaws, to not harbor or aid criminals and outlaws, and to bring any suspected malefactors to the attention of bailiffs and sheriffs.[356] Furthermore,

> ...When a hue and cry is raised for the pursuit of outlaws, robbers, thieves, or the harbourers of such, all shall join in pursuit of them to the best of their ability; and if they shall see any one, and it shall be clear that the has not joined in the said pursuit, or that he has, without permission, withdrawn himself therefrom, they shall take such same persons, as though they were offenders, and deliver them to the sheriffs, not to be set at liberty, but by the king or by his chief justice.[357]

---

353 The questions of inquest had been in place since the mid-twelfth century, but the commission of the 1194 eyre specified the range of questions and duties, or articles, to be carried out by the justices. The "articles in eyre" continued to expand through the thirteenth century.

354 Hunnisett, *Medieval Coroner*, 8-9, 37-39, 57, 61, 68-74; Warren, *Governance*, 135-136.

355 Hunnisett, *Medieval Coroner*, 99-100; H.R.T. Summerson, "Introduction," *Crown Pleas of the Devon Eyre of 1238*. ed. H.R.T. Summerson. Devon & Cornwall Record Society, New Series, vol. 28 (Torquay, England: The Devonshire Press Ltd., 1985), xvi.

356 Hoveden, vol. 2: 367-368.

357 Hoveden, vol. 2: 368; Cheney, *Hubert Walter*, 93; Hudson, *Formation of English Common Law*, 136-139; Warren, *Governance*, 142-143 also quotes this passage in his discussion of "The King's Government in the Shires."

According to Roger de Hoveden, this edict resulted in the arrest and imprisonment of many individuals, as well as in the flight of others who feared its consequences.[358] Emphasis on the pursuit and capture of criminals affirmed the long-standing practice of the hue and cry by royal order. The strength and efficacy of the hue and cry publicized wrongs and the customary obligation of all community members was backed by royal decree. Failure to fulfill this duty resulted in amercement payable to the Crown. All instances of the hue and cry were reported to the hundred courts, the shire courts, and to the justices in eyre when they visited the county, adding to the accountability and publicity of crime and criminals in the late twelfth century.[359]

Royal justice and local order were made to interact more closely through the creation of new offices, the appointment of new personnel, and by the re-affirmation of customary practices. As a result, the role of the crown in the practices of exclusion increased. Royal officials were more active in and emphasized the use of the outlawry process. Meanwhile, pardons continued to be obtained from the king by an outlaw or an abjuror; writs were issued to bring suits; juries of presentment reported justices in eyre about outlaws, abjurors, and other criminal and civil matters; and even upon clearing oneself of a crime, an individual could be required to leave the kingdom. Slowly, the Crown took a larger role in the legal aspects of exclusion as a mechanism for maintaining social order.[360]

The use of imprisonment in the late twelfth and early thirteenth centuries

Royal concerns over debt, customs, and trade during the reigns of Kings Richard and John resulted in an increased use of imprisonment in several areas of law. The Assize of Weights and Measures, issued in 1198, standardized measurements of goods throughout England and punished violators with a period of imprisonment. Furthermore, offender's chattels were seized by the crown and for

358 Hoveden, vol. 2: 369.

359 Summerson, "Introduction," *Crown Pleas*, xvi.

360 T. Rymer, *Foedera, conventiones, literæ, et cujuscunque generis acta publica, inter reges Angliæ, et alios quosvis imperatores*, Londin: J. Tonson, 1726-35, vol. 1; *Syllabus of the Documents Relating to England and Other Kingdoms: Contained in the Collection Known as "Rymer's Foedera"* by Great Britain Public Record Office, Scottish Record Office, Thomas Duffus Hardy, Thomas Rymer Compiled by Thomas Rymer (pub. by Longmans, Green, 1869), 13; Hurnard, *King's Pardon*, 175-176.

the king's use and the wrongdoer could only be freed by the king or his chief justice.[361] King John reinforced standardization in his statutes of 1199, as any vintner selling wine either by tap or in casks contrary to the assize was to be arrested and kept in the king's prison. Offenders again had their goods seized until the king or his men reached further judgment.[362]

In 1200, John proclaimed that debtors were to be punished in the following manner:

> He shall be put in the prison for that purpose named, according to the laws of the exchequer, and the debt due to the king shall be levied from the chattels of his master, in conformity with the laws of the exchequer. If also he shall not keep the faith to which he has pledged himself, so as not to appear at the time and place of payment to the sheriff, or if he shall make his appearance, and shall depart without leave given, his body shall be seized and placed in the king's prison for that purpose named, and he shall not be set at liberty but by the especial command of our lord king....[363]

Debtors were imprisoned or expected to leave the country and were at the king's mercy for their freedom. Imprisonment was becoming a royally endorsed and a regulated method of exacting payment throughout England. Royal statutes and mandates punished offenders with imprisonment, were then enforced by the sheriffs, and supervised by the justices in eyre. The use of imprisonment found in John's proclamations is indicative of how this political and legal tool, unrestricted by custom and subject to the king's will, became more common in royal law.

The use of imprisonment in response to lesser offenses, such as debt and merchant regulations, reflected royal intent to circumvent legal processes as they existed. Prior to the proclamations made by King John, all offenses were handled through local officials and proceedings. The Assizes of Clarendon and Northampton had established procedures for dealing with murderers, thieves, and the like, and this included the increased use of gaols.[364] A debtor, however, was subject neither to appeal nor to jury presentment nor to the justices in eyre; but, he was just as likely to flee and escape judgment as a felon. From the late twelfth and early thirteenth centuries, the rules began to change for nonfelonious offenses. With more royal involvement and regulation over debtors

---

361 Hoveden, vol. 2: 410-411; Warren, *Governance*, 134; Gillingham, *Richard I*, 277.

362 Hoveden, vol. 2: 466; J.C. Holt, *The Northerners: A Study in the Reign of King John* (Oxford, UK: Clarendon Press, 1961), 174-176.

363 Hoveden, vol. 2: 512-513.

364 "Assize of Clarendon, 1166," c. 2, 4, 6; "Assize of Northampton, 1176," c. 12.

and merchants came more fines, closer scrutiny of failure to pay or to find sureties, and, as a result, more imprisonment of offenders.

In addition to the use of imprisonment articulated in the Assizes, Curia Regis and eyre records from the 1190s and early 1200s indicate that custody, prison, and confinement were frequently used in the administration of justice. Appellants who had failed to prosecute a suit were amerced, but were often placed into gaol if they could not pay. Appellants could also be imprisoned for not having pledges to swear on their behalf or for failing to appear before the court at all.[365] False appeals were subject to imprisonment, as was false testimony, and suspects were often held in confinement until further information could be obtained by the jurors or until the coming of the Justices.[366]

Imprisonment continued to be a key component to the exercise of forest law in England. Without customary interference, the Crown could amerce and imprison forest offenders. Similarly, the king's justices could order a county to exact and outlaw a fugitive forest offender, placing this customary practice under the will of the Crown in specific instances. Eyre records from Northamptonshire in 1209 tell us about Roger, who was placed in custody after he was seen in the forest with his dogs, and about Peter and Richard, who were to be sought out by the sheriff after they had been seen in the forest with bows and arrows. If the latter did not appear, they were to be outlawed in the county court.[367] Likewise during the Shropshire eyre of 1209, a certain Hugh fled to a church after venison was found in his home. He later escaped and was placed in exigency and outlawed.[368]

Forest law was the king's law, and the cooperation of forest officials and local courts brought together custom and innovation. Forest eyres and general eyres functioned alongside one another and facilitated royal interaction to the localities as well as allowing for the crown to effectively use county courts in the administration of royal justice.[369] Additionally, the placement of new personnel, the county coroner, provided the crown with royal official who was involved in both the forest eyre and the general eyre and was used to keep the

365 Stenton, *Pleas before the King or His Justices*, vol. 1: no. 41; vol. 2: nos 2, 40, 44, 75, 250-252, 257, 258, 279, 285ff.

366 *Three Rolls of the King's Court in the Reign of King Richard the First, AD 1194-1194*, intro. F.W. Maitland. pub. by the Pipe Roll Society, vol. 14. (London, UK: Wyman and Sons, 1891), 2; *Curia Regis Rolls of the Reigns of Richard I and John* (Preserved in the Public Records Office. London, UK: Majesty's Stationery Office, 1922), vol. 5: 182.

367 G. J. Turner, ed., *Select Pleas of the Forest,* pub. of the Selden Society, vol. 13. (London, UK: Bernard Quaritch, 1901), 2; lxiv.

368 Turner, *Select Pleas of the Forest*, 9.

369 Vollmer, *The English Royal Forest*, 34-37, 40-44.

county sheriff in check as well as to keep better record of outlawries, abjurations, and deaths for the Crown. Involvement in local justice was one way in which the crown sought to strengthen its power within England, and while it was successful in doing so, it was unable to acquire control over the outlawry process. Instead, the increased use of arrests, gaols, and the earliest manifestations of gaol delivery in the late twelfth century illustrated the methods of punishment, governance, and order directly under the control of the crown.[370]

Within the growing systematization of law in England, outlawry, abjuration, and imprisonment were increasingly linked while their placement and function in legal and political spheres were becoming more clearly defined. The role of the king's approver illustrates this phenomenon well. An approver was a felon who turned on his fellow criminals while being held in gaol by the sheriff. By using approvers, the crown was able to bring more criminals to justice by "breaking up bands of robbers, thieves, and murders, and the receivers of stolen goods," as well as exercise its mercy, boost its coffers through the acquisition of felons" chattels, and further use royal personnel to police the realm.[371] The approver confessed his crime to the coroner with the understanding that he would subsequently appeal his accomplices in court. The approver would appeal his associates and bring them justice through battle or the county would submit those defendants to the exigent process, which would ultimately result in outlawry. If enough convictions were made from the appeals of an approver, the approver was allowed to abjure the realm or submit himself to perpetual imprisonment. The crown continued to use exclusion as a means of governance when and where it was available to them and effective, but increasingly supplemented the practice with imprisonment, confinement, and captivity.

370 Pugh, "The King's Prisons before 1250," 21; Meekings, "Introduction," *Crown Pleas of the Wiltshire Eyre of 1249*, 5; Pugh. *Imprisonment in Medieval England*, 256-257. Meekings states that while the origins of gaol delivery remain obscure, it is clear that "in the early thirteenth century gaols were being delivered by means unrecorded in the chancery enrolments. From the 1220s onwards, commissions for the delivery of some gaols…appear on the dorses of the patent rolls."

371 Hamil, "The King's Approvers," 239-241; Hunnisett, *Medieval Coroner*, 68-70.

Exile, Outlawry, and Imprisonment in the Earliest Eyre Records

Plea rolls from roughly 1198 forward reveal the function of outlawry in law and the role of exclusion in society.[372] All fugitives from the law were subject to the outlawry process. Fugitives were interrogated, or sought out and summoned before the shire court, three times before being declared to be an outlaw. Outlawry was then pronounced in the county court, after which it was recorded and presented to the justices in eyre by the juries of presentment at the next visitation to the county. An outlaw was known to the community and the crown alike, and was completely without property, friends, and protection.[373]

The outlawry process was included in the articles of the eyre, or *capitula itineris*, the series of matters and pleas that the justices in eyre would hear upon their visitations to the counties.[374] Felonies, appeals of which could result in out-

372 The earliest judicial records from England do not distinguish between civil and criminal proceedings and the documentation of the eyre is included with that of the "curia regis" or king's court. Pleas of the Crown (*Placita Coram Rege*) and Common Pleas (*Placita De Banco*) are contained in *Rotuli Curiae Regis* until the accession of Edward I in 1272, and until 1272, all eyre records are also called "assize rolls." For more on the distinctions among court records, see *The Sources and Literature of English History from the Earliest Times to about 1485*, 2nd edn (New York, NY: Peter Smith, 1951), 449 by Charles Gross. For a summary of the judiciary in the twelfth and early thirteenth centuries, see Stenton, *The Development of the Judiciary 1100-1215*, as Appendix I in vol. 3 of *Pleas before the King or His Justices, 1198-1212*, vols 1-4, ed. D.M. Stenton for the Selden Society. Selden Society vols 67, 68, 83, 84 (London, UK: Bernard Quaritch, 1967), xlvii-ccxciv.

373 *The Earliest Lincolnshire Assize Rolls AD 1202-1209*, ed. D.M. Stenton (Lincoln, UK: Printed for the Lincoln Record Society, 1926), xlviii. According to Bracton, an outlaw would be proclaimed after five successive meetings of the county court. See Bracton, *On the Laws and Customs of England*, trans. Samuel E. Thorne, ed. Gorge E. Woodbine, vols 1-4 (Cambridge, MA: The Belknap Press of Harvard UP in association with the Selden Society, 1968), vol. 2: 352-354.

374 See Walter of Coventry, 69-74, 128-133; H.M. Cam, *Studies of the Hundred Rolls*, 9-22; C.A.F. Meekings, ed. *The 1235 Surrey Eyre*. vols 1-3 The Surrey Record Society, vols 31, 32, and 33. Prepared for press by David Crook. (Guilford, UK: Surrey Record Society, 1979), vol. 1: introduction, 90; 151, notes 1-4; F.W. Maitland, *The Constitutional History of England: a course of lectures delivered*. (Cambridge, UK: Cambridge UP, 1908), 137; The earliest articles, those from the eyre of 1194, come down via the narrative chronicle of Roger de Howden, as do those from 1198. For a summary of copies of the thirteenth century articles in eyre, with particular interest in the articles as they stood c. 1235, see Meekings, 90-94.

lawry, were addressed in the earliest documented articles in eyre.[375] Justices would inquire about individuals who had been outlawed since the last visitation and confirm that the possessions of outlaws had been confiscated by the sheriff accordingly. The possessions and any amercements associated with the proclamation of outlawry would be handed over to the Crown. Justices would also inquire about any outlaw or fugitive that may have returned without warrant or pardon, as well as into the failure of a community member to pursue an outlaw or fugitive once the hue and cry had been called.[376]

Although the articles in eyre allowed for royal justices to inquire about and participate in the outlawry process, the justices failed to control its use. Royal justices visiting county courts were limited to inquiries about accountability of outlaws" sureties and forfeiture of outlaws" property. The closest they came to pronouncing outlawry was when one of their visitations was regarded as a meeting of the county court. Presentation and reenrollment of outlawry at the coming of the eyre and in coroner records brought double notoriety, as outlaws were now known locally and to the crown.[377] Not only were individuals who pledged on behalf of an outlaw fined, but the outlaws themselves were more than just local criminals. Presentment juries were required to answer to the justices in eyre about outlaws and fugitives, bringing them to the attention of the justices as agents of the king. Outlaws received royal recognition which served to strengthen the social stigma of the practice of outlawry.

The king held one unrestricted power in the outlawry process, however, as he had the authority to grant a pardon to an outlaw.[378] An outlaw would neces-

---

375 Concerned mostly with criminal offenses and royal rights, the articles were inquiries put to jurors representing each hundred. Copies of articles used in 1208 and 1218-1219 have survived from two separate London collections, allowing for a rough reconstruction of their content as they would have been carried out on visitations during the reigns of Kings Richard and John. See H.M. Cam, *Studies in the Hundred Rolls*, 19-20.

376 Meekings, "Introduction," 91-94; Cam, *Studies in the Hundred Rolls*, 17-20.

377 H.R.T. Summerson, "Criminal Law in the Age of Bracton," in *The History of English Law: Centenary Essays on "Pollock and Maitland," Proceedings of the British Academy*, vol. 89, ed. John Hudson. (Oxford, UK: Published for the British Academy by Oxford UP, 1996): 115-143 at 119; H.R.T. Summerson, "The Structure of Law Enforcement in Thirteenth Century England," 313-327 at 321.

378 The king's pardon during the early thirteenth century was the pardon *de gratia* or pardon of grace, granted at his discretion. Under Henry III, the pardon *de cursu*, or pardon of right, developed as the royal chancery began to grant pardons in homicides on lack of evidence and claims of self-defense. See Hurnard, *King's Pardon*, 68-108; M.H. Kerr, R.D. Forsyth, and M.J. Plyley, "Cold Water and Hot Iron: Trial by Ordeal in England," *Journal of Interdisciplinary History*, vol. 22: no. 4 (Spring, 1992): 573-595 at 594-595.

sarily need to find assistance in obtain a pardon, physically and financially, but if he received the mercy of the king, he was saved. Almost all pardons were granted on the condition that the outlaw stand to right if necessary. Pardons were read in county courts so that an appellor could come and announce his intent to appeal the pardoned individual. Whether an appeal was brought against a pardoned outlaw or not, granting a pardon was advantageous for the king. Not only did a pardon exhibit royal power, but the crown further benefited by maintaining all possessions of former outlaws.[379]

Court records from the late twelfth and early thirteenth centuries illustrate and provide insight into all of these aspects of outlawry and how widespread its use was within the system of justice. The Curia Regis roll from 1195 noted fugitives who had been outlawed following murders and woundings, as well as entire villages, such as Wallingford and Crendon, amerced for harboring outlaws. Tithing groups were also fined for having a member of their community declared an outlaw.[380] Within the extant portions of the assize roll from the Norfolk eyre of 1198, there are five pleas in which a man accused of homicide fled and was subsequently outlawed. There is one case of arson that had the same end result.[381] Accused criminals who failed to appear were to be sought out or summoned, while their pledges and tithings were amerced.[382] The following example of a plea from Wells in Somerset in 1201 describes the outlawry procedure:

> Robert the smith of Puckington was killed at Barrington and David and Martin of Stocklinch were suspected thereof, so that the neighbourhood followed them with the hue and cry and took [them] in flight. They deny the whole word for word. Judgment, let them purge themselves by water. Let Geoffrey Segrim who fled for that death be interrogated in the shire and outlawed according to the assize of the kingdom.[383]

---

379 Hurnard, *King's Pardon*, 59-63, 134-135, 207-212.

380 *Three Rolls*, 145-147; *Curia Regis Rolls of the Reigns of Richard I and John*. vol. 1. Preserved in the Public Records Office. London, UK: Majesty's Stationery Office, 1922.

381 *Pleas before the King or His Justices, 1198-1212*, vol. 2: nos 11, 12, 25, 33, 43, 74. There are 76 pleas of the crown extant from the Norfolk eyre of 1198, Assize Roll, London, The National Archives, JUST 1/559, m. 1.

382 *Pleas before the King or His Justices*, vol. 2: 1-15.

383 *Pleas before the King or His Justices*, vol. 2: no. 746; In *Magna Carta*, J.C. Holt speculates that cases such as this which cite law "according to the assize of the kingdom" were dangerous and ambiguous and perhaps full of empty rhetoric as the understanding of their meaning was open to argument.

The 1201 Cornish eyre records reveal similar practices. In addition to overt mentions of outlawry, suspects in woundings, deaths, and thefts who had fled were summoned to appear in court. This procedure was called interrogation. A suspect was given three opportunities to appear before the county court before formally being declared an outlaw.[384] Coroners were amerced for not enrolling fugitives" cattle properly and a jury in Cornwall was amerced for "foolish presentment" after presenting a man who had been outlawed for fifteen years.[385] In Bedfordshire, a plea from 1202 against Simon Prig for the death of Simon Brereton perhaps demonstrates the complexities of outlawry in the developing bureaucracy of common law. Simon Prig fled for the death of Simon Brereton, but was not outlawed according to the county records or the coroner rolls despite the testimony of the sheriff that outlawry had taken place. As a result, the county and coroners were held in judgment for failing to accurately record and present the case to the justices and Simon presumably went free.[386]

At the Shropshire eyre of 1203, one third of the 92 verdicts from the pleas at Church Stretton included elements of the outlawry process. Eleven pleas resulted in abjuration of the realm by the malefactor; there were nine explicit outlawry proclamations, one of waivery (the outlawry of a woman, who was technically not within the law and therefore could not be placed outside of it), and ten interrogations.[387] One notable case included the outlaw John Walensis returning to his county with letters patent from the King pardoning him from his flight and any subsequent proclamation of outlawry, providing he secured the necessary sureties.[388] In one other interesting case, Richard Wigun's appealed William, the reeve of High Ercall, for harboring outlaws at his home. The court determined that William was innocent, however, and that Richard had appealed out of hatred and disputed land rather than in accordance with the law. Richard was then amerced.[389] Assize rolls from Northamptonshire and Lincolnshire reveal similar information about the circumstances of outlawry in the first decade of the thirteenth century. Suspected criminals who had fled in appeals of wounding and

---

384*Pleas before the King or His Justices*, vol. 2: 64-69, 83-85, 117-118, 214-218, 221. See also *Select Pleas of the Crown, Volume 1: AD 1200-1215*, ed. F.W. Maitland. A Selden Society Publication (London, UK: Bernard Quaritch, 1888), 1-3.

385 *Pleas before the King or His Justices*, 2: no. 259.

386 *Select Pleas of the Crown*, no. 62.

387 *Pleas before the King or His Justices*, vol. 3: 69-87. The Shropshire Assize Roll of 1203, no. 732, contains criminal and civil pleas heart at Shrewsbury, Oxford, Gloucestershire, and Worcester.

388 *Pleas before the King or His Justices*, vol. 3: no. 717.

389 *Pleas before the King or His Justices*, vol. 3: no. 740; *Select Pleas of the Crown*, no. 78.

homicide were interrogated and outlawed, their cattle was placed in the possession of the crown, and villages and towns were held in mercy for having outlaws without frankpledge within their confines.[390]

It was also the duty of the coroner to receive the confession and oath of a sanctuary seeker wishing to abjure the realm. The majority of sanctuary seekers were either suspected felons being pursued after the hue and cry or escapees from nearby prisons. A felonious sanctuary seeker could remain in a place of refuge for forty days before having to either stand trial or abjure the realm.[391] Compared to instances of outlawry, there were relatively few recorded instances of abjuration of the realm in the assize and plea rolls from the first two decades of the thirteenth century. Records from the visitation at Shrewsbury in 1203 contained three murders and one robbery for which suspects fled to a church and abjured the realm, while in Lincolnshire in 1202, at least six accused murders and one man charged with burglary fled to churches and later abjured the realm.[392] The more prescribed form of abjuration found in the Assizes of Clarendon and Northampton is also recorded in early thirteenth century records, as at Lincoln in 1202, when a certain Jordan cleared himself of charges of falsifying money by water but was forced to abjure the realm after he could not find pledges to stand to right for him.[393]

The intricacies of the outlawry process and its carryover into daily life reveal its legal and social importance. One plea at Lincoln in 1202 revealed that a woman whose husband may have been outlawed was allowed to keep his land despite the fact that it should have been forfeited to the king. In another plea, justices instruct a claimant to return to their shire's courts until outlawry could be declared. In the presentment brought against a certain Hugh, he was outlawed for the death of Roger and later pardoned by the king, but was outlawed again for the same homicide later on a different appeal.[394] Examples such as these

---

390 *The Earliest Northamptonshire Assize Rolls AD 1202*-1203 ed. D.M. Stenton (Lincoln and London, UK: Printed for the Northamptonshire Record Society by J.W. Ruddock & Sons, 1930), 4, 9, 11, 15, 17; *The Earliest Lincolnshire Assize Rolls AD 1202-1209* ed. D.M. Stenton. (Lincoln, UK: Printed for the Lincoln Record Society, 1926), 97, 102-138, 154-159.

391 Hunnisett, *Medieval Coroner*, 37; Cam, *The Hundred and The Hundred Rolls*, 130-131. Although I use the masculine throughout, women were able to, and often did, take sanctuary and abjure the realm.

392 *Pleas before the King or His Justices*, vol. 3: nos 676, 683, 711, and 713; *The Earliest Lincolnshire Assize Rolls*, nos 547, 588, 728, 748, 763, 884, 978, 990.

393 *The Earliest Northamptonshire Assize Rolls*, no. 797, see also xxvi.

394 *The Earliest Lincolnshire Assize Rolls*, no. 512; *The Earliest Northamptonshire Assize Rolls*, no. 51; *Select Pleas of the Crown*, no. 47.

dominate early twelfth century plea rolls. They illustrate how social accountability and public notoriety played an essential part in the importance of exclusion as a punishment. A woman was able to retain the lands of her husband despite his outlaw status because social practice dictated such an allowance was possible. The eyre was well aware of the power of outlawry and instructed complaintants to continue suits in the county courts in order that they receive appropriate justice. And despite a pardon for homicide, Hugh was outlawed on the appeal of the slain man's kin.

The articles in eyre reveal a minimal concern with prisons and gaols at this stage in the development of criminal law, although the royal endorsement of gaol deliveries was addressed in the articles by 1218. Concern for the escape of thieves was included in the articles by 1221, and later all escapees were mentioned, revealing the increased existence, use, and necessity of prisons. As early as the laws of Alfred, prison escapees were considered fugitives and removed from societal protections. In the early thirteenth century, an escaped prisoner was assumed to be guilty of the offense for which he or she was charged, and if recaptured, he or she was often hanged.[395] Breaking out of prison created a presumption of guilt and an escaped prisoner was, for all intents and purposes, an outlaw.

Custody, prisons, and confinement were in no way as widespread in use or as significant in legal and social impact as outlawry. A prisoner who was held in gaol was usually there temporarily, until he or she could find sureties and was able to pay a pecuniary punishment. An appellant who had failed to prosecute a suit was amerced, but would be placed in gaol if he could not pay. Imprisonment was the result for an appellant if he did not have pledges to swear on his behalf or if he failed to appear before the court at all.[396] False appeals were subject to imprisonment, as was false testimony, and suspects were often held in confinement until further information could be obtained by the jurors about the crime in question or until the coming of the royal justices.[397] Jurors and entire juries could be imprisoned. In Devon in 1204, each member of the jury of presentment had his cattle confiscated by the crown and they were all sentenced to prison for falsely presenting an appeal to the justices.[398]

Imprisonment was used as circumstances dictated and in response to emerging legal situations. Imprisonment was a punishment inflicted upon criminals in

395 Meekings, "Introduction," 93; Pugh, *Imprisonment in Medieval England*, 224-228.

396 Stenton, *Pleas before the King or His Justices*, vol. 1: no. 41; vol. 2: nos 2, 40, 44, 75, 250-252, 257, 258, 279, 285ff.

397 *Three Rolls of the King's Court in the Reign of King Richard the First*, 2; *Curia Regis Rolls of the Reigns of Richard I and John*, vol. 5, page 182, for example.

398 *Curia Regis Rolls of the Reigns of Richard I and John*, vol. 3: 134-135.

conjunction with monetary penalty and was often used when unusual pleas arose. In 1204, one man was held in prison for exhibiting “unseemly behavior” in the shire court; in 1214, a man was sentenced to prison and had to forfeit his holdings for attempting to buy a male infant to pass the child off as his heir.[399] Neither of these occurrences was common enough to have a punishment based in custom nor were there any other reasonable responses, so imprisonment was used instead. As gaols and prisons were being used more often, it became necessary for the Crown to come up with mechanisms to clear gaols and deal with prisoners. Gaols could be delivered, or cleared, by justices in eyre, and by the king and his court when touring the country. Until roughly 1220, the relatively small use of imprisonment allowed for the mechanisms of justice already in place to simply add gaol delivery to their respective responsibilities.[400]

The relationship between outlawry, abjuration, and imprisonment in the late twelfth and early eleventh century is one of cooperation and reliance upon one another. An outlaw was removed from society and the law; an abjuror took that removal upon himself, swore to leave England, often after having escaped from confinement of some kind, and essentially became an outlaw; imprisonment was a means to exact a fine from a criminal or a method used to detain a person before bringing them to justice. Similarly, failure to appear for charges in county court or escape from prison could bring about outlawry or possible abjuration if the offender managed to make it to a church; and harboring an outlaw was subject to imprisonment, as was pledging surety for an offender who later fled. Coroners were responsible for recording abjurors and outlaws, sheriffs were accountable for prisoners and gaols, and both could be deemed responsible for monies and possessions due to the crown from offenders in any of the above categories. These officials could also be punished for failure to record and accurately report upon these matters to the justices in eyre. The complex web of methods used to exact justice and hold members of society accountable for their actions and the actions of others was in place at the local level. Through the use of writs, proclamations, and personnel the Crown was becoming increasingly integrated into local matters of justice and often used imprisonment to achieve that end.

---

399 *Curia Regis Rolls of the Reigns of Richard I and John*, vol. 3: 130; vol. 7: 169.

400 Pugh, *Imprisonment in Medieval England*, 255-266.

King John and the Magna Carta

After Richard died in 1199, John‘s only opposition for the crown was his young nephew, Arthur of Brittany. When Arthur discovered that John intended to perpetually imprison him, he fled from England to France.[401] John captured Arthur and many of his supporters in France in 1202. He incarcerated his nephew at Falaise and sent other prisoners back to England to be confined.[402] The fate of Arthur remains unknown, however, as he simply disappeared.[403] The circumstances surrounding the treatment and disappearance of Arthur caused rumors and speculation that John had murdered his nephew. When the wife of one of John‘s trusted men, William de Braose, made a comment about the fate of Arthur, John immediately coordinated the downfall of the whole family. De Braose‘s wife and son were imprisoned in 1210 while the family patriarch was driven into exile and outlawed during the same year. In heavy debt to the crown, John claimed that de Braose had failed to appear when summoned to answer charges against him and was a fugitive from the law. He manipulated the outlawry process to his own ends.[404] Similar steps were taken to outlaw Robert fitz Walter and Eustace de Vesci after they had allegedly conspired against the king in 1212.[405]

---

401 Hoveden, vol. 2: 464; Roger of Wendover, vol. 2: 183. Arthur was son of Geoffrey, Archbishop of York, who was the illegitimate son of Henry II, and Constance of Brittany, and heir to the dukedom of Brittany.

402 W. L. Warren, *King John* (London, UK: Eyre Methuen Limited, 1961), 79-80.

403 Warren, *King John*, 80-84. According to Ralph of Coggeshall, John wished to have Arthur blinded and castrated but Hugh de Burgh announced to the Bretons that Arthur was in fact dead. He tried to renounce this after the Bretons swore vengeance upon John for such a barbaric act.

404 Warren, *King John*, 184-188; Holt, *The Northerners*, 184-186; J. C. Holt, *Magna* Carta, 2nd edn (Cambridge, UK: Cambridge UP, 1992), 109; Rymer's *Foedera*, 1: 107-108; Roger of Wendover, *Flowers of History, Comprising the History of England from the Descent of the Saxons to AD 1235*, trans. J.A. Giles. vols 1-2 (London, UK: Henry G. Bohn, 1849), vol. 2: 48; Ralph V. Turner, "Briouze , William (III) de (d. 1211)", *Oxford Dictionary of National Biography*, Oxford UP, Sept 2004; online edn, Oct 2006 [http://www.oxforddnb.com/view/article/3283]. John later captured William's wife and son and imprisoned them, where they both starved to death. See Roger of Wendover, vol. ii, 254-255. For more on the "Customs of the Exchequer" see Hoveden, vol. 2, 51-513. For more on the history of the Briouze family and their relationship with the crown, see "King John, the Braoses, and the Celtic Fringe, 1207-1216" by Brock W. Holden, *Albion: A Quarterly Journal Concerned with British Studies*, vol. 33, no. 1 (Spring, 2001): 1-23.

405 Roger of Wendover, vol. 2: 257-258; Holt, *The Northerners*, 79-85; Holt, *Magna Carta*, 109; Warren, *King John*, 200; R. V. Turner, *The King and His Courts: The Role of John*

King John used exclusion to rid himself of enemies such as William de Briouze (Braose), Robert fitz Walter and Eustace de Vesci. Although he claimed to have law on his side, John simply took part in what has been called the Angevin effort "to dress up royal action in the trappings of the law."[406] He also imprisoned individuals who threatened his position as king. According to Roger of Wendover, Geoffrey, Archdeacon of Norwich was put into prison and starved to death by John in 1209.[407] As a result, the king's use of imprisonment, exile, and outlawry were at the forefront of disputes between King John and English Barons in the early thirteenth century.

Civil war broke out in England in 1212, and by 1215, willful and extra-legal outlawries had found a place among the complaints of the barons.[408] Additionally, English barons were upset that the King abused land regulations associated with outlawry.[409] Law dictated that lands of an outlaw were forfeited to the king, but this was not supposed to be a permanent arrangement. Forfeited land was supposed to be returned to its rightful lord after a year and one day, but John failed to abide by this principle. English barons brought forth their complaints against John in 1215, first in the Articles of the Barons and then in Magna Carta. As a result, the King was prohibited from holding the lands of outlaws longer

---

and Henry III in the Administration of Justice, 1199-140 (Ithaca, NY: Cornell UP, 1968), 204; Morris, *Medieval Sheriff*, 150; Matthew Strickland, "Fitzwalter, Robert (d. 1235)", *Oxford Dictionary of National Biography*, Oxford UP, Sept 2004; online edn, May 2007 [http://www.oxforddnb.com/view/article/9648]; Ralph V. Turner, "Vescy, Eustace de (1169/70–1216)", *Oxford Dictionary of National Biography*, Oxford UP, 2004 [http://www.oxforddnb.com/view/article/28253].

406 Holt, *Magna Carta*, 107-109; Turner, *King John*, 197-198; Turner, *King and His Courts*, 204.

407 Roger of Wendover, vol. 2: 250-251; 254; Warren, *King John*, 185, Clanchy, *England and Its Rulers, 1066-1272: Foreign Lordship and National Identity* (Oxford, UK: Basil Blackwell Publisher Ltd., 1983), 137-138. Wendover is the lone source regarding Geoffrey of Norwich.

408 D. Carpenter, "Justice and Jurisdiction under King John and King Henry III," in *The Reign of King Henry III* (London, UK: Hambledon Press, 1996): 17-43 at 37; For the text of and more on the title of "The Articles of the Barons" see Holt, *Magna Carta*, appendix 5, 429-440. See also "The Articles of the Barons" in *Select Charters,* ed. Stubbs, 289-296 as well as "Magna Carta, 1215," 296-306, and reissues under Henry III, 339-351, 353-355; For more on role of the Magna Carta as a response to the royal government's threats against collective unity and tradition, see Reynolds, *Kingdom and Communities*, 55ff.

409 *Curia Regis Rolls*, vol. 6: m. 3, 1212, no. 256, for example records a certain Gilbert son of William of Weston and Alan son of Turbern offering the crown money for land in Weston, Lincolnshire held by men who were outlawed for the death of William son of Wigot.

than custom allowed and from punishing a criminal or suspect without proper judgment and access to legal processes.[410]

> We will not hold for more than a year and a day the lands of those convicted of felony, and then the lands shall be handed over to the lords of the fiefs.
>
> No free man shall be arrested or imprisoned or disseised or outlawed or exiled or in any way victimized, neither will we attack him or send anyone to attack him, except by the lawful judgment of his peers or by the law of the land.[411]

The desire of the barons to protect themselves from the abusive use of outlawry and exile by John is clear. The English baronage successfully protected lords from the loss of property to the Crown when a felon was outlawed or had abjured, thus limited the power and wealth of the king.[412]

More importantly, Magna Carta limited the use of outlawry and exile by the king. Outlawry, as it had been used by Kings John, Richard and Henry II, was more akin to exile, as it was politically motivated and manipulated contrary to legal custom. Exile in this context had threatened the security of English barons and lords who were viewed as a threat to royal power or simply fell out of royal favor. As a result, the barons sought to protect themselves. The barons reminded the king that any extra-legal removal of an enemy from England exceeded his power and infringed upon baronial rights. The king could not manipulate outlawry for his own use, which limited all forms of exclusion available to the Crown. Outlawry and exile, which had been murky in their distinction from one another, were now more clearly defined in by law. Neither outlawry nor exile were processes that fell under the direct authority of the king; rather their respective processes lay in the guise of the county court.[413] The driving principle

---

410 "The Articles of the Barons, 15 June 1215," *Select Charters*, 289-296.

411 "Magna Carta, 1215," *Select Charters,* 296-306.

412 F.M. Powicke, "*Per Iudicium Parium vel per Legem Terrae*" in *Magna Carta Commemoration Essays* ed. H.E. Malden. (London, UK: Royal Historical Society, 1917): 96-121 at 103. Powicke concludes that the barons were not more concerned with form of trial than they were with protecting themselves from arbitrary actions of the King. See also H.M. Cam, *Magna Carta—Event or Document?* For more on the "intent" of the Magna Carta and the historical debate surrounding this topic. Magna Carta was reissued three times, in 1216, 1217, and finally in 1225.

413 By the reissue of Magna Carta in 1225, this clause read as follows: "No free man shall in future be arrested or imprisoned or disseised of his freehold, liberties or free customs, or outlawed or exiled or victimized in any other way, neither will we attack him or send anyone to attack him, except by the lawful judgment of his peers or by the law of the land. To no one will we sell, to no one will we refuse or delay the right of justice." "Magna Carta, 1225," *Select Charters*, 353-355. The words "in future" were additions in 1225, while "other" was added in the 1216 reissue, and clarification on disseisin was

behind the limits placed upon outlawry carried over into the reign of Henry III, and by the time of Bracton, as we will see, it is clearly stated that "outlawry at the King's suit or command is a nullity unless an inquest has been taken by the justices and the fugitive has been found guilty."[414]

Just as Magna Carta placed restrictions on the royal power to outlaw, it also made the exercise of imprisonment more defined.[415] Magna Carta limited the use of arrest and imprisonment by the King but such a concession by John was not as legally paralyzing it had been with the use of outlawry. The barons sought to protect themselves from unjust imprisonment by the king, which was presumably an easier method of restraint to be meted out by the Crown. There were no specific customary guidelines for imprisonment in the judicial process, and as a result, restrictions on imprisonment were not as effective. The barons were asserting their rights and customary law, the "law of the land," but because there was no "law of the land" dictating the use of imprisonment, they had a much weaker argument against its use.

English barons were not attempting to impinge upon the king's jurisdiction. Rather, they were protecting their access to effective justice.[416] The use of imprisonment was left open to discretion and interpretation and the barons were seeking to prevent related abuses by asserting the legality and efficacy of the outlawry process in the first quarter of the thirteenth century. The use of imprisonment became increasingly necessary and favored by royal authorities in the early thirteenth century, as it was accessible within the confines of both customary and written law.

As far back as Hubert Walter's edict of 1195, perhaps even with the reforms of Henry II's reign, administrative actions endorsing the use of imprisonment had been issued to justify the legal activity of the crown when it conflicted or differed from custom. During the course of the thirteenth century, imprisonment became increasingly important and fundamental to royal judicial authority.[417] It

---

added in 1217. See *Select Charters*, "Magna Carta, 1216," and "Magna Carta, 1217, " and Warren, *King John*, 236-240.

414 Powicke, "*Per Iudicium Parium*," 106-107; 110; Young, *The Royal Forests of Medieval England*, 68-69; *Bracton's Notebook, A Collection of Cases Decided in the King's Court During the Reign of Henry III, annotated by a lawyer of that time, seemingly Henry de Bratton*, vols 1-3, ed. F.W. Maitland (London, UK: C.J. Clay and Sons, 1887), vol. 2: no. 857.

415 "Magna Carta, 1225" in *Select Charters*, 353-355.

416 R. W. Kaeuper, *War, Justice, and Public Order: England and France in the Later Middle Ages* (Oxford, UK: Clarendon Press, 1988), 134-137; Holt, *Magna Carta*, 233.

417 Powicke argues for the 1195 date, but I see the use of imprisonment addressed and encouraged in the Assizes of Clarendon and Northampton.

has been argued that the barons sought to quell the prerogative use of imprisonment by the crown, and to some extent they did. But their actions had greater consequences. The barons inadvertently encouraged the Crown to use imprisonment against its enemies after having made alternatives increasingly difficult for the king to pursue.[418] Authorities were not restricted by custom when it came to the exercise of imprisonment, as they were with the processes of outlawry.

John had conceded the use exile, outlawry, and imprisonment without just cause and due process against his barons. This weakened the prerogative of the King, reaffirmed the position of exile and outlawry in political and legal custom, as well as helped define the growing role of imprisonment in judicial processes. Imprisonment, such as that found in forest law, still reeked of royal prerogative, but because it was based in legal proclamations, such prerogative was impenetrable by English barons.

One might in fact argue that Magna Carta inadvertently encouraged royal law in England to continue in the vein of that of the forest law. Forest law had included provisions for imprisonment in the Assize of the Forest in 1184 and still contained prison as a punishment according to the Charters of the Forest of 1217 and 1225. Forest offenders could be placed into prison for one year and one day if they could not pay the appropriate fine. Following their term of imprisonment, offenders were to abjure the realm if they were unable to find pledges.[419] Despite baronial demands to have the right to imprison individuals who trespassed in their parks and preserves, the Crown maintained authority over such offenses. Forest law continued to be the domain of the King, a principle reasserted at the council held at Merton in 1236 and later by the Statute of Westminster in 1275, in which violators of forest law could be imprisoned for three years at the discretion of the king's justices.[420]

Forest law did involve outlawry, however, to which the Charters of the Forest of 1217 and 1225 attest. Here any individual who had been outlawed from the time of Henry II to the coronation of Henry III for a forest offense could be released from outlawry as long as he had pledges to attest that he would do no wrong in the forest in the future. The king was using his one powerful tool in the outlawry process, the pardon, to have an impact in its workings.

---

418 Powicke, "*Per Iudicium Parium*," 112-113.

419 "Charter of the Forest, 1217," *Select Charters*, 347-351, no. 10; Pugh, *Imprisonment in Medieval England*, 20-21; James, *Forestry*, 11; Havins, *Forests*, 29-30; Young, "English Royal Forests Under the Angevin Kings," 5; Young, *The Royal Forests of Medieval England*, 68-69; Vollmer, *The English Royal Forest*, 42-44.

420 Powicke, *The Thirteenth Century*, 69; Turner, *Select Pleas of the Forest*, cxix; Pugh, *Imprisonment in Medieval England*, 21, 32-33.

Outlaws, Legend, and Politics during the reign of King John

In some of the earliest outlaw legends two men, the historical figures Fulk Fitzwarin and Eustace the Monk, personify the struggle between ruler and subject during the early thirteenth century. Fulk Fitzwarin was a landed yeoman from Shropshire who had allegedly been a childhood friend of King John. After a land-holding dispute that spiked the anger of the King, Fitzwarin was stripped of his familial possessions. He was outlawed in 1200, later led an outlaw band for a time, and was pardoned along with thirty-eight of his fellow outlaws by King John in 1203.[421] Eustace had been in the service of John, but once the English King allied himself with the Count of Boulogne in 1212, Eustace turned his support to the French King. Eustace, as a skilled naval commander and pirate, assisted the French invasion of England in 1215 and supported the rebel barons in England in 1216. He died at the Battle of Sandwich in 1217.[422]

In the legends which grew up concerning these outlaws, Fulk Fitzwarin was acting against a tyrannical king who had taken his land without proper judgment, while Eustace was taking a stand against the French count who failed to exercise justice upon the man who murdered his father. The legends of both Fulk and Eustace were written following the events surrounding Magna Carta and contain romanticized accounts of the rejection of the policies and actions of oppressive and tyrannical rule. These legends remind us how engrained outlawry was in thirteenth century England and demonstrate how outlaws functioned as active individuals in law and society rather than passive reactions or bi-products of weak governance. As they are portrayed in legend, Fulk and Eustace are "good outlaws," outside of the protection of the law in order that they pursue justice, a true paradox.[423]

---

421 G. S. Burgess, *Two Medieval Outlaws: Eustace the Monk and Fouke Fitz Waryn* (Cambridge, UK: D.S. Brewer, 1997), 91-198.

422 Burgess, *Two Medieval Outlaws*, 3-90; Keen, *Outlaws*, 39-63, 209-210;Eustace's lord, Rainald of Dummartin, the Count of Boulogne, allegedly failed to punish Eustace's father's murderer, Hainfrois de Maresingeuhans. After King John allied himself with the Count of Boulogne in 1212, Eustace permanently gave his service to the French king. This was an affront to both his sovereign lord Rainald of Dummartin, the Count of Boulogne, and the English King.

423 Ohlgren, *Medieval Outlaws*, xxviii-xxx.

The minority of Henry III

After John's death in 1216, power in England fell to the king's nine-year-old son, Henry. The young king's regents, William Marshal and Hubert de Burgh, took governmental and administrative control of England, while other powerful nobles acquired land, power, and authority in the kingdom. These men were concerned with their own financial gains and political authority but were also careful to not recreate any of the hardships associated with John's reign. The general eyre toured the country from 1218, and the forest eyre was sent out in the early 1220s, but no heavy taxation was put into effect until 1225.[424] The minority of King Henry III saw the continuation of legal practices in the midst of political infighting, and despite the goings-on of the aristocracy and political elite, justice and authority in the localities continued to function according to custom and law.

With respect to the general eyre, the articles of the eyre began to increase in number and widen in scope after 1215. This is indicative of ever-growing royal interest in local governance, but there was little change in the period immediately following John's death. Jury presentments fell under the general article of inquiry concerned with new matters and the information on outlaws, fugitives, and harboring of the like was often presented here rather than as part of a separate inquiry. This in no way lessened the prominence and importance of outlawry, but rather reflected the overall efficiency of the local courts and communities to record such matters, and subsequently report them to the justices upon their arrival.[425] In fact, that exigency and the outlawry process increasingly became part of jury presentments allowed for two court procedures by which a suspect could be outlawed: jury presentment and appeal. When Robert was outlawed at the suit of Agnes for the death of her husband William, it was the result of Agnes"

---

424 D. Carpenter, *The Minority of Henry III* (London, UK: Meuthun London, 1990), 93-103.

425 Meekings, *Surrey Eyre*, "Introduction," 91-92; Cam, *The Hundred and the Hundred Rolls*, 23; Carpenter, *Minority*, 97-98; For example of the Articles, see "Opening of sessions: Articles of the eyre (nos. 6-36)", *The London eyre of 1244.* eds H.M. Chew & M. Weinbaum (London, UK: London Record Society, 1970), 5-10. URL: http://www.british-history.ac.uk/report.aspx?compid=35934. Overall, the articles in eyre for the first part of the reign of King Henry III largely resemble those used during the reign of John.

appeal of felony; upon presentment to the eyre by the jurors, Radulf was put in exigency and outlawed on suspicion of killing Hugo.[426]

The crown could nominally become the plaintiff in a suit presented to the eyre by the jury of presentment. Similarly, appeals of felonies automatically fell under offenses that warranted attention of the king. These practices brought royal law into closer contact with the outlawry process. In appeals and jury presentments alike, individuals who failed to appear before the court were put to exigency as a means to outlawry. Flight after killing or theft was extremely common according to eyre documents, and when this occurred, outlawry was often the ultimate result. In all matters and circumstances, exaction and the declaration of outlawry was the duty of the county court, which used the outlawry process effectively as a judicial entity.[427]

Eyre records from York in 1218-1219 reveal the ubiquitous nature of outlawry. According to the eyre documentation, forty outlawries were declared in county court meetings prior to the arrival of the royal justices. Thirty-three more completed in the eyre session. Forty-nine criminals, mostly killers and thieves, were put in exigency by the county before the eyre arrived, with fifty-five additional exigencies recorded at the visitation of the eyre itself. There were six abjurations, ten instances of the justices instructing appellors to continue their suits to outlawry, two cases in which the justices required further information from the county courts as to the status of an outlaw, and two cases by which the outlawry of accomplices was left until the outlawry of the principal offender was proclaimed.[428] The Yorkshire pleas attest not only to the scope of exaction and outlawry, but also to their public nature and seriousness. When Simon was killed, it was suspected that Reginald, an outlaw in the county of Chester, had committed the act. The presentment knew of Reginald's status as an outlaw and relayed his wrongdoings to the justices.[429] Similarly, when John was outlawed in the shire court for the death of Ragnild but was later arrested by the sheriff, John denied being an outlaw and claimed to have gotten a writ of war-

426 *Pleas of the Crown for the County of Gloucester, 1221, Before the Abbot of Reading and his Fellows Justices Itinerant*, ed. F.W. Maitland (London, UK: MacMillan & Co. 1884), no. 58, no. 23.

427 Summerson, "Criminal Law in the Age of Bracton," 119; Summerson, "The Structure of Law Enforcement in Thirteenth Century England," 321.

428 *Rolls of the Justices in Eyre being the rolls of pleas and assizes for Yorkshire in 3 Henry III (1218-1219)*, ed. D. Stenton for the Selden Society. Selden Society vol. 56. (London, UK: Bernard Quaritch, 1937), Assize Roll no. 1053. There are 666 pleas of the crown contained in Assize Roll no. 1053.

429 *Rolls of the Justices in Eyre being the rolls of pleas and assizes for Yorkshire in 3 Henry III (1218-1219)*, no. 533.

ranty. Both the shire and the coroner attested to his outlaw status, however, and he was hanged.[430]

The Gloucester pleas of 1221 contain similar information about the role of exclusion and outlawry in society. The most notable aspect of the Gloucester records is the number of felons fleeing after the commission of a crime and the repeated failure to appear on appeal. All of these matters led to or potentially led to outlawry.[431] Records from eyre visitations at Lincoln in 1218 and 1219 Worcester in 1221 are much the same.[432] Flight could also lead to a suspect taking sanctuary in a church, then confessing to the coroner, after which he took an oath to abjure the realm. It was equally common, however, for a suspect to take refuge in a church and later escape, only to be proclaimed an outlaw by the county court.[433]

The prevalence of exclusion in the forms of outlawry and abjuration in extant records reveals how fundamental these actions were to the local administration of justice and the functioning of social order. Communities pursued offenders, county courts outlawed criminals and fugitives, and crown officials and jury members alike reported these actions to the justices upon their visit. The justices in eyre, in turn, endorsed and used local processes.[434] The cooperation of local courts with the representatives of the Crown is apparent, as is the relative autonomy of the county courts within the growing justice system.

Plea roll documentation also indicates that there were checks placed upon the localities by the visiting justices, which reflected a balance of cooperation and regulation. Customary law was endorsed and facilitated by the eyre, but jurors could be amerced several times for failing to properly conduct their judicial duties. Judgment was pronounced against juries for failure to report to the justices about the chattels of fugitives and for concealing the names of individuals who harbored outlaws.[435] In one case, judgment was made against the coro-

---

430 *Rolls of the Justices in Eyre being the rolls of pleas and assizes for Yorkshire in 3 Henry III (1218-1219)*, no. 876.

431 *Pleas of the Crown for the County of Gloucester, 1221, Before the Abbot of Reading and his Fellows Justices Itinerant*, ed. F.W. Maitland (London, UK: MacMillan & Co. 1884).

432 *Rolls of the Justices in Eyre for Lincolnshire 1218-19 and Worcestershire 1221*, ed. D. Stenton for the Selden Society. Selden Society vol. 53. (London, UK: Bernard Quaritch, 1934). For a general frame of reference, the plea rolls from Lincolnshire and Worcestershire contain a total of fifty-three outlawries.

433 *Pleas of the Crown for the County of Gloucester, 1221*, no. 315.

434 Hurnard, *King's Pardon*, 137-151.

435 *Rolls of the Justices in Eyre being the rolls of pleas and assizes for Yorkshire in 3 Henry III (1218-1219)*, no. 463 and no. 549.

ner for not inquiring into the chattels of an outlaw. Upon further investigation, it was determined that a local man had taken the outlaw's land and chattels and he was amerced for taking what "should be the lord king's, into his own hand."[436] Flight after escape from prison not only resulted in the fugitive being outlawed but also led to a heavy fine for the gaol keeper or sheriff responsible for the escape.[437]

Prisons continued to find increased use, particularly as a result of the changes in legal procedure brought about by the Fourth Lateran Council of 1215. Priestly participation in the trial by ordeal was banned by the Church and, as a result, royal and local administrators alike were forced to find other methods of gathering proof. The letters patent from January 1219 provided instructions to itinerant justices about changes in procedure:

> ...since it was in doubt and was not determined before the beginning of your eyre by what judgment those should be dealt with who are charged with robbery, murder, arson, and such like things, judgment by fire and water being forbidden by the Roman see, it is provided by our council at present that in your eyre it shall be done in this wise in regard to accusations of such crimes, that those who are accused of the aforesaid greater crimes, and are suspected of those things of which they are accused and in regard to whom, although they might abjure the realm, there is still suspicion that afterwards they might do ill, shall be held in our prison and safely guarded, so that they do not incur peril of life or limb by reason of our prison. Those who are accused of medium crimes touching which the judgment of fire and water would be suitable if it were not forbidden, and touching whom if they abjure our realm there would be no suspicion of evildoing afterwards, shall abjure our kingdom. Those who are charged with lesser crimes and in regard to whom there is no suspicion, shall find safe and secure pledges to keep our allegiance and peace and thus shall be loosed in our land....[438]

Placement of criminals into prison was left to the discretion of the justices and abjuration of the realm remained a mode of punishment for moderate offenders.

436 *Rolls of the Justices in Eyre being the rolls of pleas and assizes for Yorkshire in 3 Henry III (1218-1219)*, no. 856.

437 *Pleas of the Crown for the County of Gloucester, 1221*, no. 269, no. 316; Pugh, *Imprisonment in Medieval England*, 232.

438 *Patent rolls of the reign of Henry III, 1216-1225, preserved in the Public Record Office, printed under the superintendence of The Deputy Keeper of the Records.* vols 1-2. (London, UK: Printed for His Majesty's Stationery Office by Mackie and Co., 1901-1903), 186; Stenton, "The Trial of Criminals," in *Rolls of the Justices in Eyre being the rolls of pleas and assizes for Yorkshire in 3 Henry III (1218-1219)*, xl; S. F. C. Milsom, *Historical Foundations of the Common Law* (London, UK: Butterworths, 1969), 410.

Abjuration was not thought to be harsh enough for hardened offenders, however, and justices were encouraged to hold such criminals in prison indefinitely. Eyre records indicate that the justices took seriously the instructions from the king but were "far from rigid in their insistence on the imprisonment of the man suspected of the crime of which he was accused."[439] Suspected killers and other felons were placed in prison and kept there until their cases were determined. In one appeal of rape, Eva accused Adam of rape but failed to follow up her suit, resulting in both she and Adam being placed in custody. [440] Other lesser criminals, like those accused of false appeal for instance, were placed in gaol but paid a fine and were granted release.[441] Some criminals placed in gaol managed to escape, such as one arsonist who fled to a church and abjured the realm; others were detained while the accusations against them were further investigated; still more were placed into custody as accessories while the principle suspects in a criminal matter were tried; and many civil claimants were placed in gaol for making peace outside of the court and ordered to make payment to the Crown.[442]

Observations: Social order, law, and governance, c. 1225

By 1225, the Crown had extended its control over the increasingly centralized government in England, only to have its authority limited by baronial grievances embodied in the Magna Carta. The successors of Henry II initially held a large amount of power when it came to the use of prisons, and in some instances of exile and outlawry. This brought about political friction and complaints that the Crown was exceeding its authority. Unlawful imprisonment and outlawry were

---

439 Stenton, "The Trial of Criminals," xli.

440 *Rolls of the Justices in Eyre being the rolls of pleas and assizes for Yorkshire in 3 Henry III (1218-1219)*, nos 773, 681, 945, 757, 977, 966 for homicide; nos 522 and 759 for robbery; nos 688, 763, 955, 975 for rape; no. 594 for rape and robbery.

441 *Rolls of the Justices in Eyre being the rolls of pleas and assizes for Yorkshire in 3 Henry III (1218-1219)*, no. 946. Margery was placed into custody but paid a fine of 20 shillings; no. 449 Adam was appealed as an accessory in a homicide and in the custody of the sheriff, but "made fine by half a mark that he might be quit."

442 *Rolls of the Justices in Eyre being the rolls of pleas and assizes for Yorkshire in 3 Henry III (1218-1219)*, no. 1000 for the arsonist who abjured the realm; nos. 923, 695, 86, 766, and 996 for detention for making peace outside of court; no. 1015 for custody while further inquiry into a matter was made; nos 771, 1032, 592, and 449 for accessories.

two complaints held by barons, and thus became two aspects of governance by which the king's prerogative was limited.

The inception of the county coroner in the 1190s as an official in charge of hearing and recording abjurations and outlawries allowed for local legal actions to come under closer royal scrutiny. As the earliest eyre records indicate, outlawry continued to be prominent in England, thus creating a need for the Crown to be more involved in its processes and outcomes. The names of outlaws were given by the coroner to the Exchequer because their chattels and land became property of the Crown. The financial interest in outlawry would remain important through the course of the thirteenth century. Overall, the Crown attempted to extend its will into the role and function of county courts, but the outlawry process remained largely autonomous, and the efficacy and customary importance of outlawry endured.

The use of imprisonment in the early thirteenth century is found in response to grave crimes and suspicion. Imprisonment was a method of keeping suspected criminals safe as well as a means to coerce them to pay a fine or stand trial, and as a result, has been viewed as wholly non-punitive. Individuals were thus kept in prison until agreeing to put themselves upon the judgment of their neighbors, and if they were convicted, they could be hanged, remain in prison, find appropriate bail, or be forced to abjure the realm. Imprisonment was used to obtain sureties, receive amercements, and detain threats to the King's peace, all of which were highly punitive. Payments of fines by villages and frankpledges and of amercements by suspects were punishments, as was the detention of an accused man.[443]

Abjuration and outlawry also served as punitive actions, although in the form of removing an individual from society rather than confining them within gaol or prison walls. Outlawry and abjuration included the principles of notoriety, publicity, and exclusion that directed the operation of communal courts and the local maintenance of law and order.[444] This is clearly demonstrated in eyre records. Public knowledge of the commission of crimes was widespread, as a certain Reginald, accused of killing during the commission of a robbery and

---

443 See, for example, *Pleas of the Crown for the County of Gloucester, 1221*, nos 8, 73, 372 and 374. According to Maitland, these early attitudes towards imprisonment influenced the later development of imprisonment "peine forte et dure" during the reign of Edward I, a cruel and physically coercive method of dealing with accused individuals who refused to stand trial, see *Pleas of the Crown for the County of Gloucester, 1221*, xxxix-xl.

444 Summerson, "Criminal Law in the Age of Bracton," 121-122; Summerson, "The Structure of Law Enforcement in Thirteenth Century England," 313-327.

then fleeing, was found and hanged.[445] In another case, Robert killed John's wife and fled, after which he was captured and imprisoned in Northampton. He later escaped from prison and was said to have abjured the realm.[446] The dissemination of information about outlawries was an essential part of the administration of justice and punishments as well, exemplified when Felicia appealed Roger for robbery in Gloucestershire and when Roger did not come, it was testified that Roger was in fact an outlaw in the county of Oxford. This resulted in the immediate amercement of the men attached to him.[447]

The royal use of imprisonment in John's assizes of 1198 and 1199 as well as in the exercise of forest law was the right of the king. Imprisonment functioned as a coercive and detentive element in the administration of justice throughout the late twelfth and early thirteenth centuries and was becoming a more prominent royal, written law. Additionally, release from prison was often at the discretion of the king, which made pardons and mercy increasingly powerful royal tools. By every means available to him, the king was asserting legal authority through the use of imprisonment.

The use of outlawry, exile, and imprisonment in struggles for political power in late twelfth and early thirteenth century England represented the ebb and flow of the centralization of justice and royal authority. Expression of royal power by exclusion and imprisonment during the reign of King John resulted in conflicts between the King and his barons. These events, in turn, resulted in clear articulations of how outlawry, exile, and imprisonment could be used by the King.

The inclusion of outlawry and imprisonment in Magna Carta placed heavy restrictions upon the ancient practice of kings expelling their political enemies and threats to their authority, and increased the necessity of legal action when dealing with wrongdoers, of any kind, in England. To the minds of English Barons, King John exceeded his legal authority by using outlawry and imprisonment against political enemies, especially when these actions violated their rights. Baronial discontent rose to the point of civil war, and John was forced to acquiesce some of his royal prerogative with respect to imprisonment and outlawry as part of the Magna Carta. By the end of the reign of King John, some of the centralized royal authority of the late eleventh century had been checked by nobles and barons in England. Many of these checks involved the power to remove or imprison societal malefactors and continued into the early years of the reign of Henry III with subsequent reissues of Magna Carta.

---

445 *Pleas of the Crown for the County of Gloucester, 1221*, no. 21.

446 *Pleas of the Crown for the County of Gloucester, 1221*, no. 163.

447 *Pleas of the Crown for the County of Gloucester, 1221*, no. 103.

Chapter 6: Henry III and the Thirteenth Century: The customs, laws, and politics of outlawry and imprisonment

The outcomes from contests for authority and jurisdiction during the personal rule of Henry III defined later governmental and legal structures in England. The prominence of the eyre and legal systemization of the thirteenth century were heavily impacted by two ends of the spectrum of baronial discontent, from Magna Carta to the Baronial Reform movement. Outlawry and imprisonment alike played prominent roles in the struggle for political and legal control during the thirteenth century. By the end of Henry's rule in 1272, juridical practices that excluded wrongdoers from the realm of England were as engrained in law and custom as ever, particularly in the localities, while imprisonment was heavily relied upon by royal authorities.

Exclusion and Politics During the Personal Rule of Henry III

When Henry III took over personal rule in 1223, he affirmed his authority by neutralizing the power and prominence of magnates such as Fawkes de Breauté and Hubert de Burgh. As a result, both de Breauté and de Burgh were soon stripped of prestige and property and outlawed.

Fawkes de Breauté had a long career in England and served as sheriff of several shires during the reign of King John. He was forced to resign many of his offices after taking part in a rebellion against the young king Henry in 1223. His role in the conspiracy against the King and the abuses he committed as sheriff earned him enemies throughout England. Unlawful disseisin and disregarding royal writs were chief among his offenses, and de Breauté was formerly charged with a felony in the king's court in early 1224. The specifics of the court proceedings against him remain unclear, but Fawkes was outlawed in June of that year.[448]

---

448 *Royal and other historical letters illustrative of the reign of Henry III from the Originals in the Public Record Office*, selected and ed. W.W. Shirley. vols 1-2, *Rerum Britannicarum Medii Aevi Scriptores*. Pub. by the authority of Her Majesty's Treasury, under the direction of the Master of the Rolls. (London, UK: Green, Longman, and Roberts, 1862), vol. 1, letter CCI, 229; Matthew Paris, *Chronica Majora*, vol. 3: 85-89, 94,

De Breauté did not go easily from England, nor did his supporters help his case any. On the same day that he was outlawed, his brother, William, kidnapped one of the king's justices hearing the sixteen cases of novel disseisin brought against Fawkes. From Dunstable where the kidnapping took place, William then fled to Bedford. Fawkes fled to Chester, where he sought protection but found no assistance. He then attempted to find refuge in Wales, but failed. In a letter written to the King Henry in July 1224, the prince of North Wales, Llewellyn, denied harboring Fawkes.[449]

Meanwhile, King Henry III laid siege to Bedford castle where William and a garrison of men had fled. After eight weeks, the King captured and hanged William and his troops. Fawkes surrendered to Henry in August of 1224, after which he allowed to go into exile.[450] De Breauté attempted to gain a pardon from the King with the assistance of Pope Honorius III in 1224, but was unsuccessful and died in exile in 1226.[451]

One of the key men involved in the removal of De Breauté was the justiciar, Hubert de Burgh. De Burgh held a vast amount of power and clout with the king in 1223 but by 1232, he was in a far less stable position in England. Hubert de Burgh was one of the most important peers and officials under King John in the early thirteenth century. He held land in England and Normandy and fought on behalf of the king on both sides of the English Channel. He became justiciar under John and served as guardian of a young King Henry III as well as Chief Minister of England. Politics and governmental rivalries led De Burgh's removal from the office of justiciar in August 1232.[452] He was replaced by Stephen

---

97, 105, 119-121; D. A. Carpenter, *The Struggle for Mastery: Britain, 1066-1284* (Oxford, UK: Oxford UP, 2003), 306.

449 *Royal and other historical letters illustrative of the reign of Henry III,* vol. 1, letter CCI, 229; Matthew Paris, *Chronica Majora*, vol. 3: 85-89, 94, 97, 105, 119-121; Carpenter, *The Struggle for Mastery,* 306. The Welsh king did assert his right to receive English outlaws, however, as an independent ruler.

450 *Royal and other historical letters illustrative of the reign of Henry III*, vol. 1, letter CCIV and CCV for the siege of Bedford Castle and the safe conduct granted to de Breauté in 1224; Rymer's *Foedera,* vol. 1: 175-176 contains the August 1223 letters patent from King Henry related to his dispute with Fawkes; Powicke, *King Henry III*, 61-66; F. M. Powicke, *The Thirteenth Century: 1216-1307.* 2nd edn (Oxford, UK: Oxford UP, 1991), 25-7; Turner, *The King and His Courts*, 206-207; Roger of Wendover, vol. 2: 449-454; Morris, *Medieval Sheriff,* 162, 168; D.A. Carpenter, "The Fall of Hubert de Burgh" *The Reign of Henry III* (London, UK: Hambledon Press, 1996): 45-60 at 46.

451 *Royal and other historical letters illustrative of the reign of Henry III*, vol. 1, Appendix V, no. 19 and no. 20, no. 23.

452 *Royal and other historical letters illustrative of the reign of Henry III*, Appendix IV; Carpenter, "The Fall of Hubert de Burgh," 47-49; F. M. Powicke, *King Henry III and*

Seagrave and soon stripped of his lands and other offices. A royal writ was drafted ordering de Burgh's removal from England, and although it was never delivered, the former justiciar became a fugitive.[453]

De Burgh took refuge at the priory of Merton to prepare for his trial on September 14, but fled to St. Edmunds before that date to join his wife who had taken refuge there.[454] On his way to St. Edmunds, de Burgh stopped and stayed at the home of the bishop of Norwich in Essex. While in Essex, he was seized from the chapel by order of the King. Although de Burgh had fled to the chapel for sanctuary, he was dragged out, fettered, and taken to the Tower of London. This breach of sanctuary caused the Bishop of London to intervene on de Burgh's behalf and the former justiciar was soon restored to the chapel. De Burgh later surrendered to the kings" men however, possibly having been starved out, and was imprisoned in the Tower of London.[455] On November 10, de Burgh appeared before the King and was sentenced to imprisonment in the castle at Devizes as a prisoner of the state.[456]

---

the Lord Edward: The Community of the Realm in the Thirteenth Century (Oxford, UK: Clarendon Press, 1947), 68-83, 138-144; Powicke, *The Thirteenth Century*, 50-52; Roger of Wendover, vol. 2: 553-555; F. West, *Justiciarship in England*, 212-271; F. J. West, "Burgh, Hubert de, earl of Kent (c.1170–1243)", *Oxford Dictionary of National Biography*, Oxford UP, Sept 2004; online edn, Jan 2008 [http://www.oxforddnb.com/view/article/3991]. Carpenter's article reassesses Powicke's conclusion that a power-hungry Peter des Roches and the increasingly assertive King Henry III carefully conspired to remove an aging and unambitious de Burgh in exchange for Peter des Rivaux. Carpenter argues that de Burgh's actions as justiciar were acceptable to the king until he fell out of Henry's favor in July 1232 for inciting riots against Italian clerks, an event which Powicke dismisses as justification for the justiciar's dismissal instead of the true reason. De Burgh's demise was orchestrated by Peter des Roches and Peter des Rivaux and was as much an attack on de Burgh as an attempt at consolidation of offices and financial reform.

453 Powicke, *The Reign of Henry III*, 81; Carpenter, "The Fall of Hubert de Burgh," 45; F. J. West, "Burgh, Hubert de, earl of Kent (*c.*1170–1243)", *Oxford Dictionary of National Biography*, Oxford UP, Sept 2004; online edn, Jan 2008 [http://www.oxforddnb.com/view/article/3991].

454 *The Chronicle of Bury St. Edmunds 1212-1301*, ed. A. Grandsden (London, UK: Thomas Nelson and Sons Ltd., 1964), 7-8.

455 Roger of Wendover, vol. 2: 555-559; Matthew Paris, *Chronica Majora*, vol. 3: 220-230.

456 *Calendar of the Patent Rolls, Henry III, AD1232-1247*, Preserved in the Public Records Office (London, UK: Printed for his Majesty's Stationary office by Mackie and Co., Ltd., 1906), 17 Henry III, 27-30; Rymer's *Foedera*, vol. 1: 207ff. also contains patent letters from King Henry regarding these events as does *Royal and other historical let-*

After a series of escapes from prison, flights to sanctuary, and rescues by loyal friends, Hubert de Burgh, and the men who had assisted him, were outlawed by order of the king in late 1233. King Henry ordered the sheriff of Wiltshire to outlaw de Burgh, his two prison guards William de Millers and Thomas the Chamberlain, as well as de Burgh's two associates Gilbert Bassett and Richard Seward and their men for helping de Burgh escape from Devizes prison in September 1233. The charges were to be brought "from shire court to shire court until they were outlawed according to the law and custom of the realm."[457] All of the men were outlawed as a result of the charges, but only for a short time. The matter of de Burgh's outlawry was brought before the great council held at Gloucester in May of 1234 and it was determined that "outlawry at the king's suit or command is null and void unless an inquest has been taken by the justices and the fugitive has been found guilty as the outcome of indictment or appeal."[458] The outlawries associated with the Hubert de Burgh affair were ruled unjust, nullified, and all of the men were restored to their lands and to good standing with the king.[459]

---

ters illustrative of the reign of Henry III, vol. 1; See also Matthew Paris, *Chronica Majora*, vol. 3: 233-234 and Powicke, *The Reign of Henry III*, 81-83.

457 *Close Rolls of the reign of Henry III: Preserved in the Public Record Office, A.D. 1231-*1234 (London, UK: His Majesty's Stationery Office by Mackie and Co., Ltd., 1905), 18 Henry III, m. 34d, at 545; *Royal and other historical letters illustrative of the reign of Henry III*, vol. 1, letter CCCLVII, 429 for the King's orders to the sheriff of Wiltshire; Powicke, *The Reign of Henry III*, 140; Roger of Wendover, vol. 2: 568-572, 585-594; N. Vincent, *Peter des Roches: an alien in English politics, 1205-1238* (Cambridge, UK: Cambridge UP, 1996), 410-417 for the role of Roches in the De Burgh matter. After 1204, Peter des Roches spent the most successful part of his life and career as an exile in England. He served as Justiciar during the reign of John and regent during the minority of Henry III.

458 Powicke, *The Reign of Henry III*, 140; G. O. Sayles, *The Functions of Medieval Parliament in England* (London, UK: Hambledon Continuum, 1987), 12-14; The case appears in Bracton's Notebook, no. 857. For more on the king being "below the law" during this period of English law, see Pollock and Maitland, *History of English Law*, vol. 1: 181-183; B. Tierney, "Bracton on Government," *Speculum*, vol. 38, no. 2. (Apr., 1963): 295-317.

459 *Royal and other historical letters illustrative of the reign of Henry III,* vol. I, letters CCCLXVI, CCCLXVII, and CCCLXVIII, 439-40, all dated 26 May 1234 for the pardons of Marshall, de Burgh and Seward; letter CCCLXXI, 443, dated 8 June 1234, from Henry III to the Sheriffs of Berkshire annulling the outlawry of de Burgh as illegal; Matthew Paris, *Chronica Majora*, Edited by H.R. Luard, pub. by the authority of the lords commissioners of Her Majesty's Treasury, under the direction of the master of the rolls, vols 1-7 (London, UK: Longman & Co. 1872-83), 3: 291-292; D. Carpenter, "Justice and Jurisdiction under King John and King Henry III," in *The Reign of King Henry*

The importance of this case and the precedent it set for future outlawries cannot be overstated. Outlawry was a tool of order that resisted succumbing to the will of the king. We have seen how the crown slowly encroached upon aspects of the outlawry process in the late twelfth and early thirteenth century, but now the king was explicitly forbidden from using outlawry outside of appropriate legal processes.

Thirteenth-Century Outlawry, Imprisonment, and Abjuration as described by Bracton

In order to understand the significance of the case of Hubert de Burgh, outlawry as a process based both in customary practices and in legal procedure must be assessed. *On the Laws and Customs of England*, a thirteenth century legal treatise attributed to royal justice Henry Bracton, articulates how outlawry functioned during this period in England.[460] Bracton's work, which was not intended to formulate policy, reports on contemporary practice, much of which was derived from and influenced by pre-existing law and custom. *On the Laws and Customs of England* details many of the intricacies of the outlawry process while informing the reader about changes in law and how these two things coexisted and functioned together.[461]

Bracton describes the distinction between "true" and "presumptive" outlawry:

III, 17-43 at 40; Powicke, *The Reign of Henry III*, 139-140; Powicke, *The Thirteenth Century*, 59-60; Turner, *The King and His Courts*, 177. Hubert de Burgh entered into court proceedings to get his lands returned to him, as did most outlaws, but each case was different in its outcome. An outlaw could only be pardoned by the king and the only thing that could be restored was what the king had to give. See Turner, *The King and His Courts*, 151-152, 248 and Pollock and Maitland, *History of English Law*, vol. 2: 580-584.

460 Bracton, *On the Laws and Customs of England*, trans. Samuel E. Thorne, ed. Gorge E. Woodbine, vols 1-4 (Cambridge, MA: The Belknap Press of Harvard UP in association with the Selden Society, 1968). For a summary and assessment of the authorship, date, and role of Bracton and the work attributed to him, see P. Brand, "The Age of Bracton," in *The History of English Law: Centenary Essays on "Pollock and Maitland,"* Proceedings of the British Academy, vol. 89, ed. J. Hudson (Oxford, UK: Oxford UP, 1996): 65-90.

461 Bracton, vol. 2: 352-378; Pollock and Maitland, *History of English Law*, vol. 1: 206-210.

> True, when wickedly and feloniously in breach of the king's peace, in the presence of many bystanders and onlookers, or at least within the sight and hearing of one who has an interest enabling him to appeal, a man has been slain, or seriously wounded and maimed, [or] robbed, imprisoned and chained, provided there is someone who sues ([if] he cannot sue on his own behalf) when the wrongdoer takes to flight and cannot be arrested, and provided that the deed constitutes a felony.[462]

Presumptive outlawry, on the other hand, was the result of flight in the face of impending legal action, even if his offense was not serious, no one was dead, or a crime was never committed. The matter necessarily proceeded through exaction to outlawry with a properly brought suit. Bracton stressed the importance of cause and a proper suit in county court as the impetus to outlawry, as mere suspicion, accusation, or rumor, were insufficient.[463]

The exaction process was the precursor to a formal declaration of outlawry. A man appealed of a felony was given five chances to appear before the county court. The appeal against the accused man had to be read in its entirety before each meeting of the court and could only be brought by the afflicted party or an appropriate kinsman. During the exaction process, an appellee could surrender himself to prison, either in person or through friends, and then stand trial. If he was found innocent, he retained his lands and his social standing but lost his chattels, which were forfeited to the king for having taken flight. If a man accused of a crime failed to appear at five consecutive county courts, he was considered a "lawless man," an outlaw. An outlaw forfeited all rights, his country, property, obligations, familial and friendship ties, and could be killed with impunity if he resisted arrest.[464]

Men under the age of twelve could not be outlawed, nor could women. Minors were considered outside of the law before the age of twelve, while women were never "under the law."[465] Women could be waived, however, which left them in the same social standing as an outlaw. Waivery meant that a woman was abandoned by all, lacked all claims, and lived outside of all social protection.[466] If an outlaw was later arrested or surrendered to authorities, he was at the mercy of the king. Anyone who harbored, assisted, or communicated with an outlaw was subject to loss of life and property as well.[467] During the exaction process, an appellor could interrupt his suit without having to abandon it, and if

---

462 Bracton, vol. 2: 355-356.
463 Bracton, vol. 2: 356-357.
464 Bracton, vol. 2: 352-354.
465 Bracton, vol. 2: 353.
466 Bracton, vol. 2: 353-354.
467 Bracton, vol. 2: 352-354, 361-363, 378.

he withdrew from his suit, died, or became ill, the justices would either conduct an inquest or order the county court to complete the suit on the king's behalf.[468] In suits involving a "principal" and an "accessory", the outlawing of an accessory was most often reserved until actions against the principal were complete.[469] Outlaws could not accuse others individuals of criminal offenses, although they could turn approver. Outlawry could, however, be used as an argument against an approver. By arguing against the credibility and trustworthiness of an approver, a defendant could raise enough doubt about the accusations of an approver to gain an acquittal.[470]

Presentment juries were required to present all information about fugitives, exactions, and outlaws, including accounts of chattels, to royal justices. The chattels of all fugitives and outlaws were forfeited to the king. Any free land held by an outlaw also became the possession of the crown. The king would hold lands held by an outlaw and reap profits from them for a year and one day, after which they would be restored to the chief lord.[471] Bracton claims that when an inheritance was common to a woman and her outlawed husband or son, she did not lose her possession due to the actions of her kinsman, but rather kept her share of the land.[472]

Within this process, the king had very little independent power. The power to void or pardon an outlaw, however, rested solely with the king. Bracton articulated clear distinctions between "void" and "pardon" as well as discussed steps taken to "inlaw" an outlaw. An outlawry could be pronounced void regardless of whether the cause was true or presumptive. An invalidation of outlawry was the result of the process or suit being improperly carried out according to the law of the land. For the latter, Bracton offers examples such as if the county court proceeded without proper cause or without a sufficient inquest, an appellee would be restored to right. A pardon or remittance of outlawry was to be given if an appellee had been outlawed for an untrue cause through the proper outlawry process. The king could not void a pronouncement that was in accordance with the law, but could show mercy and grace when it came to "inlawing" the individual in question.[473]

An outlaw would obviously have a difficult time obtaining a pardon himself, so he would employ an intermediary to work on his behalf in order to obtain pardon. A fugitive would need two pardons or would need to have his flight as

---

468 Bracton, vol. 2: 354-355.

469 Bracton, vol. 2: 360-361.

470 Bracton, vol. 2: 331, 335-337.

471 Bracton, vol. 2: 363-364, 367.

472 Bracton, vol. 2: 368.

473 Bracton, vol. 2: 357-359; Hurnard, *King's Pardon*, 214-217.

well as his original crime pardoned in the same document. Pardons were also granted for outlawry alone, on the condition that the accused would appear in court to answer charges against him. The individual's chattels, however, still became the possessions of the Crown. The same was true of an abjuror. A pardoned outlaw could enter into new agreements and could come and go from the country as he pleased, but could not be restored to previous obligations, oaths, loyalties, or actions. Pardoned outlaws were "so to speak, new-born infants and new men, as though newly created, because after outlawry properly done nothing of the past abides in their persons but (after inlawry) only the present and the future take its place."[474] Understandably so, it was advisable for all former outlaws to carry their pardons with them at all times.[475]

"Inlawing" an outlaw involved allowing an outlaw back into the king's peace and back into full protection of the law. Necessary for the safety of an outlaw, this could be done whether the outlawry was voided or pardoned, although circumstances did often dictate the forgiveness and restoration granted by the king.[476] If an outlawry involved an appeal of felony but was voided due to an improper suit, it was necessary for the offender to answer the charges against him in court prior to being accepted back into the king's peace, if he was ever given the king's grace at all.[477] If an outlaw was lawfully and properly outlawed but without cause, then he was to be admitted into grace without difficulty; if outlawry was declared with no cause and without proper law, then the appellee was to be fully restored as if he had never been an outlaw.[478] Writs of remittance for outlawries were issued when a man had turned himself into the king's prison but was outlawed anyway, as well as when a man said to be slain in a suit of homicide returned or was found to be alive and well.[479]

The circumstances of outlawry and any subsequent inlawry dictated the restoration of property and any further legal action against the former outlaw. This

---

474 Bracton, vol. 2: 373-374; Pollock and Maitland, *History of English Law*, vol. 2: 580-584.

475 Hurnard, *King's Pardon*, 32-34, 63-65; 132-139; 179-182, 287-290; Bracton, vol. 2: 357; *Calendar of Patent Rolls*, 11 Henry III, 1227, at page 124 (abjuror pardoned); 12 Henry III, 1228, at page 177; 14 Henry III, 1230, at pages 328-329; 15 Henry III, 1231, at page 423; 16 Henry III, 1232, at page 462-463 (pardons of outlawry and abjuration), 487. According to Hurnard, a pardon for outlawry alone was "a process to compel the appearance in court of persons sued for trespass or for failing to render account."

476 Bracton, 2: 357, 369-378.

477 Bracton, 2: 369; Hurnard, *King's Pardon*, 207-213.

478 Bracton, vol. 2: 373. For more on the circumstances of pardoning fugitives and how it relates to outlawry, see Hurnard, *King's Pardon*, 132-142, 145.

479 Bracton, vol. 2: 369-372.

often affected inheritance disputes as well. If a person bringing a claim, or any of that claimant's ancestors, had been an outlaw or abjured the realm and was only later restored to the king's peace, his land rights depended on the manner by which he had been outlawed and later inlawed. The same was true with respect to individuals against whom claims were brought.[480] Land rights of former outlaws brought the criminal processes of outlawry into the civil legal sphere.

In a related course of action, outlawry began to take on a variant form and became a punishment in English civil law during this period as well. "Minor outlawries" could be pronounced upon fugitives who, in pleas involving money and/or injury, chattels, and possessions, did not appear in court or failed to pay the taxation of the offense as assessed by the judiciary. Such an offense was seen as…

> …contumacy and disobedience to the lord king…and accordingly ought to be outlawed, not, however, to lead to death or loss of limbs if they have afterwards returned or have been intercepted, since the cause of their outlawry has not been criminal, but to perpetual imprisonment or the abjuration of the realm, or excommunication from all those who are within the peace of the lord the king; and as the cause of the excommunication makes the excommunication and the penalty of minor degree, so the cause of the outlawry makes the outlawry and the penalty of minor degree, and he ought more easily to find grace, that having been outlawed under such circumstances he should be restored to the peace [of the king]. For excommunication and outlawry are in many respects judged alike.[481]

Outlawry in this context was civil rather than criminal and the use of imprisonment and abjuration to mitigate outlawry was not new in the administration of law in England. Imprisonment and abjuration were supplements to or options in response to an adapted form of outlawry used by the Crown. They were more controllable punitive actions used in the interest of expressing royal judicial authority.

The use of abjuration and imprisonment as alternatives to outlawry was best demonstrated in the treatment of approvers. A confessed felon who turned approver, for example, would be allowed to abjure the realm if a certain number of his accomplices and associates were convicted on his appeals. Allowing a felon to become an approver was under the sole discretion of the king, and Bracton

480 Henry Bracton, *De Legibus et Consuetudinibus Angliae*. vols 1-6, trans. T. Twiss (London, UK: Longman & Co., 1878-1883), vol. 6: 327. Bracton is either implying that a guilty criminal who was inlawed due to a technical violation in the outlawry procedure was still able to receive full legal rights or that the inlawry procedure, i.e. the mercy of the king, was infallible.

481 Bracton, *De Legibus et Consuetudinibus Angliae*, trans. T. Twiss, vol. 6: 480-481.

states that confessed thieves, robbers, killers, and even outlaws, abjurors, and escaped prisoners were able to become approvers if the king so allowed. An approver saved his life by agreeing to "rid the country" of a certain number of criminals "by his body or by the country or by flight."[482] Appellees of good social standing could plead exceptions against approvers, but appellees that could not find sureties in the face of an approver's appeal were forced to abjure the realm. Appellees who fled were put to the exaction process in county court and later outlawed; and those convicted were often hanged. The approver himself was allowed to abjure the realm or endure perpetual imprisonment, but only after an agreed upon number of felons had been successfully appealed. Such agreements are found within Bracton's text and writs permitting successful approvers to abjure are found in the Close Rolls of Henry III.[483]

According to Bracton, imprisonment was a tool of law and governance in its own right in thirteenth-century England. There are numerous references to prisons, gaols, and confinement in *On the Laws and Customs of England*, but Bracton clearly states that imprisonment was not to be used as a method of punishment, but rather as one of detention.[484] This conception of imprisonment, which dates back to Roman legal doctrine, was closely associated with the use of imprisonment as a means of exacting monetary compensation, fines, and amercements from both criminal and civil offenders.[485] To state that imprisonment was not a method of punishment does not mean that it was not punitive in its application. The use of prisons and gaols was becoming more common in the English Common Law and was increasingly relied upon as an instrument of order.[486] The legally prescribed use of imprisonment and the presence of prisons in judicial and political processes as discussed by Bracton are important to understand-

---

482 Bracton, vol. 2: 346, 429. Hamil, "King's Approvers," 239-40, states that those who had been outlawed, abjured, or convicted of a felony were unable to become approvers.

483 Bracton, vol. 2: 429-435; Hamil, "King's Approvers," 240, 242, 245-247

484 Pugh, *Imprisonment in Medieval England*, 16-17; Bracton, vol. 2: 298-299; Pollock and Maitland, *History of English Law*, vol. 1: 206-210.

485 Ulpian, *Digest of Justinian*, 48.19.8.9. For a brief discussion of imprisonment in Roman law, see Geltner, *Medieval Prison,* 45-56.

486 Pollock and Maitland, *History of English Law*, vol. 2: 516-518; Pugh, *Imprisonment in Medieval England*, 14-17; See Powicke, *King Henry III*, 331, "Just as the penalty of imprisonment was used as a way of inducing an offender to bring the matter to an end by making a fine with the king, undertaking him to pay money to him, so the grim conception of falling into the king's mercy prepared the way for the more genial writs and devices by which a man who had harmed his neighbour, in small ways as well as in great, was brought to a stand by the infliction of damages."

ing how confinement functioned in law and society and how it interacted with other methods of authority.[487]

Gaols had been in place in all counties in England since the reign of Henry II and by the mid-thirteenth century, gaol delivery commissions were the main mechanism by which prisoners were brought to justice. Gaols were to be delivered, or cleared, and jurors were to report upon the conduct of officials who kept prisoners.[488] Appellees were…

> …usually released by sureties, except in the case of homicide, since no one who can provide pledges is to be thrust into prison unless it is evident that he has perpetrated so serious a crime that he ought not to be handed over to sureties or soldiers but suffer the penalty of imprisonment and confinement, the sheriff ought to determine whether he is to be taken into custody or committed to sureties, after taking into consideration the nature and gravity of the crime of which he is accused, or his distinguished rank and great wealth or his integrity or official position.[489]

From 1225 to the Baronial Reform movement of the 1250s, gaol delivery commissions varied in regularity, geography, and number of gaols visited. Gaol delivery functioned alongside the main vehicle in the administration of law, the general eyre. [490] Imprisonment was also prescribed for accusers in offenses against the crown, such as forgery and treason, who could not find sureties. These crimes were deemed serious enough that the accused were to be held in gaol without the possibility of bail or sureties until the matter could be investigated.[491] In cases of homicide, the coroner‘s inquest determined who was suspected of the crime and, therefore, dictated the use of imprisonment. Anyone found at the body of a slain man was to be put in gaol without possibility of bail or sureties, and if a stranger was killed, anyone known to have hosted him or who associated with him was detained. Coroners also determined the severity of wounding and breaches of the king's peace, dictating again who was to be arrested and imprisoned. In the most serious offenses, appellees were not to be released on

---

487 Pugh, *Imprisonment in Medieval England*, 17; Pollock and Maitland, *History of English Law*, vol. 2: 516-517.

488 Bracton, vol. 2: 330-332, 334-336; Pollock and Maitland, vol. 1: 200-202; Pugh, *Imprisonment in Medieval England*, 255-277.

489 Bracton, vol. 2:349-350.

490 Pugh, *Imprisonment in Medieval England*, 255-260; Meekings, "Introduction," *Wiltshire Crown Pleas 1249*, 5-6. For example, patent rolls demonstrate that in 1236, the justices in eyre were to deliver the gaol at Coventry (160) while in 1237, four men were commissioned with the single task of delivering the gaol at Carlisle (182). The latter was later cancelled. See *Calendar of the Patent Rolls, Henry III, AD 1232-1247*, 20 Henry III, page 160 and 21 Henry III, page 182.

491 Bracton, vol. 2: 335-336; Powicke, *King Henry III*, 336.

sureties unless by the specific action of the king. Furthermore, Bracton stated that if an individual was arrested "for theft or homicide or some other felony he may only be kept in the prison of him who could judge them in his court."[492]

Unlike outlaws, prisoners did not lose their land while confined nor could a prisoner in one county could be outlawed in another county for failure to appear. Inquests were conducted to make sure that prisoners were not held on appeals brought out of "hate and spite" instead of actual criminal conduct. Escape from prison usually resulted in more a severe punishment than the original crime may have warranted, even if an accused was found to be innocent of his crime. Individuals who escaped from prison were pursued as outlaws. This was the opposite of the image described by Bracton in which an outlaw could surrender himself to a prison in the hopes of being cleared of any wrongdoing.[493]

The scene depicted by Bracton is one in which outlawry was omnipresent in law and society and imprisonment was used creatively, as circumstances dictated, and with more discretion by the crown. Frankly, the crown was limited in how it could function with and within exaction and outlawry, as demonstrated by the case of Hubert de Burgh, and found that imprisonment was much more accessible and applicable. Within this context, abjuration served to fill some sort of middle ground as a mitigated form of outlawry considered to be less severe and less dangerous than the alternative.

Outlawry, Imprisonment, and Abjuration leading up to the Baronial Reform: Legal Records

The general eyre functioned as another meeting of the county court, supplementing the judicial processes already underway and following them through to completion. The eyre and the royal justices could not and did not pronounce outlawries independently of the county court, but rather as an extension of it. As a visitor to the county, the eyre was thus an intermediary between local adjudication and that of the Crown.

The general eyre reached its zenith during the reign of Henry III. Plea rolls extant from the period prior to the baronial actions of the 1250s and 1260s supplement Bracton's account of thirteenth century law in England, particularly with respect to outlawry, imprisonment and abjuration. In Yorkshire in 1231, Hugh was charged with larceny, did not appear and was ordered to exigent and

492 Bracton, vol. 2: 342-345.

493 Bracton, vol. 2: 346-348, 350, 358. Criminous clerks were to be delivered to the appropriate Episcopal prison for purgation.

outlawry; William fled following suspected involvement in burglary and home invasion and was put in exigency; and Jordan was suspected of larceny, fled to a church, confessed his crime to the coroner and abjured the realm.[494] Similarly, a certain John was captured and held in Essex in 1235 until he answered charges of theft against him. He defended himself against all felonies and put himself upon the jury. No one in the vill stood surety for him and he was placed back into gaol, but before he could find pledges, he escaped and abjured the realm.[495] Crime, suspicion, and flight created a complex web of exclusion intertwined with confinement.

Plea roll evidence reveals the strength of exclusion and its social importance as a means to remove a malefactor from the community. Prior to the arrival of an eyre, most of the legal business in the country had been carried out in a county court; much of this local justice included both outlawry and abjuration processes and it becomes difficult to talk of one practice independently of the other. Flight following the commission of a serious offense often resulted in outlawry or abjuration. The difference in outcome simply depended on whether or not an individual was able to flee to a church, confess, and abjure the realm. This option was, of course, contingent upon the proximity of a holy place. The 1232 crown pleas from Buckinghamshire record forty-one outlawries and fifteen abjurations, while the Surrey eyre of 1235 records sixty-three instances of outlawry and only four abjurations.[496] In Oxfordshire in 1241, eighty-one pleas of the crown presented by jurors had resulted in outlawry. Twenty-seven culminated in abjurations. There were also five appeals in which the justices instructed the appellant to continue his suit in the county court until outlawry could be declared.[497]

---

494 London, The National Archives, JUST 1/1043.

495 London, The National Archives, JUST 1/230, m. 3.

496 London, The National Archives, JUST 1/62; *The 1235 Surrey Eyre*, ed. by C.A.F. Meekings, prepared by D. Crook for the Surrey Record Society, vols 1-3 (Ilkley, UK: The Scolar Press, 1979). There is one case of trespass in Surrey that was a continuation of an earlier suit that resulted in an outlawry, but the outcome the follow-up is unknown. See *The 1235 Surrey Eyre*, vol. 2, no. 523; also discussed in the "Introduction" on page 122 of vol. 1.

497 *The Oxfordshire Eyre, 1241*, ed. Janet Cooper. The Oxfordshire Record Society, vol. 56. (Oxford, UK: Parchment Ltd., 1986), no. 1037. There were 278 pleas of the crown for the Oxfordshire Eyre. Based on the number of abjurations, there were presumably more churches in Buckinghamshire than in Surrey. In Oxfordshire, the pervasiveness of churches is clear, as one single plea of homicide saw the three men accused of homicide flee to three different churches and subsequently abjure the realm. Three men were accused of killing William and Robert of Aston, namely Ives, son of Almer, Robert Ar-

Just like outlawry, abjuration was very public and highly punitive. When Emma fled to a church at Puddington in Cheshire, admitted to thievery and then abjured the realm, she sealed her own fate when she was arrested and imprisoned at Exeter a short time later. Emma was hanged upon presentation to the justices at gaol delivery in 1238.[498] Thomas was luckier, as following his confession to thievery and abjuration, he was arrested and imprisoned at Tavistock in Devon, only to then escape from captivity.[499] There were flaws in the system, however, for when the outlaw Robert was arrested by the sheriff Thomas, Thomas did not know he was an outlaw and took pledges from him. Robert, of course, failed to appear and both his pledges and Thomas were in mercy as a result.[500]

Outlawry and abjuration as common legal processes can be seen in sequential Devonshire eyres. During the Devon eyre of 1238, 118 killers were put to exigent and outlawed while sixteen abjured the realm. Similarly, thirty-three suspected thieves were put in exigent and thirty-five abjured the realm. There were four additional outlawries from suits of wounding brought by those offended, and two for harboring thieves. One man also fled to a church, confessed to harboring thieves, and then abjured the realm. In 1244, Devon eyre plea rolls recorded fifty-six killers and twenty-eight suspected thieves subjected to exigency and outlawry, as well as twenty-eight killers and twelve suspected thieves who abjured the realm. The Devon eyre of 1249 again resulted in fifty-six killers put in exigent and outlawed, while thirty-six suspected thieves were put in exigent. The same eyre saw seven killers and eighteen thieves abjure the realm.[501] Serious offenses such as killing and theft were problematic in Devon and as a result, these were the types of offenders that found themselves removed from society.

Plea records from London in 1244 include twenty-one outlawries and sixteen abjurations, as well as one instance of waivery; roll and writ records from

---

zuner, and Ralph Arzuner, Ives fled to St. John's Church in Oxford, Robert to Moreton Church, and Ralph to the church of Hagbourne.

498 *Crown Pleas of the Devon Eyre of 1238*, ed. H.R.T. Summerson. Devon & Cornwall Record Society, New Series, vol. 28 (Torquay, England: The Devonshire Press Ltd., 1985), no. 369.

499 *Crown Pleas of the Devon Eyre of 1238*, no. 645.

500 *Crown Pleas of the Devon Eyre of 1238*, no. 653.

501 *Crown Pleas of the Devon Eyre of 1238*, "Appendix III: Statistics of Crime from Devon Eyres," 130; "Introduction," xxviii-xxxix. There were 776 crown pleas during the Devon eyre of 1238. According to Summerson, "most of the thieves put in exigent seem likely to have been outlawed." For the woundings, see nos 90, 571 and 576; for harboring, see no. 157 and no. 635.

the Berkshire eyre of 1248 tell us of eleven outlawries by the county court by appeal, with two more by suit of the king, fifty-one overall exactions leading to outlawry and six instances of waivery. [502] Similarly, there were twenty-six abjurations, two of which were concealed by the jury, one more of a felon being outlawed prior to abjuration, and one instance of abjuration without mention of sanctuary.[503] At the Coventry session of the crown pleas heard during the Warwickshire eyre of 1247, the jury was amerced by the itinerant justices for concealing an appeal of homicide and the subsequent outlawry of the two accused men.[504]

Crown pleas from the 1249 Wiltshire eyre include the outlawry of thirty criminals presented to the justices in eyre: four for robbery, two for rape, one for mayhem, one for an unknown breach of the king's peace, and the rest for homicide. These individuals had been outlawed in the county courts on appeal prior to the arrival of the eyre, although two cases of outlawry were later determined by the eyre to have been wrongfully pronounced.[505] From the fifty-three presentments of homicide to the eyre, forty-seven men were ordered to be exacted and outlawed, while three women were ordered exacted and waived.[506] The Wiltshire eyre records twenty-two persons outlawed for appeals of homicide in the county courts, with fifteen more outlawed in eyre. Three individuals were outlawed in eyre for default on sureties for robbery charges held over from the county court.[507] Wiltshire records also attest to presentment of the abjurations of seventeen murderers, twenty-eight thieves, two coiners and two other unspecified criminals, with two sanctuary seekers escaping from their church prior to swearing the oath to abjure.[508]

---

502 *The London Eyre of 1244*, eds. H.M. Chew and M. Weinbaum. Contains crown pleas for years 10 Henry III to 27 Henry III, plus appeals, articles, constitutions and related material. By kind permission of the London Record Society. London, UK: London Record Society, 1970. accessed at: http://www.british-history.ac.uk/source.aspx?pubid=153.

503 *The Roll and Writ File of the Berkshire Eyre of 1248*, ed. by M.T. Clanchy for the Selden Society (London, UK: William Clowes & Sons Ltd., 1973).

504 "The Warwickshire Eyres" in *Early Records of Medieval Coventry*, ed. P. Coss (London, UK: pub. for the British Academy by Oxford UP, 1986), ""Extracts from the Crown Pleas of the Warwickshire Eyre, held 8 April to 9 May 1247," no. 36.6.

505 *Crown Pleas of the Wlitshire Eyre, 1249*. ed. C.A.F. Meekings. (Wiltshire Archaeological and Natural History Society. Devizes, UK: Northumberland Press, 1961), 57, 79-80; See numbers 317-318 and 373.

506 *Crown Pleas of the Wiltshire Eyre, 1249*, 58.

507 *Crown Pleas of the Wlitshire Eyre, 1249,* 65, 79, 80.

508 *Crown Pleas of the Wiltshire Eyre, 1249*, 38, 53-54.

Exclusion as an overwhelming and engrained force in social and legal order in England is clear. Individuals were in close contact with the law and were active participants in governing their surroundings. They dutifully reported on this to the royal justices as law dictated and brought appeals that encouraged the use of exclusion. Community members could also participate in assisting, aiding, or protecting outlaws. This practice was an affront to royal interests in law and order, and harboring outlaws was an element of law that the crown punished with vigor. For example, in Wiltshire, one man who harbored his outlawed son was ordered to be exacted and outlawed; a woman who was arrested for harboring an outlaw, although she later escaped; and an outlaw who was arrested outside of the county's liberty after being the subject of the local hue and cry.[509] Similarly, Robert and Agnes were amerced for harboring Batinus, a known outlaw who was later captured traveling through the county. Batinus was placed in gaol after being pursued by the hue, where he reportedly died.[510]

The pre-Baronial reform eyres well illustrate the amount of justice that had run its course in county courts prior to the arrival of the justices, as well as the accountability those courts were subject to upon arrival of the itinerant officials. There were two instances in the 1249 Wiltshire eyre in which the county was amerced for wrongful outlawry, first for outlawing an alleged robber in what was determined to be a civil plea rather than a felony, and later as a result of its outlawry of accessories prior to the determination of the appeal against the principle offender.[511] Similarly, abjurations concealed in Berkshire resulted in the amercement of the presentment juries and the Oxfordshire eyre of 1241 contains instances of the justices amercing jurors and counties for improperly exercising justice. Jurors were amerced for falsely presenting the wounding of one Richard of Grettenham while failing to mention that said Richard later killed his attacker, who the jurors had proceeded to outlaw. Additionally, the county was in mercy for concealing the chattels of a certain Walter outlawed for fleeing after the death of Robert and was amerced for taking no action against accused thief Richard Puck when he failed to appear before the county court.[512]

Royal checks on local court proceedings and judicial matters reveal a certain amount of discretion practiced by the itinerant justices. Minor thieves and other criminals were required to abjure the realm for lack of sureties, which was con-

509 *Crown Pleas of the Wiltshire Eyre, 1249*, 65.

510 *Crown Pleas of the Wiltshire Eyre, 1249*, no. 146 and no. 144.

511 *Crown Pleas of the Wiltshire Eyre, 1249*, no. 373 and nos 317-318, also discussed on pages 53, 57-58, 75 in the "Introduction"; Morris, *The Early English County Court*, 116; H.M. Jewell, *English Local Administration in the Middle Ages* (Newton Abbot, Devon, UK: David & Charles Ltd., 1972), 139-140.

512 *The Oxfordshire Eyre, 1241*, nos 1056, 955, 920.

sidered excessive at times. In one instance, the coroner and bailiffs were amerced for causing a certain Helen to abjure for a crime considered "petty larceny."[513] A similar instance is found in the Berkshire eyre of 1241 where justices found the coroner to be unjust in causing a minor thief to abjure the realm.[514] The importance of this, however, is in the use of abjuration as a punishment. Abjuration as a form of pronounced outlawry was practiced by royal officials and indicates the endorsement of exclusion as part of law and order.

Much of the criminal and civil business of the realm was carried out in county courts prior to the coming of the eyre, but the county courts were increasingly held accountable by the justices and royal officials. Sureties, tithings, and vills were amerced when criminals fled, for failing to pursue or report these flights, or for receiving an individual in flight. Individuals present at the eyre faced punishments of heavy fines, imprisonment until finding sureties or making payment, or hanging, depending on the severity of the offense.[515] Royal officials were held also answerable to the justices in eyre. Sheriffs and bailiffs were to account for the chattel of fugitives and abjurors, coroners could be amerced for mistakes in the outlawry or abjuration processes, and all men could be fined for procedural and record-keeping errors.

As the articles in eyre continued to expand, the king's personnel came under still closer scrutiny due to the ability of everyday individuals to report on injustices, grievances, and oppressions committed by sheriffs and the like. Between 1246 and 1254, nineteen new articles of the eyre were introduced, many of which emphasized community accountability and enforcement of customary duties. The articles reflected heightened concerns over the forfeitures of outlaws and the failure of individuals to participate in the hue and cry and detain outlaws.[516] Several of the new articles also addressed concerns related to the abuses of authority by local officials.[517] Charges of extortion, unjust imprisonment, wrongful amercement, and the taking of bribes against royal officials were all found in the crown pleas of the eyre rolls from the 1250s and 1260s. The Shropshire eyre of 1256, for example, contains thirteen cases of wrongful imprison-

513 *Crown Pleas of the Wiltshire Eyre, 1249*, no. 557.

514 *Crown Pleas of the Wiltshire Eyre, 1249*, 55-56. Meekings speculates that these are the early signs of the division between petty and grand larceny.

515 For example, see Meekings' discussion on *Crown Pleas of the Wiltshire Eyre, 1249*, 77-78.

516 Cam, *Studies in the Hundred Rolls*, 22-24; Meekings, *Crown Pleas of the Wiltshire Eyre*, 39-55.

517 A. Harding, ed. *The Roll of the Shropshire Eyre of 1256* (London, UK: Selden Society, 1981), "Introduction," xviii-xix; Cam, *Studies in the Hundred Rolls*, 22-24; Meekings, *Crown Pleas of the Wiltshire Eyre*, 39-55.

ment and the taking of bribes for release.[518] The subjective yet increasingly common use of imprisonment was becoming defined through the abuses of those officials, the charges brought against them, and the punishments meted out for their offenses.

Overall, the crown's involvement in matters of the local courts continued to increase. Because county courts were the lone courts in which outlawry could be pronounced, they retained an independent, fundamental power in the exercise of justice in thirteenth century England. This power would be encroached upon further through the course of the thirteenth century and by mid-century, royal letters were issued directly to county courts ordering that offenders be placed in exigency.[519] Just as the eyre was used as an extension of the county, so too was the county an extension of royal prerogative and authority.

Outlawry, Abjuration, and Imprisonment leading up to the Baronial Reform: Narrative Accounts

Matthew Paris, the chief chronicler for the reign of Henry III, tells us that when appropriate, the King was able to exclude his enemies from England. For example, Richard Seward was banished by suit of the king for a short time in 1236.[520] In 1239, Simon de Montfort was allowed to leave England after Henry's efforts to arrest and imprison him failed.[521] In 1245, another enemy of the

---

518 Harding, "Introduction," xvii.

519 Morris, *The Early English County Court*, 159, from Close Roll 65, m. 3d.

520 Matthew Paris, *English history from the year 1235 to 1273*, (hereafter *Matthew Paris*), vols 1-3, trans. J. A. Giles (London, H. G. Bohn, 1852,), vol. 1: 30; Powicke, *King Henry III*, 141; David Crouch, "Siward, Sir Richard (*d.* 1248)", rev. *Oxford Dictionary of National Biography*, Oxford University Press, 2004 [http://www.oxforddnb.com/view/article/37971, accessed 21 May 2012]. Seward had been outlawed and pardoned with Hubert de Burgh in 1234 and would later be imprisoned by the king.

521 *Matthew Paris*, vol. 1: 195-196; J.R. Maddicott, *Simon de Montfort* (Cambridge, UK: Cambridge UP, 1994), 25-30. The king accused de Montfort of seducing his married sister Eleanor, but after the intervention of Richard, earl of Cornwall, de Montfort and the king's sister Eleanor were forced or encouraged to leave England rather than face arrest. Montfort, who had earlier taken the Cross and pledged to go on Crusade, returned to England for a brief time during April 1241 in order to raise money for his journey. At this time, Montfort and the King reconciled. This demonstrates an instance of exile that echoed the Norman practice of exclusion as a period in which tempers were meant to cool.

king, Geoffrey Marisco, died while in exile. Geoffrey had been imprisoned after siding with Richard Marshall against the king in the war in Ireland in 1234, and in 1235, Geoffrey took sanctuary after being implicated in the death of Henry Clement. Henry Clement allegedly killed Richard Marshal, son of the former regent of the king and the first Earl of Pembroke, William Marshal. Geoffrey had spent time in gaol in 1234 for suspected betrayal, and sought refuge at a hospital following the death of the King's messenger Henry Clement in 1235. Geoffrey's son William, was believed to have been the chief assassin in the death of Henry Clement and was outlawed with his associates for the death. In all likelihood, Geoffrey was not a participant in Clement's murder and fled for protection due to the wrath that his son endured. Geoffrey was restored to royal favor in 1235, but lost all of his lands and was driven out of England after he was suspected of being involved in an assassination attempt on the King in 1238. [522]

Seward and de Montfort were driven into exile and not formerly outlawed, however, as the charges brought against them had not undergone the necessary inquest and full exaction process. Clearly, royal influence and intimidation still had a place in removing undesirables from England. Marisco, on the other hand, was legally outlawed for "the death of a man" at some point between 1238 and 1244. Geoffrey fled to Scotland but was driven out in 1244 and died the following year in France. [523]

Information from Matthew Paris is not limited to the exploits of the King and his enemies. The harsh treatment of an adulterer and his murderers in 1248 reminds us of the strength of personal action in thirteenth century disputes:

> The following circumstance I think ought not to be passed over, although it may appear ridiculous…for a certain knight of Norfolk, named Godfrey de Millers…secretly entered the lodgings of John the Briton, a knight, for the purpose of lying with his daughter, but was seized by some persons concealed, with the connivance of the harlot herself, who was afraid of being thought a married man's mistress, violently thrown to the ground, and severely beaten and wounded. After this he was suspended to a beam, with his legs stretched apart, and, when thus exposed to the will of his enemies, he was disgracefully mutilated to such a degree that he would have preferred decapitation, and, thus wounded and mutilated, was ejected, half-dead, from the house. A complaint of this proceeding having reached the king, the

---

522 *Matthew Paris*, vol. 2: 58; Powicke, *King Henry III*, Appendix B, 742-759. For his crimes, William Marisco was captured by William Bardolf in 1242 and executed after supposedly being betrayed by one of his own men. For more on William Marisco and the assassination attempt in 1238, see *Matthew Paris*, vol. 1: 138-139, 406-409; Powicke, *King Henry III*, 751-759.

523 *Matthew Paris*, vol. 2: 58; Powicke, *King Henry III*, Appendix B, 742-759; Powicke, *King Henry III*, 758-759.

> authors of this great cruelty were seized, and John the Briton being found guilty of it, he was disinherited and banished for ever....all who were present at the perpetration of this deed of enormous cruelty, were dispersed in exile, homeless fugitives and thus this inhuman and merciless crime involved many nobles in a lamentable calamity.[524]

The men who killed Godfrey were outlawed accordingly. Due to the violent nature of whole affair, the King intervened:

> However, the king, touched with compassion and deeply grieved, ordered it to be proclaimed as a law by herald, that no one should presume to mutilate another for adultery except in the case of his wife.[525]

Hoping to limit the feuding behaviors of a woman's kindred, any action taken against an adulterer was to solely lie in the hands of the cuckold husband. Private vengeance and independent action included violence, which the king could not eliminate but hoped to contain. The king did this by engaging legal custom and encouraging the banishment and outlawry of the criminal offenders while simultaneously dictating changes in law.

Matthew Paris also describes an elaborate highway robbery in Hampshire in 1249. He claims that thirty individuals were hanged as a result of the robbery and thirty more were imprisoned. According to Paris, the king intervened directly in the matter to order the imprisonment of the whole jury presenting the matter when they refused to name the thieves. Matthew Paris also mentions this robbery in *Historia Anglorum* and inflates his numbers even more, claiming that 100 offenders were hanged.[526] In 1249, the entire city of Winchester was essentially imprisoned when King Henry III ordered that the city gates be locked and its inhabitants renounce the criminals within their midst.[527]

Comparison of the plea roll of the Hampshire eyre and Matthew Paris's account reveals inaccuracies contained in both. Eyre records are much more explicit in detailing how imprisonment, outlawry, and abjuration cooperated in the aftermath of the robbery. Matthew Paris, on the other hand, focuses much more on imprisonment and execution as instruments of law and order. According to

---

524 *Matthew Paris*, vol. 2: 277-278.

525 *Matthew Paris*, vol. 2: 277-278.

526 Matthew Paris, *Chronica Majora*, vol. 5: 56-60; M.T. Clanchy, "Highway Robbery and Trial by Battle in the Hampshire Eyre of 1249," in *Medieval Legal Records: edited in memory of C.A.F. Meekings*, eds. R.F. Hunnisett and J.B. Post (London, UK: Her Majesty's Stationery Office: 1978), 26-63. Clanchy compares Matthew Paris's narrative account with KB 26/223 and JUST 1/776.

527 *Matthew Paris*, vol. 2: 294-298.

the plea rolls, of the sixty-four people accused in conjunction with the Hampshire robbery, thirteen were outlawed, and two escaped custody, took sanctuary and later abjured the realm. Twelve men were held in custody on lesser offenses, while two principal robbers were placed in custody at the Tower of London in late 1248 and later appeared before the king's justices at Reading.[528] William Pope was accused of harboring outlaws from the robbery in Hampshire, and was said to be guilty by the jury. No sentence was recorded, but the Close rolls indicate that he abjured the realm in 1294.[529] This may mean that he had turned approver and was finally allowed to abjure after almost fifty years. Two jurors were placed in gaol after complaint by their fellow jurors for not speaking the truth concerning the robbery. Both later paid a fine and were released.[530]

The King had an obvious role in how justice was meted out following the highway robbery of 1249. It was, after all, the king's messengers that were robbed. The exercise of royal justice in Matthew Paris's accounts about legal matters in England is insightful into what methods were being implemented by the King. The connection between royal interest and imprisonment speaks volumes about how the latter was used as an instrument of royal authority and law. Imprisonment was used in response to administrative abuse and breach of duty, while outlawry was encouraged in response to felonious offenses. This case illustrates how imprisonment and outlawry were working alongside one another as well as how the Crown could engage each to meet its ends.

Similar insight can be gleaned from the royal use of imprisonment with respect to forest law. During the 1230s, English barons attempted to obtain the right to imprison violators of forest law, but had been unsuccessful. The King maintained complete jurisdiction and could imprison for forest offenses, and the barons could not infringe upon this right. In 1236, when Richard Seward ordered his woods to be cut down and sold in order to raise money to go on Crusade, the King became angry and ordered that Richard be imprisoned.[531] Ten years later, there was a compromise and barons gained the power to imprison poachers for a

---

528 Clanchy, "Hampshire Highway Robbery," 36-37.

529 KB 26/223, m. 1 in Clanchy, "Hampshire Highway Robbery," 51, see also 35.

530 London, The National Archives, JUST 1/779, m. 27, in Clanchy, "Hampshire Highway Robbery," 54; In his version of the Hampshire robbery, Matthew supplements his words with illustrations of pillories, prisons, and gallows. *The Illustrated Chronicles of Matthew Paris: Observations of Thirteenth Century Life*, trans. and ed. R. Vaughn (Stroud, Gloucestershire, UK: Alan Sutton Publishing, 1993), 28, 92-97.

531 *Matthew Paris*, vol. 1: 34. This is the same Richard Seward who was outlawed in 1234 and exiled to Scotland in 1236. This imprisonment was the result of having been turned over to the king by Simon de Montfort and Peter de Rivaulx, but Seward was soon released.

year and a day. After this period of time, prisoners could be freed upon payment of a large fine and giving surety. The Crown received either one-third or one-half of the fines, depending on the circumstances of the poacher's capture.[532] The barons gained some control of their own lands and forest offenses therein, but not without continued oversight by the King.

Imprisonment was a discretionary tool of justice and order. Officials often ransomed individuals for release from prison or extorted funds from wrongdoers so that they avoid prison. In 1250, the King required a forger by the name of Aaron to pay the crown a large sum to remain out of prison.[533] It was possible to avoid imprisonment all together by throwing oneself upon the mercy of the king and paying a large fine to the crown. Walter de Clifford was guilty of mistreating a king's messenger in 1250, but rather than face imprisonment and stand trial, he forfeited all of his liberties and possessions to the king.[534]

Officials used imprisonment as a demonstration of power and as a means to their own ends. Bailiff Geoffrey Langley was reportedly guilty of imprisoning his enemies or any noble who spoke in opposition to him.[535] In 1256, the sheriff of Nottingham imprisoned a herdsman, a man whom he had hated for a number of years and tortured him near to death. He spared the herdsman's life only after he agreed to denounce his master as a thief at the next eyre.[536] The sheriff of Northampton was also convicted of misdeeds and injustice by Justiciar Hugh Bigod in 1258 and confined to prison, narrowly escaping with his life.[537] At times, imprisonment was harsh and led to the death of the prisoner. When Robert Chandros was captured in 1251 for arson, rape and murder, he was weighed down in fetters and died a brutal death in prison.[538] These actions came to be viewed as abuses of power and factored into the grievances brought by the Barons during the middle of the thirteenth century.

---

532 Pugh, *Imprisonment in Medieval England*, 21; Turner *Select Pleas of the Forest*, cxix-cxxii. The Statute giving the Barons such power has not survived, but Matthew Paris quotes it in his *Chronica Majora*, vol. 6: 117.

533 *Matthew Paris*, vol. 2: 357-358.

534 *Matthew Paris*, vol. 2: 324-325. Matthew Paris says that Walter de Clifford, a Welsh baron, violently mistreated the king's messenger, making him eat the royal letters and seal that he was supposed to deliver.

535 *Matthew Paris*, vol. 2: 358.

536 *Matthew Paris*, vol. 3: 187-191. Charges were subsequently brought against the sheriff for inappropriate, greedy, and malicious behavior after the justices learned of his unjust deeds. His live was only spared after his wife pleaded to the king and queen of Scotland to intercede on the sheriff's behalf with the king of England.

537 *Matthew Paris*, vol. 3: 303.

538 Matthew Paris, *Chronica Majora*, vol 5: 234.

The Baronial Reforms and the Administration of Justice

The Baronial Reform movement of the mid-thirteenth century grew out of long-standing tensions between the King and his barons. Chief among the complaints of the barons was the abuse of power by royal officials, especially sheriffs. In 1258, when the barons sent their grievances to Henry III, they demanded that unjust imprisonments and amercements by sheriffs come to an end.[539] The Provisions of Oxford of 1258 called for limits to be placed upon who could hold the office of sheriff and for how long. The position of sheriff was limited to loyal and good landholders could hold office and for no more than one year. The Provisions also demanded increased accountability of sheriffs to the Exchequer, reinstated the office of Justiciar, established an elected council of fifteen men to advise the king on matters of government, and ordained that three parliaments per year be held to conduct the common business of the kingdom.[540] The Provisions called for an inquest through all counties in England "by four knights in each county into all excesses, trespasses, and acts of injustices." [541] An ordinance of the sheriffs was circulated in the counties in October 1258 detailing the responsibilities and limitations of the office, and a special eyre was commissioned to tour the country to hear grievances against unjust and corrupt officials. They responsibility of the eyre was given to the new Justiciar, Hugh Bigod, and began in late 1258. [542]

---

539 R.E. Treharne, *Documents of the Baronial Movement of Reform and Rebellion, 1258-1267 (DBM)* (Oxford, UK: Clarendon Press, 1973), 76-89. 90-95; *Matthew Paris*, vol. 3: 310-311; 321-322.

540 *DBM*, 96-113 at c. 17; See also *Select Charters*, ed. Stubbs, 378-400; Powicke, *King Henry III and the Lord Edward*, 395-398; Clanchy, *England and its Rulers*, 195-198.

541 *DBM*, 112-115; 118-123; *Matthew Paris*, vol. 3: 301; 306; *Royal and other historical letters illustrative of the reign of Henry III*, vol. 2, letter DxIX, 130-131; R. F. Treharne, *The Baronial Plan of Reform, 1258-1263* (Manchester, UK: Manchester UP, 1971), 108-110, 119-122; David Carpenter, "What Happened in 1258" in *The Reign of Henry III*, 183-197.

542 *DBM*, 112-115; 118-123; *Matthew Paris*, vol. 3: 301; 306; *Royal and other historical letters illustrative of the reign of Henry III*, vol. 2, letter DxIX, 130-131; Treharne, *Baronial Plan of Reform*, 108-110, 119-122; D. Carpenter, "What Happened in 1258" in *The Reign of Henry III*, 183-197. The Provisions of Oxford prompted the commission of a series of special eyres to hear grievances throughout England. These special eyres were conducted in three phases between 1258 and 1270. See E.F. Jacob, *Oxford Studies in Social and Legal History, Vol. VIII Studies in the Period of Baronial Reform and Rebellion*, ed. P. Vinogradoff. (Oxford, UK: Clarendon Press, 1925), 71, 96-120. The use of special eyres was conducted in three phases. The first phase was in response to the

As the successors of the Provisions of Oxford, the Provisions of Westminster issued in 1259 further emphasized legal and administrative procedure, accountability of local officials, a stronger central authority, and a more efficient system of justice throughout England. Specifics of procedure and responsibility were more clearly defined. The mechanisms of justice put into place used local government as it functioned in the shires to "cut away…all the obstacles to sound administration which the barriers between the royal demesne and the franchises had created."[543] Government responsibility was to be shared: the exchequer and men of the county cooperated in the selection of sheriffs; officials were reported upon and held accountable by the justiciar; itinerant justices were given the 'same power as sheriffs" when on eyre; and the justice of the forest was to be assisted by three knights from each county in his inquiries.[544]

The early reform movement also sought to drive foreign landholders out of England, most importantly the powerful Poitevins. In 1258, Guy de Rochfort, a Poitevin who held the castle at Colchester, was exiled from England due to his oppression and injurious treatment of his subjects. According to Matthew Paris, his status as a foreigner had as much to do with his banishment as his misdeeds.[545] This is indicative of the grievance held by the barons in the mid-thirteenth century: that there were too many powerful foreigners in positions of power within England.

Men such as the King's half-brothers William de Valence and Aymer de Lusignan personified the abuse, excess, and injustice the Barons sought to correct.[546] The barons alleged that the Poitevins encouraged Henry III to break the oath he had taken to abide by the Provisions of Westminster in 1259 and submit-

---

Provisions of Oxford in 1258 and 1259. The second phase, from 1259-62, were conducted by royal justices and were guided by the Provisions of Westminster. The final phase dealt with matters heard as a result of the Dictum of Kenilworth from 1266. The cases and punishments found during each phase of the special eyre reflect changes in law and society in England and the measures taken by the Crown to assert its authority while meeting the needs of these changes.

543 "The Provisions of the Barons, 1259," *Select Charters*, 400-405; Powicke, *King Henry III and the Lord Edward*, 404; Powicke, *Thirteenth Century*, 129-154; P. Brand, *Kings, Barons, and Justices: The Making and Enforcement of Legislation in Thirteenth-century England* (Cambridge, UK: Cambridge UP, 2003), 15-106.

544 "The Provisions of the Barons, 1259," *Select Charters*, 400-405; Treharne, *Baronial Plan of Reform*, 169-191, 204-212.

545 *Matthew Paris*, 3: 314; Treharne, *Baronial Plan of Reform*, 125.

546 *DBM*, "The Provisions of Oxford," 97-113. The Provisions of Oxford were distributed throughout the realm and read in all of the shires in October 1258. They were replaced by the Provisions of Westminster in 1259, which were denounced by Henry III in 1261.

ted a list of offenses, abuses, and crimes committed by these men to the Papacy in order to strengthen their cause. As a result, the king's half-brothers returned to Poitou in late 1260, having been forced from England by baronial pressures. The Poitevin sheriff of Somerset and Dorset, Elias de Rabayn, was given the option of taking an oath of exile or remaining in prison. He chose to leave England, as did John of Valence, both of whom were exiled in 1260. [547] In fact, all of the Poitevins had the option of remaining in prison or being exiled. Although they all chose to leave England, most were able to return after swearing to abide by the Provisions of Westminster and the law of the land.[548] Physically controlling powerful men through exile or imprisonment was a means for the Barons to protect their own interests. The battle for authority of England during the period of the Baronial Reform movement often came down to control of confinement and exclusion as tools of political power.[549]

Special and General Eyres, 1259-1262

The special eyres of 1258-1259 and 1259-1262 were commissioned to address problems of local governance by collecting grievances against officials. These eyres represent "a return to earlier and less formal methods of pleading," as justices heard both formal complaints and *querela* related to administrative abus-

547 *Matthew Paris*, vol. 3: 332, 334-335, 337; Powicke, *Thirteenth Century England*, 138; 162; Powicke, *King Henry III*, 384-392; 415; Maddicott, *Simon de Montfort*, 127-128; Treharne, *Baronial Plan*, 125-126; H. Ridgeway, "King Henry III and the "Aliens", 1236-1272" *Thirteenth Century England*, vol. 2 (1987): 81-92. Aymer of Lusignan died in 1260, but the other three brothers returned to England in 1261. The removal of "aliens" at the insistence of the Barons had previously been an issue in 1233 and 1234 and had resulted in the temporary removal of Poitevins such as Peter des Rivaulx from England.

548 Ridgeway, "King Henry III and the "Aliens"," 91-92. Ridgeway suggests that these exiles, who were never dispossessed of their lands, were able to return out of landholder solidarity rather than as a result of the Poitevins submitting to any reform principles held by the barons.

549 Matthew Paris, vol. 3: 334; Treharne, *Baronial Plan of Reform*, 64-81, 119, 125-130; Powicke, *The Thirteenth Century*, 140; Hyams, *Rancor and Reconciliation*, 245 states that the language of the Provisions of Oxford is that of enmity discourse.

es.[550] The increased use of *querelae*, or informal, often oral, complaints, allowed individuals who were unable to afford a writ or make a formal appeal to take an action to court. *Querelae* were not inventions of mid-century law and governance but did become more common in the administration of justice during the second half of the thirteenth century.[551]

During the special eyre of 1258-1259, corrupt officials who had misused their power in local administration were brought before royal justices to answer charges against them. One-time bailiff Henry Garget unjustly took oats and hay worth two shillings from Roger de Redhill as well as extorted two shillings from Adam de Murehill. Garget was ordered to make payment on these offenses and was committed to gaol.[552] Similarly, a certain Henry was committed to gaol for distraining Walter for king's debt with undue force; former sheriff Walter de Bursted had to answer for the money he kept after he made men pay him for the escape of a thief; and Thomas Aubeney was amerced because, while sheriff, he imprisoned a certain Richard and his family, only releasing them after they had made payment of 40 shillings.[553]

In addition to the rolls of the eyres themselves, information contained within *Cronica Maiorum et Vicecomitum Londoniarum* reveals that Hugh Bigod and his special eyres of the late 1250s both amerced and imprisoned bailiffs convicted of offenses.[554] Coroners were also held accountable for errors and injustices,

---

550 Jacob, *Studies in the Period of Baronial Reform,* 36-70; 138; For *querela* and its relationship to bills in eyre, see Harding, "Plaints and Bills in the History of English Law, mainly in the period 1250-1350," in *Legal History Studies, 1972: Papers presented to the legal history conference, Aberystwyth, 18-21 July 1972* (Cardiff, Wales: University of Wales Press, 1975), 65-86.

551 A.H. Hershey, "Success or Failure? Hugh Bigod and Judicial Reform during the Baronial Movement, June 1258-February 1259" in *Thirteenth Century England: Proceedings of the Newcastle Upon Tyne Conference.* eds P.R. Coss and S.D. Lloyd, vol. 5. 1993): 65-85 at 77; A. H. Hershey, "Justice and Bureaucracy: The English Royal Writ and "1258"" *The English Historical Review,* vol. 113, no. 453 (Sept., 1998): 829-851; Jacobs, *Period of Baronial Reform,* 106ff; Harding, "Introduction," xvi-xvii, xxiv; F.W. Maitland: *Equity also, The forms of action at common law: two courses of lectures,* eds A.H. Chaytor and W.J. Whittaker (Cambridge: Cambridge UP, 1910), Lectures 3, 4, and 6.

552 *The 1258-9 Special Eyre of Surrey and Kent,* ed. A.H. Hershey. Surrey Record Society, vol. 38. (Bristol, UK: J.W. Arrowsmith Ltd., 2004), no. 79; no. 81.

553 *1258-1259 Special Eyre,* no. 335, no. 337, no. 363 and no. 364.

554 E. fitz Thedmar, *Cronica Maiorum et Vicecomitum Londoniarum,* ed. T. Stapleton. Camden Society no. 34. (London, UK: Published for the Camden Society, 1865), 39; Hershey, "Success or Failure?" 70; E.F. Jacob, *Studies in Period of Baronial Reform,* 71-125;Treharne, *Baronial Plan of Reform,* 144-156.

punished for omissions and inconsistencies in their records as well as for sending clerks to inquests rather than attending themselves.[555]

Extant documentation from the 1259-1262 special eyre reveals similar concerns with corruption and wrongdoing by local officials.[556] Charges of forcible ejection, unnecessary distraint, wrongful detention of cattle, unjust imprisonment, and extortion were commonly brought against royal and seigniorial officials alike. These offenses often resulted in amercement and imprisonment of the offenders.[557]

Special eyres contain decidedly more references to gaols, gaol committals, and imprisonments than in their general counterparts. The use of imprisonment is telling as to how governmental authority interacted with local justice. It also demonstrates how imprisonment in legal and social proceedings played a key role in the pursuit of judicial and administrative control. By finding a way to punish their own officials for abuses, the crown and the barons were, at least in principle, jointly prescribed the use of imprisonment upon and on the behalf of individuals in the shires. The mere increased use of imprisonment as a tool of justice brought it more to the forefront of society.

In contrast to general eyres of the same period, the special eyre of 1258-1259 contains only one instance of outlawry. A certain Roger le Warrener fled after being accused of imprisoning a man who later died. The eyre ordered that Roger be exacted and outlawed and that his chattels be confiscated by the crown following testimony by the jury that he could not be found in the county.[558] Here is a clear example of how the reform eyres used the procedures of the county courts to exact justice, namely the outlawry process, while simultaneously incorporating and imposing internal methods of constraint as appropriate.

General eyres functioned alongside special eyres during the 1250s and 1260s.[559] Records from the general eyres are again rife with outlawry, waivery,

---

555 See for example, *The 1256 Shropshire Roll*, no. 486, no. 506, and no. 652.

556 Jacob, *Period of Baronial Reform*, 71, 96-120.

557 *Royal and other historical letters illustrative of the reign of Henry III*, vol. 2, letter DXVII, 141, for example, is a letter close from Henry III to the Sheriff of Nottingham ordering justices to go around and redress grievances; Jacob, *Period of Baronial Reform*, 71-125, 137-143.

558 *1258-1259 Special Eyre*, no. 194.

559 Jacob supplies an incomplete list of the extant assize rolls from 1259-1262 in *Period of Baronial Reform*, 101-102. On pages 103-106, Jacobs goes on to distinguish between the county records from the eyre commissioned by the Provisions of Westminster, and those of the general eyre commissioned by Henry III in November 1260. The special eyres heard matters of the general eyre as well, but were especially concerned with *querelae* of transgressions by officials. See Treharne, *Baronial Plan of Reform*, 189-204.

and abjuration as tools of justice and order. As noted above, the Oxford eyre of 1241 recorded 85 instances of outlawry or continuation of the outlawry process. The Wiltshire eyre of 1249 ordered the exaction and outlawry of 206 men and the exaction and waivery of 9 women.[560] There were over 150 outlawries declared during the Norfolk eyre of 1250, 204 at the Yorkshire eyre of 1257, and 138 during the Surrey eyre of 1263.[561] The crown pleas from Shopshire in 1256 contained sixteen continuations to outlawry and twenty-three abjurations of felons and the eyre roll from the 1261 Cambridgeshire eyre contains 52 outlawries, three waiveries, and 32 abjurations.[562] Similarly, crown pleas from the 1262 eyre of Buckinghamshire record 29 instances of outlawry and 21 abjurations.[563]

Imprisonment in the general eyres remained a lesser-used custodial or coercive exercise, often associated with amercements. In many cases, imprisonment led to escape and subsequent outlawry or abjuration of the realm. When Walter was placed in gaol at Coventry in 1262 for possessing false money, he escaped, fled to a church, and abjured the realm.[564] In another case from the same Warwickshire eyre, it was alleged that bailiffs Ranulf and Walter placed Hugh in stocks and later in prison so that his feet rotted and fell off of his legs. Hugh later died, and the justices ordered that Walter be placed in gaol, as he had recently taken up a clerical habit. Ranulf, who had fled, was ordered to be exacted and outlawed.[565]

Gaol Commissions and Forest Eyres

Existing alongside special and general eyres were gaol delivery commissions and the forest eyre. The form and frequency of gaol delivery continued to vary

---

560 Meekings, *Wiltshire Crown Pleas*, 98. Meekings discusses exigent rolls, on which the names of those ordered to be exacted and outlawed were recorded. These rolls were probably always made with crown plea rolls, although they are only extant from 1285.

561 Harding, *The Shropshire Eyre of* 1256, xvi; *Oxfordshire Eyre, 1241*; For the Norfolk eyre, London, The National Archives, JUST 1/563, JUST 1/564, and JUST 1/565; *The 1263 Surrey Eyre*, ed. S. Steward. Surrey Record Society, vol. 40 (Bristol, UK: 4Word Ltd., 2006); For Yorkshire, London, The National Archives, JUST 1/1109.

562 London, The National Archives, JUST 1/82, m. 23ff; Jacob classifies JUST 1/82 as a "general eyre" roll, *Period of Baronial Reform and Rebellion*, 106.

563 London, The National Archives, JUST 1/61. The totals are by my own calculations.

564 "Extracts from the Crown Pleas of the Warwickshire Eyre held 5 June-20 July 1262," in *Early Records of Medieval Coventry*, no. 37.11.

565 "Extracts from the Crown Pleas of the Warwickshire Eyre held 5 June-20 July 1262," in *Early Records of Medieval Coventry*, no. 37.17.

under Henry III. By roughly 1280, some 125 gaols were being visited, although the personnel and number of commissioners could include anywhere from one to four local knights or royal justices. During Henry III's reign, commissions were more likely to be composed of non-professional judges than they had been under John. Gaols were delivered only by royal warrant and the commissions continued to cooperate with the eyre and other legal processes. [566]

Forest law remained relatively consistent during the reign of Henry III and the prerogatory nature of the law held true. Violation of the king's forest resulted in amercement and imprisonment and failure to appear before the justices of the forest could bring about exigency and outlawry. Forest offenders were detained in prison after conviction of a trespass against the king's vert or venison and could be held for up to a year and a day. In Northamptonshire in 1255, John was detained in prison after being accused of taking the king's fawn. Once it was determined that the fawn was already dead, that John had no "evil intent" and that he had been held in prison for more than a year, he was pardoned by the King for any amercement owed to the crown. At the same eyre, it was presented that Ralph took a beast from the king's forest, but afterwards fled. Exaction and outlawry were ordered. [567] In another instance, one man was held in prison for a year and a day due to his inability to make fine, after which time he abjured the realm. He was later pardoned by the king "because of his poverty, his imprisonment, and the debility of his body."[568]

The mechanisms of law and governance all functioned together in the administration of thirteenth century justice. They all used outlawry, imprisonment, and abjuration in order to maintain order. Special and general eyres, gaol commissions, and forest eyres brought together custom and innovation in the formation of English Common law. As a result, the heightened presence of the Crown in local matters and administration increased the prominence of confinement and imprisonment. It also used and altered the local system of social order based on exclusion.

---

566 Pugh, *Imprisonment in Medieval England*, 260-266, 276.

567 Turner, *Select Pleas of the Forest*, 29, 36. For more on the functioning of the forest system and its officials, see Young, *The Royal Forests of Medieval England*, 74-113, 135-141 Concerns over inquests and perambulations of the forest were among the grievances brought by the Barons during the Baronial Reforms of the 1250s and 1260s. After the barons were defeated at Evesham, the king maintained control over the forests and reaffirmed the Charter of the Forests in the Dictum of Kenilworth in 1266.

568 From the London National Archives Exchequer records, "Treasury of Receipt, Forest Proceedings," 2, m. 2, in Young, *The Royal Forests of Medieval England*, 103.

Trespass and Outlawry – bridging the gap between criminal and civil processes

In large part due to use of *querelae*, an increasing number of trespass complaints were brought against officials and fellow freeman alike. Trespass originated as a complaint of injury resembling an appeal, and although it was not a felony, it did fall under the authority of the king as a breach of his peace. Trespass came to incorporate injuries of one's person as well as property, making it a form of civil and criminal legal recourse. The action of trespass and its connection with a breach of peace, as well as the link it provides between criminal and civil complaints, is essential to the changes to outlawry and its connections to the growth of imprisonment.

Trespass was usually an action of minor significance. It was often not followed through or was settled out of court before the arrival of the justices in eyre. However, that trespass was becoming something of a "writable" offense within the county courts was an extension of royal power into local courts and processes. An action of trespass could, in theory, lead to exigency and outlawry. Writs are most commonly associated with civil pleas while appeals and the like were used in criminal cases. Trespass combined the legal tools of civil and criminal complaints as "a method, not for a long time a substantive concept: a method of remedying before the king a large variety of cases for which specific procedures had not yet been provided there…it illuminates wide social developments as much as technical and legal ones."[569] Bracton provides an example of such a "writ of trespass" from Devonshire as early as the Hillary and Easter term of 1220 and an instance from *Coram Rege* proceedings in Herefordshire in 1237.[570] By the 1250s, writs of trespass had developed to "a desirable…[and] common remedy for private wrongs," and, combined with the *querela*, these two actions gave plaintiffs two courses by which to pursue a complaint.[571]

---

569 Harding, "Introduction," liv; Hyams, *Rancor and Reconciliation*, 226-228. See also S.F.C. Milsom, "Trespass from Henry III to Edward III, Part I: General Writs," *Law Review Quarterly* vol. 74 (April 1958): 195-224; S.F.C. Milsom, "Trespass from Henry III to Edward III, Part II: Special Writs," *Law Review Quarterly* vol. 74 (July 1958): 407-436; S.F.C. Milsom, "Trespass from Henry III to Edward III, Part III: More Special Writs and Conclusions," *Law Review Quarterly* vol. 74 (October 1958): 561-590; Kaeuper, *War, Justice, and Public Order,* 157-160.

570 *Bracton's Notebook*, vol. 2: no. 85; vol. 3: no. 1232.

571 *Bracton's Notebook*, vol. 2: 76, note 1; Plucknett, *Concise History*, 366-373; Harding, "Introduction," xxxvii-lviii; Kerr, "Angevin Reform of Felony," 377-381.

Many of the complaints of trespass resulted in fine and imprisonment of the offender. The increased use of imprisonment in this context served to foster the growing prominence of imprisonment in law, justice, and politics in mid-thirteenth century English society. Trespass cases, as non-felonious, personal, and under royal pervue, blended civil recourse and remedy with criminal complaint and punishment. Default on damages, recovery of goods, and amercement would result in imprisonment through a writ of *capias*, as would a false complaint and failure to prosecute once proceedings had begun. Imprisonment in civil and criminal contexts could be united in matters of trespass, and in the growing number of trespass actions, imprisonment became much more common in the administration of the Common Law.[572]

Just as the concept of "criminal trespass" developed in mid-thirteenth century law, so too did "civil outlawry." These were the "minor outlawries" to which Bracton referred. During the early part of the thirteenth century, as we have seen, criminal outlawry was restricted to felony and treason. Outlawry, much like arrest, was soon used as one of the tools by which civil processes were changed during the second half of the thirteenth century.[573] Outlawry became part of the civil process, specifically in actions of trespass, replacing less efficient methods such as attachment and distraint. In the 1250s, new procedures used against contumacious defendants in personal actions of trespass brought together writs of *capias* and the exigency (*exigas*) process, resulting in "a modified form of outlawry." This "minor" or "civil" outlawry did not result in death, as the sanctions practiced within the *mesne* process could not result in penalties more serious than those brought about through conviction.[574]

The schema of the combined use of *capias* and *exigas* required the sheriff to return a writ of attachment stating that a defendant had no property. It was then ordered three times by writ of *capias* that the defendant be arrested. Following that, if the defendant had not been found nor had he surrendered to the court, he was placed in exigency and the process proceeded to outlawry. This made the *mesne* process against defendants with no property relatively efficient, while allowing the defendant ample opportunity to attempt to make peace with the crown, to find mainpernors, and to surrender himself to the charges brought

---

572 Harding, *The Roll of the Shropshire Eyre of 1256*, "Appendix of Cases Illustrating the History of Trespass," lxi-lxxiv traces changes in cases of trespass from the eyre of 1235 at Essex to the 1292 eyre in Hertfordshire.

573 N. Levy, "Mesne Process in Personal Actions at Common Law and the Power Doctrine" *The Yale Law Journal* vol. 78, no. 1 (Nov., 1968): 52-98 at 80-81.

574 D. W. Sutherland, "The Mesne Process upon Personal Action in the Early Common Law," *Law Quarterly Review* vol. 82 (October, 1966): 482-496 at 484.

against him and "reverse" the process.[575] Civil exigency and outlawry were now part of the judicial process as well as the possible end result of the process of personal action.[576] The use of outlawry in civil actions would be extended during the reign of Edward I and still further from the mid-fourteenth century on.[577]

Baronial and Royal Authority in England from 1261-1265

Throughout 1261, there was a decided decline in the efforts of the reforming council. Royal authority rose in complement to this phenomenon. Election of sheriffs promised in the Provisions of Oxford was not conducted and, instead, Henry appointed his own men to the positions.[578] The special eyre was suspended for a time by Henry III in 1260 and, in 1261, the king received papal absolution from having to abide by the promises he made in accordance with the Provisions of Oxford. In 1261, a general eyre was commissioned to conduct usual business of the crown, rather than to right injustices as its special counterpart had done, and powerful Poitevins, such as William de Valence, returned to England to reap generous rewards from the King.[579]

Power in England was shifting back to the King. Henry reacquired the right to appoint local administrative and judicial officials as well as to control the use of political exile and exclusion related to his kingdom. In 1260, magnates hostile to the king were prohibited from entering the city of London, as were soldiers bearing arms from the city. The king also declared that armed men attempting to enter England at the ports at Dover and the Cinque Ports without special license were to be arrested.[580] The leader of the Baronial Reform effort, Simon de Montfort, went into exile in France in 1261, and despite several short returns to Eng-

---

575 Sutherland, "Mesne Process," 489, 486.

576 Levy, "Mesne Process," 80-81; J.G. Bellamy, *Crime and Public Order in England in the Later Middle Ages* (London: Routledge & Kegal Paul, Ltd., 1073), 106.

577 Levy, "Mesne Process," 81-83, 85. Civil outlawry was abolished in 1879.

578 *DBM*, 190-193; 238-241; Powicke, *King Henry III and the Lord Edward*, 419-420; Treharne, *Baronial Plan of Reform*, 247-250, 262-265.

579 *Matthew Paris*, vol. 3: 333-334, 338; Treharne, *Baronial Plan of Reform*, 251-257; 274-275; Powicke, *The Thirteenth Century*, 160-169.

580 Treharne, *Baronial Plan of Reform*, 229-231; *DBM*, 192-195; J.R. Maddicott, *Simon De Montfort* (Cambridge, UK: Cambridge UP, 1994), 192-193.

land, he remained on the Continent until he was recalled to lead the baronial effort in 1263.[581]

By 1263, the King's power in England had weakened again. He was engaged in conflicts with the Welsh and there was so much renewed baronial discontent in England that a group of nobles met to reinstate their oath to uphold the Provisions of Oxford. They vowed to treat all individuals opposed to the Provisions as enemies and sent a written statement to the King demanding that he observe the Provisions as well. The King refused, which led to renewed rebellion and civil war.[582]

Barons in England took aim at those in England who abused authority and power and sought to right injustices throughout the kingdom. The "statute" against aliens was promulgated in 1263, and called for foreigners to be expelled from the kingdom. Although the 'statute" was condemned by arbitrator King Louis IX of France in 1264, it again placed the power to cast out political and legal undesirables from England into the hands of the barons.[583] Attempts at peace and settlement were made but soon the royalists were driven out of power in England. Prince Edward, Earl Richard of Cornwall (the king's brother), and King Henry III himself were imprisoned following the Battle of Lewes on May

---

581 Maddicott, *Simon De Montfort*, 197-198, 213-214, 219-225, 267; *DBM*, 194-210; Treharne, *Baronial Plan of Reform*, 233-242.

582 The failed arbitration by King Louis IX of France produced a document commonly known as the "Mise of Amiens" in which the French monarch declared victory for his English counterpart. Simon De Montfort was not present at the meeting at Amiens, as he had broken his leg after falling off of his horse on the way to board a ship to France. See Maddicott, *Simon De Montfort*, 259. See also *DBM*, 280-293; Treharne, *Baronial Plan of Reform*, 301; Powicke, *The Thirteenth Century*, 170-177; Brand, *Kings, Barons, Justices*, 140-184.

583 Carpenter, "King Henry III's "statute" against aliens," 927-931, 936; Maddicott, *Simon De Montfort*, 228-232. Carpenter argues that the so-called "statute against aliens" was in place in 1263 rather than in 1258, after having been constructed from clauses of the petitions of the barons and the *forma pacis* of 1263. This petition of the barons is found in the *Cronica Maiorum et Vicecomitum*, 54 and the *forma pacis* is contained in a letter from the bishops of Lincoln, London, and Coventry and Lichfield sent to Henry and Edward on behalf of the barons found in *Flores Historiarum* and the *Calendar of Patent Rolls, 1258-1266*. Carpenter includes them as an appendix to his article at 943-944. These documents were created in early 1263 after the king had nullified the Provisions of Oxford. The action in 1258 was directed at one group of aliens, the Lusignans, while the "statute" of 1263 was xenophobic and sought to rid England of all aliens, Lusignans, Savoyards, and foreign mercenaries alike. See also H.W. Ridgeway, "Foreign Favourites and Henry III's Problems of Patronage, 1247-1258," *The English Historical Review* vol. 104, no. 412 (Jul., 1989): 590-610.

14, 1264. This led to the rise of Earl Simon Montfort as the ruler of England for a period of fifteen months.[584]

As part of Montfort's negotiated victory at Lewes, he released many of the prisoners he had taken during the battle, namely the Marcher barons Roger Mortimer, James of Audley, and Roger of Leyburn.[585] The Marcher barons were obliged to leave England and go to Ireland for a year and a day as well as return for the next meeting of Parliament so that they may stand trial.[586] Simon De Montfort kept Prince Edward, Earl Richard, and King in his custody, a triumph for Montfort and a symbolic exercise of his authority. Unfortunately, the Marcher barons would play a heavy role in Montfort's defeat in 1265.[587] For the time being, the government of England under Simon de Montfort was to be based on the ideals that justice had triumphed over an oppressive monarch and the English had rightfully defeated harmful and disruptive foreigners. The *Song of Lewes*, a lengthy Latin poem written sometime between the Battle of Lewes and the Battle of Evesham, asserted that Montfort and his men intended to create a "community of the realm" to advise the king and speak for the people.[588] The Provisions of Oxford were restored in principle and the power of the crown was offset by the baronial council's authority over the kingdom and appointments.[589]

---

584 *Matthew Paris*, vol. 3: 338-351; Clanchy, *England and its Rulers*, 190; Maddicott, *Simon De Montfort*, 270-278, 280; D. Carpenter, *The Battles of Lewes & Evesham, 1264/65* (Staffordshire, UK: Mercia Publications Ltd., 1987), 34-51.

585 After the Battle of Lewes, peace was promised in the so-called Mise of Lewes, although no version of this document exists. See J.R. Maddicott, "The Mise of Lewes, 1264," *The English Historical Review*, vol. 98, no. 388 (July, 1983): 588-603; D. Carpenter, "Simon de Montfort and the Mise of Lewes," in *The Reign of Henry III*, 281-291; D. Carpenter, *Lewes & Evesham*, 35; Maddicott, *Simon De Montfort*, 270-278, 307; Simon Lloyd, "Audley, James (*d.* 1272)", *Oxford Dictionary of National Biography*, Oxford University Press, 2004 [http://www.oxforddnb.com/view/article/894, accessed 21 May 2012]; Kathryn Faulkner, "Leybourne (Leyburn) , Sir Roger of (*c.*1215–1271)", *Oxford Dictionary of National Biography*, Oxford University Press, 2004; online edn, Jan 2008 [http://www.oxforddnb.com/view/article/16624, accessed 21 May 2012].

586 Maddicott, *Simon De Montfort*, 307; A. Lewis, "Roger Leyburn and the Pacification of England, 1265-7," *English Historical Review*, vol. 54, no. 214 (Apr. 1939): 193-214. None of the men followed through on this promise and continued to fight in England on behalf of the King.

587 Carpenter, *Lewes & Evesham*, 35.

588 *The Song of Lewes: A Latin political song of the time of the Barons" war, 1264, justifying Simon de Montford and his cause, and setting forth the true theory of kingship,* ed. C.L. Kingsford (Oxford, UK: Clarendon Press, 1890); Clanchy, *England and its Rulers*, 202-203.

589 Maddicott, *Simon De Montfort*, 279-295; Maddicott, "The Mise of Lewes, 1264," 588-603; D. Carpenter, "Simon de Montfort and the Mise of Lewes," 281-291. Treharne in-

Montfort and the Barons were increasingly met with opposition to their authority. In an attempt to restore peace to the kingdom, King Henry and Prince Edward, now held together under house arrest at Hereford, ceded a limited amount of royal authority to consular supervision during the spring of 1265. [590] If either the king or the prince broke their respective oaths, they could lawfully be resisted and their supporters subjected to arrest and outlawry.[591] By May 1265, however, former exiles William of Valence and John of Warenne had returned to England to join forces with the Marcher barons who refused to leave England. Together, these men put into a motion a plan that led to Edward's escape from captivity.[592] Once free, the Prince reformed his army and defeated a force of Montfort's allies at Kenilworth. Soon after, he met Montfort's forces at Evesham on August 4, 1265. The Battle of Evesham was a complete victory for the English Prince. Earl Simon died at Evesham and following the battle, Henry III was restored to the crown.[593]

cludes "The form of peace accepted by the king and the community of the realm, 22-28 June 1264, c. 15 August 1264" in *DBM*, 294-301. See also Treharne, *DBM*, 46-55, 302-309. Attempts at peace in England were made and a Parliament was called, but the reforming government of Montfort faced challenges from within the kingdom and abroad. In France, King Louis IX refused to accept the Peace of Canterbury that had been signed by Montfort and Henry III in August 1264. This document that called for consular supervision of the King, reinforced the "Magna Carta", "the Charter of the Forests", "the Provisions of Oxford", and required observance of the statutes regarding grievances.

590 Maddicott, *Simon De Montfort*, 296-307; Carpenter, *Lewes & Evesham*, 37.

591 *DBM*, 309-315; Maddicott, *Simon De Montfort*, 320-321; Powicke, *King Henry and the Lord Edward*, 497-499.

592 *Royal and other historical letters illustrative of the reign of Henry III*, vol. 2: 282-284, letter DCXXXIV, dated 10 May 1265, is from King Henry III to the Sheriff of York that states that the exiles had arrived in England against royal will and that the ports should be watched more carefully; letter DCXXXCII, vol. 2: 188, from mid-June 1258 states that Prince Edward and William de Valance besieged Gloucester while the king and Simon de Montfort remained at Hereford; See also Robert of Gloucester's *Chronicle*, vol. 2: 756.

593 *Matthew Paris,* vol. 3: 353-356; See also Carpenter, *Lewes & Evesham*, 38ff; Maddicott, *Simon De Montfort*, 306-308, 333-345; Powicke, *The Thirteenth Century*, 178-206; Prestwich, *Edward I*, 40-53; Powicke, *King Henry III and the Lord Edward*, 497-502.

Post-Baronial Reform Governance and Order

In the aftermath of the Baronial Revolt, Henry sought to reassert his power and pacify England.[594] In 1266, Henry issued the Dictum of Kenilworth, in which he seized the right to banish any individual perceived to be a threat to his realm and reaffirmed his royal authority to remit banishments and outlawries. Individuals who had been banished during the 1250s and 1260s as a result of the rebellions were at the mercy of the king for any sort of forgiveness. The king also dictated that he and his lord legate would take action against anyone feared to be making war against the king through "banishments out of the kingdom for a time or otherwise." Anyone wishing to stand trial could submit to the king's judgment by January 13, 1267, and if such an offender was outside of the country, he was granted a "stay of proceedings for being overseas in accordance with the law and custom of the land" if he was willing to submit to the peace of the king.[595]

Most trials related to the period of rebellion were brought to the court of the King starting in 1265. These matters continued to be heard *coram rege* well into the reign of Edward I. The Curia Regis rolls from 1265 to 1268 "yield in great numbers two types of cases...pleas of trespass, where violence and robbery have been done to loyal subjects; and pleas initiated under special royal provision by loyalists for recovery of lands of which they had been deprived during the rising."[596] Corporeal punishments were relatively absent from the Dictum, as most of the cases heard resulted in fines and amercements. Edward would later cite the Dictum of Kenilworth in his instructions to the justices in eyre, reminding them that offenses committed under the guise of war were not to be punished with loss of life, limb, or by perpetual imprisonment.[597]

A special eyre was commissioned to hear land matters and "presentments of offences committed throughout the whole period of disturbance."[598] The articles

594 *Matthew Paris*, vol. 3: 358ff; Powicke, *King Henry and the Lord Edward*, 503-530; Brand, *Kings, Barons, Justices*, 185-204. Peace was officially proclaimed at Winchester on 16 September 1265.

595 *DBM*, "The Dictum of Kenilworth, 1266," 317-337; "The Dictum of Kenilworth," *Select Charters*, 419-425, provision no. 14, no. 20, no. 21; Powicke, *Thirteenth Century England*, 209-213; Powicke, *King Henry III*, 522-538, 555-556, see specifically note 2 on page 556; Hyams, *Rancor and Reconciliation*, 255; Pollock and Maitland, *History of English Law*, vol. 1: 179-180.

596 Treharne, *Period of Baronial Reform*, 159. A list of sessions of the where rebellion trials were heard has been compiled from Curia Regis rolls found on page 157.

597 Powicke, *The Thirteenth Century*, 209; Powicke, *King Henry III*, 522-526.

598 Treharne, *Period of Baronial Reform*, 162-163, 167-201. This is the third phase of the special eyres, mentioned above.

from this eyre contained interrogatories as to land possession and loyalty to the King, and required that juries present anyone who had committed a criminal act, as well as outlaws who had returned.[599] But, as noted, the majority of cases heard in the post-rebellion period involved land matters and invoked the Dictum of Kenilworth. As a result, many cases brought before the eyre were removed from local jurisdiction to the *coram rege* by way of writ of *certiorari*.[600]

The Statute of Marlborough, issued on November 18, 1267, emphasized the restoration of order in England. Revenge, retribution, and vigilante justice had run rampant following the rebellion, and it was ordered that any unlawful disseize of land by neighbor or lord was to be met with a heavy amercement and possible imprisonment. Release of a defendant held for redisseisin without authorization by the king and payment of a fine was punishable for county sheriffs and could result in further punishment of the defendant. The Statute of Marlborough reaffirmed the Magna Carta, and writs were to be freely issued for infringements upon it. This placed those offenses directly into the court of the king or under the prevue of the itinerant justices.

The exercise and rule of law was trusted to justices in eyre and sheriffs, as agents of the King and his council. Ultimately, the law that these officials were to enforce contained many of the provisions of the barons from 1258.[601] The extension of trespass and protection from unjust and forceful land and property actions were prominent in the Statute of Marlborough. As a result, by 1267, the crown had incorporated all offenses *contra pacem Regis* and those involving false judgment into its jurisdiction. Royal authority was now stronger than ever, while the lesser county courts were further weakened, save their exclusive control of the outlawry process.[602]

The events of the Baronial Reform call attention to the uses of outlawry and exile and their relations to imprisonment. Outlawry played a very small role in the operation of the special eyres in the late 1250s, while imprisonment was brought to a heightened awareness and prominence in the exercise of local jus-

---

599 Treharne, *Period of Baronial Reform*, 182-183.

600 Treharne, *Period of Baronial Reform*, 217; F.J. Goodnow, "The Writ of Certiorari," *Political Science Quarterly*, vol. 6, no. 3 (Sep., 1891): 493-536, see specifically 493-501 for the writ in England and its prerogatory history.

601 "The Statute of Marlborough, 52 Henry III, (18 November 1267)," *The statutes of the realm*, Volume 1, 1235-1377. Printed at the command of His Majesty King George III. [n.d.], 19-25; Brand, *Kings, Barons, Justices*, 188-204, 379-380; Powicke, *The Thirteenth Century*, 216-218; Powicke, *King Henry III*, 547-549.

602 "The Statute of Marlborough, 52 Henry III (18 November 1267)," c. 20; Brand, *Kings, Barons, Justices*, 192-192, see also Appendix III, pages 456-462; Plucknett, *Concise History*, 93.

tice. The general eyres, when commissioned, demonstrate how prominent outlawry and abjuration were in the shire courts and their prominent respective positions within the law. Eyre records from Dorset in 1268 contain a mixture of outlawry, abjuration and imprisonment. Simon fled to a church, confessed to robbery, and abjured the realm in the care of the coroner; Thomas was captured and imprisoned following an accusation or wrongdoing by John, only to escape and be placed in exigency; and Robert burgled the home of Randolph and fled, he was suspected and outlawed.[603] Abjuration and outlawry were common according to the Wiltshire eyre of the same year, with twelve abjurations and eleven outlawries recorded on just one sheet from that year's eyre records.[604] Individuals accused of felonies such as larceny and homicide fled, and whether their flight was to a church, a forest, a neighboring village, or to a destination unknown, those offenders were considered guilty, removed from the law and excluded from society. As had always been the case, abjurors were required to confess upon abjuration and those placed in exigency and outlawed were always 'suspected" of the crime of which they were accused and perceived to be guilty. The cattle of the abjurors and outlaws went to the Crown and the official who had allowed their escape was amerced. Numerous suspects evaded prison and fled to a church to abjure or were simply placed in exigency and outlawed upon flight.[605]

The crown had not gained control over the outlawry process but was reforming justice in a way that incorporated the increased use of imprisonment as circumstance and context dictated.[606] The use of exile against political enemies continued, although confinement played a key role in the Baronial movement and the government of the Barons under Simon De Montfort. The captivity of Edward and Henry Almain following the Battle of Lewes in 1264 was key in the negotiations for peace that followed. By limiting the King's physical and political movements through the method of house arrest, Montfort was able to exercise unlimited control over his political enemies. It was only when Edward was free after escaping confinement that the Royalists rallied, defeated De Montfort at Evesham, and recaptured the kingdom of England.

603 London, The National Archives, JUST 1/20, m. 2, m. 4, m. 6.
604 London, The National Archives, JUST 1/998a, m. 34.
605 London, The National Archives, JUST 1/998a, m. 24, m. 27, m. 33.
606 Hyams, *Rancor and Reconciliation*, 242-266.

Observations: Outlawry, Imprisonment, Violence and Justice during the reign of Henry III

The reign of Henry III saw the struggle for power in England between the Crown and Baronage extend from Runnymede and Magna Carta to the Battle of Lewes and the Statute of Marlborough. The events of the Baronial Reform resulted in a compromise over power which had been in the works since 1215. However, the struggle for authority in England was not over and unified methods of dealing with wrongdoers were not found. The Crown lost the ability to outlaw without legal cause, nor was it to use imprisonment unjustly. As matters of politics and law became distinguished, so too did mechanisms of social order and royal authority.

As a result of new limitations placed upon the use of outlawry, aspects of the outlawry process were interfered with and modified by the Crown. County courts maintained control of the outlaw process as a whole, but the methods of outlawry, such as writs and pardons, were in place such that the Crown could exercise influence if necessary and extend its will into a local court. The turbulence of the 1250s and 1260s left England open to the reform efforts of Henry's son, Edward I.

Chapter 7: Edwardian legislation, the end of the Eyre, and Outlawry at the end of the thirteenth century

Following the Baronial Reforms of the 1250s and 1260s, the inquests and legislation which occurred during the reign of Edward I were intended to reform legal and administrative processes, quell the abuses committed by royal personnel throughout England, and reestablish order throughout the realm.[607] By the suspension of the eyre in 1294, the Crown had refined local legal processes and had further solidified its control over the administration of justice. Outlawry, abjuration, and imprisonment played key roles in these changes and by the mid-1290s, the practices were adapted to function in the new legal setting.

Edwardian Reforms, Legislation, Outlawry and Imprisonment

The Edwardian reforms began with mass investigations into administrative and legal affairs in England. Upon Edward I's accession to the throne in 1272, the general eyre was suspended and a countrywide inquest into the hundreds was conducted. Royal officials carried out the inquest, the likes of which had not been undertaken in England since the Domesday Survey. Justices inquired into financial and judicial matters in the hundreds. Many of the articles of inquiry resembled the earlier articles in eyre, but now, far more specific and substantive chapters were added.[608] Much of the inquest focused upon the duties and deeds of royal officials, specifically sheriffs, and abuses related to their peace-keeping, judicial, and financial capacities. Concerns over the mistreatment of prisoners and injustice resulting from bribes, extortion, or excess resulted in heightened accountability of royal officials maintaining gaols. Sheriffs who had failed to capture and bring felons to justice or released guilty men were also brought un-

---

607 See generally, Powicke, *Thirteenth Century England*, Chapter 8, 322-380; M. Prestwich, *Edward I* (London, UK: Methuen London Ltd., 1988), 93-98; 233-237; 267-297; M. Prestwich, *The Three Edwards: War and State in England 1272-1377*, 2nd edn (London, UK and New York, NY: Routledge, 2003), 18-22.

608 Cam, *Studies in the Hundred Rolls*, 29-56.

der review.[609] Similarly, corruption by officials who mistreated, threatened, and coerced prisoners to turn approvers was investigated.[610]

When the general eyre was reinstated in 1278, it took on many of the same characteristics as the inquest and, by 1281, the articles in eyre included many of the topics that had been of central focus during the inquest of 1274-1275. The eyre inquired into franchise and administrative abuses, corruption and conspiracy, and trespasses concerning the crown.[611] As many as one hundred five articles were added to the eyre during the period between 1244 and 1278, greatly expanding the eyre as a tool of governance used to bring local matters under closer royal scrutiny. However, after 1278, only eight additions were made to the articles in eyre, a sign that the eyre was losing its efficacy and efficiency. The decline of the eyre in the last two decades of the thirteenth century is clear, as the articles leading up to the suspension of the eyre in 1294 remain consistent with those of 1278.

Thirteenth century reformers clarified the duties of the office of coroner, specifically with respect to criminal procedure and its relationship with the office of sheriff. The coroner, as we have seen, inquired into all deaths and homicides, heard abjurations, and recorded outlawries, as well as viewed injuries in appeals of rape, wounding, or other physical assaults. The *Officium Coronatoris* of 1275/6 listed the duties of the coroner and formally detailed how the coroner was to use imprisonment in the coronal processes. The coroner was required to place all homicide suspects in the custody of the sheriff who would place them in gaol until the coming of the justices.[612] From the perspective of the Crown, the role of the sheriff in the late thirteenth century remained fundamental to the local administration of justice and there was little change in his duties. Sheriffs held the sole records for civil pleas in the county, were in charge of arrests and writs, as well as supervised their staffs, the growing number of men who worked

609 Cam, *The Hundred and the Hundred Rolls*, 107-128 and Appendix I, most relevant to this discussion are nos 26-27; Cam, *Studies in the Hundred Rolls*, 152-188. Many of the new articles had been influenced by the Baronial Reforms and late-thirteenth century statutes.

610 Hamil, "King's Approvers," 250; Cam, *The Hundred and the Hundred Rolls*, 67-74; Morris, *The Medieval Sheriff*, 232-233, 281-282. Sheriffs and bailiffs would often keep approvers in prison for long periods of time in order that they make false appeals in order to extort money, and although the hundred rolls contain numerous complaints of this type of extortion, none of Edward's legislation addressed the problem.

611 Cam, *Studies in the Hundred Rolls*, 56-62.

612 *The Statutes of the Realm: Printed by Command of his Majesty King George the Third*, vol. 1, 1235-1377, "*Officium Coronatoris,*" 40-41; Cam, *The Hundreds and the Hundred Rolls*, 128-132. The coroner was also responsible for inquiring into treasure finds and home invasions.

below the sheriff in the county. Some sheriffs had undersheriffs, who presided over county and hundred the courts and at times knew more about the law then their superiors. Sheriffs also employed bailiffs and clerks to assist with their judicial and financial duties, who in turn appointed sub-bailiffs and the like to round out the growing county bureaucracy.[613]

Further efforts to reform and clarify law, governance, and authority in England were contained in late thirteenth century legislation. Within the text of the first Statute of Westminster (1275), the treatment of outlawry illustrated the royal desire for legal uniformity in the way it was carried out:

> ...because it has been the practice in some counties to outlaw people appealed of command, force, aid and receipt during the period that one is in the process of outlawing him who his appealed of the deed, it is provided and granted by the king that no one is to be outlawed because of appeal of commandment, force, aid or receipt until the one appealed of the deed is convicted, so that there may be one uniform law for this throughout the land; but he who appeals shall not because of this omit to make his appeal of them in the next county as well as those appealed of the deed but the exigent shall wait in their case until those appealed of the deed have been attained by outlawry or otherwise.[614]

The Statute clarified procedures for dealing with accessories to outlaws, in whatever context they were at issue. Bracton had articulated the proper treatment of "principles" and "accessories" as participants in the outlaw process, but due to discrepancies and inconsistencies in practice throughout the realm, "proper" custom now found itself explicitly stated within Edwardian statutory law.[615] Furthermore...

> ...it is commanded by the king that prisoners previously outlawed, those who have abjured the land, approvers, and all who are taken with the mainour (stolen property), those who have broken the king's prison, common or notorious thieves, those appealed by approvers as long as the approver is alive (if they are not of good repute) those arrested for arson feloniously done or for counterfeiting money or forging the king's seal, persons excommunicate arrested at the request of the bishop, those arrested for manifest crime and those arrested for treason touching the king

613 Palmer, *County Courts*, 41-55; Cam, *The Hundreds and the Hundred Rolls*, 132ff.

614 "Statute of Westminster I, 3 Edward I (1275)," *The statutes of the realm*, Volume 1, 1235-1377. Printed at the command of His Majesty King George III. [n.d.], 26-39, c. 14.

615 Bracton, vol. 2: 360-362.

> himself are to be in no wise replevisable by the common-law writ or without writ....[616]

Former outlaws were grouped with traitors, thieves, and killers, reflecting the seriousness and importance of outlawry in law and society. Outlaws were a very real threat to social order and the king sought to control them by using the legal methods in place for other significant malefactors. Previously outlawed men could not be released on sureties or writ, nor could they take legal action to recover personal property. Bracton had already made clear to us that this was a matter of custom, but once again, practice found its place and clarity within statutory law and under royal authority.[617]

In addition to modifying the outlawry process, Edwardian legislation incorporated uses of imprisonment into aspects of criminal and civil law. In the passage quoted above from the first Statute of Westminster, irreplevisable or unbailable offenses were clarified. Certain prisoners were not bailable once in custody and were to remain in gaol until they appeared before the king or his justices.[618] By denying suspects bail, the Statute eliminated the possibility such an individual would flee after release upon surety or bail and flee the jurisdiction. Imprisonment was used to prevent flight from legal process. In fact, because later thirteenth century society was "more fluid and as the frankpledge system decayed...in certain circumstances, imprisonment on suspicion became the rule."[619] Furthermore, the Statute punished any undersheriff, constable or bailiff who released a prisoner without the consent of his lord to three years imprisonment and a fine.[620] Criminals and wrongdoers were imprisoned and the officials who confined them were subject to similar penalties if they failed to fulfill their duties.

Imprisonment for specific offences and for particular lengths of time is found throughout the statutes of the 1270s and 1280s. According to the first Statute of Westminster, violators of royal statutes were to be placed in the king's

---

616 "Statute of Westminster I, 3 Edward I (1275)," c. 15; *Fleta*, vols 1-3, ed. H.G. Richardson and G.O. Sayles, (London, UK: Bernard Quaritch for the Selden Society, 1955), vol. 2: Book 1, 7.

617 Bracton, vol. 2: 362-363; Hurnard, *King's Pardon*, 173-174.

618 "Statute of Westminster I, 3 Edward I (1275)," c. 15.

619 Bellamy, *Crime and Public Order*, 162; Morris, *The Frankpledge System*, 151-166.

620 "Statute of Westminster I, 3 Edward I (1275)," c. 15; Pugh, *Imprisonment in Medieval England*, 28. The Oxford English Dictionary provides an appropriate definition for "replevisable" as "that which may be replevied" and "replevy" in this context as "the bailing of, or bail for, a person."

prison in order that they pay a fine determined by the courts and the crown.[621] Judicial personnel and common freemen alike were subject to imprisonment for failure to maintain peace and for neglecting to take part in the arrest and pursuit of felons.

> If the default is in the bailiff he shall have one year's imprisonment and then be heavily fined, and if has not the means he is to have two years" imprisonment. And if a sheriff or other bailiff, within liberties or without, for reward or on request or because of any sort of relationship, conceal or consent to or procure concealment of felonies committed in their bailiwicks, or pretend to arrest or to attach wrongdoers when in reality they could, or otherwise pretend to perform their office as any sort of favour to the wrongdoers, and are convicted of it, they shall have one year's imprisonment and be heavily fined, and if they have no means they shall have four years imprisonment.[622]

Similarly, a bailiff who excessively tolled a plaintiff without orders from his lord was to be imprisoned for forty days.[623]

Conditions of custody came under closer scrutiny and types of imprisonment changed. Felons who were of ill repute and failed to plead to undergo an inquest were subject to "a prison strong and hard," the *prison forte et dure*.[624] Any man who forced himself upon any woman against her will was to spend two years in prison, followed by payment of a fine or a longer term of imprisonment if he did not have means to pay. Those convicted of doing wrong in a forest of the king were to be imprisoned for three years if they could not make fine; debtors to the king were subject to imprisonment at the king's pleasure; individuals who took more from the king's coffers than needed for completing a royal task were to repay the king threefold and spend forty days in the king's prison.[625] Anyone who spoke mistruths about the king was to be kept in prison for an undetermined length of time, and any party who sought to deceive the king's court in any way was to spend at least a year and a day in prison.[626] A disseisor determined to be at fault by an assize of novel disseisin had to spend some time in prison prior to making fine for the offense. Even if the disseisin

---

621 "Statute of Westminster I, 3 Edward I (1275)," c. 1; Prestwich, *Edward I*, 279-280.

622 "Statute of Westminster I, 3 Edward I (1275)," c. 9; Pugh, *Imprisonment in Medieval England*, 34.

623 "Statute of Westminster I, 3 Edward I (1275)," c. 31.

624 "Statute of Westminster I, 3 Edward I (1275)," c. 12; Pugh, *Imprisonment in Medieval England*, 25; A. Babbington, A. *The Power to Silence: A History of Punishment in Britain*. (London, UK: Robert Maxwell Publishing, 1968), 8.

625 "Statute of Westminster I 3 Edward I (1275)," c. 13, c. 20, c. 32, c. 34; T.F.T. Plucknett, *Edward I and Criminal Law* (Cambridge, UK: Cambridge UP, 1960), 90-92.

626 "Statute of Westminster I 3 Edward I (1275)," c. 34, c. 29.

took place absent any robbery, any such action done by "force and arms," offenses against the king, was to be punished with imprisonment and amercement.[627]

The increased use of imprisonment in the first Statute of Westminster, particularly for a fixed period of time, represented a break from earlier criminal law and legislation. Imprisonment was most often used to exact financial payment or as a temporary custodial tool, but by the reign of Edward I, it had taken on more punitive characteristics. Terms of imprisonment for forest offenses had increased from one year under Henry II, John, and Henry III to as many as three years under Edward I. Similarly, when one of the King's officials or an individual in service of the king violated or failed to fulfill his duty, he was subjected to a specific period of imprisonment. Here, the Crown exercised its authority over matters directly within its prevue by articulating tangible, exact, and punitive terms of imprisonment.

Similarly, the Statute of Gloucester (1278) lengthened the time in gaol spent by suspected killers. No writ of inquiry, and therefore bail, was to be granted in cases where one man killed another by misadventure, in self-defense, or by felony. All such cases were to be brought to the attention of the justices in eyre. Suspects in gaol were to place themselves upon the country and the processes of justice were to proceed. If he proved himself to be innocent, he was restored to the king's peace.[628] If he was unable to prove his innocence, he was presumably hanged.

Imprisonment at the discretion of the king or until a criminal could make fine were the oldest forms of imprisonment in England. Imprisonment had often been reserved for offenses or political misdeeds that specifically touched the crown. Once an offender was released, he was very likely required to leave the kingdom within a specified period of time. The same was true if a prisoner was an individual of ill-repute, as he was required to abjure the realm upon release. This type of abjuration was included in the Assizes of Clarendon and Northampton and continued throughout the thirteenth century according to Bracton. In this context, abjuration was at once the end result of imprisonment and a mitigated form of outlawry. Abjuration as outlawry of sorts was essentially pro-

---

627 "Statute of Westminster I, 3 Edward I (1275)," c. 37; Pugh, *Imprisonment in Medieval England*, 32-33.

628 "Statute of Gloucester, 6 Edward I (7 August 1278)," *The statutes of the realm*, Volume 1, 1235-1377. Printed at the command of His Majesty King George III. [n.d.], 45-50, c. 9; Pollock and Maitland, *History of English Law*, vol. 2: 480-481, 588-589 Commentators such as Sir Edward Coke contented that the writ in question in the Statute of Gloucester was the writ of *odio et atia* but Pollock and Maitland dismiss this claim. See their discussion in note 2, 589.

nounced by the Crown and had a long tradition and gave royal officials the authority to rid the kingdom of malefactors, nuisances, and threats to the king's peace. The practice was endorsed and strengthened by the increased use of imprisonment. More prisons meant more abjurations following release. Similarly, by evoking the familiarity and usefulness of abjuration and outlawry in association with imprisonment, the latter increasingly became a part of the common law.

The familiarity and usefulness of outlawry and abjuration as related to imprisonment is nowhere more apparent than in the practice of *prison forte et dure*, "prison strong and hard." *Prison forte et dure* was used to compel defendants who refused to plead in matters of felony against them. The earliest articulation of *prison forte et dure* is found in *Placita corone* from the mid-1270s. The later *peine forte et dure*, a deviant form of the *prison forte et dure*, is first found in documentation from about 1290. The authors of *Britton* and *Fleta*, as well as chronicler Bartholomew Cotton, comment on the treatment of prisoners imprisoned strong and hard although the specifics of the treatment of prisoners do not always agree. *Prison forte et dure* generally included deprivation of food and water, heavy irons, and very little clothing. Prisoners were only allowed water (usually stagnant) on days they did not eat, and food (stale bread) on days that they did not drink. In addition, prisoners often had only one linen garment and were placed into heavy fetters, "on bare ground...loaded with irons from the hands to the elbows, and from the knees to the feet."[629] According to plea rolls from 1292 forward, a silent defendant was met with strong and hard imprisonment more often, presumably due to a reissue of the first Statute of Westminster.

629 *Britton*. Containing the ancient pleas of the crown, translated; and illustrated with references, notes, and ancient records by Robert Kelham. (London, UK: 1762), vol. 1: 26-27; *Fleta*, vol. 2: 85; "Bartholomaei de Cotton, monachi norwicensis," *Historia anglicana* (A.D. 449-1298), necnon ejusdem Liber de archiepiscopis et episcopis Angliae / ed Henry Richards Luard, pub. by the authority of the Lords Commissioners of Her Majesty's Treasury, under the direction of the Master of the Rolls (London, UK: Longman, Green, Longman and Roberts, 1859), 227-28. The sources do not agree on the use of fetters and irons. See H.R.T. Summerson, "The Early Development of *Peine Forte et Dure*," *Law, Litigants, and the Legal Profession: Papers Presented to the Fourth British Legal History Conference at the University of Birmingham 10-13 July 1979*. eds E. W. Ives & A. H. Manchester. Royal Historical Society Studies in History Series, vol. 36. (London, UK: Humanities Press, 1983): 116-125 at 118-120; and Plucknett, *Concise History*, 118-119.

By remaining silent, a defendant who declined to plead "refused to stand to the Common Law of the Land."[630] He forfeited his property and chattels to the king and deprived himself of that…

> protection against ill-treatment that the law afforded to ordinary prisoners and was thereby reduced to a situation not far removed from that of an outlaw. The one was outside the law, the other refused it.[631]

The principles of outlawry are here applied to imprisonment in its harshest form. To be removed from the protection of the law was fundamental to the outlawry process, and by the late thirteenth century, that same removal had become a key component to prison strong and hard. During the second half of the thirteenth century, the increased use of prisons to hold criminals had led to concern over the treatment of prisoners. Holding recalcitrant defendants who would not plead was problematic. They could be considered guilty and hanged or be allowed to abjure the realm, but most often they were kept in custody until they cooperated with royal officials. By not pleading in court, silent offenders denied the common law, an act that, in the opinion of judicial authorities, absolved them of any responsibility for the well-being and safety of the prisoner until he surrendered himself back into law. From this, the *prison forte et dure*, a type of imprisonment that was so painful the prisoner had no other choice than to submit to legal process, found its way into law.[632] Prisoners lost all property and chattels, forfeited legal protections and were at the mercy of their gaolers, and either gave surrendered to law or died. Such attitudes echo those taken with respect to outlaws for centuries. Outlaws had no possessions, were no longer protected by any law, and could be killed with impunity if found. Prisoners and outlaws were now on legal and social equals.

The second Statute of Westminster, issued in 1285 stressed the maintenance of social order and addressed continued matters of local accountability, royal and manorial officials were brought under closer scrutiny. [633] Bailiffs, sergeants, and other servants of lords who were guilty of embezzlement or fraud were to be arrested and imprisoned. The debtor servant was to be "committed to prison in irons and in good custody and remain in that prison living at their own

---

630 "Statute of Westminster I, 3 Edward I (1275)," c. 12; Summerson, "*Peine Forte et Dure*," 121; C. Harding, et al. *Imprisonment in England and Wales: A Concise History* (London, UK: Croom Helm Ltd., 1985), 45; Pollock and Maitland, *History of English Law*, vol. 2: 651-652.

631 Summerson, "*Peine Forte et Dure*," 121.

632 Summerson, "*Peine Forte et Dure*," 122; Pugh, *Imprisonment in Medieval England*, 25-27; Pollock and Maitland, *History of English Law*, vol. 2: 651-652.

633 Prestwich, *The Three Edwards*, 20-21.

expense until they have rendered full satisfaction to their master for the arrears." If royal auditors were appointed to assess the account and the servant was found to owe money to his lord, he was placed in Fleet prison in the manner stated above by order of a writ of *capias*. If the individual fled when audited, he was to be exacted accordingly and outlawed. If an offender was captured, he was not allowed out of custody upon sureties.[634]

The threat of outlawry in matters of debt was perhaps just that, a threat intended to cause the debtor to appear in court, "an engine for compelling the contumacious to abide the judgment of the courts."[635] Even if outlawry was just a threat, up until this time, it had been a mostly criminal proceeding. Its inclusion in the second Statute of Westminster marked "the first extension of outlawry to a purely civil action."[636] Such an extension would not have proved necessary had outlawry been a weak and ineffective method of maintaining order as the likes of Maitland have argued. The continued manipulation and extension of outlawry at the hands of the Crown indicates its effectiveness rather than weakness as well as its engrained position in the exercise of the law. The Crown was using the existing practice to expand its power and control over law and order in England. This extension of outlawry continued, as *Fleta*, c. 1290, stated that exigency and outlawry were not available to matters of debt because there was no breach of peace, but by the mid-fourteenth century, civil outlawry would extend to actions of debt, detinue and replevin.[637]

The formulaic plan outlined in clause thirty-five of the second Westminster statute regarding lawful marriage echoes this manipulation of legal custom. The clause elaborated upon the earlier Statutes of Merton and Westminster with respect to regulations over an individual's right to restrict or withhold marriage of his heirs. Previously, violators of marriage and wardship customs had been sub-

634 "Statute of Westminster II, 13 Edward I (1285)," *The statutes of the realm*, Volume 1, 1235-1377. Printed at the command of His Majesty King George III. [n.d.], 71-95, c. 11; Prestwich, *Edward I*, 275.

635 Pollock and Maitland, *History of English Law*, vol. 2: 449.

636 T.F.T. Plucknett, *Legislation of Edward I* (Oxford, UK: Clarendon Press, 1949), 156, note 1.

637 Levy, "Mesne Process," 81-83, 85; Brand, *Kings, Barons, Justices*, 321. Statutory law made outlawry applicable in actions of account (1285, Westminster II), debt, detinue and replevin (1350), trespass on the case (1503), and convent, annuity and forcible entry (1531). During the late sixteenth century, there were 'secret" outlawries procured through proceedings remote from defendant's dwellings or without notice – this evoked a statute which laid out more procedures for civil outlawry, and brought in the use of bail. An act of 1692 allowed civil outlaws to appear by attorney and reverse outlawries without bail unless special bail was outlawed, and those already in custody could obtain freedom through special bail. Civil outlawry was abolished in 1879.

ject to amercement and imprisonment, and the inevitable prospect of outlawry may have been implied. Outlawry was now explicitly mentioned as the result should amercement and imprisonment fail to bring an offender to justice through a writ of trespass.[638] Seizure of a child to whom no right of marriage was held, even if that child was restored to his or her rightful position, was punishable by two years in prison. Failure to restore, marry the heir by a marriageable age, or recompense for the marriage resulted in perpetual imprisonment or abjuration of the realm. The Westminster clause articulated writs issued to complainants in such instances, and the statute ordered that if a ravisher failed to appear as a result of a complaint, he was to be exacted and outlawed for contumacy.[639] Outlawry was more than a mere threat; it was an actuality and a strong punitive outcome.

Additional matters contained in the second Statute of Westminster affected writ procedures, appeals of felony, and the eyre, as well as the role of the county court and its processes in the administration of justice. Writs, specifically writs of trespass, were to be granted only before justices of the king's court or eyre.[640] The Statute included still more references to imprisonment, with a sentence of one year prescribed for false accusations of felony and for a discretionary period of imprisonment as punishment for false imprisonment and for false testimony.[641] This now meant that individuals who had been falsely imprisoned by the sheriff could bring action against him following their release. Two years imprisonment was the punishment for hindering the collation of a bishop and refusing to pay damages, and abduction of a nun resulted in three years in prison, even if the nun consented to being taken from her house.[642] Bailiffs or any men who impeded or delayed the will of the crown were imprisoned at the discretion

---

638 "Statute of Westminster II, 13 Edward I (1285)," c. 35; Plucknett, *Legislation of Edward I*, 112-115. According to Plucknett, clause thirty-five is surprisingly thorough, as it "anticipates many of those contingencies which normally were left as puzzles for the courts to solve as they rose," taking into account what would happen if the heir, the plaintiff or the defendant were to die during the process.

639 "Statute of Westminster II, 13 Edward I (1285)," c. 35. For more on marriage and wardship, see Pollock and Maitland, *History of English Law*, vol. 2: 319-329.

640 "Statute of Westminster II, 13 Edward I (1285)," c. 29. There were two exceptions to this, as the king could grant a writ at the request of a litigant. The king could issue a writ of trespass as an act of special grace if it was "a heinous trespass where it is necessary to apply a speedy remedy." A writ *de odis et atia* was granted to litigants to prevent "appealed or indicted persons being kept in prison a long time…as stated in Magna Carta and other statutes."

641 "Statute of Westminster II, 13 Edward I (1285)," c. 12, c. 13; Pugh, *Imprisonment in Medieval England*, 198. The term of imprisonment was at the discretion of the justices.

642 "Statute of Westminster II, 13 Edward I (1285)," c. 5, c. 35; Prestwich, *Edward I*, 280.

of the king.[643] There is an inconsistent, hodge-podge feel to the offenses being addressed by imprisonment, a reflection of its flexibility, growing use, and relative ease of application by royal authority.

The second Statue of Westminster also detailed the specific assignments of justices of the bench and of the eyre, inquest procedures, enrollment practices, and writ delivery, all of which clarified judicial action as it took place in the localities and incorporated more royal control into legal and administrative processes in order to expedite justice.[644] By reaffirming and redefining the authority of the Crown in the lower courts and stressing the superiority of the King, his courts, and his justices, the county courts were reminded of their status as agents of the king's law and the king's justice. The Crown used imprisonment to enforce this principle and simultaneously prescribed the use of imprisonment in a manner that kept its own officials in check. This was done in a way that incorporated existing exigency and outlawry practices in order to compel order and exercise its will.

The second Statue of Winchester expressed royal concern for crime and order in society and increased accountability of the counties with respect to crimes. The weakening of the frankpledge system throughout England was perhaps one reason behind the crown's increased concern for policing the localities, as the overall reluctance and decline of presentments by local juries to royal officials was addressed.[645] Penalty for the whole of a county, district, hundred, or neighborhood was established for failure to present any felony and bring offenders forward to royal justices. Public proclamation and pursuit of wrongdoers was re-emphasized, as was the watch-and-ward, capture of strangers, and arrest and imprisonment of malefactors.[646] This system would be entrusted to the *custos pacis*, or keeper of the peace, a position that had been an area of contention during the Baronial Reform movement of Henry III's reign.[647] In 1287, keepers

643 "Statute of Westminster II, 13 Edward I (1285)," c. 11, c. 39; Plucknett, *Legislation of Edward I*, 153-156.

644 "Statute of Westminster II, 13 Edward I (1285)," c. 30, 39.

645 H.R.T. Summerson, ""The enforcement of the Statute of Winchester, 1285-1327," *The Journal of Legal History*, vol. 13, no. 3 (1992): 232-250; Morris, *The Frankpledge System*, 151-155.

646 "Statute of Winchester II, 13 Edward I (1285)," c. 1-4; Summerson, "The enforcement of the Statute of Winchester," 232-234; Prestwich, *Edward I*, 280.

647 D.W. Sutherland, *The Eyre of Northamptonshire, 3-4 Edward III, AD 1329-1330*, vols 1-2 (London, UK: Selden Society, 1983), vol. 1: xxiv; A. Harding, "The Origins and Early History of the Keeper of the Peace," *Transactions of the Royal Historical Society*, 5th ser., vol. 10 (1960): 85-109, specifically 85-96 for the earliest manifestations of the Keepers, pages 102-109 for how Keepers gained judicial authority and their role in the later creation of the office of Justice of the Peace; A. Harding, "Early trailbaston pro-

were appointed to each county to police "the land and to arrest felons and trespassers and hold them for trial," tasks that would require their continued presence in the administration of law and order in England.[648] The Statute of Winchester was aimed at reconnecting local and royal governments, a connection that was damaged by the decline of the eyre, but ultimately the Crown failed to place the necessary supervision in the counties to ensure its success.[649]

The Statute of Merchants of 1283 was intended to facilitate the recovery of debts owed to creditors and instructed that a debtor was to be placed into prison if he had no other way of raising money or levying his possessions to repay his debt. Creditors were to maintain their debtors in prison if the malefactors were unable pay, but costs to maintain imprisonment were added to the amount of what the debtor previously owed.[650] Two years later, the Statute of Merchants echoed this action and elaborated upon the responsibilities of the debtors, creditors, and authoritative personnel. Debtors were again subject to arrest and imprisonment, although it was now upon initial default. This was similar to the arrest of bailiffs who failed to make full payment to lords found in the second Statute of Westminster.[651] If the gaoler did not receive a debtor or allowed him to escape, then he or his lord assumed the debt. This was done in order to make local authorities fulfill their duties in keeping debtors within the confines of their gaols as well as to eliminate corruption or any reluctance to changing processes. Immediately following the debtor's arrest, it was lawful for him to sell his land and tenements to repay his debts. After the first quarter of a year, however, the merchant acquired the goods and lands of the debtor, all the while the latter remained in prison until the debt was repaid in full. There is an obvious change in

---

ceedings from the Lincoln roll of 1305", eds R. F. Hunnisett & J. B. Post, *Medieval Legal Records edited in Memory of C. A. F. Meekings* (London: H. M. Stationery Off., 1978): 144-169 at 149; H.M. Cam, "Some Early Inquests before "Custodes Pacis"" *English Historical Review* vol. 40, no. 159 (Jul., 1925): 411-419; See also B. Putnam, "The Transformation of the Keepers of the Peace into the Justices of the Peace, 1327-1380," Transactions of the Royal Historical Society, 4th ser., vol. 12 (1929): 19-48 at 22-23.

648 Harding, "Keeper," 99-100; Morris, *The Frankpledge System*, 106.

649 Summerson, "The enforcement of the Statute of Winchester," 246.

650 "Statute of Merchants, 11 Edward I (1283)," *The statutes of the realm*, Volume 1, 1235-1377. Printed at the command of His Majesty King George III. [n.d.], 53-54; Plucknett, *Legislation of Edward I*, 138-139.

651 "Statute of Westminster II, 13 Edward I (1285)," c. 11; Plucknett, *Legislation of Edward I*, 153.

procedure from the 1283 statute to the 1285 legislation, but it is unclear as to why such a shift took place.[652]

In addition to increased legislative use of imprisonment, turning approver in the thirteenth century brought an increased number of criminals into the king's gaols. Previously approvers had been taken from county to county, but from the mid-thirteenth century forward, approvers and appellees were brought to the court of the king to make and reply to their appeals. Prisons in London, specifically Newgate, grew in part due to this procedural shift.[653] Unsuccessful approvers were hanged outright, and successful approvers were to abjure the realm, as were successful appellees if they could not find sureties.[654] Matthew Paris provides information as to one approver who abjured the realm after successfully appealing six men, while the close rolls from the reign of Edward I tell us that in Cumberland, Simon of Cockermuthe was allowed to abjure the realm after successfully appealing seven thieves.[655] By the mid-1290s, pardons were issued for approvers who had successfully appealed as many as fifteen, and in one case, seventy men.[656]

The use of a statute as a mechanism of change during the reign of Edward I again altered the political and legal spheres. From the late twelfth century and the Assize of Clarendon, there was an impetus in England for the criminal law "to be one, and uniform, and royal."[657] Edwardian statutes facilitated this, as well as sought to unify civil law, by streamlining and clarifying judicial processes and punishments. Systemization of the eyre, gaol delivery and oyer and terminer commissions, royal officials such as sheriffs and coroners, and actions such as writs, appeals, and *querelae*, demonstrate royal intent to bring outlawry

---

652 "Statute of Merchants, 1285," *Statutes of the Realm*, 98-100; Plucknett, *Legislation of Edward I*, 140-144, 149; Prestwich, *Edward I*, 278.

653 Hamil, "King's Approvers," 241-242; Pugh, *Imprisonment in Medieval England*, 105, 115-116, 192, 315-316. M. Bassett, "Newgate Prison in the Middle Ages," *Speculum*, vol. 18, no. 2 (Apr., 1943): 233-246; Meekings, *Crown Pleas*, 91-92. In 1300, it became law that appellees were to be arrested and brought to approvers held in deliverable gaols. For a general discussion of the processes of law, see A.L. Brown, *The Governance of Late Medieval England, 1272-1461* (Stanford, CA: Stanford UP, 1989), 100-112.

654 Hamil, "King's Approvers," 246.

655 Matthew Paris, *Chronica Maiorica*, vol. 60; *Calendar of Close Rolls*, 5 Edward I, 400, August 4, 1277; Hamil, "King's Approvers," 247.

656 *Calendar of Close Rolls*, 22 Edward I, January 27, 1291 at page 61; See also H.R.T. Summerson, "The criminal underworld of Medieval England," *The Journal of Legal History* vol. 17, no. 3 (1996): 197-224, at 202.

657 Plucknett, *Edward I and Criminal Law*, 77.

under closer control as well as an increased reliance upon imprisonment in matters of law and order.[658]

Legal writings and Court documentation during the reign of Edward I

Legal treatises from the late thirteenth century provide insight into the changes and uses of outlawry during the last years of Henry III's reign and the early years of Edward I's kingship. *Fleta*, mentioned above, summarizes Bracton's discussion of fugitives and outlaws, incorporates some provisions of statutory law, and at times adds information as to the process and efficacy of outlawry.[659] According to the author of *Fleta*, the appeals which could be brought by women that could result in outlawry expanded from "the death of her husband, slain in her arms, and injury done to her person" to include the death of a child *in utero* and rape.[660] An individual could only be outlawed at the county court by specific suit or "at the coming of the justices in eyre, before whom the accused will be indicted on the presentment of the jurors." In the latter, the accused was exacted once at the eyre as if it were on meeting of the county court, and subsequently at county court meetings until outlawry could be pronounced. If outlawry was pronounced too soon, too late, or without proper writ or order of the justices, the county was subject to amercement.[661] This method had previously only been available to men continuing the uncompleted suits of others who had died, refused to sue, or had become seriously ill, a practice which continued according to *Fleta* as well.[662]

As Bracton told us, if an instance of outlawry had been remitted by the king, the outlaw was to carry his charter of pardon with him at all times; if new charges were brought against him, he was only able to defend himself by jury, as he was "forbidden to defend himself by his body, to mark the detestation in which

658 Prestwich, *Edward I*, 267-297; Plucknett, *Edward I and Criminal Law*, 77-101.

659 *Fleta*, eds H.G. Richardson and G.O. Sayles, (1955); *Britton*, trans. Robert Kelham, (1762); Pollock and Maitland, *History of English Law*, vol. 1: 210. *Fleta* was written in Latin while *Britton* was composed in French. Also emerging from this period was the *Mirror of Justices*, a work of doubted authenticity and unknown authorship published by the Selden Society in 1895. See *The Mirror of Justices*, ed. W.J. Whittaker. Selden Society vol. 7 (London, UK: Bernard Quaritch for the Selden Society, 1895).

660 Bracton, vol. 2: 353, 359; *Fleta*, vol. 2, book 1: 69, 88.

661 *Fleta*, vol. 2, book 1: 70.

662 Bracton, vol. 2: 355; *Fleta*, vol. 2, book 1: 71.

flight and outlawry held." If he refused a jury, he was considered convicted and then committed to perpetual imprisonment. According to *Fleta*, refusing to defend oneself by jury resulted in the wrongdoer having to leave the realm.[663] In that same vein, anyone who sued a man to outlawry in a county court out of malice was to be punished and faced banished from the kingdom.[664]

The increased use of imprisonment did not go unnoticed by contemporaries of the late-thirteenth century legal and administrative changes. The anonymous legal treatise *Mirror of Justices*, written c. 1290, called the use of long-term imprisonment and the pain of *peine forte et dure* in the second Statute of Westminster "reprehensible."[665] The use of imprisonment accompanied by fine or "ransom" was considered to be double punishment by the author of *Mirror*, an opinion reiterated throughout his text. The prescription of imprisonment for ravishing in the second Statute of Westminster was deemed inappropriate, for corporal punishment was only to be used in matters of public safety. Similarly, according to the author of *Mirror*, imprisonment for debt as articulated in the Statute of Merchants was considered contrary to the principles of Magna Carta and therefore unjust.[666]

As imprisonment was becoming more common in legal contexts, outlawry was by no means removed from English law. Outlawry remained common in county court proceedings and eyre visitations. There continued to be the shift in the use of outlawry from strictly criminal to civil, or what some may call semi-criminal, offenses. Civil outlawry, or what Bracton described as "minor outlawry," and the legislation of the later thirteenth century articulated its use within English law.[667] Actions of trespass had become increasingly popular during the later years of Henry III's reign, and because refusal to comply or appear in such instances was an offense against the king, it was within the king's prevue to pronounce an appropriate punishment. The end result was often outlawry. As was seen in the second Statute of Westminster's assertion that fugitive officials were subject to outlawry upon disobedience, so too were civil offenders. The king had the power to remit or lessen an outlawry in this context but there was still no manifestation of outlawry that fell under the full authority of the king.

663 *Fleta*, vol. 2, book 1: 75-76; Bracton, vol. 2: 376-377.

664 *Britton*, 11, 79.

665 *Mirror of Justices*, 184-187. While the intent and usefulness of *Mirror* as a legal text remain murky, the attitudes reflected within its pages are important to this project. See the introduction to the Selden Society publication written by F.W. Maitland for more on authorship and purpose of the *Mirror of Justices*.

666 *Mirror of Justices*, 195-196; 199-200.

667 Bracton, trans. Twiss, vol. 6: 480-481; Pugh, *Imprisonment in Medieval England*, 19-20; 26; Plucknett, *Concise History*, 456-457.

Heightened royal supervision of appeals from Angevin reforms of the late twelfth century, through the period of Magna Carta, and into the 1260s, indicates the continuous jurisdictional power-struggle of sorts between county courts and royal justices. Removing an appeal from the county court could be achieved by claiming bias of some kind. It was widely believed that the higher the court, the lesser the bias and the more authoritative a decision.[668]

From 1292, and possibly earlier, county courts could not proclaim outlawry in appeals of homicide until the court obtained a warrant from the king to do so. For the early stages of the exigent process, the case could and often would remain in the county court, but before the process could culminate in the proclamation of outlawry, the case was removed to the king's court. If the accused did not appear there, the case was again moved back to the county court for outlawry proceedings.[669] Palmer provides one example of such a case from the Court of Common Pleas in 1292. Records indicate that after John failed to appear in county court four times for the death of Thomas, the case was moved to the court of the King by writ. Cecilia, wife of Thomas and the appellor, appeared in the king's court, but John did not. It was then ordered that the case should be sent back to the county court and that the sheriff and coroner should proceed to outlawry against John.[670] Here, the king itself was a step in the pronunciation of outlawry.

In a significant shift of power, the county exigent process was also being used by the crown to obtain a proclamation of outlawry.

> Cases of appeal and trespass brought in the king's court could utilize this process when the defendant could not be found. The county court was ordered to initiate the process by the writ *exigere facias*…[this] was soon extended to actions of account and then, later on, more generally, even to actions of debt.[671]

The exigent process had been used by the county courts in matters of appeal was now ordered directly by the crown. This bound the county courts more closely to

---

668 Palmer, *County Courts*, Appendix 7, 322. Palmer observes that justices seemed to dislike the appeal and "discouraged its use whenever possible," quashing actions and allowing exceptions so that cases could be discontinued on the county level and taken up instead on behalf of the king. The discouragement of appeals is also apparent in "the regularization of removal of cases involving the death of a man."

669 Palmer, *County Courts*, Appendix 7, 322.

670 Palmer, *County Courts*, Appendix 7, 324; CP 40/98, m. 81, accessed at http://aalt.law.uh.edu/E1/CP40no98/aCP40no98fronts/IMG_0167.htm. This case is to appear in a forthcoming Selden Society publication on Medieval County Courts, ed. R. Palmer.

671 Palmer, *County Courts*, Appendix 7, pages 324-325.

those of the king and in many ways gave county courts a heightened position in the administration of justice. The use of the exigent process and outlawry by the crown reveals how the crown came to see outlawry much the same as it saw imprisonment in previous centuries. Outlawry could be used as a threat against criminals and could be used to extort pecuniary punishments. This is very much the role that imprisonment played in the Anglo-Saxon and Anglo-Norman periods.

Tolt and *pone*, discussed above, were actions by which royal authorities and the King's Court itself could acquire direct jurisdiction over local litigation. During the reign of Edward I, these measures were further extended and still more cases were brought to the attention of the King's Court by way of *pone* and *recordari*. A writ of *pone* removed a case begun by writ from the county court to that of the king, and a writ of *recordari* relocated cases begun by plaint from the county court to the court of the king. Prior to 1275, *recordari* was limited in use to matters of land, but it was extended to include personal actions such as trespass and debt.[672] One appeal of assault from 1276 reveals Richard Lombe appearing before the King's Bench on the "fourth day" against his alleged attackers, who do not appear. The sheriff was then ordered by writ to bring the accused men to court; if they were located, they were to be placed in prison; if they were not found, they were to be subjected to the exigent process. The processes of the county court were being conducted by the King's Court.[673]

Toward the end of the thirteenth century and up until the suspension of the eyre in 1294, the relationship between royal courts and county courts changed such that the Crown had found ways to manipulate local procedures as a means to its own ends. It became possible to use the exigent process in personal actions involving property wrongs and obligations brought before the king's court. Exigency in this context required that an offender submit himself to royal justice. The exigency process never became available for use in personal actions adjudicated in county courts themselves, but the proclamation of outlawry remained under the authority of county courts.[674]

---

672 Palmer, *County Courts*, 163, 168, and chap. 8, 232-262; Plucknett, *Concise History*, 345; Morris, *The Medieval Sheriff*, 167-206. For an example of a writ *pone*, see Morris, *The Early English County Court*, 168.

673 G.O. Sayles, ed. *Select Cases in the Court of the King's Bench under Edward I, Volume 1*, ed. for the Selden Society (London, UK: Bernard Quaritch, 1936), no. 21. It was later recorded that the accused were outlawed by the earlier writ, but because it was issued in error to the sheriff of Norfolk rather than the sheriff of Huntingdon, where the assault had allegedly taken place, the outlawry was annulled.

674 Palmer, *County Courts*, 223. Personal actions involved property wrongs and obligations but were not actions that determined any rights of real property.

These changes, as steps taken by the Crown to hold more control of adjudicated matters, backfired, however, and the Crown was forced to limit the number of cases bought to its attention. Between 1275 and 1278, the number of trespass cases brought to the Court of Common Pleas had risen exponentially, and as a result, the Second Statute of Westminster and the Statute of Gloucester set limits upon the kinds of trespass cases that could be brought to higher courts.[675] This relegated some of that authority back down to the counties as well as to special commissioners.

Special commissions had been used in England since the early thirteenth century to relieve some of the stress placed upon the eyre by the growth in legal business. Commissions also facilitated further change in procedure of the administration of justice. Commissions of gaol delivery and possessory assizes had functioned since the 1220s. The frequency with which gaol deliveries were commissioned increased steadily through the reign of Henry III and by the accession of Edward I as many as seventy commissions were sent out annually.[676] Commissions were sent out to deliver specific types of prisoners, certain gaols, or particular criminals, especially those who had been in exigent but surrendered to gaol. For example, in January 1288, four prisoners who had been in exigency and then surrendered to Gloucester gaol were ordered by the royal chancery to be delivered.[677] The second Statute of Westminster (1285) articulated that gaol deliveries were to take place at each gaol at least once annually, although not more than three times per year. Slowly, the use of local knights was replaced by personnel consisting of professional judges and permanent commissioners. In 1293, four gaol delivery circuits, each staffed by two commissioners, were established in order to make the process uniform and consistent and by 1299, the assize circuits and gaol delivery circuits, as well as assize and gaol delivery justices, were one and the same.[678]

Two types of commissions were implemented on a grand scale during the reign of Edward I. Oyer and terminer commissions were initiated as a means by

---

675 Palmer, *County Courts*, 236-246, 249-251; "Statute of Gloucester, 6 Edward I (7 August 1278)," c. 8; "Statute of Westminster II, 13 Edward I (1285)," c. 29.

676 Pollock and Maitland, *History of English Law*, vol. 1: 200; Pugh, *Imprisonment in Medieval England*, 256-257.

677 *Patent Rolls, Edward I, 1281-1292*, 16 Edward I, 291.

678 Pugh, *Imprisonment in Medieval England*, 260-282; "Statute of the Justices of the Assize, 21 Edward I (1293)," *The statutes of the realm*, Volume 1, 1235-1377. Printed at the command of His Majesty King George III. [n.d.], 111. By 1330, the piecemeal system of gaol delivery of the late thirteenth century had transitioned to a process in which professional judges traveled from county to county, from gaol to gaol, trying felons and civil suits at the same time and place.

which a king could investigate matters of trespass.[679] Oyer and terminer commissions were intended to provide a speedy response to wrongs, to ease the workload of the eyre, and to, presumably, facilitate order in society.[680] From 1304, commissions of the trailbaston were issued in response to complaints of crime and disorder in England. Trailbaston commissions, criminal bands, and forest law are intimately linked and, although they fall out of the chronological scope here, their uses altered interactions between Crown and county.[681]

The changes during the reign of Edward and commission put into place reflect a shifting "social threshold for the perception of violence and toleration of disorder."[682] Matters were brought before the King personally as well, for when Edward was in Norwich in 1285, the entire town of Ipswich was accused of crimes before his court. The king heard the complaint and heavily fined the individuals involved. Additionally, "thirteen of the townsmen of a better sort were sent to prison in different parts of England for half a year."[683] In 1284, Edward I commissioned two justices to inquire into forest offenses and the death of George the Forester in Northumbria; in 1287, four justices were commissioned to deliver the gaol at Cambridge of two criminals, Ralph Sumpter and Bartholomew Metleaske, who had surrendered after being put in exigent by the last eyre.[684] In many ways, commissions met the needs of royal authority in a more

679 R. W. Kaeuper, "Law and Order in Fourteenth-Century England: The Evidence of Special Commissions of Oyer and Terminer, " *Speculum*, vol. 54, no. 4 (Oct., 1979): 734-784 at 742-743; Cam, *Studies in the Hundred Rolls*, 72-79. There were a few oyer and terminer commissions sent out sporadically during the reign of Henry III. For the first twenty-two years of Edward I's reign, the number of commissions coincides with eyre cycles, their suspensions, and their resumptions. When the eyre was in session, oyer and terminer commissions decreased; with the inception of trailbaston commissions in 1305, oyer and terminer commissions saw a significant decline. See *Calendar of Patent Rolls*, 32 Henry III, 15 June 1248 one of the earliest recorded commissions.

680 Kaeuper, "Law and Order," 752-753, 773-774; "Statute of Westminster II, 13 Edward I (1285),"c. 29.

681 Harding, "Early trailbaston proceedings from the Lincoln roll of 1305."

682 Kaeuper, "Law and Order," 737. Until 1287, forest law remained relatively untouched, although the Charter of the Forest had been confirmed early in Edward's reign. See Young, *The Royal Forests of Medieval England*, 136-148.

683 *The Chronicle of Florence of Worcester: With the Two Continuations; Comprising Annals of English History, from the Departure of the Romans to the Reign of Edward I*, (Florence's chronicle ends with the year 1117; the first continuation, 1117-1141, was written by John of Worcester; the second, 1152-1295, was the work of John De Taxster to 1265, continued to 1295 probably by John of Eversden), ed. T. Forester (H. G. Bohn, 1854), 372.

684 *Calendar of Patent Rolls*, 13 Edward, 1284, 200; 16 Edward, 1287, 265.

efficient manner than the eyre, but after a significant rise in the use of commissions from 1275 to 1285, the crown issued criteria limiting the cases that could be brought to commission to those of "heinous trespass".[685] By 1292, the letters patent contain numerous commissions of gaol delivery, oyer and terminer, and matters of assize, as well as those of inquiry into specific criminal offenses.

Commissions and royal investigations of appeals, writs, and judicial processes were conducted to insure that actions were not being brought out of hate and malice. They exhibit an obvious desire of the crown to quell vengeance and violence. The increased use of imprisonment in the thirteenth century can be viewed in these terms, as removing a criminal from society and placing him or her into gaol was means to end the cycle of violence, at least for a time, and attempted to bring wrongs and wrong-doers to court.[686] Similarly, the use of writs allowed for the Crown to control the treatment of malefactors within the administration of justice while exercising its own authority. The writ of *monstravit de compoto*, for example, could be obtained from the royal chancery by a lord who wished to compel a bailiff who owned him money. The writ of *monstravit de compoto* required that a lord appear before the chancery personally and request that measures be taken to secure "attachment of the body" of the bailiff in question. Once the royal writ was issued, it authorized sheriffs to take any means necessary to secure the accused in court, including by arrest and imprisonment. If the writ of *monstravit de compoto* failed to bring the defendant to court, then a writ of *capias* could be issued, which according to the second Statute of Westminster, could lead to exaction and outlawry of the defendant.[687]

685 Kaeuper, "Law and Order," 744, 775-776; "Statute of Westminster II, 13 Edward I (1285)", c. 30. Oyer and terminer commissioners were to be chosen from justices of the bench or the eyre according to the second statute of Westminster, although this was not always the case.

686 Hyams, *Rancor and Reconciliation*, 242-266.

687 Brand, *Kings, Barons, Justices*, 312-333, 402-403; "Statute of Westminster II, 13 Edward I (1285)," c. 11; Prestwich, *Edward I*, 275. Although a creation of the Provisions of Westminster in 1260, this writ was not commonly used until after 1267. According to Brand, most of the writs *monstravit de compoto* issued between 1267 and 1280 were to men closely associated with the king. The first instance of exaction in the case of a *monstravit* defendant is found on CP 40/63, m. 5 (1286).

Outlawry and the Eyre During the Reign of Edward I

According to plea roll documentation, vagabonds were commonly put to exigency and outlawed. Vagabonds, itinerant social drifters, lacked support from peers and often became legal outsiders as a result. A certain Richard was shooting at targets with a crossbow when he accidentally hit Walter on the head with an arrow so that he died. Richard at once fled to the church of St. Magnus where he remained for three days. He then escaped from the church and absconded, after which he was exacted and outlawed. He had no chattels nor frankpledge because he was a vagabond.[688] In another example, John and Martin were drinking together in a tavern and a quarrel arose between them. John killed Martin with a staff and was at once arrested and taken to the house of the sheriff, where he was imprisoned. Afterwards he escaped and took sanctuary, where he remained for fifteen days. He escaped again, after which he was to be exacted and outlawed according to the custom of the City. The sheriff was amerced for the escape and nothing was known of John‘s frankpledge because he was a vagabond.[689] Outlawry in this context continued to serve a local need of removing strangers and potential criminals from legal protections.

One other notable case from the London eyre involved the surrender of an outlaw. When Henry died on London Bridge, Robert le Taylour absconded and because he was suspected to have caused his death. Robert was to be exacted and outlawed according to the custom of the City. Afterwards Robert was arrested but did not wish to put himself upon the verdict of his country, so he was committed to gaol and nothing resulted from his outlawry.[690] There are two instances from the Berkshire eyre of 1275 of men abjuring the realm following flight to a church and confession to a coroner, but as the coroner had not recorded the abjurations (or they had never taken place), the offenders were declared outlaws instead.[691]

---

688 “Crown Pleas: 39 Henry III - 41 Henry III (nos 50-77)”, *The London eyre of 1276* (1976), no. 61. URL: http://www.british-history.ac.uk/report.aspx?compid=35993.

689 “Crown Pleas: 42 Henry III - 44 Henry III (nos 78-107)”, *The London eyre of 1276* (1976), no. 83. URL: http://www.british-history.ac.uk/report.aspx?compid=35994.

690 “Crown Pleas: 42 Henry III - 44 Henry III (nos 78-107)”, The London eyre of 1276 (1976), no. 107. URL: http://www.british-history.ac.uk/report.aspx?compid=35994.

691 London, The National Archives, JUST 1/10, m. 29, m. 31. Abjuration of the realm was more common according to the London eyre of 1276 due to the fact that there were twenty-eight churches in London from 1251-1276. Nearly two thirds of abjurors recorded during the London eyre were strangers or vagabonds and only two were women. No information is provided on the ports of abjuration to which they were assigned. *The*

The connections between abjuration, imprisonment, and outlawry continue to exhibit themselves though late thirteenth century documentation. According to the Oxford eyre of the mid-1280s, abjuration by a suspect commonly resulted from flight to a church after evading prison. The pleas of the crown from 1285 at Oxford contain six cases of evasion that led to abjuration of the realm.[692] As always, some entity, whether it was the sheriff or the town or village, was held accountable for any escape. In one instance, the King's Court ordered that the estate of a sheriff named Nicholas, who had actually died before the coming of the justices, be held accountable for the evasion.[693] There are two accounts of clerks rescuing suspects from gaol, one that resulted in the abjuration of a criminal who had been on his way to the gallows. One of the rescuers, a certain Robert Tursway, later absconded and was outlawed. The fate of the other rescued man is unknown, but his codefendant in the robbery of which he was accused was said to have been allowed to escape from gaol by the bailiff and was later outlawed.[694] In yet another notable case, a certain John Ardern fled to a church after being accused of theft with his associate Robert Pennoby, who then abjured the realm. John, however, left the church and surrendered to the peace of the king, and was placed into prison at Oxford.[695]

London Eyre of 1276. ed. M. Weinbaum (London, UK: London Record Society, 1976), "Introduction," xv. Also at *The London Eyre of 1276*, ed. M. Weinbaum. Contains crown pleas for years 36 Henry III to 4 Edward I, plus civil pleas, assizes, and related material. By permission of the London Record Society. (London, UK: London Record Society, 1976), Accessed at: http://www.british-history.ac.uk/source.aspx?pubid=156. London eyres of the thirteenth century were essentially crown plea sessions. London was excluded from general eyres and had its own judicial customs, which were reaffirmed by Henry III in a 1268 charter. If a felon or suspected felon was absent, the justices ordered his exaction and outlawry, exaction and waivery for a woman. The process was continued in accordance with what had been explained to the justices in 1244: "fugitives were put in exigent at three hustings held fortnightly and then outlawed by precept of the king at the folkmoot at St. Pauls. The justices considered that the time for exaction and outlawry was very short and should be amended. No record of the form then provided has survived nor does the plea roll of 1276 provide further evidence concerning the process of outlawry."

692 "Pleas of the Crown, before the Justices in Eyre, 14 Jan. 1285 (*Twyne*, ms. IV, p. 617 sqq.)" in *Oxford City Documents: Financial and Judicial, 1268-1665*, ed. J.E. Thorold Rogers. (Oxford, UK: Printed for the Oxford Historical Society at the Clarendon Press, 1891): 182-236, no. 22, no. 23, no. 30, no. 36, no. 82.

693 "Pleas of the Crown," ed. Rogers, 189-190; no. 82. no. 86.

694 "Pleas of the Crown," ed. Rogers, 189; no. 86, no. 77.

695 "Pleas of the Crown," ed. Rogers, no. 88.

In 1286 during the Suffolk eyre, justices were presented with two men who had escaped custody after being imprisoned for robbery. Both men were suspected and subsequently exacted and outlawed. During the same eyre, it was reported that a certain John was captured and placed into custody. He escaped, fled to church where he confessed to robbery, and abjured the realm.[696] In the Huntington eyre of 1286, Adam withdrew himself following the death of Margery, was suspected by the jury and was to be outlawed. He later surrendered to gaol and placed himself before the country, where it was determined by oath that he was not culpable and was quit of the crime.[697] In another case of homicide, Eustace and Andreas fled and were placed in exigency, although the former was later captured and placed into the custody of the sheriff. He was delivered to the justices at the coming of the eyre, although his fate is unknown. Andreas was outlawed at the order of the county.[698] One more notable example involves Eustace Pudche, who was captured and imprisoned by the village of Spaldwick on suspicion of theft. Eustace escaped from prison, fled, and was put to exigency to be outlawed. Eustace was then said to have been captured at Huntingdon and placed in the King's prison under guard of the sheriff, where he again escaped. After consultation of the rolls of the coroner, however, it was determined that following his escape from Spaldwick, Eustace had fled to church, confessed to theft, and abjured the realm. This nullified the outlawry pronounced by the county.[699] For the first escape, the village of Spaldwick was to respond, for the second, the sheriff was held responsible, and the ultimate fate of Eustace is unknown.[700]

Overall, the pleas of the crown from the Huntington eyre of 1286 and the Ramsey Abbey banlieu court of 1287 contain seventy-one exactions leading to outlawry, as well as six additional occurrences of waivery. There are forty-one abjurations of the realm, six of which were instances of suspects escaping custo-

---

696 London, The National Archives, JUST 1/835a, m. 8. m. 15.

697 *Royal Justice and the Medieval English Countryside: The Huntingdonshire Eyre of 1286, the Ramsey Abbey Banlieu Court of 1287, and the Assizes of 1287-1288*, eds. A.R. Dewindt and E.B. Dewindt, vols 1-2 (Toronto, Canada: Pontifical Institute of Medieval Studies, 1981), no. 354.

698 *Royal Justice and the Medieval English Countryside*, no. 363. There are no extant corresponding gaol delivery rolls from Huntingdon.

699 *Royal Justice and the Medieval English Countryside*, no. 519.

700 See the amercement records for the hundred of Leghtanstan, particularly *Royal Justice and the Medieval English Countryside*, no. 703, liii, liv.

dy or prison, fleeing to a church and then abjuring the realm.[701] There are two escapes from sanctuary, one by a cleric who escaped by night, and the other by a thief who was later outlawed.[702] During the Lancashire eyre of 1292, William was pursued to a church but fled immediately after arrival there. He was put to exigent and outlawed. He was later captured by Gilbert the sheriff, who failed to hold him for gaol delivery. Geoffrey was called before the justices and claimed that William's two sons had been attached for their father and that William had appeared but claimed that his case fell under the liberty of the bishop rather than the jurisdiction of the hundred. Gilbert was placed into gaol for a time until it was determined that he was quit of any charges or maljustice.[703] From the Cumberland eyre of 1292, we learn that a certain Hugo, son of Stephen, was a suspected thief who fled and was outlawed, but that his father who had attached himself on his son's behalf was placed into gaol.[704] Geoffrey fled after Adam died, whom he had wounded three weeks prior, and was outlawed. The language of the entry on the plea rolls is interesting in that it reads Geoffrey had only been an outlaw in the county (prior to the arrival of the justices, presumably), but was truly an outlaw now.[705]

Exigent lists, which included the names of all those of individuals ordered to be exacted, begin to appear in the eyre records from Edward I's reign, the earliest extant from 1285.[706] The inclusion of an exigent list reflected the growing bureaucratization of the outlawry process.[707] According to the Assize of Northampton, all outlaws were to be recorded and their names were to be handed over to the Exchequer. It is likely that exigent lists and lists of outlaws were made at the eyre together, but the exact methods of compilation are unknown. Exigent lists were to be used within the county and were given to sheriffs and coroners for further action. They would have been consulted by the justices at their next visit to the county and used by commissioners after the end of the eyre in 1294

701 *Royal Justice and the Medieval English Countryside*, nos 519, 554, 565, 573, 600, 815. See also "Huntingdonshire Crown Pleas, 1286-1287" in *Royal Justice and the Medieval English Countryside*, 40-100.

702 *Royal Justice and the Medieval English Countryside*, no. 802, no. 507.

703 London, The National Archives, JUST 1/413, m. 8.

704 London, The National Archives, JUST 1/137, m. 16.

705 London, The National Archives, JUST 1/137, m. 4.

706 London, The National Archives, JUST 1/623, m. 32-33. This is from the Northampton Eyre of 1285. See Meekings, *Crown Pleas*, 98-99. Additional exigent lists assessed for this project include, but are not limited to, those found in London, The National Archives, JUST 1/351a, m. 14 (1286), JUST 1/284, m. 44-46 (1287), JUST 1/213, m. 53 (1288).

707 "Huntingdonshire Crown Pleas, 1286-1287," in *Royal Justice and the Medieval English Countryside*, 40-100.

as well.[708] By the end of the thirteenth century, Edward I had rearticulated the exigency and outlawry procedures for his officials:

> Note that, although one who is appealed of a death of a man, or for some other felony, make default at three County Courts, yet at the fourth County Court may appear and give mainprise to appear at the fifth County Court: and then, if he do not come he will be outlawed: and if the appellor abandon the prosecution, the Exigent at the King's suit shall try until the Eyre; and then he shall be tried (for he may return to the peace if he will) at the suit of the King. And if he will not come, he shall be called at three County Courts; and if he do not come at the third, he shall be outlawed at the fourth County Court, if he do not come or give mainprise to come at the fifth County Court.[709]

Outlawry in this form had been customarily carried out for centuries. The detailed procedure found here would later be used by commissioners of the trailbaston during the early fourteenth century when conducting trials.[710]

Corruption, Justice, and Governance: The "State Trials" of the 1290s

When Edward I returned to England in 1289 following his military campaigns in Wales and a long stay in Gascony, he was met with grievances about the whole of his judicial administration. Many of the complaints were against his chief justices and other high royal officials. As a result, King Edward came to believe that corruption and abuse of power had run rampant during his absence and took action against the offenders. In September 1289, Thomas de Weyland, chief justice of Common Pleas from 1278, was accused of aiding two of his men suspected of homicide after the fact. As a result, Weyland was deprived of his property and placed into custody. He escaped and fled to the Bury of St. Edmunds, but was starved into submission and taken to the Tower of London.

---

708 *Calendar of London Trailbaston Trials under Commissions of 1305 and 1306.*, ed. R. Pugh. (London, UK: Her Majesty's Stationery Office, 1975), 33-34; *Wiltshire Gaol Delivery and Trailbaston Trials, 1275-1306*, ed. R.B. Pugh. Wiltshire Record Society, Volume XXXIII. (Stoke-on-Trent, UK: JG. Fenn Ltd., 1978), 23-24. Exigent list were necessary tools of oyer and terminer and trailbaston commissions in the early fourteenth century.

709 *Year Books of the Reign of King Edward the First, Years XXXII and XXXIII*, ed. and trans. A. Horwood (Rolls Series xxxi), 386-387.

710 *Calendar of London Trailbaston Trials under Commissions of 1305 and 1306*, 33-34; *Wiltshire Gaol Delivery and Trailbaston Trials, 1275-1306*, 23-24.

When Parliament met in late 1289, Weyland was given the choice of standing trial, submitting to perpetual imprisonment, or abjuring the realm. He chose the latter.[711]

Ralph de Hengham, chief justice of the King's Bench, Adam de Stratton, high official of the Exchequer, and Henry Bray, the king's former clerk and Justice of the Jews, were also imprisoned and fined for offences committed during the king's absence.[712] Hengham had been chief justice of the King's Bench from 1274 and while the specifics concerning the accusations against him remain unclear, he was convicted of misconduct in 1290. He paid a hefty fine to be released from prison and for his subsequent pardon.[713] Adam de Stratton was deprived of his office in the Exchequer and put on trial for felony in 1289, although the specific charges remain unknown. Stratton had previously been suspended from office in 1279 for fraud and forgery, but was cleared of charges and reinstated as Exchequer after paying a bribe. In 1291, Stratton received a pardon from the king, only to be placed on trial for felony again that same year for forging charters. He was placed in the Tower of London, convicted in late 1292, and died in 1294 of unknown causes.[714] Henry Bray had served as the king's personal clerk from 1273 and in 1281 or shortly after became Justice of the Jews. He was charged with levying Jewish debts that had come into the

---

711 *State Trials of the Reign of Edward the First, 1289-1293*, eds. T.F. Tout. and H. Johnstone (London, UK: Office of the Royal Historical Society, 1906), xxix; Bartholomew Cotton, 171-172; *The chronicle of Pierre de Langtoft, in French verse from the earliest period to the death of King Edward I*, ed. T. Wright, pub. by the authority of the lords commissioners of Her Majesty's Treasury, under the direction of the master of the rolls (London, UK: Longmans, Green, Reader, and Dyer, 1866-68), 184-187; Prestwich, *Edward I*, 339; P. Brand, "Weyland, Sir Thomas (c.1230–1298)", Oxford Dictionary of National Biography, Oxford UP, Sept 2004; online edn, Jan 2008 [http://www.oxforddnb.com/view/article/29154].

712 *State Trials of the Reign of Edward the First, 1289-1293*, xiii; Prestwich, *Edward I*, 339.

713 *State Trials of the Reign of Edward the First, 1289-1293*, xxx; P. Brand, "Hengham, Ralph (b. in or before 1235, d. 1311)", *Oxford Dictionary of National Biography*, Oxford UP, Sept 2004; online edn, Jan 2008 [http://www.oxforddnb.com/view/article/12924].

714 *State Trials of the Reign of Edward the First, 1289-1293*, xxx; *Chronicles of the Reigns of Edward I and Edward II, Volume I, Annales Londonienses and Annales Paulini*, ed. Wm. Stubbs. Rolls Series. *Rerum Britannicarum Medii Aevi Scriptores*. no. 76, vol. 1 (London, UK: Longman & Co., 1882), 98; Bartholomew Cotton, 171-172, 180; R.C. Stacey, "Stratton, Adam of (d. 1292x4)", *Oxford Dictionary of National Biography*, Oxford UP, Sept 2004; online edn, Jan 2008 [http://www.oxforddnb.com/view/article/26652].

hands of the King. In May 1290, Bray was deprived of office, arrested and placed in the Tower of London for unknown causes, where he remained until October of that year. He paid a fine for his release, but was arrested and imprisoned again at the Tower in 1292 at Winchester Castle in 1294. He was released only after agreeing to pay yearly installments of his large fine to the King.[715]

Among the many officials charged with judicial misconduct during the State Trials of 1289-1293, William de Brompton, a judge from the court of Common Pleas, John de Lovetot, a justice from the King's Bench, and royal justice Solomon of Rochester were also imprisoned and later released upon payment of heavy fines.[716] Royal justices were being punished with periods of imprisonment followed by fines or abjuration of the realm. This was the same as the punishments given to lesser offenders. Reforms of the legal system under Edward I were being exercised upon the highest legal officials. The notable use of imprisonment in this context reflected shifting norms in the overall legal structure of the late thirteenth century.

Edward I, Pardons, and Outlawry

Royal pardon of outlawry had a long tradition in England by the reign of Edward I, but pardons were usually issued in individual cases, upon a king's acces-

---

715 Bartholomew Cotton, 171-172; P. Brand, "Bray, Henry (b. before 1248, d. 1311x13)", rev. Oxford Dictionary of National Biography, *Oxford UP*, 2004; online edn, Jan 2008 [http://www.oxforddnb.com/view/article/37530]. Bray arranged to pay 300 marks of his 2,000 mark fine to the king. In 1299, Bray gave some of his lands in Northamptonshire to the king in exchange for remission of his remaining financial debts.

716 *State Trials of the Reign of Edward the First, 1289-1293*, xixxi-xxxii; P. Brand, "Lovetot, Sir John de (b. in or before 1236, d. 1294)", rev. *Oxford Dictionary of National Biography*, Oxford UP, 2004; online edn, Jan 2008 [http://www.oxforddnb.com/view/article/37606]; P. Brand, "Rochester, Solomon of (c.1240–1293)", *Oxford Dictionary of National Biography*, Oxford UP, Sept 2004; online edn, Jan 2008 [http://www.oxforddnb.com/view/article/23919]. By late 1293, the State Trials had run their course and legislation was put into place to regulate and more clearly defined the processes by which counties would be subjected to the itinerant system. "The Statute of the Justices of the Assize" and "The Statute of Persons to be put in Assizes and Juries" defined the four itinerant circuits, listed qualifications of jurors, detailed the duties of royal officials in the counties, and set limits upon what cases could be transferred to the King's Bench at Westminster, namely trespass cases only involving at least forty shillings. See *The Statutes of the Realm: Printed by Command of his Majesty King George the Third*, vol. 1, 1235-1377, "The Statute of Justices of the Assize" and "The Statute of Persons to be put in Juries and Assizes," 112-113.

sion to the throne, or to commemorate some other momentous event. Edward I, however, issued pardons in two distinct ways that altered outlawry in England.

During the reign of Edward I pardons were issued for outlawries stemming from larceny, trespass, and robbery provided the individual surrender himself to a specified gaol within a certain amount of time. This was in contrast to pardons during the reign of Henry III, which were issued contingent upon the pardoned individual standing to right if anyone brought further appeal. In 1274, pardon was granted to Mabel, who had abjured the realm for larceny, contingent upon her surrender to prison and placement before the county for judgment. A similar pardon was issued in 1279 to the outlaw Ralph Machon, so long as he surrendered himself to prison and put himself on the county to answer the charges against him.[717] More pardons are as follows:

> Pardon of the ban and outlawry of a criminal accused of trespass on the isle of Jersey provided he surrender himself to the gaol and undergo a trial according to Jersey custom.[718]
>
> Pardon to William de Harecurt of his outlawry for a trespass in the forest of Rutland, provided that he surrender within forty days to Qakham gaol.[719]
>
> [Pardon] to John le Baillif of Corsham of outlawry for robberies, whereof he was indicted before John de Berewyk and his fellows, justices in eyre in the county of Salop, provided that he surrender within forty days to Shrewsbury gaol.[720]
>
> Pardon, at the instance of William de Monte Reville, to Adam son of John de Bukenhull of his outlawry for the death of Cradoe le Waleys provided that he surrender within forty days to Hereford gaol.[721]

The exchange of outlawry for imprisonment reflects changing legal and social sensibilities and realities in England. In one instance, Edward I ordered the sheriff of Devon to supercede the exaction and outlawry of Richard of Bamfeld on account of his having surrendered to the court of the king on appeal of homicide.[722] Royal pardon and remittance of outlawry articulated in the close and patent rolls from Edward‘s reign varied from pardons granted by his predecessors. From the time of Henry II, outlawry was remitted completely except for the obligation that the offender stand to right if necessary, not contingent upon time spent in gaol. Edward‘s use of pardon altered the outlawry process in such

717 *Calendar of Close Rolls*, 3 Edward I (1274), 140; 7 Edward I (1279), 545.

718 *Calendar of Patent Rolls*, 8 Edward I, (4 January 1280), 358.

719 *Calendar of Patent Rolls*, 23 Edward I, (11 June 1293), 23.

720 *Calendar of Patent Rolls*, 23 Edward I, (6 November 1293), 40.

721 *Calendar of Patent Rolls*, 24 Edward I, (22 January 1294), 60.

722 *Calendar of Close Rolls*, 7 Edward I (10 February 1279), 521. For similar supercession, see also 18 Edward I (23 May 1290), 81, and 17 Edward I (16 February 1289), 6.

a way that placed control of a malefactor within the hands of royal officials, weakened the thrust of a proclamation of outlawry, and increased the importance of gaols and imprisonment in the administration of justice.

Edward proclaimed in a royal letter that all outlaws in the realm would be pardoned if they agreed to provide military service for his wars in Gascony.[723] Patent rolls from Edward's reign contain numerous pardons for outlaws, vagabonds, and indicted individuals in hiding in exchange for their service, or that of their kin, in Gascony, Wales, and Scotland.

> Pardon to Robert de Corbrigg of Bywell of his outlawry for the death of Richard le Tayllour, as it appears *by* testimony before the king that his son, John de Corbrigg of Bywell has, for this reason, offered of his own free will to go to Gascony on the king's service in the company of Edmund, the king's brother.[724]
>
> ...Power, at the request of the prelates, earls, barons and others of council...to take bond of all persons charged with offences, who are willing to come into the king's peace, (1) that they will immediately set forth on the king's service to Wales, and remain there at the king's wages, during pleasure, and thence set forth on the king's service to Gascony, and remain there at the king's wages, during pleasure, (2) that upon their return from Wales, or from Gascony, if they should go there, they will stand their trial, if any one wishes to implead them for homicides, robberies and other crimes, and trespasses, whereof they are charged or appealed, or for which they are imprisoned, outlawed, or in hiding; and for such manucaption testified by the said justices before the Chancery, they are to have letters patent of pardon of the king's suit.[725]
>
> Remission and pardon to Stephen de London of the condition attached to a late pardon to him for a robbery committed by him upon Philip de Shillingford, to wit, that he should go to Wales and thence to Gascony and serve the king at the king's wages during pleasure, as in the former letters patent is more fully set forth; and he is to take his trial if indicted.[726]

---

723 Bartholomew Cotton, 235-236.

724 *Calendar of Patent Rolls*, 22 Edward I, (5 October 1294), 96.

725 *Calendar of Patent Rolls*, 22 Edward I, (12 November 1294), 107. The entry continues "The king is moved to this by pity as well as by the re-conquest of the Council, because so many and such different kinds of men are frequently in danger of losing life or limb; some being charged, indicted or appealed by approvers, of homicides, robberies and other crimes against the peace; some wandering about the country for trespasses in the forest doing much mischief so that part of them come to be imprisoned, or outlawed, or are in hiding."

726 *Calendar of Patent Rolls*, 23 Edward I, (22 January 1295), 129.

Close rolls from 1293 contain a letter to sheriffs and coroners in Dorset to delay until further ordered the exigency and outlawry for trespass of forty-nine men who were defending the Cinque Ports in service to the barons and the king.[727]

There were also individual gaol deliveries commissioned by Edward to address individuals in exigent who had surrendered and were held in gaol. Through the course of the 1280s, Edward commissioned justices to deliver gaols to which men placed in exigent at previous eyres for homicide, breach of the king's peace, unspecified trespass, larceny, and other offenses had surrendered. For example, in November 1286, six such commissions were issued, thirty-one were ordered in February 1287, and another six in January 1288.[728] Both the threat and actuality of exigency and outlawry remained effective up through the early 1290s and the King continued to commission justices. In January 1294, Edward commissioned two justices to deliver Maydenstan gaol in Kent of "persons who were put in exigent for outlawry after the last eyre…and upon rumor had surrendered."[729] Similar commissions were sent to Northumbria in February 1294 and to York in June 1295. According to the writ from 1295, the gaol in York was overflowing with individuals in exigent since the last visitation of the justices due to the suspension of the eyre.[730]

As a result of Edward's changes to legal processes, individuals placed into exigency began surrender themselves to gaol and remain there until the next gaol delivery or the next eyre. Depending on the offense he or she was accused, the end result could be continued imprisonment with possible amercement. Imprisonment was functioning at both a coercive and punitive level in the administration of justice. To correspond with the increasing use of imprisonment within the common law, the 1295 statute concerning prison-escapees dictated that escaped suspects were not to be punished in any way that exceeded the punishment that corresponded to their original crime.[731] During the reign of Henry III, prison-breaking was considered its own crime and suspects who escaped were considered guilty of the original offence by which they were charged. Escapees were usually killed if recaptured and were otherwise considered outlaws. Measures taken during the reign of Edward I encouraged the recapture of pris-

727 *Calendar of Close Rolls*, 21 Edward I, (8 May 1293), 282-283.

728 *Calendar of Patent Rolls*, 15 Edward I, (1287), 283-286; 16 Edward I, (1288), 291.

729 *Calendar of Patent Rolls*, 22 Edward I, (4 January 1294), 109. The justices were also instructed to deal with any other criminals who were in custody.

730 *Calendar of Patent Rolls*, 22 Edward I, (7 February 1294), 109; *Calendar of Close Rolls*, 23 Edward I, (8 June 1295), 161.

731 "The Statute of Breaking Prisons, 23 Edward I (1295)," *The statutes of the realm*, Volume 1, 1235-1377. Printed at the command of His Majesty King George III. [n.d.],, 113; Pugh, *Imprisonment in Medieval England*, 228-229.

oners, and perhaps even their surrender, followed by a proper trial. Prison-breaking was no longer a separate offense, which transitioned the status of an escapee from that of a double-criminal or an outlaw to a mere criminal on the run. The distinction was subtle, but with the elimination of a death penalty for the latter, it was an important differentiation to be made with respect to methods of punishment and social order and the administration of royal justice.

By the end of the thirteenth century, imprisonment could be the long-term outcome of a case, depending on circumstances, and the preference of judicial authorities to inclusively constrain criminals was becoming clear. To be sure, outlawry still existed, functioned, and played a large role in the judicial administration of medieval England, but the interchangeable properties of these practices cannot go unnoticed. Exchanging imprisonment for outlawry through gaol escape and flight from justice had been common in the twelfth and thirteenth centuries. Now the opposite was true. Outlaws could surrender to prison. In many ways, outlawry and imprisonment had become inverted in their legal and social functions.

The Suspension of the Eyre, 1294

The effective end of the eyre in 1294 was due to the start of Edward I's war with France, although its abandonment may have been in part "a favour to the people," who viewed the eyre as cumbersome and inconvenient.[732] The decline of the eyre had been a lengthy process and was the result of an over-extended system unable to handle the increased business brought to the attention of the court.[733] The eyre had lost its effectiveness in the localities through the course of the thirteenth century and as matters of its concern increased, the Crown used

---

732 D. W. Sutherland, *Quo Warranto Proceedings in the Reign of Edward I, 1278-1294* (Oxford, UK: Clarendon Press, 1963), 213; Prestwich, *Edward I*, 289.

733 D. Crook, "The Later Eyres," *The English Historical Review*, vol. 97, no. 383 (Apr., 1982): 241-268, at 243; C. Burt, "The Demise of the General Eyre in the Reign of Edward I," *The English Historical Review* (February, 2005): 1-14 at 8; Harding, "Plaints and Bills in the History of English Law," and Harding, "Early trailbaston proceedings from the Lincoln roll of 1305". Harding argues that the "flood" of *querelae* and bills of trespass at eyre played a large part to the decline of the institution, but Burt argues that Harding overstates his case, as well as the number of complaints brought against royal officials and the impact plaints and bills had on the decline of the eyre. She acknowledges that overall, the business of the courts outweighed its practical abilities, but denies the tendency to conflate end of the eyre with any breakdown in law and order in the fourteenth century.

writs and commissions to bring actions out of the eyre and into the hands of other judicial mechanisms.

The eyre, with its broader geographical and legal scope and relative regularity, was essentially replaced by royal commissions and writs, which ultimately decreased royal presence in the shires. "During the period of a flourishing eyre system…[it] brought royal justice into the shires as a solemn, periodic part of normality," which ended in 1294.[734] The abandonment of the eyre in 1294 and failed attempts to revive it "ended an integral part of the fabric of judicial administration."[735] The end of the eyre in 1294 was very much a relief to many in the localities of England and reflects not only the refocused attention of the Crown but also the need for other royal methods of dealing with malefactors in the localities. The commissions that became increasingly common through the reign of Edward I facilitated the administration of justice and were intended to be more focused, more specific than the general eyre had been in its waning days.

Observations: Outlawry at the end of the Thirteenth Century

Outlawry and abjuration as legal practices found in late thirteenth century eyre records do not reflect ineffectual forms of legal processes, but rather demonstrate strong local practices that endured in the face, alongside, and as a result of royal intervention and adaptation. The business of the eyre had outgrown the eyre itself. As new legal procedures were put into place, the use of imprisonment increased. This was in part due to failed attempts by the crown to control local processes, namely outlawry. Royal law substituted and incorporated imprisonment, its efforts were largely unsuccessful. The strength of outlawry had resulted in an increased use of imprisonment by the end of the thirteenth century and facilitated the inclusion of carceral methods of punishment and order in

734 Hyams, *Rancor and Reconciliation*, 265, Hyams continues, "the kings" men managed to keep themselves informed of virtually all unnatural deaths and to deter concealment along with most efforts at private settlement out of court…overt feud action, whether for blood or money, became so much rarer. Nevertheless, the king's justices were fully aware that their courtrooms seethed with hatreds…hence the justices struggled to control jurors out to nullify the letter of the law."

735 R W. Kaeuper, "Law and Order," 738, quoting Meekings, unpublished "List of Gaol Delivery Rolls and Files;" see also Crook, "The Later Eyres," 241-268. "Oyer and terminer" is from the French for to "hear" and "determine".

English Common Law. By attempting to control outlawry, the Crown had found it necessary to use imprisonment more often.

Many administrative changes that took place during the reign of Edward I restructured and reordered legal processes in the interest of strengthening royal justice and solidifying the king's peace throughout the realm. With respect to outlawry, the Crown both succeeded and failed. Pardons and writs were used to control aspects of outlawry and imprisonment was emphasized more heavily under Edward I, but eyre records indicate that outlawry and abjuration were just as common as they had always been in the local administration of justice. The eyre, and by extension the Crown, had failed to fully incorporate local processes into its control. Indeed, justice in the county courts was conducted in the name of the king and the eyre's visitations supervised its workings. The fact that the Crown created an entire species of commission, the trailbaston, to deal with malefactors in society and address the presence of outlaws throughout England illustrates the importance of local courts and their processes in late thirteenth century law and society.

Chapter 8: Reassessing Outlawry

From late Anglo-Saxon England to the end of the judicial eyre in 1294, outlawry, exile, and banishment underwent vast changes in governance, politics, and law. Not only were outlawry and the like essential in maintaining social order, but investigation into their use, strength, and importance has rejected the narrow view that these practices were ineffective and weak practices of law and governance in Medieval England.

During the Anglo-Saxon period, exile and outlawry were used without legal restrictions but in accordance with perceived customary rights. They were conceptually identical practices, with the latter being a more regional form of the former. Anglo-Saxon kings exiled their enemies just as county courts outlawed societal malefactors. As Anglo-Saxon law came to be written down, there were attempts by the Crown to take a role in the regional process of outlawry, but the practice remained in the hands of the county courts. Outlawry was a strong, effective tool of social order that allowed for community members to rid themselves of local malefactors, publicize the wrongs that had been committed, and create a punitive culture of exclusion.

Little changed with respect to outlawry when the Normans invaded England in 1066, but there were alterations to law that impacted local order. Forest law introduced an aspect of royal law that had been absent prior to the Battle of Hastings. Forest offenses fell under the prerogative of the king and punishments associated with forest wrongs began to use imprisonment. Politically, enemies of the Crown were exiled just as they had been for centuries, but Norman kings also imprisoned their foes. This was particularly true for men of noble status and relatives, such as William the Conqueror‘s half-brother Odo, Henry I‘s brother Robert, and the repeatedly bothersome Robert Belleme.

By the reign of Henry I in the early twelfth century, the king held nominal authority in the legal process of outlawry and could exile political enemies at his discretion. Law and custom were not in opposition to one another, and were much less easily distinguished. Imprisonment was not a practice that met the needs of English society or politics, and was used if no other option existed or in special circumstances.

The reforms that took place during the reign of Henry II (1154-1189) changed the social, legal, and political landscapes of England and the roles of outlawry, exile, and banishment within those spheres. The relationship between church and government reflected changing sensibilities on external and internal forms of punishment and constraint. The Constitutions of Clarendon prohibited clerics from leaving England without royal permission, hoping to control the relationship between the English prelates and Rome. For felonious offenses, however, the church was more prone to imprison a criminal or force them to abjure, punishments that were either not severe enough in the eyes of the king, or simply left his will out of the process. The reign of Henry II brought clarified criminal jurisdiction and strengthened the royal administration of justice. A criminal could plead benefit of the clergy and, if proven, would be punished by the bishop, most commonly with a term of imprisonment.

The Assizes of Clarendon and Northampton altered the customary law, and while the customary changes associated with presentment and ordeal are well acknowledged, those associated with the principles of exile and outlawry have been ignored. The Crown and its officials were able to effectively use and monitor outlawry while incorporating imprisonment and abjuration into the sphere of punishment in ways that served their interests. Casting an offender out of society actually gained royal strength with the endorsement of abjuration of the realm for individuals who had cleared themselves at trial though the ordeal. Controls over abjuration of the realm and its pronouncement upon criminals or suspects of ill-repute allowed the Crown to essentially outlaw individuals who were not subject to the exigent process because they had appeared in court. Outlawry and its principles were being altered to fit the needs of the Crown in the legal sphere. We will see, however, that this severely limited the use of outlawry and exile by the Crown for its own political gain.

Outlawry continued to function at the county level but the need for increased use of confinement was also felt in the localities. Custodial imprisonment was the most common form of confinement used, but with the building of a gaol in every English county as ordered by the Assize of Clarendon, gaols and the concept of internal constraint under authority of the Crown were gaining recognition and awareness in society. However, without the outlawry process, the justices in eyre would not have been able to punish offenders who did not appear for trial and malefactors would have remained unknown to the communities. That crime existed and was problematic is not in dispute, and given the social framework, outlawry was an effective way of dealing with these issues.

With the reign of King John in the early thirteenth century, the power-struggle within England shifted and his use of both imprisonment and outlawry outside of the specified legal perimeters created political unrest. As the law became more defined, so too were breaches of it. John, in a way, was the victim of his father's reforms. The demands of the early thirteenth-century barons that the king cease the use of unlawful imprisonment and outlawry attested to misuse of both practices. The association of outlawry and imprisonment with one another reveals perceptions about the punitive nature of each as well as the similar threat each posed. Henry III (1216-1272) was met with resistance when he attempted to exile and outlaw his political enemies, demonstrated clearly by the case of Hugh de Burgh. In 1234, the exclusive right of the county courts to pronounce outlawries was affirmed. Royal prerogative and custom had finally clashed with all clarity and the crown was denied use of the powerful tool of outlawry thanks to its own increased centralization. The recognition that legal backing to drive out enemies was necessary did not go unrealized, however, as the barons brought charges against the Poitevins, pushed for the "Statute of Aliens" and brought about prosecution against corrupt officials that resulted in the choice of imprisonment or self-imposed exile by the accused.

The use of outlawry by the Crown was subject to scrutiny and opposition based on custom. After outlawry by royal prerogative disappeared during the mid-thirteenth century, there was a decided royal concern with maintaining order through checks on the outlawry process in the counties. The administration of justice was increasingly bureaucratized and consequences of mistakes and abuses are clearly explained to us by Bracton. The Crown found innovative ways to use the outlawry process for its own ends, however, as it issued royal writs ordering county courts to place men in exigency. Local resentment ensued and communities attempted to hold on to their rights and responsibilities while resisting royal interference.[736] With this increased litigation, a growing number of felonies, and corruption of legal processes in the thirteenth century, however, more men were brought to courts or fled prior to being called to appear. This increased the number of fugitives in society, led to more exigents and outlawries, and likely resulted in heightened resentment for the crown and its men. Antipathy could result in sympathy, or perhaps just apathy, towards outlaws, rendering outlawry less effective as a punitive social practice.

All the while, the justices in eyre continued to interact with the outlawry process during their visitations. From its earliest days, outlawry was an essential part of the eyre's visitations to county courts. Outlawry continued to be pronounced in the counties throughout the thirteenth century in matters brought by appeal, presentment, and *querela*. Outlawry was a common response to a wrong– flight by a criminal occurred in a moment of panic, fear caused suspects to evade authorities, and after an appropriate period of time, outlawry was pronounced in the local court attended by community members.

736 The relationship between resentment and law is also mentioned by W.C. Jordan in "A Fresh Look at Medieval Sanctuary," in *Law and the Illicit in Medieval Europe*. eds R. M. Karras, J. Kay, and E. A. Matter (Philadelphia, PA: University of Pennsylvania Press, 2008): 17-32 at 28.

The notoriety and publicity of outlawry functioned well in medieval England. Within the outlawry process, the Crown did maintain certain rights and control. The possessions of outlaws went to royal coffers, although this was limited to "a year and a day" later as lords wished to have their property returned to them following the outlawry of one of their subjects. Royal officials were responsible for presenting outlaws to the justices in eyre, enrolling them for royal records, and holding individuals accountable for the behavior and treatment of outlaws within their communities. Although the crown attempted to garner control of the local courts through the use of personnel, increased presence, and more clearly defined legal processes, it was only moderately successful.

By the end of the thirteenth century, however, many responses to wrongdoing that involved outlawry were suppressed, replaced, and altered by the increased use of imprisonment, gaols, and confinement. It was becoming easier to obtain a pardon or avoid recourse for being an outlaw. A pardon could be bought but the process was being recorded so closely that outlawry could be remitted on a technicality or exchanged for imprisonment, which could then be commuted for a fine. During the reign of Edward I (1271-1307), outlawry could even be remitted in exchange for military service. In practice, outlawry was still a strong force and where the Crown could control its process, it continued to do so. Pardons were issued or sold, cattle was taken, land was seized and the eyre was still concerned with outlaws. The articles of the eyre, the duties of the coroner, and the role jury of presentment are all elements of the Crown's attempt to have a greater amount of authority within the outlawry process, a desire that was never fulfilled.

The increased use of imprisonment was both a cause and a result of the failed royal effort to control order in England. The Crown slowly found legal mechanisms other than outlawry. Imprisonment met this need. Similarly, as imprisonment became more common and more of a legal and social threat, flight from this threat found more use. Just as the rise in litigation in the late thirteenth century changed the legal culture and social order in England, so too did the use of imprisonment.

By the first decade of the fourteenth century, Edward I had become entangled in wars in Wales, Gascony, and Scotland, the eyre had been abandoned, and there was a need for renewed order within England. The Crown was forced to find another means to deal with the legal, economic, social, and political duties previously exercised by the eyre. Special commissions, specifically those termed "trailbaston", were one part of effort to thwart disorder. [737] Trailbaston

737 "Ordinance of the Inquiry, 33 Edward I (1305)," *The statutes of the realm*, Volume 1, 1235-1377. Printed at the command of His Majesty King George III. [n.d.], 143;

commissions had been used sporadically in the 1290s, but in 1304-1305 "came large-scale country-wide enquiry by justices in five circuits into murder, arson, robbery, and other breaches of the peace, into complicity in these and into confederacies, intimidation, maintenance, bribery, and extortions since 1297."[738] In addition to commissions, peacekeeping officers were also used, first as the "keeper" and later as the better-known "justice of the peace". During the last part of Edward I's reign, keepers of the peace continued to enforce the Statute of Winchester of 1285 and also received extended authority to hear and punish complaints associated with Magna Carta and the Charter of the Forest.[739] With the trailbaston commissions and keepers of the peace, gaols were increasingly used to hold wrongdoers and stress was placed upon local accountability for offenders, prisoners, and outlaws. Developments such as these remind us that the story of the relationship between outlawry and imprisonment does not end with the end of the eyre in 1294, nor with the trailbaston in 1305, nor with the death of Edward I in 1307. Justice and the maintenance of law and order were always related to these practices, which were constantly adapting as a result, and the fourteenth century would bring still more interaction between outlawry and imprisonment.

"Trailbaston Proceedings at Derby, 4 July 1306," 612-620; A. Harding, "Early trailbaston proceedings"; *Calendar of London Trailbaston Trials Under Commissions of 1305 and 1306*, ed. R.B. Pugh; Brown, *Governance in Late Medieval England*, 116-128; Prestwich, *Edward I*, 285-288.

738 Brown, *Governance in Later Medieval England*, 118; "Ordinance of the Inquiry, 33 Edward I (1305)," 143; Crook, "The Later Eyres," 246.

739 Kaeuper, *War, Justice, and Public Order;* 176-181; Sutherland, *Quo Warranto*, 185-189; Putnam, "The Transformation of the Keepers of the Peace into the Justices of the Peace, 1327-1380," 19-48; A. Musson, "Sub-keepers and Constables: the Role of Local Officials in Keeping the Peace in Fourteenth Century England," *English Historical Review* (Feb. 2002): 1-24; Brown, *Governance in Later Medieval England*, 122-123. Musson focuses on local peacekeeping officials as part of the sum of justice in England in the fourteenth century while Putnam emphasizes a divide between "local" and "central" justice. In my estimation, Putnam's articulation is necessary in understanding how local and central related to one another while Musson's emphasis on understanding the whole system is obvious and can be accomplished even while recognizing that some sort of disconnect did exist.

Why Imprisonment?

T.F.T. Plucknett observed:

> A most striking feature of our older criminal law and legislation is the reluctance to use imprisonment; even when it does appear, it is often merely a means to the end of extracting money from the offender. A fixed term, imposed as a penalty, seems to be a novelty – and a rare one – in Edward I's legislation, where it seems reserved for those cases which aroused indignation; thus poaching incurs three years plus a fine, and ultimately outlawry; a bailiff of a franchise who does not pursue a felon may get one or two years, and the lawyer, be he the eminent sergeant-at-law or any other, who is guilty of any manner of deceit in the king's court may get a "year at least".[740]

And James Bellamy states:

> ...that there were more sentences to imprisonment in the later middle ages than in preceding centuries cannot be doubted. One reason seems to have been the popularity, from the later thirteenth century, of the actions of trespass following misdeeds like assault or petty larceny which men claimed had broken the king's peace. When the courts found a man guilty on this count he was liable both to the payment of damages and to a period in gaol. Another reason was the increased promulgation of laws which contained clauses imposing imprisonment, often precisely defined as to duration, on those who broke them.... These laws...first appear in the first half of the thirteenth century and suggest popular support for their penal provisions in that they were fabricated with the consent of the whole community.[741]

Overall, the act of casting a malefactor out of society was increasingly being replaced by mechanisms of social, political, and judicial control that included imprisonment. Outlawry and the like were modified and alternatives were used, but not as a result of its ineffectiveness. Rather it was in response to attempts by the crown to "routinize" outlawry and the resistance and strength of outlawry in the face of prerogatory kingship and statutory law. The kings used the law to solidify, shape, and control outlawry, but as a result tied their own hands in the use of it and its principles. Abjuration was still available to the crown, but only in specific circumstances, and imprisonment became the only viable option for much of what the crown wanted to do in political and legal spheres.

Hurnard and Bellamy state that law and order declined under the reign of Edward I due to his preoccupation with foreign wars and use of pardons, which

740 Plucknett, *Concise History*, 90.

741 Bellamy, *Crime and Public Order*, 163-164.

had set a contagious example for disrespect in the law. Similarly, the end of the eyre in 1294 resulted in the cessation of full investigations into county matters by royal officials.[742] Summerson argues that it was this decline in law and order in the late thirteenth century that saw the downfall of outlawry. According to Summerson, the growing population and the resulting emergence of a "vagrant class" caused the exclusion and publicity provided by outlawry as a form of law enforcement to become less effective from the perspective of the Crown.[743] In the face of the growing use of imprisonment, it seems hardly the case that outlawry and the like represent a weak or ineffective system of justice. Rather, outlawry represents the part of a system of justice of which the Crown failed to seize control.

Later medieval kings copied the Angevins, who made use of imprisonment to compel officials to make payments and restitutions as well as used it to make reluctant accusers prosecute appeals.[744] Bellamy argues that by the fifteenth century, the crown realized that they needed to limit popular control over trial procedures and sought to close loopholes, such as the benefit of the clergy and sanctuary, however were challenged by the realization that the king's law and Common Law were not the same thing. The increased use of pardons and fines show a novel approach to punishment, even if the king welcomed them as a means of royal profit, and a way to reconcile to society offenders he was unable to bring to trial.[745]

While Bellamy is accurate in his assertion, we need not wait until the fifteenth century to see this royal realization take place. Limits were placed, or at least attempted, on judicial processes in the statutes of Edward I, particularly within the Statute of Winchester, where the Crown was just not able to follow-up and control local justice. The need for greater authority of the counties and a strengthened link between local and royal governance had been realized, and attempts to reform law and order are found in the increased use of imprisonment in the thirteenth century and royal attempts to adapt and control the outlawry process. The relationship between outlawry and imprisonment and their respective changes since the tenth century clearly demonstrate attempts at the centralization of power. Some of these efforts had been successful, some had not.

Punishment and mechanisms of public order, as we have seen, included outlawry and imprisonment, as well as fines, mutilation, and even death. In this

---

742 Hurnard, *King's Pardon*, 313-317; Prestwich, *Edward I*, 284.

743 Summerson, "The Structure of Law Enforcement in Thirteenth Century England," 313-327.

744 Bellamy, *Crime and Public Order*, 164.

745 Bellamy, *Crime and Public Order*, 202-204.

context, why did imprisonment become more common in the later middle ages? What would have been accomplished by a term of imprisonment? What purpose did it serve for the complaint bringer; the presiding authorities; or the system of law? Did it reform or deter an offender?

For a complainant, imprisonment could act as a means to receive repayment or recompense from a wrongdoer. Although terms of imprisonment in the Middle Ages appear to be short, "to late medieval people even a fortnight behind bars was intolerable."[746] Imprisonment in the Middle Ages would have been harsh by any modern standard, although conditions would be relative to social rank. This is why gaolers were often viewed as corrupt extortionists, as they would often use the prison and their words as a means to profit. An offender paid his own way while in prison, and if he had the resources, he could buy food, warmth, and a higher level of comfort. The poor were reliant upon charity or friends for assistance, although distribution of these items was also subject to the gaoler's discretion.

Since the reign of Henry II and the Assize of Clarendon, the use of prisons as a physical display of authority and a social representation of royal power was a factor in the increased existence and use of goals and prisons. Imprisonment allowed for repayment of fines due to the Crown as well, and could also result in royal seizure of land or possessions.[747] From the thirteenth century, imprisonment was used for a large variety of crimes: misbehavior of officials with respect to justice or tax collection, corruption of justice, riots, forcible entry, disseisin, economic crimes such as fraudulent mercantilism, and offenses against statutes of laborers. These crimes all, in theory, touched the king directly. Just as no law was regarded as a new law, not even a statute, neither was the punishment found within that law. Rather, it was "the discovery and affirmation of some rule of previous centuries."[748]

As the law developed, particularly that which was written, so did the punishments for offenses and means of righting wrongs. What we perceive to be innovations were thought to be assertions of previously unwritten law or adaptations of law ideally based in custom. In that context, it makes sense that imprisonment "to gain compliance" was used.[749] Imprisonment was not arbitrary, as Dunbabin suggests, but was initially used in matters that touched the King, his peace, and his subjects, but only in instances where the Crown could exercise

746 T. Dean, *Crime in Medieval Europe 1200-1550* (London, UK: Pearson Education, Ltd., 2001), 122.

747 Dean, *Crime in Medieval Europe*, 122-124.

748 Bellamy, *Crime and Public Order,* 164.

749 Bellamy, *Crime and Public Order*, 164.

constraint without treading upon custom. This is why forest law had taken shape as it did. That the Normans brought forest law to England is a relative certainty, but post-Conquest law-makers sought to find justification in its enforcement in the Anglo-Saxon laws of Cnut and Edward the Confessor. In reality, forest law was not subject to the scrutiny of custom and community. As a result, the Crown could punish and enforce according to its will. This is why imprisonment was used to punish offenders.

The same can be said of matters of trespass. As the distinctions between civil and criminal law began to hash themselves out in late thirteenth century law, penalties and punishments received new definition and use as well. Trespass was not a felony, nor was it limited to criminal or civil matters, but it fell under the peace of the King nonetheless. As a writable offense, the King was able to extend his reach to private wrongs that had previously been heard as appeals in the county courts. As trespass developed, new mechanisms of dealing with offenders did as well. Trespassers were subject to terms of imprisonment and fines and as the number of trespass complaints grew, so too did the use of the prison.

That said, how does one reconcile imprisonment in England with the Roman law tradition resisting its punitive application? Justinian's *Digest* asserted that prisons were to be used to hold men, not to punish them. Medieval jurists "abhorred" the use of punitive imprisonment but in late medieval England, "the king and his legal advisors had no objection to imprisonment on principle."[750] Imprisonment had been long used in England in matters of law and politics, and "in the case of punitive imprisonment in the Middle Ages, legislation lagged behind practice and...departed from contemporary, mainstream penal thought."[751] Distinguishing between punitive, coercive, and custodial imprisonment is not easily done, nor is it entirely helpful or relevant, as all time spent in confinement was surely viewed as punishment by the incarcerated individual.

> Many of those who languished in later medieval gaols were there not awaiting trial but having already been tried and sentenced to imprisonment, either as their sole punishment or as part of it. Condemnation to a term of incarceration in gaol was not a particularly common form of punishment. This was because there were other penalties available which provided the king with reward rather than expense; in many cases a fine was much to be preferred.[752]

750 Geltner, *Medieval Prison*, 44-56; Bellamy, *Crime and Public Order*, 163.
751 Geltner, *Medieval Prison*, 44.
752 Bellamy, *Crime and Public Order*, 163.

Legal terms of imprisonment in England were accompanied by fines, ransoms, and forfeiture of property, measures that may have been viewed by authorities as the primary punishment placed upon a criminal.

Furthermore, the Church's use of imprisonment "to punish unpurged clerks was a constant reminder of the favour it enjoyed in other quarters, and the king must have been aware of the argument that it might effect a change of heart through the time it gave the misdoer to reflect on his crime and predicament."[753] Monastic orders had long used seclusion, excommunication, and pilgrimage as forms of penance imposed upon members needing correction or punishment. In the eleventh century, monasteries in England also began to use prisons for the moral correction of monks.[754] By the twelfth century, bishops used prisons as well, and in 1298, Pope Boniface VIII "overturned the "rule" that prisons should be for custody, not punishment, in allowing bishops to incarcerate clerics who committed crimes."[755]

A combination of all of these factors influenced the use of imprisonment, which had been slow to come to the forefront of English legal and social authority, as a tool that was adapted to meet the needs of the overall administration of justice. The changes in judicial processes in the early fourteenth century, particularly the commissions of the trailbaston in 1305, again altered legal and political frameworks in England and the relationship between the Crown and its subjects.

Did Outlawry Lose its Place in the Administration of Justice?

Prior to this work, the transition to a system of law and order based more on confinement has not been assessed in terms of the forms of punishment and methods of maintaining order that preceded this increased use of imprisonment. Exile, banishment, and outlawry dominated the legal and political processes in England from the tenth through the thirteenth centuries, and continued to do so well into the fourteenth and beyond. By the end of the thirteenth century, however, the Crown had asserted, or at least had attempted to, assert, control over

753 Geltner, *Medieval Prison*, 56; Dean, *Crime in Medieval Europe*, 120-121; Bellamy, *Crime and Public Order*, 163.

754 Pugh, *Imprisonment in Medieval England*, 374-383; Lanfranc, *Monastic Constitutions of Lanfranc*, eds D. Knowles and C.N. Brooke (Oxford, UK: Oxford UP, 2002), 148, 153; E. Vodola, *Excommunication in the Middle Ages*, 1-111, 191-193.

755 Dean, *Crime in Medieval Europe*, 121; Plucknett, *Edward I and Criminal Law*, 95-98.

aspects of outlawry, exile, and later abjuration. The increased use of imprisonment contained in legislation and judicial processes must be assessed in this context. Royal efforts attempted to bring as many components of the respective processes of each into the centralized control of the Crown.

Likewise, the Crown applied many of the same principles of outlawry to imprisonment, creating methods of punishment that were under their control yet resembled in some ways what was customary and traditional in England. The preceding discussion of the role of outlawry in the development of common law – viewed as an attempt by the crown to "routine" of the custom of casting a malefactor via outlawry, exile, banishment, or abjuration – does just that. Outlawry was altered and replaced as politics and justice necessitated. This resulted in an emphasis upon imprisonment as a political and legal tool. Through the course of the central Middle Ages, outlawry, abjuration, and imprisonment all functioned together, used and facilitated one another, and ultimately caused the increased use of the latter.

Without any doubt, gaols and prisons were commonly used at various levels of legal and administrative processes by the end of the thirteenth century. This was in large part influenced by the role of outlawry, exile, and banishment in law and governance in Medieval England. No matter how many royal officials were put into English counties, regardless of how many inquests and statutes were intended to rectify abuses and restore royal order, and in spite of political alliances and agreements, exclusion remained an effective means of punishment and tool of social in England. Local courts held the power to proclaim outlaws and individuals pulled the strings as to criminal presentments and the treatment of fugitives.

Law, Literature, and Legend

By the end of eyre in 1294, the needs of justice in England had outgrown their own ability. They eyre had experienced an increased number of duties and disputes to hear with each tourn of the country, a workload that caused its inefficiency and decline. Whether out of judicial ineptitude or simply from more complaints being brought to law, there seems to have been a corresponding rise in outlawry in medieval England in the late thirteenth century.[756] Although imprisonment was much more common and more widely used in England by the end of the thirteenth century, outlawry had in no way disappeared.

756 For example, see the prominence of outlawry contained in London, The National Archives, JUST 1/563 of 1293.

To most historians of later medieval England, Edward I's trailbaston commissions of the early fourteenth century were issued as a response to the number of outlaws and outlaw bands running rampant in England. In 1305, royal justices were sent out to the counties to elicit presentments of felony, trespass, and other offenses. Whether the commissions were sent as a response to the decay of public order or as part of the continued royal responsibility for law and society, they were meant to provide local citizens with a royal avenue by which corruption, violence, and crime could be brought to justice. However, the commissions were viewed by contemporaries as instruments of that very corruption and as a means for the Crown to profit financially.[757] According to *The Outlaw Song of the Trailbaston*:

> Some will become robbers who never used to be,
> who dare not lead a peaceful life for fear of jail;
> they lack what it takes to keep them alive each day.
> Whoever began this business embarked on a great task.
>
> Well may merchants and monks give a curse
> to all those who ordained the Trailbaston.
> The royal protection will not be worth a garlic head
> unless they hand over the coins without getting anything back.
>
> You who are indicted, I advise you, come to me,
> to the green wood of Belregard, where there is no entanglement,
> just wild animals and pleasant shade;
> for the common law is too unreliable.[758]

The Crown had not been able to control or adapt outlawry for its own purposes so it altered the systems of justice and constraint, which led to the rampant flight of suspected criminals. Commission justices would place these fugitives in exigent and they would be outlawed in the county court. The flight and outlawry of these suspects came to be seen as necessary, righteous, and as a valiant act in response to an oppressive legal system. Such sentiments influenced what be-

757 A. Harding, "Early trailbaston proceedings from the Lincoln roll of 1305"; Kaeuper, *War, Justice and Public Order*, 139-142; Kaeuper, "Law and Order," 734-784.

758 *The Political Songs of England*, ed. Thomas Wright (Camden Society, 1839), 231-236, stanzas 12-14; C. Revard, "The Outlaw Song of the Trailbaston," in *Medieval Outlaws: Twelve Tales in Modern English Translation*, ed. T.H. Olgren (Parlor Press, LLC: 2005), 151-164.

came an idealized notion of outlawry, with the emergence of legends of Robin Hood and other notorious outlaws fleeing prosecution from overzealous governing authorities.

The conflicts between outlaw and authority found in medieval legends had long been used to represent the struggle against despotism and abuse of law. The earliest outlaw legends were penned in the twelfth century, and the early stories of Hereward, Eustace, and Fulk Fitzwarin, later those of Gamelyn and William Wallace, remind us how literature came to be used to as statements against injustice. These legends culminate in the best-known medieval outlaw, Robin Hood. Robin Hood was a timeless proud, devout, and courteous outlaw, the antithesis to the corrupt royal official, the Sheriff of Nottingham, as well as a romanticized literary response to unjust and misguided royal administration.[759] Discontent in England was expressed through these literary works that contained "an amalgam of outraged idealism and pure pragmatism."[760] They reflect…

> …that kings did take their responsibility seriously, within the limits of practical politics, sometimes as an instrument of practical politics…for their part subjects did want more order, and did place much hope for improvement of the public peace royal leadership, retaining always a belief, perhaps even a fondness, for violent self-help in circumstances of their own choosing.[761]

An outlaw was not always a criminal on the run, but rather was a champion of good and justice against a corrupt and flawed royal administration. This is not to say that crime and violence were glamorous or lawlessness was preferred, but it attests to dissatisfaction with the mechanisms of justice. The literary trope of the "good outlaw" offers a reader the outlaw complete with a sense of empowerment, superiority, and heroism in the face of tyranny.[762]

---

759 "The Matter of the Greenwood," pages 1-9 in M.H. Keen, *Outlaws of Medieval Legend*, see also 95ff and 191-218; T.H. Olgren, "General Introduction" and "The Gest of Robyn Hode" in *Medieval Outlaws*, xv-xxxv and 356-396, respectively; G. Seal, *The Outlaw Legend: A Cultural Tradition in Britain, America and Australia* (Cambridge, UK: Cambridge UP, 1996), 20-30; Kaeuper, *War, Justice, and Public Order*, 335-346, 374; Prestwich, *The Three Edwards*, 204-205.

760 Kaeuper, *War, Justice, and Public Order*, 143.

761 Kaeuper, *War, Justice, and Public Order*, 143.

762 Henry Summerson, "The criminal underworld of Medieval England," 197-224, at 219-220; Ohlgren, *Medieval Outlaws*, xxviii-xxx.

Implications for the Administration of Justice in Fourteenth Century England

Edward I was heavily engaged in wars in Scotland for the last decade of his rule and faced opposition from his magnates over liberties, taxation, and money-borrowing.[763] An overall assessment of Edward‘s policies reveals that while “the development of legislation by statute may not have been consciously deliberate…it transformed the process of legal change.” Edward‘s statutes were responses to needs and grievances within society: they corrected wrongs and increased judicial and administrative efficiency, no intent or principle guided their inception.[764] Oyer and terminer commissions, particularly those of the trailbaston, and peacekeeping officials were further agents of Edward‘s policy. As main avenues of royal administration in the early fourteenth century, they weigh heavily on discussion of law and order during the last years of Edward I’s reign and beyond.

That Edward I was concerned with criminal and civil law in England is not in doubt. The reign of Edward I’s son, Edward II, was plagued by the inherited war with Scotland (which he would lose in 1314), skeptical barons, and political in-fighting. Edward II was unable to successfully fill the role of soldier and leader as his father had done and is usually characterized by his interests in entertainment and male companions.[765] Exile and outlawry remained heavily engrained in politics and law in England, as demonstrated by the demand of the permanent removal of Piers Gaveson, one of the king’s favorites, from England in 1308 and again in the Ordinances of 1311, as well as to the exile of the Despencers in the 1320s.[766]

---

763 Prestwich, *Edward I*, 517-567.

764 Prestwich, *Edward I*, 560.

765 Prestwich, *The Three Edwards*, 71-101.

766 “The New Ordinances of 1311, 5 Edward II (1311),” *Statutes of the Realm*, 157-168, specifically at c. 20; P. Chaplais, *Piers Gaveston: Edward II’s adoptive brother* (Oxford, UK: Oxford UP, 1994), 69-72; N. Fryde, *The Tyranny and Fall of Edward II 1321-1326* (Cambridge, UK: Cambridge UP, 2004); Stubbs, *Constitutional History of England*, vol. 3: 313-332; 345-353. The Ordinances were compiled by a group of twenty-one men in England to place restrictions upon the King and his power. For more on (and a significant amount of speculation about) the relationship between Gaveston and Edward II, see Chaplais *in toto*, J.S. Hamilton, *Piers Gaveston, Earl of Cornwall, 1307-1312: Politics and Patronage in the Reign of Edward II* (Detroit, MI: Wayne State UP,1992); Prestwich, *The Three Edwards*, 71-101; and the play *Edward II* by Christopher Marlowe.

The tools of law, justice, and order from previous centuries continued to be used during the fourteenth century. Edward II took an active interest in criminal justice by way of the court of the King's Bench. In 1318, the court delivered the gaol at York and in 1323, Edward II ordered that it tour the country to hear trespass and felony indictments, much the same way as the trialbaston commissions had done. In the 1350s, the court of the King's Bench was even used as an eyre, sent throughout England to hear various matters.[767] In 1328, the parliament commissioned trailbastons in the vein of those conducted in 1305 and 1307. Keepers of the peace as agents of royal law and order were appointed in 1310, 1314, and 1326, and were extended further duties and power throughout the fourteenth century. Keepers were allowed to arrest upon suspicion without indictment from 1314-1327, as well as given the power to impose amercements for trespass in 1326 and to try charges of felony in 1329. And in 1329, the eyre of previous centuries was briefly revived.[768]

There was limited use of the eyre in the early fourteenth century, in 1313-1314 in Kent and in 1321 in London for example, but no regular or general eyre had been conducted since the end of the thirteenth century. The 1329-1330 eyre had two circuits, one in Nottinghamshire and one in Northamptonshire, and was charged with hearing all matters, especially those which fell out of the purview of royal commissions and keepers of the peace, such as escapes and other offenses that fell under the responsibility of sheriffs, coroners, and other officers of the law.[769] Justices also ordered the county courts to outlaw any identifiable fugitive felons. This could also be done in county court by appeal or by indictment before the trailbaston commissioners or keepers of the peace, but "only in the eyre with its comprehensive series of presentments…was every case certain to be covered."[770] The eyre also escheated the values of lands and chattels of felons, fugitives, outlaws, and abjurors, which demonstrates one argument in favor of the eyre. Without the thorough, systematized visitation of the eyre, the Crown could not receive the chattels of fugitives and others. Financial motives aside, the desire to maintain peace and exercise effective justice were also met,

767 S. L. Waugh, *England in the Reign of Edward III* (Cambridge, UK: Cambridge UP, 2001), 164.

768 D.W. Sutherland, "Introduction," *Northamptonshire Eyre, 1329-1330*, xxiv-xxvi; B.H. Putnam, "Records of the Keepers of the Peace and Their Supervisors, 1307-27," *The English Historical Review*, vol. 45, no. 179 (Jul., 1930): 435-444; A. Verduyn, "The Politics of Law and Order during the Early Years of Edward III," *English Historical Review*, vol. 108, no. 429 (Oct., 1993): 842-867; Kaeuper, "Law and Order," 734-784.

769 Sutherland, "Introduction," xxii-xxx.

770 Sutherland, "Introduction," xxx.

as until escheats were carried out, the sanctions "the common law laid against felons and their families" were not fulfilled.[771]

For a variety of reasons, not the least of which was continued resentment by local men at the coming of the royal justices, the general eyre only visited four counties in 1329 and 1330.[772] This disconnect between local and royal power only fostered what Bellamy identified as the three levels of problems of law enforcement England by the reign of Edward III: the lawlessness experienced by townsmen and villagers, the crown's duty to maintain order, and in the middle of those two as ends of a spectrum, local power, exercised by office or retainer. "Everything the crown did had to be mediated through county, town, village elites. That is precisely where much of the problem lay."[773] Edward III's policy was to confer with the localities in matters war, taxation, and appointments of officials. This guided statutory law and parliamentary development during his reign.[774]

By 1330, outlawry had been turned into a much less effective tool of justice and order than it had been in previous centuries. As demonstrated by the actions of prominent outlaws such as the Folvilles and the Coterel gang, fourteenth century outlawry had become a pseudo-profession, the result of which was wealth and notoriety. The ease with which outlaws eluded and escaped capture as well as obtained pardons was facilitated by measures taken by the Crown, essentially resulting in the Crown being its own biggest hurdle to law and order.[775] The

---

771 Sutherland, "Introduction," xxx.

772 Sutherland, "Introduction," xxxiii-xl; H.M. Cam, "The General Eyres of 1339-1330," *The English Historical Review*, vol. 39, no. 154 (Apr., 1924): 241-252; Crook, "The Later Eyres," 261-263. Sutherland discusses financial factors, the inconvenience of the eyre, and perceived unreasonable demands as causes for local resistance to the proceedings.

773 Waugh, *England in the Reign of Edward III*, 167.

774 Waugh, *England in the Reign of Edward III*, 167-169; J.G. Bellamy, *The criminal trial in later medieval England: felony before the courts from Edward I to the sixteenth century* (Toronto, CA: University of Toronto Press, 1998), 149; Brown, *Governance in Late Medieval England*, 156-179; *Statutes of the Realm*, vol. 1, 1235-1377; According to Bellamy, the statutes of Edward III contained the first use of imprisonment as a governmental measure. In the Ordinance of Laborers in 1349, men who refused to work at pre-plague wages were imprisoned until suretities could be found. Edward I's use of imprisonment was found in procedures and offenses that touched or were close to felony, but were not comparable to later uses of confinement.

775 E.L.G. Stone, "The Folvilles of Ashby-Folville, Leicestershire, and Their Associates in Crime, 1326-1347," *Transactions of the Royal Historical Society*, 5th ser., vol. 7 (1957): 117-136; J.G. Bellamy, "The Coterel Gang: An Anatomy of a Band of Fourteenth-Century Criminals," *English Historical Review*, vol. 79, no. 313 (Oct., 1964): 698-717.

ability to kill an outlaw with impunity was revoked in c. 1330, thus weakening the process as a threat or a punishment still further.[776]

Final Remarks

From the Anglo-Saxon period through the end of the thirteenth century, the most effective methods of punishment and social control transitioned from outlawry, exile, and banishment to imprisonment. As exile, banishment, and outlawry took on distinct forms and specific uses, control over their applications and processes became increasingly important. The Crown attempted to control exile, banishment, and outlawry by establishing processes for abjuration as well as by incorporating the use of gaols, prisons, and confinement into law and order in Medieval England.

776 Brown, *Governance in Late Medieval England*, 105-106.

Index

A

abjuration, 6, 8, 12, 16, 78, 79, 89, 96, 97, 103, 104, 114, 124, 129, 130, 132, 142, 143, 145, 156, 157, 160, 161, 162, 163, 165, 166, 169, 177, 178, 179, 188, 191, 197, 200, 213, 214, 219, 225, 229, 238, 245
abjure, 8, 78, 79, 85, 86, 96, 97, 100, 103, 104, 111, 117, 120, 125, 130, 138, 142, 143, 145, 157, 161, 162, 163, 164, 165, 170, 189, 197, 198, 204, 229
abjured the realm, 94, 111, 130, 144, 146, 156, 161, 162, 169, 178, 179, 188, 204, 214, 220
abjuror, 121, 132, 155
Æthelred, King of England, 22, 24, 28, 29, 31, 32, 33, 35, 36, 80
Æthelred, King of the English, 24
Æthelstan, 23, 26, 27, 35, 41, 52
Æthelstan, King of the English, 23
Æthelwine, Bishop of Durham, 55, 65
Alfgar, Earl of East Anglia, 37
Alfred, King of the English, 6, 23, 25
Anglo-Saxon Chronicle, 19, 21, 22, 26, 32, 37, 38, 55, 56, 59, 63
Anselm, Archbishop of Canterbury, 65, 66, 89
approver, 79, 80, 103, 124, 154, 157, 170, 194, 204
Arnold d'Courville, 47
Arnulf, 68
Arthur of Brittany, 133
articles of the eyre, 119, 120, 126, 140, 166, 231
Assize of Clarendon, 92, 93, 94, 95, 96, 98, 99, 100, 104, 107, 111, 119, 123, 204, 229, 235
Assize of Northampton, 96, 97, 98, 104, 111, 123, 216
Assize of the Forest, 77, 102, 137
Assize of Weights and Measures, 122
Assizes of Clarendon and Northampton, 94, 96, 107, 123, 130, 137, 197, 229
Aymer de Lusignan, 174

B

bajulus, 38
Baldwin de Redvers, Count of Anjou, 73
banishment, 6, 7, 8, 10, 11, 15, 19, 20, 22, 25, 26, 27, 29, 32, 33, 38, 41, 42, 44, 45, 46, 47, 50, 51, 62, 70, 71, 74, 76, 80, 81, 84, 85, 86, 87, 89, 92, 96, 105, 115, 116, 169, 174, 228, 238, 244
Baronial Reform, 148, 159, 160, 167, 172, 173, 175, 176, 177, 178, 182, 186, 187, 188, 189, 202
Baronial Revolt, 186
Barons, 16, 93, 134, 135, 146, 171, 172, 173, 174, 179, 183, 184, 185, 186, 188, 189, 200, 212
Battle of Evesham, 179, 184, 185, 186, 189
Battle of Lewes, 184, 189
Bayeux Tapestry, 50
Becket, Thomas, 75, 85, 86, 87, 88, 89, 90, 91, 104, 110, 111
botless, 28, 29
Bracton, 13, 125, 127, 136, 140, 145, 151, 152, 153, 154, 155, 156, 157, 158, 159, 160, 161, 180, 181, 193, 194, 197, 205, 206, 207, 230
Braose, William, 133, 134

C

Canon law, 12, 13
Charters of the Forest, 137, 138
Cnut, King of England, 28, 29, 30, 32, 33, 34, 35, 36, 37, 38, 41, 51, 52, 53, 67, 77, 80, 236
Common Law, 6, 7, 14, 17, 72, 81, 84, 88, 92, 93, 94, 96, 99, 102, 108, 121, 143, 158, 181, 198, 225, 234
Constitutions of Clarendon, 67, 77, 87, 88, 89, 90, 91, 104, 110, 111, 228, 237
coroner, 109, 119, 120, 124, 125, 126, 129, 130, 141, 142, 144, 159, 161, 165, 188, 192, 207, 213, 215, 231
County coroners. See coroner
county court, 27, 52, 54, 70, 71, 99, 108, 124, 125, 126, 128, 132, 136, 140, 141, 142, 153, 154, 155, 158, 160, 161, 163,

164, 165, 201, 205, 206, 207, 208, 240, 243
county courts, 27, 53, 54, 77, 92, 95, 98, 104, 107, 108, 111, 120, 124, 126, 127, 131, 141, 142, 145, 153, 163, 164, 165, 166, 177, 180, 188, 202, 207, 208, 209, 225, 228, 230, 236, 243
Course of the Exchequer, 77
curia, 72, 125
custos pacis, or keeper of the peace, 202

D

danegeld, 31, 33
de odio et atia, appeals of, 103
Dialogue of the Exchequer, 77
Domesday Survey, 57, 67, 94, 191
Dudo of St. Quentin, 45
Duke Richard II, 48, 49
Duke Richard III, 49
Duke Robert, 46, 64, 67, 68, 69
Duke William, 47, 49, 81
Duke William II in Normandy. See William of Normandy, King William of England

E

Edgar, King of the English, 23, 28, 35, 56
Edith, 38, 39
Edmund, King of East Anglia, 6, 23, 28, 32, 221
Edward (the Confessor), King of England, 8, 16, 19, 23, 24, 26, 28, 31, 32, 36, 37, 38, 39, 40, 49, 50, 56, 57, 77, 78, 88, 92, 97, 102, 125, 145, 150, 172, 173, 180, 182, 183, 184, 185, 186, 191, 192, 193, 194, 195, 196, 197, 198, 199, 200, 201, 202, 203, 204, 205, 209, 210, 211, 212, 213, 218, 219, 220, 221, 222, 223, 224, 231, 232, 233, 234, 237, 241, 242, 243, 244
Edward and Guthrum, laws of, 26
Edward I, King of England, 182, 184, 185, 186, 187, 189, 191, 196, 204, 205, 208, 209, 210, 211, 216, 217, 219, 220, 221, 222, 223, 224, 225, 231, 232, 234, 236, 239, 241
Edward II, King of England, 241, 242
Edward III, King of England, 243, 244
Edwin, 21, 40, 55, 56, 81
Eleanor of Aquitaine, Queen of England, 91, 114, 115, 116, 167
Emma, 31, 36, 162
Eric, Earl of Northumbria, 32
Eustace de Vesci, 134
Eustace the Monk, 138
exchequer, 72, 80, 81, 98, 101, 108, 111, 122, 173
excommunication, 6, 7, 13, 25, 59, 72, 111, 157, 237
exile, 6, 7, 8, 9, 10, 11, 12, 13, 15, 16, 19, 20, 21, 22, 25, 26, 27, 29, 30, 31, 32, 33, 36, 37, 38, 39, 40, 41, 44, 45, 47, 48, 50, 51, 52, 54, 55, 56, 57, 60, 63, 64, 65, 66, 68, 69, 70, 71, 73, 74, 76, 78, 79, 80, 81, 84, 86, 89, 90, 96, 97, 102, 110, 112,116, 117, 118, 133, 134, 135, 137, 144, 146, 149, 151, 167, 168, 174, 182, 188, 189, 228, 229, 230, 238, 242, 244

F

Fawkes de Breauté, 148, 149
First Statute of Westminster, 193, 194, 195, 196, 198
Forest eyres, 124
forest law, 66, 77, 123, 137, 146, 170, 211, 236
Forest offenders, 137, 179
forisbannitio, 52, 53
Foucault, Michel, 13
Fourth Lateran Council, 143
Fulk Fitzwarin, 138, 139, 240

G

Gamelyn, 240
gaol, 100, 101, 114, 117, 123, 124, 131, 132, 142, 144, 145, 159, 161, 162, 164, 167, 170, 176, 178, 179, 192, 194, 196, 205, 209, 210, 211, 212, 213, 214, 215, 216, 220, 221, 222, 223, 229, 233, 237, 242
gaols, 6, 100, 104, 112, 123, 124, 131, 132, 158, 159, 176, 178, 191, 203, 204, 210, 221, 222, 229, 231, 232, 237, 238, 245
gemot, 23
general eyres, 124, 177, 178, 179, 188, 213
Geoffrey Marisco, 167, 168

Geoffrey of Mowbray, 62
Geoffrey Talbot, 73
Gesta Stephani, 73, 74, 75, 76
Gilbert Bassett, 151, 204
Gilbert de Lacy, 73
Glanvill, 92, 105
Glanville, 54, 94, 105, 106, 107, 108
Godwin, Earl of Wessex, 10, 36, 38, 39, 40
Guy de Rochfort, 173
Guy of Abbeville, 49
Guy of Burgundy, 47

H

Harold Harefoot, 36, 38
Harold, Son of Godwin, King of England, 36, 38, 40, 49, 50, 81
Harthacnut, 36, 37, 38
Henry Bray, 218
Henry I, 28, 65, 67, 68, 69, 70, 71, 72, 73, 77, 78, 79, 81, 89, 93, 99, 102, 228
Henry II, 6, 14, 16, 73, 77, 80, 84, 85, 87, 88, 89, 90, 91, 92, 93, 94, 96, 99, 100, 101, 102, 105, 106, 107, 108, 109, 110, 111, 112, 114, 115, 118, 119, 133, 135, 137, 138, 144, 159, 196, 221, 228, 235
Henry III, 16, 114, 127, 134, 136, 138, 139, 140, 141, 142, 143, 144, 146, 148, 149, 150, 151, 152, 155, 158, 159, 160, 163, 167, 168, 169, 172, 173, 174, 176, 177, 178, 180, 182, 183, 184, 185, 186, 187, 188, 189, 196, 202, 205, 207, 209, 210, 212, 213, 220, 223, 230
Hereward, 38, 55, 57, 58, 240
homicide, 6, 26, 30, 34, 53, 85, 87, 95, 107, 120, 128, 129, 130, 144, 156, 159, 162, 163, 188, 192, 207, 215, 218, 221, 222
Hubert de Burgh, 139, 148, 149, 150, 151, 152, 160, 167
Hubert Walter, 119, 120, 121, 137
hue and cry, 24, 93, 97, 120, 121, 126, 128, 130, 164, 166
Hugh Bigod, 171, 173, 175, 176
Hugh of Grandmesnil, 47
Hugh of Salisbury, 62

I

imprisonment, 6, 7, 8, 12, 13, 14, 15, 16, 17, 24, 25, 44, 48, 49, 50, 54, 55, 56, 57, 58, 60, 65, 66, 69, 73, 74, 75, 76, 79, 81, 85, 86, 99, 100, 102, 104, 106, 107, 110, 112, 114, 115, 118, 121, 122, 123, 124, 131, 132, 134, 136, 137, 143, 144, 145, 146, 148, 151, 157, 158, 159, 160, 161, 166, 169, 170, 171, 174, 176, 178, 179, 180, 187, 188, 189, 191, 192, 194, 195, 196, 197, 198, 200, 201, 202, 203, 204, 205, 206, 208, 212, 214, 218, 219, 221, 223, 225, 228, 229, 231, 232, 233, 234, 235, 236, 237, 238, 239, 244
inlaw, 155
Inquest of the Sheriff, 99
itinerant justices, 93, 99, 143, 163, 165, 173, 187, See justices in eyre, See justices in eyre

J

John de Lovetot, 219
John of Salisbury, 75, 89, 90
judicial eyre, 6, 119, 228
juries of presentment, 92, 93, 100, 104, 111, 121, 125, See also presentment juries
justices in eyre, 93, 94, 98, 100, 102, 108, 121, 122, 123, 125, 126, 127, 132, 142, 163, 166, 180, 187, 205, 229, 230, 231, See also itinerant justices, See also itinerant justices, See also itinerant justices, See also itinerant justices
justiciar, 38, 116, 118, 119, 149, 150, 173

K

keepers of the pleas of the crown. See coroners
King Alfred, 131
King Edmund, 6
King Edward, 38, 39, 40, 217, 218
King Edward I, 16
King John, 14, 16, 19, 31, 32, 37, 38, 39, 40, 51, 59, 67, 75, 89, 90, 114, 116, 117, 118, 122, 123, 126, 127, 129, 131, 132, 133, 134, 135, 136, 137, 138, 139, 140, 141, 146, 148, 149, 151, 152, 161, 162,

168, 174, 178, 179, 188, 196, 207, 208, 211, 212, 213, 214,219, 220, 221, 229
King Richard, 16, 114, 116, 117, 123, 131
King Stephen, 73, 74, 75, 76, 93
King William, 55, 59, 62, 63
king's peace, 28, 57, 94, 111, 156, 159, 163, 197, 222, 225, 233

L

Leges Eadwardi Confessoris, 40, 41
Leges Edwardi Confessoris, 78
Leges Henrici Primi, 70
Leis Willelme, 52
Leofa, 26
Lillebonne, Council of, 85, 86, 87

M

Magna Carta, 16, 72, 128, 133, 134, 135, 136, 137, 139, 144, 146, 148, 185, 187, 189, 201, 206, 207, 232
manslaga, 6
Matilda, Empress, 73, 74, 75, 76
mercy, 23, 30, 35, 60, 70, 71, 78, 79, 96, 97, 103, 106, 115, 118, 122, 124, 127, 129, 146, 154, 155, 156, 158, 162, 165, 171, 186, 199
Morcar, 40, 55, 56, 61
morte d'ancestor, writ of, 92

N

New Forest, 66, 67
Newgate Prison, 100, 204
novel disseisin. writ of, 92, 149

O

Odo of Bayeux, 55, 58, 59, 60, 62, 63, 64, 65, 74, 81, 228
On the Laws and Customs of England, 126, 152, 158
Orderic Vitalis, 45, 46, 47, 55, 56, 57, 59, 60, 61, 62, 63, 64, 68, 69, 74, 76
Osgod Clapa, 37
Osred, King of Northumbria, 21, 22
ostracism, 8, 9
outlaw, 8, 10, 11, 16, 24, 25, 26, 29, 31, 32, 34, 35, 37, 39, 40, 44, 51, 52, 57, 58, 70, 71, 72, 77, 80, 94, 96, 105, 109, 110, 121, 123, 125, 126, 127, 128, 129, 130, 131, 132, 133, 135, 136, 138, 141, 142, 146, 151, 152, 153, 154, 155, 156, 160, 162, 164, 165, 189, 193, 198, 206, 213, 216, 220, 223, 229, 230, 231, 239, 240, 241, 243, 244
Outlaw Song of the Trailbaston, 239, 240
outlawry, 6, 7, 9, 10, 11, 12, 14, 15, 16, 17, 19, 25, 26, 27, 28, 29, 30, 31, 32, 33, 34, 35, 37, 38, 39, 41, 42, 44, 45, 51, 52, 53, 54, 57, 58, 70, 71, 72, 76, 77, 78, 80, 81, 84, 85, 86, 89, 91, 92, 96, 97, 98, 102, 103, 104, 105, 109, 110, 111, 112, 114, 115,121, 124, 125, 126, 127, 128, 129, 130, 131, 132, 133, 134, 135, 136, 137, 138, 139, 140, 141, 142, 144, 145, 146, 148, 151, 152, 153, 155, 156, 157, 160, 161, 162, 163, 165, 166, 169, 170, 177, 178, 179, 180, 181, 182, 185, 188, 189, 191, 193, 194, 197, 198, 199, 200, 202, 205, 206, 207, 208, 209, 212, 213, 214, 215, 216, 220, 221, 222, 223, 225, 228, 229, 230, 231, 232, 233, 234, 235, 238, 239, 240, 242, 244
Oyer and terminer Commissions, 210, 211, 225, 241

P

pardon, 23, 30, 35, 64, 78, 79, 105, 115, 126, 127, 131, 138, 149, 155, 156, 206, 218, 220, 221, 222, 231
peine forte et dure, 145, 197, 206
penance, 6, 23, 71, 86, 90, 237
Penda, King of Mercia, 21
Philip de Broi, 87
pilgrimage, 6, 13, 30, 35, 85, 237
prison, 6, 13, 14, 36, 48, 49, 55, 56, 57, 58, 60, 62, 65, 67, 69, 74, 75, 82, 106, 107, 114, 115, 117, 122, 123, 131, 132, 134, 137, 142, 143, 145, 146, 151, 153, 156, 159, 160, 171, 174, 178, 179, 189, 192, 193, 195, 197, 198, 199, 200, 201, 203, 209, 211, 214, 215, 218, 220, 223, 235, 236
prison *forte et dure*, 6, 195, 197, 199
Provisions of Oxford, 146, 172, 173, 174, 175, 182, 183, 185
Provisions of Westminster, 173, 174, 177, 212

Q

querela, 175, 180, 230
querelae, 175, 177, 179, 205, 224

R

Ralf of Tosny, 47
Ralph de Hengham, 218
Ralph Torta, 46
Ranulf de Glanville, 119
Ranulf Flambard, 67, 105
reeve, 24, 25, 129
Regesta regum Anglo-Normannorum, 64
Richard Seward, 151, 152, 167, 168, 170
Richard the Fearless, 46
Robert fitz Walter, 134
Robert Malet, 68
Robert of Bellême, 68, 69
Robert of Brampton, 73
Robert of Gloucester, 73, 75, 185
Robert of Mortain, 60, 62
Robert of Mowbray, 62
Robert of Normandy, 70
Robert of Pontefract, 68
Robert of Saint-Evroul, 47
Robert of Stuteville, 69
Robin Hood, 240
Roger of Lacy, 62
Roger of Montgomery, 62
Roger the Poitevin, 68
Rollo, 46
Roman law, 12, 158, 236
Rome, 12, 59, 64, 65, 66, 88, 91, 110, 229
Royal forests, 66

S

sanctuary, 8, 24, 79, 97, 120, 130, 142, 150, 151, 163, 164, 167, 169, 213, 215, 234
Second Statue of Winchester, 202
Second statute of Westminster, 211
Second Statute of Westminster, 199, 201, 203, 206, 207, 210, 212
sheriff, 53, 54, 71, 72, 80, 93, 98, 99, 104, 107, 108, 109, 122, 124, 126, 129, 141, 142, 144, 148, 151, 159, 162, 171, 172, 174, 176, 181, 192, 195, 201, 207, 208, 209, 213, 214, 215, 216, 221
Simon de Montfort, 69, 167, 168, 170, 174, 182, 183, 184, 185, 186, 189
Solomon of Rochester, 219
Song of Lewes, 184
special eyres, 173, 175, 176, 177, 187, 188
Stature of Aliens, 174, 230
Statute of Gloucester, 196, 197, 209
Statute of Marlborough, 187, 188, 189
Statute of Merchants, 203, 204, 206
Swein, Earl of Herefordshire, Son of Godwin, 38

T

Theobald, Archbishop of Canterbury, 74, 75, 89
Thomas de Weyland, 217
Thorkell, Earl of East Anglia, 31, 32, 33
Thurstan Goz, 47
Tinchebray, 68
tolt, 107
Tostig, Son of Godwin, 40, 41
Tower of London, 67, 150, 169, 218
Trailbaston Commissions, 202, 210, 211, 217, 224, 225, 231, 232, 237, 239, 241, 243
Trespass, 179, 180, 181, 236

U

utlaga, 34, 72

V

Vita Aedwardi Regis, 38, 40

W

waivery, 129, 163, 177, 213, 215
Waltheof, Earl of Northumbria, 55, 56, 81
wergeld, 24, 29
William Busac, 47
William de Brompton, 219
William de Valence, 174, 182
William Fitz Osbern, 55, 59
William Longchamp, 116, 118
William Longsword, 46
William Marshal, 139, 167
William of Arques, 47
William of Calais, Bishop of Durham, 63, 64, 65, 66
William of Jumièges, 45, 46

William of Mortain, 69
William of Normandy, 41, 50
William of Poitiers, 49, 50, 59
William Rufus, 60, 61, 62, 63, 64, 65, 66, 67, 72, 81, 89
William the Conqueror, 40, 41, 44, 45, 46, 50, 52, 56, 58, 60, 61, 62, 63, 64, 66, 74, 78, 80, 81, 85, 86, 87, 94, 118, 228
William Werlenc, 47
wolf's head, 11
writ of *capias*, 181, 199, 212
writ of *certiorari*, 187
writ of exigency (*exigas)*, 181
writ of *monstravit de compoto*, 212
writ of pone, 107, 108, 208
writ of *recordari*, 208
writ of right, 92
writ of trespass', 180
Wulfnoth, 61
Wulfstan, Archbishop of York, 29, 33, 35

Bibliography

Unpublished Sources

United Kingdom. London, National Archives, Kew. Justices in Eyre, of Assize, of Oyer and Terminer, and of the Peace, etc: Rolls and Files. 1198-1528. (JUST 1). JUST 1/4, 6, 10, 16, 36, 37, 61-62, 82, 92, 93, 130a, 137, 155, 174-176, 201-202, 223, 229-231, 271-271, 300a, 300c, 321, 351a, 413-414, 456, 536, 562-565, 568, 569b, 614a, 652, 703, 721, 733b, 756, 863, 911, 953, 1043, 1109, 1172-1173, 1181, 1187-1204.

United Kingdom, London, National Archives, Kew. Coroners' Rolls and Files, with Cognate Documents. 1228-1426. (JUST 2). JUST 2/261, 262, 278.

United Kingdom, London, National Archives, Kew. Court of Common Pleas and King's Bench, and Justices Itinerant: Early Plea and Essoin Rolls. (KB). KB/26, 27.

Primary Works

The 1235 Surrey Eyre, ed. C.A.F. Meekings, prepared by D. Crook for the Surrey Record Society. vols 1-3. Ilkley, UK: The Scolar Press, 1979.

The 1258-9 Special Eyre of Surrey and Kent, ed. A.H. Hershey. Surrey Record Society. vol. 38. Bristol, UK: J.W. Arrowsmith Ltd., 2004.

The 1263 Surrey Eyre, ed. S. Steward. Surrey Record Society. vol. 40. Bristol, UK: 4Word Ltd., 2006.

The Anglo-Saxon Chronicle, trans. A. Savage. New York, NY: St. Martin's/Marek, 1983.

*The Anglo-Saxon Chronicle***,** trans. and ed. D. Whitelock with D.C. Douglas. New Brunswick, N.J., Rutgers UP, 1961.

De Antiquis Legibus Liber, Cronica Maiorum et Vicecomitum Londoniarum et quedam, que contingebant temporibus illis ab anno MCLXXVIII ad annum MCCLXIV cum appendices, ed. T. Stapleton. London, UK: Camden Society, 1846.

Asser's Life of King Alfred and other contemporary sources, trans. S. Keynes and M. Lapdige. New York, NY: Penguin Books, 1983.

Bede, *Ecclesiastical History of the English People*, trans. L. Sherley-Price. London, UK: Penguin Books, Ltd., 1955.

Bedfordshire Coroners' Rolls, ed. R.F. Hunnisett. Publications of the Bedfordshire Historical Record Society, Volume XLI. Streatley, Bedfordshire, UK: The Bedfordshire Historical Society, 1961.

Bracton. *On the Laws and Customs of England (De Legibus et Consuetudiinibus Angliae)*, trans. S.E. Thorne. Ed. G.E. Woodbine. vols 1-4. Cambridge, MA: Published in Association with the Selden Society at Belknap Press of Harvard UP, 1968.

Bracton. *De Legibus et Consuetudinibus Angliae*, trans. T. Twiss. vols 1-6. London, UK: Longman & Co., 1878-1883.

Bracton's Notebook: A Collection of Cases Decided in the King's Court During the Reign of Henry the Third, Annotated by a lawyer that of that time, seemingly by Henry of Bratton, ed. F.W. Maitland. vols 1-3. London, UK: CJ Clay and Sons, 1887.

Britton. Containing the ancient pleas of the crown, translated; and illustrated with references, notes, and ancient record by Robert Kelham. London, 1762. Based on information from English Short Title Catalogue. Eighteenth Century Collections Online. Gale Group. http://galenet.galegroup.com/servlet/ECCO.

Calendar of London Trailbaston Trials Under Commissions of 1305 and 1306, ed. R.B. Pugh. London, UK: Her Majesty's Stationery Office, 1975.

Calendar of the Close rolls preserved in the Public record office. vols 1-5. Prepared under the superintendence of the deputy keeper of the records. Edward I. 1272-[1307]. London, UK: Printed for H. M. Stationery office by Eyre and Spottiswoode by Mackie, 1900-08.

Calendar of the Patent Rolls, Henry III, AD1232-1247, Preserved in the Public Records Office. London, UK: Printed for his Majesty's Stationary office by Mackie and Co., Ltd., 1906.

Calendar of the patent rolls. Preserved in the [Great Britain] Public Record Office. vols 1-4. Prepared under the superintendence of the Deputy Keeper of the Records. Edward I. 1272-1307. London, UK: Eyre and Spottiswoode, 1893-1901.

Historical Works of Gervase of Canterbury, Vol. 1, The Chronicle of the Reigns of Stephen, Henry II, and Richard I, ed. W. Stubbs. London, UK: Kraus Reprints Ltd., 1965.

Close Rolls of the reign of Henry III: Preserved in the Public Record Office, A.D. 1231-1234. London, UK: His Majesty's Stationery Office by Mackie and Co., Ltd., 1905.

Close Rolls (Supplementary) of the Reign of Henry III, Preserved in the Public Record Office, 1244-1266, ed. A. Morton. London, UK: Her Majesty's Stationery Office, 1975.

The Chronicle of Battle Abbey, ed. and trans. E. Searle. Oxford, UK: Clarendon Press, 1980.

The Chronicle of the Bury of St. Edmunds, 1212-1301, ed. A. Grandsden. London, UK: Thomas Nelson and Sons Ltd., 1964.

The Chronicle of John of Worcester, eds. R.R. Darlington and P. McGurk. Trans. J. Bray and P. McGurk. vols 1-2. Oxford, UK and New York, NY: Clarendon Press, 1995.

The Chronicle of Florence of Worcester: With the Two Continuations; Comprising Annals of English History, from the Departure of the Romans to the Reign of Edward I, (Florence's chronicle ends with the year 1117; the first continuation, 1117-1141, was written by John of Worcester; the second, 1152-1295, was the work of John De Taxster to 1265, continued to 1295 probably by John of Eversden), ed. T. Forester. H. G. Bohn, 1854.

Chronicles of Matthew of Paris: Monastic Life in the Thirteenth Century, ed. and trans. R. Vaughn. Gloucester, UK: Alan Sutton, 1984.

The chronicle of Pierre de Langtoft, in French verse from the earliest period to the death of King Edward I, ed. T. Wright. Published by the authority of the lords commissioners of Her Majesty's Treasury, under the direction of the master of the rolls. London, UK: Longmans, Green, Reader, and Dyer, 1866-68.

Chronicles of the Reigns of Edward I and Edward II, Volume I, Annales Londoniensies and Annales Paulini, ed. Wm. Stubbs. Rolls Series. Rerum Britannicarum Medii Aevi Scriptores. No. 76, vol. 1. London, UK: Longman & Co., 1882.

Civil Pleas of the Wiltshire Eyre, 1249, ed. M.T. Clanchy. Wiltshire Record Society. Gloucester, UK: Glevum Press Ltd., 1971.

Corpus iuris canonici, ed. A. Friedberg. vols 1-2. Leipzig, Germany: Bernhardi Tauchnitz, 1879-81.

Cotton, Bartholomew. *Historia anglicana* (A.D. 449-1298), ed. H.R. Luard, Published by the authority of the Lords Commissioners of Her Majesty's Treasury, under the direction of the Master of the Rolls. London, UK: Longman, Green, Longman and Roberts, 1859.

Cronicon Richardi Divisensis De Tempore Regis Richardi Primi or The Chronicle of Richard of Devizes of the Time of King Richard the First, ed. J.T. Appleby. London, UK: Thomas Nelson and Sons, Ltd., 1963.

Crown Pleas of the Devon Eyre of 1238, ed. H.R.T. Summerson. Devon & Cornwall Record Society, New Series, vol. 28. Torquay, England: The Devonshire Press Ltd., 1985.

Crown Pleas of the Wlitshire Eyre, 1249, ed. C.A.F. Meekings. Wiltshire Archaeological and Natural History Society. Devizes, UK: Northumberland Press, 1961.

Curia Regis Rolls of the Reigns of Richard I and John. vols 1-6. Preserved in the Public Records Office. London, UK: Majesty's Stationery Office, 1922.

'*Dialogus de Scaccario*' or *The Course of the Exchequer* by Richard Fitz Nigel, ed. and trans. C. Johnson. Corrections by F.E.L. Carter and D.E. Greenway. Oxford, UK: Clarendon Press, 1983.

The Digest of Justinian, ed. T. Mommsen with the aid of P. Krueger; English translation ed. by A. Watson. vols 1-4. Philadelphia, PA: University of Pennsylvania Press, 1985.

Documents of the Baronial Movement of Reform and Rebellion, 1258-1267. ed. R.F. Treharne. Oxford, UK: Clarendon Press, 1973.

Dudo, Dean of St. Quentin, fl. 1030. *De moribus et actis primorum Normanniae ducum. (History of the Normans),* trans. E. Christiansen. Woodbridge, Suffolk, UK: Boydell Press, 1998.

Eadmer. *Historia Novella in Anglia et opuscula duo de vita Sancti Anselmi et quibusdam miraculis ejus*, ed. M. Rule. Rolls Series. Rerum Britannicarum Medii Aevi Scriptores. Vol. 81. London, UK: Longman & Co., 1884.

Eadmer, *Historia Novorum in Anglia or Eadmer's History of Recent Events in England*, trans. G. Bosanquet. London, UK: The Cresset Press, 1964.

Eadmer. *The Life of St. Anselm*, ed. R.W. Southern. London, UK: Thomas Nelson and Sons, Ltd., 1962.

The Earliest Lincolnshire Assize Rolls AD 1202-1209, ed. D.M. Stenton. Lincoln, UK: Printed for the Lincoln Record Society, 1926.

The Earliest Northamptonshire Assize Rolls AD 1202-1203, ed. D.M. Stenton. Lincoln and London, UK: Printed for the Northamptonshire Record Society by J.W. Ruddock & Sons, 1930.

English Historical Documents, Vols. 1-3, ed. D. Douglas. New York, NY: Oxford UP, 1953-1979.

The Eyre of Northamptonshire, 3-4 Edward III, AD 1329-1330, ed. D. W. Sutherland. vols 1-2. London, UK: Selden Society, 1983.

Fasti Ecclesiae Anglicanae 1066-1300: volume 2: Monastic cathedrals (northern and southern provinces), ed. Diana E. Greenway. (1971).

Fitz Nigel, Richard. *Dialogus de Scaccario, The Course of the Exchequer*, ed. and trans. C. Johnson. Oxford, UK: Clarendon Press, 1983.

Fleta, eds. H.G. Richardson and G.O. Sayles. vols 1-3. London, UK: Bernard Quaritch for the Selden Society, 1955.

Flodoard of Reims. *The Annals of Flodoard of Reims, 919-966*, ed. and trans. S. Fanning and B.S. Bachrach. Toronto, Canada: Broadview Press, Ltd., 2004.

Foedera, conventiones, literæ, et cujuscunque generis acta publica, inter reges Angliæ, et alios quosvis imperatores, Londin: J. Tonson, 1726-35., vol. 1; Syllabus of the Documents Relating to England and Other Kingdoms: Contained in the Collection Known as 'Rymer's Foedera' by Great Britain Public Record Office, Scottish Record Office, Thomas Duffus Hardy, Thomas Rymer. Compiled by Thomas Rymer. Pub. by Longmans, Green, 1869.

Geoffrey of Monmouth. *The History of the Kings of Britain*, trans. L. Thorpe. Middlesex, UK: Penguin Books, 1966.

Gesta Normannorum Ducum of William of Jumièges, Orderic Vitalis, and Robert of Torigni, Volume II, Books V-VIII, ed. and trans. E.M.C. Van Houts. Oxford, UK: Clarendon Press, 1995.

Gesta Regis Henrici Secundi Benedicti Abbatis, The Chronicle of the Reigns of Henry II and Richard I, A.D. 1169-1192, known commonly under the name of Benedict of Peterborough, ed. Wm. Stubbs. vols 1-2. London, UK: Krause Reprint, Ltd., 1965.

Glanville, Ranulf. *The treatise on the laws and customs of the realm of England (commonly called Glanvill)*, ed. and trans. G.D.G. Hall. London, UK: Nelson, 1965.

The Great Roll of the Pipe for the Reign of King Henry the Second as part of The Great Rolls of the Exchequer, commonly called The Pipe Rolls, and other documents prior to the year AD 1200. Published by the Pipe Roll Society. London, UK: Wyman and Sons, 1884, vol. 7, 1163.

Henry of Huntingdon, *The Chronicle of Henry of Huntingdon, comprising the History of England from the Invasion of Julius Caesar to the Accession of Henry II, also the Acts of Stephen, King of England and Duke of Normandy*, trans. and ed. T. Forester. London, UK: Henry G. Bohn, Covent Garden, 1853.

Henry, Archdeacon of Huntington. *Historia Anglorum, The History of the English People*, ed. and trans. D. Greenway. Oxford, UK: Clarendon Press, 1996.

Herman of Tournai. *The Restoration of the Monastery of Saint Martin of Tournai*. trans. L. H. Nelson. Washington, DC: The Catholic University of America Press, 1996.

'De Iniusta Vexacione Willelmi Episcopi Primi per Willelmum Regem Filium Willemi Magni Regis,'ed. H.S. Offler in *Chronology, Conquest and Conflict in Medieval England, Camden Miscellany XXIV*. Cambridge: Cambridge UP (Camden Society, Fifth Series, vol. 10), 1997.

Lanfranc, *Monastic Constitutions of Lanfranc*, ed. D. Knowles and C.N. Brooke, Revised edn. Oxford, UK: Oxford UP, 2002.

The Laws of the Earliest English Kings, ed. and trans. F.L. Attenborough. New York, NY: Russell & Russell, Inc., 1963.

Leges Henrici Primi, ed. and trans. L.J. Downer. Oxford, UK: Clarendon Press, 1972.

Le très ancien coutumier de Normandie. vol. 1 of *Coutumiers de Normandie,* ed. Ernest-Joseph Tardiff. Rouen, E. Cagniard, 1881-1903.

Liebermann, F. *Die Gesetze der Angelsachsen.* Halle an der Saale: Max Niemeyer, 1903.

List of Assize Rolls, 1206-1481. Preserved in the Public Records Office. List and Index Society, Vol. 220. London, UK: Swift Printers, 1986.

The London Eyre of 1244, eds. H.M. Chew and M. Weinbaum. Contains crown pleas for years 10 Henry III to 27 Henry III, plus appeals, articles, constitutions and related material. By kind permission of the London Record Society. London, UK: London Record Society, 1970. accessed at: http://www.british-history.ac.uk/source.aspx?pubid=153.

The London Eyre of 1276, ed. M. Weinbaum. London, UK: London Record Society, 1976.

Master Walter Map's Book, 'De Nugis Curialium' (Courtiers' Trifles). trans. by F. Tupper and M.B. Ogle. London, UK: Chatto & Windus, 1924.

Materials for the History of Thomas Becket archbishop of Canterbury (canonized by Pope Alexander III., A. D. 1173). Rerum britannicarum medii ævi scriptores; or, Chronicles and memorials of Great Britain and Ireland during the middle ages. Vols 1-7, ed. J. C. Robertson. London, UK: Longman, 1875-1885.

Matthew of Paris. *English history from the year 1235 to 1273,* trans. J. A. Giles. vols 1-3. London, UK: H. G. Bohn, 1852.

Matthew Paris's English history: From the year 1235 to 1273, ed. J. A. Giles. London, UK: H.G. Bohn, 1853.

Matthew of Paris, *Chronica Majora*, ed. H.R. Luard. Published by the authority of the lords commissioners of Her Majesty's Treasury, under the direction of the master of the rolls. vols 1-7. London, UK: Longman & Co., 1872-83.

Medieval Handbooks of Penance, trans. McNeill, J.T. and H.M. Gamer. New York: Columbia UP, 1938.

'Memoriale Fratis Walteri de Covenetria' or The Historical Collections of Walter of Coventry, ed. Wm. Stubbs. vols 1-2. In Rerum Britannicarum Medii Aevi Scriptores or Chronicles and Memorials of Great Britain and Ireland during the Middle Ages (Rolls Series). vol. 58, parts 1 and 2. London, UK: Her Majesty's Stationary Office, 1872; Kraus Reprint Ltd., 1968.

The Mirror of Justices, ed. W.J. Whittaker for the Selden Society. Selden Society vol. 7. London, UK: Bernard Quaritch, 1895.

Orderic Vitalis. *The Ecclesiastical History of Orderic Vitalis*, ed. M. Chibnall. vols 1-6. Oxford, UK: Clarendon Press, 1980.

The Oxfordshire Eyre, 1241. Ed. J. Cooper. The Oxfordshire Record Society, vol. 56. Oxford, UK: Parchment Ltd., 1986.

Patent rolls of the reign of Henry III, 1216-1225, preserved in the Public Record Office, printed under the superintendence of The Deputy Keeper of the Records. vols 1-2. London, UK: Printed for His Majesty's Stationery Office by Mackie and Co., 1901-1903.

Pleas before the King or His Justices, 1198-1212. vols 1-4, ed. D. M. Stenton for the Selden Society. Selden Society vols 67, 68, 83, 84. London, UK: Bernard Quaritch, 1967.

Pleas of the Crown for the County of Gloucester, 1221, Before the Abbot of Reading and his Fellows Justices Itinerant, ed. F.W. Maitland. London, UK: MacMillan & Co. 1884.

Pleas of the Crown for the Hundred of Swinehead and the township of Bristol, AD 1221, ed. E.J. Watson. Bristol, UK: W. Crofton Hemmons, 1902.

'Pleas of the Crown, before the Justices in Eyre, Jan. 14, 1285 (*Twyne*, ms. IV, p. 617 sqq.)' in *Oxford City Documents: Financial and Judicial, 1268-1665*, ed. J.E. Thorold Rogers. (Oxford, UK: Printed for the Oxford Historical Society at the Clarendon Press, 1891.

The Political Songs of England, ed. T. Wright. London, UK: Camden Society, 1839.

Regesta regum anglo-normannorum, 1066-1154 ed. H. W. C. Davis with the assistance of R. J. Whitwell and B. Litt. vols 1-3. Oxford, UK: Clarendon Press, 1913-69.

Roger of Wendover. *Flowers of History*, ed. J.A. Giles. vols 1-2. London, UK: Henry G. Bohn, 1849.

The Roll and Writ File of the Berkshire Eyre of 1248, ed. M.T. Clanchy for the Selden Society. London, UK: William Clowes & Sons Ltd., 1973.

The Roll of the Shropshire Eyre of 1256, ed. A. Harding for the Selden Society. Selden Society Publication, vol. 96. London, UK: Selden Society, 1981.

Rolls of the Justices in Eyre for Lincolnshire 1218-19 and Worcestershire 1221, ed. D. Stenton for the Selden Society. Selden Society vol. 53. London, UK: Bernard Quaritch, 1934.

Rolls of the Justices in Eyre being the rolls of pleas and assizes for Yorkshire in 3 Henry III (1218-1219), ed. by D. Stenton for the Selden Society. Selden Society vol. 56. London, UK: Bernard Quaritch, 1937.

Rotuli hundredorum temp. Hen. III. & Edw. I. in Turr' Lond' et in curia receptae Scaccarij Westm. asservati. Printed by command of His Majesty King

George III. in pursuance of an address of the House of Commons of Great Britain. vols 1-2. London, UK: 1812-18.

Royal and other historical letters illustrative of the reign of Henry III from the Originals in the Public Record Office. ed. W.W. Shirley. vols 1-2. Rerum Britannicarum Medii Aevi Scriptores. Published by the authority of Her Majesty's Treasury, under the direction of the Master of the Rolls. London, UK: Green, Longman, and Roberts, 1862.

Royal Justice and the Medieval English Countryside: The Huntingtonshire Eyre of 1286, the Ramsey Abbey Banlieu Court of 1287, and the Assizes of 1287-1288, eds. A.R. Dewindt and E.B. Dewindt. vols 1-2. Toronto, Canada: Pontifical Institute of Medieval Studies, 1981.

Select Cases in the Court of the King's Bench under Edward I, Volume 1, ed. by G.O. Sayles for the Selden Society. London, UK: Bernard Quaritch, 1936.

Select Charters and other Illustrations of English Constitutional History from the Earliest Times to the Reign of Edward the First, ed. Wm. Stubbs. Oxford, UK: Clarendon Press, 1890.

Select Pleas of the Crown, Volume 1, AD 1200-125I, ed. F.W. Maitland. Selden Society vol. 1. London, UK: Spottiswoode and Co., 1887.

Select Pleas of the Forest, ed. G.J. Turner. Publications of the Selden Society, vol. 13. London, UK: Bernard Quaritch. 1901.

Scriptores Rerum Gestarum Willelmi Conquestoris, ed. J. Giles. Publications of the Caxton Society, vol. 3. New York, NY: Burt Franklin, 1845, reprint 1967.

The Song of Lewes: A Latin political song of the time of the Barons' war, 1264, justifying Simon de Montford and his cause, and setting forth the true theory of kingship, ed. C.L. Kingsford. Oxford, UK: Clarendon Press, 1890.

The statutes of the realm, Volume 1, 1235-1377. Printed at the command of His Majesty King George III. [n.d.].

Symeon of Durham. *Libellus de Exordio atque Procursu Istius, hoc est Dunhelmensis Ecclesie*, ed. and trans. D. Rollason in *Tract on the Origins and Process of this Church of Durham.* Oxford, UK: Clarendon Press, 2000.

Symeon of Durham, History of the Kings of England, trans. J. Stevenson in *The Church Historians of England, Vol. III, Part II: The Historical Works of Simeon of Durham*. London, UK: Seeley, 1860.

Thedmar, E. fitz. *Cronica Maiorum et Vicecomitum Londoniarum*, ed. T. Stapleton. Camden Society no. 34. London, UK: Published for the Camden Society, 1865.

Three Rolls of the King's Court in the Reign of King Richard the First, AD 1194-1194. Intro. F.W. Maitland. pub. by the Pipe Roll Society, vol. 14. London, UK: Wyman and Sons, 1891.

Vita Aedwardi Confessoris or The Life of King Edward who rests at Westminster, ed. F. Barlow 2nd edn. Oxford, UK: Clarendon Press, 1992.

Vita Quorundum Anglo-Saxonum (Original Lives of Anglo-Saxons and Others Who Lived Before the Conquest), ed. J. Giles. Publications of the Caxton Society, XVI. New York, NY: Burt Franklin, 1854, reprint 1967.

Wace. *Le roman de Brut*, ed. I. Arnold. vols 1-2. Paris: Société des anciens textes francais, 1938-40.

'The Warwickshire Eyres' in *Early Records of Medieval Coventry*, ed. P. Coss. London, UK: Published for the British Academy by Oxford UP, 1986.

William of Malmesbury. *Chronicle of the Kings of England: From the earliest period to the reign of King Stephen*, ed. J.A. Giles. London, UK: George Bell and Sons, 1904.

William of Newburgh. *The History of English Affairs, Book I*, eds. P.G. Walsh and M.J. Kennedy. Warminster, UK: Aris & Phillips Ltd., 1988.

William of Poitiers. *The Gesta Gvillelmi*, ed. and trans. R.H.C. Davis and M. Chibnall. Oxford: Clarendon Press: 1998.

Wiltshire Gaol Delivery and Trailbaston Trials, 1275-1306, ed. R.B. Pugh. Wiltshire Record Society, Volume 33. Stoke-on-Trent, UK: JG. Fenn Ltd., 1978.

The laws of the kings of England from Edmund to Henry I, ed. and trans. A. J. Robertson. Cambridge, UK: Cambridge UP, 1925; New York, NY: AMS Press, 1974.

Van Caenegem, R.C., ed., *English Lawsuits from William I to Richard II*, vols 1, 2. The Publications of the Selden Society, vols 106, 107. London, UK: Selden Society, 1991.

-----., ed., *Royal Writs in England from the Conquest to Glanvill: Studies in the Early History of the Common Law*. A Selden Society Publication, vol. 77. London, UK: Bernard Quaritch, 1959.

Van Houts, E.M.C., ed. *The gesta Normannorum ducum of William of Jumièges, Orderic Vitalis, and Robert of Torigni*. vols 1-2. Oxford, UK: Clarendon Press, 1992-1995.

Wilkins, D., ed., *Concilia Magnae Britanniae et Hiberniae, A Synodo Verolamiensi A.D. CCCXLVI ad Londinensem A.D. [MDCCXVII]. Accedunt constitutiones et alia ad historiam Ecclesiae Anglicanae spectantia*. vols 1-4. London, UK: R. Gosling, 1737.

Year Books of the Reign of King Edward the First, Years XXXII and XXXIII, ed. and trans. A. Horwood. Rolls Series 31.

Vita Aedwardi Confessoris or The Life of King Edward who rests at Westminster, ed. F. Barlow 2nd edn. Oxford, UK: Clarendon Press, 1992.

Secondary Works

Appleby, J.T. *England Without Richard, 1189-1199*. Ithaca, NY: Cornell UP, 1965.

Appleby, J.C. and P. Dalton, eds. *Outlaws in Medieval and Early Modern England: Crime, Government and Society, c. 1066-1600*. Surrey, UK: Ashgate Publishing Ltd., 2009.

Arnold, M.S, T.A. Green, S.A. Scully, and S.D. White, eds. *On the Laws and Customs of England: Essays in Honor of Samuel E. Thorne*. Chapel Hill, NC: The University of North Carolina Press, 1981.

Babington, A. *The English Bastille: A History of Newgate Gaol and Prison Conditions in Britain 1188-1902*. London, UK: MacDonald and Company, 1971.

-----. *The Power to Silence: A History of Punishment in Britain*. London, UK: Robert Maxwell Publishing, 1968.

-----. *The Rule of Law in Britain: From the Roman Occupation to the Present Day, The Only Liberty*. 3rd edn. Chichester, UK: Barry Rose Publishing, 1995.

Barlow, F. *Edward the Confessor*. Berkeley and Los Angeles, CA: University of California Press, 1970.

-----. *The English Church, 1000-1066: A History of the Later Anglo-Saxon Church*. London and New York: Longman Inc., 1979.

-----. *The English Church, 1066-1154: A History of the Anglo-Norman Church*. London and New York: Longman, Inc., 1979.

-----. *The Feudal Kingdom of England 1042-1216*. 4th edn. London and New York: Longman Inc., 1961.

-----. *The Godwins: The Rise and Fall of a Noble Dynasty*. London, UK: Pearson Education Ltd., 2002.

-----. *William Rufus*. Los Angeles and Berkeley, CA: University of California Press, 1983.

Bartlett, R. *England under the Norman and Angevin Kings, 1075-1225*. Oxford, UK: Clarendon Press, 2000.

-----. *Trial by Fire and Water: The Medieval Judicial Ordeal*. Oxford, UK: Clarendon Press, 1986.

Bassett, M. 'Newgate Prison in the Middle Ages,' *Speculum*, vol. 18, no. 2 (Apr., 1943): 233-246.

Bates, D. *Normandy before 1066*. New York, NY: Longman Inc., 1982.

-----. 'The Character and career of Odo Bishop of Bayeux (1049/50-1097),' *Speculum*, vol. 50, no. 1 (1975): 1-20.

-----. 'The Earliest Norman Writs.' *English Historical Review*, vol. 100, no. 395 (April 1985), 266-284.

-----. 'Normandy and England after 1066.' *English Historical Review*, vol. 104, no. 413 (Oct., 1989): 851-880.

Bates, D. and A. Curry, eds. *England and Normandy in the Middle Ages*. London, UK: The Hambledon Press, 1994.

Bellamy, J.G. *Crime and Public Order in England in the Later Middle Ages*. London: Routledge & Kegal Paul, Ltd., 1973.

-----. *The criminal trial in later medieval England: felony before the courts from Edward I to the sixteenth century*. Toronto, CA: University of Toronto Press, 1998.

-----. *The Law of Treason in the Later Middle Ages*. Cambridge, UK: Cambridge UP, 1970.

-----. 'The Coterel Gang: An Anatomy of a Band of Fourteenth-Century Criminals,' *English Historical Review*, vol. 79, no. 313 (Oct., 1964): 698-717.

Bender, John. *Imagining the Penitentiary: Fiction and the Architecture of Mind in Eighteenth-Century England.* Chicago and London: The University of Chicago Press, 1987.

Bennett, M. 'Violence in eleventh-century Normandy: feud, warfare and politics,' in *Violence and Society in the Early Medieval West*. Ed. Guy Halsall. Woodbridge, Suffolk, UK: The Boydell Press, 1998: 126-140.

Berthrum, D. *The Homilies of Wulfstan*. Oxford, UK: Clarendon Press, 1957.

Biancalana, J. 'For Want of Justice: Legal Reforms of Henry II.' *Columbia Law Review*. vol. 88, no. 3. (April 1988): 433-536.

Bisson, T.N. *Tormented voices: power, crisis, and humanity in rural Catalonia, 1140-1200*. Cambridge, MA: Harvard UP, 1998.

Bloch, M. *Feudal Society*, trans. L.A. Manyon. Chicago, IL: University of Chicago Press, 1961.

Bonner, G., Rollason, D. and C. Stancliffe, eds. *St. Cuthbert, His Cult and His Community to AD 1200*. Woodbridge, Suffolk: The Boydell Press, 1989.

Bouet, P. and V. Gazeau, eds. *La Normandie et l'Angleterre au Moyen Age*. Caen, France: les Publications du CRAHM Universite de Caen Basse-Normandie, 2003.

Bradbury, J. *Stephen and Matilda, The Civil War of 1139-53*. Gloucestershire, UK: Alan Sutton Publishing Ltd., 1996.

Brand, P. Edward I and the Judges: the 'State Trials' of 1289-1293.' *Thirteenth Century England I: Proceedings of the Newcastle Upon Tyne Conference* (1985): 31-40.

-----. *Kings, Barons and Justices: The Making and Enforcement of Legislation in Thirteenth-Century England.* Cambridge, UK: Cambridge University Press, 2003.

-----. *The Making of the Common Law*. London, UK: The Hambledon Press, 1992.

Braswell, M.F. *The Medieval Sinner: Characterization and Confession in the Literature of the English Middle Ages*. East Brunswick, NJ: Associated UP, Ltd., 1983.

Brown, A. L. *The Governance of Late Medieval England, 1272-1461*. Stanford, CA: Stanford UP, 1989.

Brown, R.A. *The Norman conquest of England: sources and documents*. Woodbridge, Suffolk, UK ; Rochester, NY: Boydell Press, 1995.

-----. *The Normans*. New York, NY: St. Martin's Press, 1984.

-----. *The Normans and the Norman Conquest*. New York, NY: Crowell, 1969.

-----. *Origins of English Feudalism.* London, UK: Allen & Unwin, Barnes and Noble, 1973.

Burgess, G. S. *Two Medieval Outlaws: Eustace the Monk and Fouke Fitz Waryn*. Cambridge, UK: D.S. Brewer, 1997.

Burt, C. 'The Demise of the General Eyre in the Reign of Edward I,' *English Historical Review*, vol. 120, no. 1 (February, 2005): 1-14.

Calisse, C. *A History of Italian Criminal Law*, Continental Legal History Series, vol. 8, (Boston, 1928).

Cam, H. M. 'The General Eyres of 1339-1330,' *The English Historical Review*, vol. 39, no. 154 (Apr., 1924): 241-252.

-----. *The Hundred and the Hundred Rolls: An Outline of Local Government in Medieval England.* London, UK: Merlin Press Ltd., 1963.

-----. *Magna Carta—Event or Document?* Selden Society Lecture, delivered on July 7th, 1965. Printed by the Selden Society. London, UK: Bernard Quaritch, 1965.

-----. 'Some Early Inquests before 'Custodes Pacis'' *English Historical Review* vol. 40, no. 159 (Jul., 1925): 411-419.

-----. *Studies of the Hundred Rolls: Some Aspects of Thirteenth-Century Administration, Volume VI, Oxford Studies in Social and Legal History.* ed. P. Vinogradoff. Oxford, UK: Clarendon Press, 1921.

Campbell, J., ed. *The Anglo-Saxons*. Ithaca, NY: Cornell UP, 1982.

Campbell, J. *Essays in Anglo-Saxon History*. London, UK: The Hambledon Press, 1986.

Capua, J. V. 'Feudal and Royal Justice in Thirteenth-Century England: The Forms and the Impact of Royal Review.' *The American Journal of Legal History*. vol. 7, no. 1 (Jan., 1983): 54-84.

Carpenter, D.A. *The Battles of Lewes & Evesham 1264/65*. Staffordshire, UK: Mercia Publications, Ltd., 1987.

-----. 'The Decline of the Curial Sheriff in England 1194-1258.' *The English Historical Review*. vol. 91, no. 358 (Jan., 1976): 1-32.

-----. 'King Henry III's 'Statute' against Aliens: July 1263.' *The English Historical Review*. vol. 107, no. 425 (Oct., 1992): 925-944.

-----. 'Kings, Magnates, and Society: The Personal Rule of King Henry III, 1234-1258.' *Speculum*. vol. 60, no. 1 (1985): 39-70.

-----. *The Minority of Henry III.* London, UK: Meuthun London, 1990.

-----. *The Reign of Henry III*. London, UK: Hambledon Press, 1996.

-----. *The Struggle for Mastery: Britain, 1066-1284*. Oxford, UK: Oxford UP, 2003.

Chaplais, P. *Piers Gaveston: Edward II's adoptive brother*. Oxford, UK: Oxford UP, 1994.

Charlton, J., ed., *The Tower of London: Its Buildings and Institutions*. London, UK: Dept. of the Environment, H.M. Stationery Office, 1978.

Cheny, C.R. *Hubert Walter*. London, UK: Thomas Nelson & Sons Ltd., 1967.

-----. 'The Punishment of Felonous Clerks' *The English Historical Review* vol. 51, no. 202 (April 1936): 215-236.

Chibnall, M. *Anglo-Norman England, 1066-1166*. Oxford, UK: Basil Blackwell, Ltd. 1986.

-----. 'Charter and Chronicle: The Use of Archive Sources by Norman Historians' in *Church and Government in the Middle Ages: Essays Presented to C. R. Cheney on his 70th Birthday*, eds. C. N. L. Brooke et al. Cambridge, UK: Cambridge UP, 1976.

-----. *The Normans*. Oxford, UK: Basil Blackwell Publisher Limited, 2000.

-----. *The World of Orderic Vitalis*. Oxford, UK: Clarendon Press, 1984.

Chibnall, M., ed. *The Debate on the Norman Conquest*. Manchester, UK and New York, NY: Manchester UP, 1999.

Clanchy, M. T. *England and Its Rulers, 1066-1272: Foreign Lordship and National Identity*. Oxford, UK: Basil Blackwell Publisher Ltd., 1983.

-----. *From Memory to Written Record: England, 1066-1307*. 2nd edn. Oxford, UK and Cambridge, MA: Blackwell Publishers, 1993.

-----. 'Highway robbery and trial by battle in the Hampshire eyre of 1249' in *Medieval Legal Records: Edited in memory of C.A.F. Meekings*. eds R.F.

Hunnisett and J.B. Post. London, UK: Her Majesty's Stationery Office, 1978.

Clover, C. J. 'Regardless of Sex: Men, Women, and Power in Early Northern Europe,' *Speculum*, vol. 68, no. 2 (Apr., 1993): 363-387.

Cowdrey, H.E.J. *Lanfranc: Scholar, Monk, and Archbishop*. Oxford, UK: Oxford UP, 2003.

Cox, J.C. *The Sanctuaries and Sanctuary Seekers of Mediaeval England*. London, UK: George Allen & Sons, 1911.

Cronne, H.A. 'The Royal Forest Under Henry I.' In *Essays in British and Irish History In Honour of James Eadie Todd*. eds H.A. Cronne, T.W. Moody, and D.B. Quinn. London, UK: Frederick Muller Ltd., (1949): 1-23.

Crook, D. *Records of the General Eyre*. PRO Handbooks, vol. 20. London, UK: HMSO, 1982.

-----. 'The Later Eyres,' *The English Historical Review*, vol. 97, no. 383 (Apr., 1982), pp. 241-268.

Crossley-Holland, K. *The Anglo-Saxon World, An Anthology*. Oxford, UK: Oxford UP, 1982.

Crouch, D. *The Normans: The History of a Dynasty*. London, UK: Hambledon and London, 2002.

-----. *William Marshall: Court, Career, and Chivalry in the Angevin Empire, 1147-1219*. London, UK: Longman Group UK Ltd., 1990.

Danziger, D. and J. Gillingham. *1215: The Year of the Magna Carta*. London, UK: Hodder & Stoughton, 2003.

Darby, H.C. and E.M.J. Campbell, *The Domesday Geography of South-East England*. Cambridge, UK: Cambridge UP, 1962.

Dean, T. *Crime in Medieval Europe 1200-1550*. London, UK: Pearson Education, Ltd., 2001.

Douglas, D. *The Norman Achievement.* Berkeley and Los Angeles, CA: University of California Press, 1969.

-----. *The Norman Fate.* Berkeley and Los Angeles, CA: University of California Press, 1976.

-----. *William the Conqueror: The Norman Impact Upon England.* Berkeley and Los Angeles, CA: University of California Press, 1964.

Duckett, E.S. *Alfred the Great: The King and His England.* Chicago and London: The University of Chicago Press, 1956.

Duggan, C. *Canon Law in Medieval England: The Becket Dispute and Decretal Collections*. London, UK: Variorum Reprints, 1982.

Dunbabin, J. *Captivity and Imprisonment in Medieval Europe, 1000-1300*. London, UK: Palgrave Macmillan, 2002.

-----. *France in the Making: 843-1180*. 2nd edn. Oxford, UK: Oxford UP, 2000.

Elias, N. *On Civilization, Power, and Knowledge: Selected Writings.* eds S. Mennell and J. Goudsblom. Chicago, IL: University of Chicago Press, 1998.

Fleming, R. *Domesday Book and the law: Society and legal custom in early medieval England.* Cambridge, UK: Cambridge UP, 1998.

Fletcher, R. *Bloodfeud: Murder and Revenge in Anglo-Saxon England.* Oxford, UK: Oxford UP, 2003.

Flori, J. *Richard Coeur De Lion: Le roi-chevalier*. Paris, France: Payot & Rivages, 1999.

Forsdyke, S. *Exile Ostracism, and Democracy: The Politics of Expulsion in Ancient Greece*. Princeton, NJ and Oxford, UK: Princeton UP, 2005.

Foucault, M. *Discipline and Punish: The Birth of the Prison*, trans. A. Sheridan. New York, NY: Vintage Books, 1977.

Fournee, J. *Les Culte Populaire des Saints en Normandie*. Paris: Societe Parisienne D'Histoire et D'Archeologie Normandes, 1973.

Freeman, E. *The Reign of William Rufus and the Accession of Henry the First*, vols 1-2. 3rd edn. Oxford, UK: Clarendon Press, 1922.

Fryde, N. *The Tyranny and Fall of Edward II 1321-1326*. Cambridge, UK: Cambridge UP, 2004.

Ganshof, F. L. *Feudalism*. trans. Philip Grierson. 3rd. edn. New York, NY: Harper & Row Publishers, 1961.

Garland, D. 'Frameworks of Inquiry in the Sociology of Punishment.' *The British Journal of Sociology*, vol. 41, no. 1. (Mar., 1990): 1-15.

Punishment and Modern Society: A Study in Social Theory. Chicago, IL: University of Chicago Press, 1990.

-----. 'Sociological Perspectives on Punishment.' *Crime and Justice*, vol. 14. (1991): 115-165.

Garnett, G. and J. Hudson, eds. *Law and Government in Medieval England and Normandy: Essays in honour of Sir James Holt*. Cambridge, UK: Cambridge UP, 1994.

Geltner, G. *The Medieval Prison: A Social History*. Princeton, NJ: Princeton UP, 2008.

Gerth, H.H. and C. Wright Mills, ed. *From Max Weber: Essays in Sociology*. New Edition. London, UK: Routledge, 1991.

Gillingham, J. *The English in the Twelfth Century*. Woodbridge, Suffolk: The Boydell Press, 2000.

-----. 'The Introduction of Chivalry into England,' in *Law and Government in Medieval England and Normandy: Essays in honour of Sir James Holt*, G. Garnett and J. Hudson, eds. Cambridge, UK: Cambridge UP, 1992): 31-55.

-----. *Life and Times of Richard I*. London, UK: Weidenfeld and Nicolson Ltd., 1973.

-----. *Richard I*. New Haven, CT and London, UK: Yale UP, 1999.

-----. *Richard the Lionheart*. London, UK: Weidenfeld and Nicolson, 1978.

Gibson, M.T. *Lanfranc of Bec*. Oxford, UK: Clarendon Press, 1978.

Goebel, J. *Felony and Misdemeanor: A Study in the History of English Criminal Procedure, Volume One*. New York, NY: The Commonwealth Fund, 1937.

Goodnow, F. J. 'The Writ of Certiorari,' *Political Science Quarterly*, vol. 6, no. 3 (Sep., 1891): 493-536.

Gransden, A. *Historical Writing in England c. 550 to c. 1307*. London, UK: Routledge & Kegan Paul, 1974.

Green, J.A. *The Government of England Under Henry I*. Cambridge, UK: Cambridge UP, 1986.

-----. *Henry I: King of England and Duke of Normandy*. Cambridge, UK: Cambridge UP, 2006.

Green, T.A. 'The Jury and the English Law of Homicide, 1200-1600,' *Michigan Law Review* vol. 74, no. 3 (Jan. 1976): 413-499.

Groot, R.D. 'The Jury of Presentment before 1215.' *The American Journal of Legal History*. vol. 26, no. 1 (Jan., 1982): 1-24.

Gross, C. *The Sources and Literature of English History from the Earliest Times to about 1485*. 2nd edn. New York, NY: Peter Smith, 1951

Grupp, S. 'Some Historical Aspects of Pardon in England.' *The American Journal of Legal History*. vol. 7, no. 1 (Jan., 1963): 51-62.

Guterman, S.L. *The Principle of Personality of Law in the Germanic Kingdoms of Western Europe from the Fifth to the Eleventh Centuries*. New York, NY: Lang, 1990.

Halsall, G. 'Violence and Society: an introductory survey,' in *Violence and Society in the Early Medieval West*, ed. G. Halsall (Woodbridge, Suffolk, UK: The Boydell Press, 1998): 1-45.

Hamil, F.C. 'The King's Approvers: A Chapter in the History of English Criminal Law.' *Speculum* vol. 11, no. 2 (April, 1936): 238-258.

Hamilton, S. *The Practice of Penance: 900-1050.* Woodbridge, UK: The Boydell Press, 2001.

Hamilton, J. S. *Piers Gaveston, Earl of Cornwall, 1307-1312: Politics and Patronage in the Reign of Edward II.* Detroit, MI: Wayne State UP, 1992.

Hanawalt, B.A. *Crime and Conflict in English Communities, 1300-1348*. Cambridge, MA: Harvard UP, 1979.

Harding, A. 'Early trailbaston proceedings from the Lincoln roll of 1305', eds R.F. Hunnisett and J.B. Post, *Medieval Legal Records Edited in Memory of C.A.F. Meekings.* London, UK: H. M. Stationery Office, 1978.

-----. *England in the Thirteenth Century*. Cambridge, UK: Cambridge UP, 1993.

-----. 'The Origins and Early History of the Keeper of the Peace,' *Transactions of the Royal Historical Society*, 5th series, 10 (1960): 85-109.

-----. 'Plaints and Bills in the History of English Law, mainly in the period 1250-1350,' in *Legal History Studies, 1972: Papers presented to the legal history conference, Aberystwyth, 18-21 July 1972*. Cardiff, Wales: University of Wales Press, 1975.

-----. *The Social History of English Law*. Gloucester, MA: Peter Smith, 1973.

Harding, C. et al. *Imprisonment in England and Wales: A Concise History*. London, UK: Croom Helm Ltd., 1985.

Hardy, T. D. *A Description of the Close Rolls in the Tower of London; with an account of the early courts of law and equity and various historical illustrations*. London, UK: Eyre and Spottiswoode, 1833.

Harper-Bill, C. and E. van Houts, eds. *A Companion to the Anglo-Norman World.* Woodbridge, UK: The Boydell Press, 2003.

Haskins, C.H. 'The Norman 'Consuetudines et Iusticie' of William the Conqueror,' *The English Historical Review*, vol. 23, no. 91 (Jul., 1908): 502-508.

-----. *Norman Institutions.* New York, NY: Frederick Ungar Publishing Co., 1960.

-----. 'Normandy under William the Conqueror' *The American Historical Review*, vol. 14, no. 3 (Apr., 1909): 453-476.

-----. *The Normans in European History.* Boston and New York: Houghton Mifflin Company, 1915.

-----. *The Renaissance of the 12th Century.* New York, NY: World Publishing Co., 1957.

Haskins, G.L. 'Executive Justice and the Rule of Law: Some Reflections on Thirteenth-Century England.' *Speculum* vol. 30, no. 4 (Oct., 1955): 529-538.

Havins, P.J.N. *The Forests of England.* Devon, UK: Robert Hale & Company, 1976.

Hayward, J. 'Hereward the Outlaw,' *Journal of Medieval History* vol. 14 (1988): 293-304.

Heiser, R.R. 'Castles, Constables, and Politics in Late Twelfth-Century English Governance.' *Albion: A Quarterly Journal Concerned with British Studies*. vol. 32, no. 1 (Spring, 2000): 19-36.

Helmholz, R.H. 'Magna Carta and the *ius commune*.' *The University of Chicago Law Review*. vol. 66, no. 2 (Spring, 1999): 297-371.

Hershey, A.H. 'Justice and Bureaucracy: The English Royal Writ and '1258'.' *The English Historical Review*. vol. 113, no. 453 (Sept, 1998): 829-851.

-----. 'Success or Failure? Hugh Bigod and Judicial Reform during the Baronial Movement, June 1258-February 1259.' *Thirteenth Century England V*. Proceedings of the Newcastle Upon Tyne Conference. (1989): 65-87.

Hogg, R.M. 'Henry III, the Justiciarship, and the Court *coram rege* in 1261.' *The American Journal of Legal History*. vol. 30, no. 1 (Jan. 1986): 59-78.

Holden, B.W. 'King John, the Braoses, and the Celtic Fringe, 1207-1216.' *Albion: A Quarterly Journal Concerned with British Studies*. vol. 33, no. 1 (Spring, 2001): 1-23.

Hollister, C.W. ed. *Anglo-Norman Political Culture and the 12th-Century Renaissance*. Woodbridge, UK: The Boydell Press, 1997.

Hollister, C.W. 'Greater Domesday Tenants-in-Chief,' in *Domesday Studies. Papers read at the Novocentenary Conference of the Royal Historical Society and the Institute of British Geographers*, Winchester, 1986. ed. J.C. Holt. pp. xix, 347. Woodbridge, Suffolk: Boydell & Brewer, 1987.

-----. *Henry I*. ed. and completed by A. C. Frost. New Haven, CT and London, UK: Yale UP, 2001.

-----. 'Normandy, France and the Anglo-Norman Regnum.' *Speculum*, vol. 51, no. 2 (April 1976): 202-242.

Holt, J.C. *Magna Carta*. 2nd edn. Cambridge, UK: Cambridge UP, 1992.

-----. *Magna Carta and Medieval Government*. London, UK: The Hambledon Press, 1985.

-----. *The Northerners: A Study in the Reign of King John*. Oxford, UK: Clarendon Press, 1961.

Hudson, J. *The Formation of the English Common Law: Law and Society in England from the Norman Conquest to Magna Carta*. London, UK: Addison Wesley Longman Limited, 1996.

Hudson, J., ed. *The History of English Law: Centenary Essays on 'Pollock and Maitland'*. Proceedings of the British Academy, vol. 89. Oxford, UK: Published for the British Academy by Oxford UP, 1996.

Hunnisett, R.F. *The Medieval Coroner*. Cambridge, UK: Cambridge UP, 1961.

-----. 'The Medieval Coroners' Rolls.' *The American Journal of Legal History*. vol. 3, no. 3 (July, 1959): 205-221.

-----. 'The Origins of the Office of Coroner.' *Transactions of the Royal Historical Society*. 5th Series, vol. 8 (1958): 85-104.

Hurnard, N.D. 'The Anglo-Norman Franchises.' *English Historical Review,* vol. 64, no. 252 (July, 1949), 289-327.

-----. 'The Anglo-Norman Franchises (Continued).' *English Historical Review*, vol. 64, no. 253 (Oct., 1949), 433-460.

-----. 'The Jury of Presentment and the Assize of Clarendon.' *The English Historical Review*. vol. 56, no. 223 (July, 1941): 374-410.

-----. *The King's Pardon for Homicide before A.D. 1307*. Oxford, UK: Clarendon Press, 1969.

Hyams, P.R. 'Feud and the State in Late Anglo-Saxon England.' *The Journal of British Studies*, vol. 40, no. 1. (Jan., 2001): 1-43.

-----. *Rancor and Reconciliation in Medieval England*. Ithaca, NY: Cornell UP, 2003.

Ireland, R.W. 'Theory and Practice within the Medieval English Prison.' *The American Journal of Legal History*. vol. 31, no. 1 (Jan. 1987): 56-67.

Ives, George. *A History of Penal Methods: Criminals, Witches, Lunatics.* Montclair, NJ: Patterson Smith, 1970.

Jacob, E. F. *Oxford Studies in Social and Legal History, Vol. VIII Studies in the Period of Baronial Reform and Rebellion*, ed. P. Vinogradoff. Oxford, UK: Clarendon Press, 1925.

James, N.D.G. *A History of English Forestry.* Oxford, UK: Basil Blackwell, 1981.

Jewell, H.M., *English Local Administration in the Middle Ages.* Newton Abbot, Devon, UK: David & Charles (pub.) Ltd., 1972.

John, E. 'Edward the Confessor and the Norman Succession.' *English Historical Review*, vol. 94, no. 371 (Apr., 1979): 241-267.

Johnson, E. 'The Process of Norman Exile into Southern Italy,' in *Exile in the Middle Ages: Selected Proceedings from the International Medieval Congress, University of Leeds, 8-11 July 2002*, eds Laura Napran and Elisabeth van Houts. Vol. 13, Turnhout, 2002: 29-38.

Jolliffe, J.E.A. *Angevin Kingship*. London, UK: A. and C. Black Ltd., 1955.

Jordan, W. C. 'A Fresh Look at Medieval Sanctuary,' in *Law and the Illicit in Medieval Europe*. eds, R. M. Karras, J. Kay, and E. A. Matter. Philadelphia, PA: University of Pennsylvania Press, 2008: 17-32.

Jurasinski, S. '*Reddatur Parentibus*: The Vengeance of the Family in Cnut's Homicide Legislation,' *Law and History Review*, vol. 20, no. 1 (Spring, 2002): 157-180.

Kantorowicz, E. H. *The King's Two Bodies: A Study in Mediaeval Political Theology*. Princeton, NJ: Princeton UP, 1957.

Kaeuper, R.W. 'Law and Order in Fourteenth-Century England: The Evidence of Special Commissions of Oyer and Terminer,' *Speculum*, vol. 54, no. 4 (Oct., 1979): 734-784.

-----. *War, Justice, and Public Order: England and France in the Later Middle Ages*. Oxford, UK: Clarendon Press, 1988.

Keen, M. H. *The Outlaws of Medieval Legend.* London, UK: Routledge and Kegan Paul, Ltd., 1987.

Keeton, G.W. *The Norman Conquest and The Common Law*. London, UK: Ernest Benn Ltd., 1966.

Kelly, A. *Eleanor of Aquitaine and the Four Kings*. Cambridge, MA: Harvard UP, 1959.

Kerr, M. H. 'Angevin Reform of the Appeal of Felony,' *Law and History Review*, vol. 13, no. 2 (Autumn, 1995): 351-391.

Kerr, M. H., Forsyth, R.D., and M.J. Plyley, 'Cold Water and Hot Iron: Trial by Ordeal in England,' *Journal of Interdisciplinary History*, vol. 22, no. 4 (Spring, 1992): 573-595.

Keynes, S. ''Crime and Punishment in the Reign of King Æthelred the Unready,' in *People and Places in Northern Europe, 500-1600. Essays in Honor of Peter Hayes Sawyer*, eds Ian Wood and Niels Lund. Woodbridge, Suffolk, UK: The Boydell Press, 1991.

King, E. B. and S. J. Ridyard, eds. *Law in Mediaeval Life and Thought*. Sewanee, TN: The Press of the University of the South, 1990.

Kirby, D. P. *The Earliest English Kings*. London, UK: Unwyn Hyman Ltd., 1991.

Koziol, G. *Begging pardon and favor: ritual and political order in early medieval France*. Ithaca, NY: Cornell UP, 1992.

Knowles. D. *The monastic order in England; a history of its development from the times of St. Dunstan to the Fourth Lateran council, 943-1216*. Cambridge, UK: Cambridge UP, 1940.

-----. *The Religious Houses of Medieval England*. London, UK: Sheed & Ward, 1940.

Kuttner, S. *The History of Ideas and Doctrines of Canon Law in the Middle Ages*. London, UK: Variorum Reprints, 1980.

Langbein, I.L. 'The Jury of Presentment and the Coroner.' *Columbia Law Review*, vol. 33, no. 8. (Dec., 1933): 1329-1365.

Langdon-Davies, J. *1066: a collection of contemporary documents*. London, UK: Cape, 1966.

Lawson, M. K. 'Archbishop Wulfstan and the Homiletic Element in the Laws of Æthelred and Cnut,' *The English Historical Review*, vol. 107, no. 424 (Jul., 1992): 565-586.

-----. *The Battle of Hastings 1066*. Stroud, UK: Tempus, 2002.

Lear, F.S. *Treason in Roman and Germanic Law, Collected Papers*. Austin, TX: University of Texas Press, 1965.

Le Patourel, J. 'The Norman Succession, 996-1135.' *English Historical Review*, vol. 86, no. 339 (April 1971), 225-250.

Lea, H.C. *A History of Auricular Confession*. 3 vols. Philadelphia, PA: Lea Brothers & Co., 1896.

Levy, N. 'Mense Process in Personal Actions at Common Law and the Power Doctrine.' *The Yale Law Journal* vol. 78, no. 1 (Nov., 1968): 52-98.

Lewis, A. 'Roger Leyburn and the pacification of England, 1265-7.' *The English Historical Review*. vol. 54, no. 214 (Apr. 1939): 193-214.

Logan, F.D. *Excommunication and the Secular Arm in Medieval England: A Study in Legal Procedure from the Thirteenth to the Sixteenth Century*. Toronto, Canada: Pontifical Institute of Mediaeval Studies, 1968.

Loyn, H. R. *The English Church, 940-1154*. London, UK: Pearson Education Ltd., 2000.

-----. *The Governance of Anglo-Saxon England, 500-1087*. London, UK: Edward Arnold Publishers, Ltd., 1984.

-----. *The Making of the English Nation: From the Anglo-Saxons to Edward I*. London, UK: Thames and Hudson Ltd., 1991.

Maddicott, J.R. 'Edward I and the Lessons of the Baronial Reform: Local Government, 1258-1280.' in *Thirteenth Century England I: Proceedings of the Newcastle Upon Tyne Conference*. 1985: 1-30.

-----. 'Magna Carta and the Local Community 1215-1259.' *Past and Present*. no. 102 (Feb., 1984): 25-65.

-----'The Mise of Lewes, 1264.' *The English Historical Review*. vol. 98, no. 388 (July, 1983): 588-603.

----- *Simon De Montfort*. Cambridge, UK: Cambridge UP, 1994.

Maitland, F.W. *The Constitutional History of England: a course of lectures delivered*. Cambridge, UK: Cambridge UP, 1908.

-----. 'Henry II and the Criminous Clerks.' *The English Historical Review*, vol. 7, no. 26 (April, 1892): 224-234.

-----. 'The 'Praerogativa Regis'.' *The English Historical Review*. vol. 6, no. 22 (April, 1891): 367-372.

-----. *Equity also, The forms of action at common law: two courses of lectures*, Edited by A. H. Chaytor and W. J. Whittaker. Cambridge, UK: Cambridge UP, 1910. Lectures 3, 4, 6.

Mansfield, M.C. *The Humiliation of Sinners: Public Penance in Thirteenth Century France*.
Ithaca and London: Cornell UP, 1996.

Matthew, D. *King Stephen*. London, UK: Hambledon and London, 2002.

Matthew, H.C.G. and B. Harrison, eds. *Oxford dictionary of national biography: in association with the British Academy : from the earliest times to the year 2000*. Oxford, UK: Oxford UP, 2004. http://www.oxforddnb.com/.

McKitterick, R. *The Frankish Kingdoms Under the Carolingians: 751-987*. London, UK: Longman Group Ltd., 1983.

Meekings, C.A.F. *Studies in 13th Century Justice and Administration*. London, UK: Hambledon Press, 1981.

Meens, R. 'Penitentials and the practice of penance in the tenth and eleventh centuries.' *Early Medieval Europe*. vol. 14, no. 1. (2006): 7-21.

Miller, W. I. 'In Defense of Revenge' in *Medieval Crime and Social Control*, eds. B.A. Hanawalt and D. Wallace. *Medieval Cultures* vol. 16. Minneapolis, MN: University of Minnesota Press, 1999: 70-89.

Miller, W. I. *Bloodtaking and Peacemaking: Feud, Law and Society in Saga Iceland.* Chicago, IL: University of Chicago Press, 1990.

Milsom, S.F.C. *Historical Foundations of the Common Law*. London, UK: Butterworths, 1969.

-----. *The Legal Framework of English Feudalism*. Cambridge, UK: Cambridge UP, 1976.

-----. 'Trespass from Henry III to Edward III, Part I: General Writs,' *Law Review Quarterly* vol. 74 (April 1958): 195-224.

-----. 'Trespass from Henry III to Edward III, Part II: Special Writs,' *Law Review Quarterly* vol. 74 (July 1958): 407-436

-----. 'Trespass from Henry III to Edward III, Part III: More Special Writs and Conclusions,' *Law Review Quarterly* vol. 74 (October 1958): 561-590

Morris, N. and D. J. Rothman, eds. *The Oxford History of the Prison*. Oxford, UK: Oxford UP, 1998.

Morris, W.A. *The Early English County Court: An Historical Treatise with Illustrative Documents*. University of California Publications in History. vol. 14, no. 2. Berkeley, CA: University of California Press, 1926: 89-230.

-----. *The Frankpledge System*. Cambridge, MA: Harvard UP, 1910.

-----. *The Medieval English Sheriff to 1300*. Manchester, UK: Manchester UP, 1968.

Mortimer, R. *Angevin England: 1154-1258*. Oxford, UK: Blackwell Publishers, 1994.

Musset, L. *The Bayeux Tapestry*. trans. Richard Rex. Woodbridge, Suffolk, UK: Boydell Press, 2005.

Musson, A. 'Sub-keepers and Constables: the Role of Local Officials in Keeping the Peace in Fourteenth Century England,' *English Historical Review* vol. 117, no. 1 (Feb. 2002): 1-24.

Napran, L. and E. van Houts, eds. *Exile in the Middle Ages: Selected Proceedings from the International Medieval Congress, University of Leeds, 8-11 July 2002*. Turnhout, UK: Brepolis, 2004.

Norwich, J. J. *The Normans in Sicily.* London: Penguin Books Ltd., 1992.

Oakley, T.P. *English Penitential Discipline and Anglo-Saxon Law in their Joint Influence.* 2nd edn. New York, NY: AMS Press, 1969.

O'Brien, B.R. *God's Peace and King's Peace: The Laws of Edward the Confessor*. Philadelphia, PA: University of Pennsylvania Press, 1999.

H.S. Offler, H.S., '*The Tractate de Iniusta Vexacione Villelmi Episcopi Primi.*' *The English Historical Review* vol. 66, no. 260 (July, 1951): 321-341.

Ohlgren, T.H., ed. *Medieval Outlaws: Ten Tales in Modern English.* Stroud, Gloucestershire, UK: Sutton Publishing, 1998.

Oliver, L. *The Beginnings of English Law.* Toronto, Canada: University of Toronto Press, 2002.

Painter, S. *William Marshall: Knight-Errant, Baron and Regent of England.* Baltimore, MD: The Johns Hopkins Press, 1933.

Palmer, P, ed. *Sources of Christian Theology, Vol. II: Sacraments and Forgiveness: History and Doctrinal Development of Penance, Extreme Unction and Indulgences*. Westminster, MD: The Newman Press, 1959.

Palmer, R. C. *The County Courts of Medieval England, 1150-1135*. Princeton, NJ: Princeton UP, 1982.

-----. 'The Origins of Property in England,' *Law and History Review*, vol. 3, no. 1 (Spring, 1985): 1-50.

Peters, E. 'Prison before the Prison' in *Oxford History of the Prison: the Practice of Punishment in Western Society*, eds N. Morris and D. J. Rothman. New York, NY: Oxford UP, 1995: 13-23.

Petit-Dutaillis, C. *Studies and notes supplementary to Stubbs' Constitutional history down to the Great charter*. trans. by W. E. Rhodes. vols 1-3. Manchester, UK: Manchester UP, 1908-1929.

Pluckett, Theodore F. T., *A Concise History of the Common Law*. 5th edn. Boston, MA: Little, Brown and Company, 1956.

-----. *Edward I and Criminal Law*. Cambridge, UK: Cambridge UP, 1960.

-----. *Legislation of Edward I*. Oxford, UK: Clarendon Press, 1962.

-----. *The Mediaeval Bailiff*. London, UK: The Athlone Press, 1954.

Pollock, F. and F.W. Maitland. *The History of English Laws Before the Time of Edward I*. vols. 1-2. 2nd edn. Washington, D.C.: Lawyers' Literary Club, 1959.

Poole, A.L. *From Domesday Book to Magna Carta, 1087-1216*. 2nd edn. Oxford, UK: Clarendon Press, 1964.

-----. 'Outlawry as a Punishment of Criminous Clerks.' In *Historical Essays in Honour of James Tait*. eds J.G. Edwards, V.H. Galbraith, and E.F. Jacob. Manchester, UK: Manchester UP, 1933: 239-246.

Poole, R. L. *The Exchequer in the Twelfth Century*. Oxford, UK: Clarendon Press, 1912.

Poschmann, B. *Penance and the Anointing of the Sick*. trans. F. Courtney. New York, NY: Herder and Herder, 1964.

Potts, C. *Monastic Revival and Regional Identity in Early Normandy*. Woodbridge, UK: The Boydell Press, 1997.

Powicke, F.M. *King Henry III and the Lord Edward: The Community of the Realm in the Thirteenth Century*. Oxford, UK: Clarendon Press, 1947.

-----. '*Per iudicium parium vel per legem terrae*.' In *Magna Carta Commemoration Essays*. ed. H.E. Malden. London, UK: Royal Historical Society, 1917: 96-121.

-----. *The Thirteenth Century: 1216-1307.* 2nd edn. Oxford, UK: Oxford University Press, 1991.

Prestwich, M. *Edward I.* London, UK: Methuen London Ltd., 1988.

-----. *The Three Edwards: War and State in England 1272-1377*, 2nd edn. London, UK and New York, NY: Routledge, 2003.

Pugh, R.B. 'Early Registers of English Outlaws.' *The American Journal of Legal History*. vol. 27, no. 4 (Oct., 1983): 319-329.

-----. *Imprisonment in Medieval England.* Cambridge, UK: Cambridge UP, 1968.

-----. 'The King's Prisons before 1250,' Transactions of the Royal Historical Society, 5th Series, vol. 5, (1955): 1-22.

Pulsiano, P. and K. Wolf, eds. *Medieval Scandinavia: An Encyclopedia.* New York, NY: Garland, 1993.

Putnam, B.H. 'Records of the Keepers of the Peace and Their Supervisors, 1307-27,' *English Historical Review*, vol. 45, no. 179 (Jul., 1930): 435-444.

-----. 'The Transformation of the Keepers of the Peace into the Justices of the Peace, 1327-1380,' *Transactions of the Royal Historical Society*, 4th Series, vol. 12 (1929): 19-48.

Reville, A. 'L'Abjuratio Regni, Histoire d'une Institution Anglaise.' In *Revue Historique*. ed. Felix Alcan. vol. 50, Septembre-Decembre 1982 (Paris, France: Ancienne Librairie Germer Balliere): 1-42.

Reynolds, S. *Fiefs and Vassals: The Medieval Evidence Reinterpreted.* Oxford: Clarendon Press, 1994.

-----. *Kingdoms and Communities in Western Europe, 900-1300.* New York, NY: Oxford UP, 1997.

Richardson, H.G. 'Glanville Continued.' *The Law Quarterly Review*. vol. 54 (1938): 381-395.

-----. ‘The Letters and Charters of Eleanor of Aquitaine,’ *The English Historical Review*, vol. 74, no. 291 (Apr., 1959): 193-213.

Richardson, H.G. and G.O. Sayles. *The Governance of Mediaeval England from the Conquest to the Magna Carta*. Edinburgh, UK: Edinburgh UP, 1963.

Ridgeway, H. ‘King Henry II and the ‘Aliens’, 1236-1272.’ *Thirteenth Century England II: Proceedings of the Newcastle Upon Tyne Conference* (1987): 81-92.

Robertson, L. ‘Exile in the Life and Correspondence of John of Salisbury, in *Exile in the Middle Ages*. eds L. Napran and E. van Houts. Turnhout, Belgium: Brepols Publishers, 2004: 181-197.

Round, J. H. *Geoffrey De Mandeville: A Study of the Anarchy*. New York, NY: Burt Franklin, 1892.

-----. ‘King John and Robert Fitzwalter.’ *The English Historical Review*. vol. 19, no. 76 (Oct. 1904): 707-711.

Russell, J. C. ‘Ranulf de Glanvill’ *Speculum* vol. 45, no. 1. (Jan., 1970): 69-79.

Sayles, G. O. *The Functions of Medieval Parliament in England.* London, UK: Hambledon Continuum, 1987.

Seal, G. *The Outlaw Legend: A Cultural Tradition in Britain, America and Australia*. Cambridge, UK: Cambridge UP, 1996.

Searle, E. *Predatory Kinship and the Creation of Norman Power, 840-1066*. Los Angeles and Berkeley, CA: University of California Press, 1988.

Seipp, D.J. ‘The Mirror of Justices,’ in *Learning the Law: Teaching and the Transmission of Law in England, 1150-1900*. eds J. Bush and A. Wijffels. Proceedings of the Thirteenth British Legal History Conference (1999): 85-112

Shaw, C. *Politics of Exile in Renaissance Italy*. Cambridge, UK: Cambridge UP, 2000.

Shirley, Kevin L. *The Secular Jurisdiction of Monasteries in Anglo-Norman and Angevin England.* Woodbridge, Suffolk, UK: The Boydell Press, 2004.

Shoemaker, K. *Sanctuary and Crime in the Middle Ages, 400-1500.* New York, NY: Fordham UP, 2010.

Shopkow, Leah. *History and Community: Norman Historical Writing in the Eleventh and Twelfth Centuries.* Washington, D.C.: The Catholic UP, 1997.

Slocombe, George E. *Sons of the Conqueror: Robert Curthose, William Rufus, Henry Beauclerc and the grandson, Stephen.* London, UK: Hutchinson & Co. Publishers Ltd., 1960.

Smail, D.L. 'Hatred as a Social Institution in Late-Medieval Society.' *Speculum.* vol. 76, no. 1 (Jan., 2001): 90-126.

Southern, R.W. *Medieval Humanism and Other Studies.* Oxford, UK: Basil Blackwell, 1970.

-----. *Saint Anselm: A Portrait in a Landscape.* Cambridge, UK: Cambridge UP, 1990.

-----. *St. Anselm and his Biographer: A Study of Monastic Life and Thought, 1059-c. 1130.* Cambridge, UK: Cambridge UP, 1963.

Spierenurg, P. *The Spectacle of Suffering: Executions and the evolution of repression: from a preindustrial metropolis to the European experience.* Cambridge, UK: Cambridge UP, 1984.

Starn, R. *Contrary Commonwealth: The Theme of Exile in Medieval and Renaissance Italy.* Berkeley and Los Angeles, CA: University of California Press, 1982.

Stenton, D.M. *English Justice between the Norman Conquest and the Great Charter: 1066-1215.* Philadelphia, PA: The American Philosophical Society, 1964.

-----. *English Society in the Early Middle Ages, 1066-1307.* 4th edn. Baltimore, MD: Penguin Publishing, 1965.

Stenton, F.M. *Anglo-Saxon England.* Oxford, UK: Clarendon Press, 1943.

-----. *The first century of English feudalism, 1066-1166.* Oxford, UK: Clarendon Press, 1961.

-----. *William the Conqueror and the rule of the Normans.* New York, NY: Barnes & Noble, 1966.

Strickland, M. *The Conduct and Perception of War in England and Normandy, 1066-1217.* Cambridge, UK: Cambridge UP, 1996.

-----. *War and Chivalry: The Conduct and Perception of War in England and Normandy, 1066-1217.* Cambridge, UK: Cambridge UP, 1994.

Stringer, K.J. *The Reign of Stephen: Kingship, Warfare and Government in Twelfth-Century England.* London, UK: Routledge, Inc., 1993.

Stone, E. L. G. 'The Folvilles of Ashby-Folville, Leicestershire, and Their Associates in Crime, 1326-1347,' *Transactions of the Royal Historical Society*, 5th Series, vol. 7 (1957): 117-136.

Stubbs, Wm. *The Constitutional History of England in its Origin and Development.* vols 1-3. 6th edn. Oxford, UK: Clarendon Press, 1903.

-----. *Historical Introduction to the Rolls Series.* ed. A. Hassall. New York, NY: AMS Press, 1971.

Summerson, H.R.T. Summerson, H.R.T. 'The criminal underworld of Medieval England,' *The Journal of Legal History*, vol. 17, no. 3 (1996): 197-224.

-----. 'The Early Development of *Peine Forte et Dure*,' *Law, Litigants, and the Legal Profession: Papers Presented to the Fourth British Legal History Conference at the University of Birmingham 10-13 July 1979.* eds E. W. Ives & A. H. Manchester. Royal Historical Society Studies in History series 36. (London, UK: Humanities Press, 1983): 116-125.

-----. 'The Structure of Law Enforcement in Thirteenth Century England,' *The American Journal of Legal History*, vol. 23, no. 4 (Oct., 1979): 313-327.

Sutherland, D.W. 'The Mense Process upon Personal Action in the Early Common Law,' *Law Quarterly Review,* vol. 82 (October, 1966): 482-496.

-----. *Quo Warranto Proceedings in the Reign of Edward I, 1278-1294*. Oxford, UK: Clarendon Press, 1963.

Symons, T. *The Monastic Agreement of the Monks and Nuns of the English Nation*. London, UK: Thomas Nelson and Sons, Ltd., 1953.

Thomas, H.M. *The English and the Normans: Ethnic Hostility, Assimilation, and Identity, 1066-c.1220*. Oxford, UK: Oxford UP, 2003.

Thompson, F. *The First Century of Magna Carta: Why It Persisted As a Document*. New York, NY: Russell & Russell, 1967.

Thorpe, L. *The Bayeux tapestry and the Norman invasion: with an introduction and a translation from the contemporary account of William of Poitiers*. London, UK: The Folio Society, 1973.

Tout, T.F. and J. Johnstone. *State Trials of the Reign of Edward the First, 1289-1293*. London, UK: Office of the Royal Historical Society, 1906.

Treharne, R. F. *The Baronial Plan of Reform, 1258-1263*. Manchester, UK: Manchester UP, 1971.

Trenholme, N. M. *The Right of Sanctuary in England: An Institutional History*. Columbia, MO: University of Missouri Press, 1903.

Turner, R.V. *The English Judiciary in the Age of Glanvill and Bracton, c. 1176-1239*. Cambridge, UK: Cambridge UP, 1985.

-----. *The King and His Courts: The Role of John and Henry III in the Administration of Justice, 1199-1240*. Ithaca, NY: Cornell UP, 1968.

-----. *King John*. London, UK: Longman Group UK, Ltd., 1994.

-----. *Judges, Administrators and the Common Law in Angevin England*. London, UK: The Hambledon Press, 1994.

-----. 'The Origins of Common Pleas and King's Bench.' *The American Journal of Legal History*. vol. 21, no. 3 (July, 1977): 238-254.

Van Caenegem, R.C. *The Birth of English Common Law*. Cambridge, UK: Cambridge UP, 1973.

-----. 'Public Prosecution of Crime in Twelfth-Century England.' *Church and Government in the Middle Ages: Essays Presented to C.R. Cheney on his 70th Birthday*. eds. C.N.L. Brooke et al. Cambridge, UK: Cambridge UP, 1976: 41-76.

Van Houts, E. ' L'Exile dans l'Espace Anglo-Normand,' in *La Normandie et l'Angleterre au Moyen Age, 4-7 Octobre 2001 Colloque Cerisy-la Salle*, ed. V. Gazeau. Turnhout, Belgium: Brepols, 2003.

-----. 'Historical Writing' in *A Companion to the Anglo-Norman World*, eds Christopher Harper-Bill and Elisabeth Van Houts. Woodbridge, Suffolk: The Boydell Press, 2003.

-----. 'The Vocabulary of Exile and Outlawry in the North Sea Area around the First Millenium,' in *Exile in the Middle Ages*, eds L. Napran and E. van Houts. Turnhout, Belgium: Brepols Publishers, 2004: 13-28.

Vaughn, S.N. *The Abbey of Bec and the Anglo-Norman State, 1034-1136*. Woodbridge, UK: The Boydell Press, 1981.

Verduyn, A. 'The Politics of Law and Order during the Early Years of Edward III,' *English Historical Review*, vol. 108, no. 429 (Oct., 1993): 842-867.

Vincent, N. *Peter des Roches: an alien in English politics, 1205-1238*. Cambridge, UK: Cambridge UP, 1996.

Vinogradoff, P. 'Magna Carta, c. 39.' In *Magna Carta Commemoration Essays*. ed. H.E. Malden. London, UK: Royal Historical Society, 1917: 78-95.

Vodola, Elisabeth. *Excommunication in the Middle Ages*. Berkeley, CA: University of California Press, 1986.

Vollmer, *The English Royal Forests: A Communication in Power and Politics*. Unpublished Ph.D. dissertation. University of California-Berkeley, 2005.

Von Bar, C. L. *History of Continental Criminal Law*, Continental Legal History Series, vols 1-6. Boston, MA: Little, Brown, and Co., 1916.

Warren, W.L. *The Governance of Norman and Angevin England, 1086-1272.* London, UK: Edward Arnold Publishers, Ltd., 1987.

-----. *Henry II.* London, UK: Eyre Methuen, 1973.

-----. *King John.* London, UK: Eyre Methuen Ltd., 1961.

Watkins, O.D. *A History of Penance.* vols 1-2 New York, NY: Burt Franklin, 1961.

Waugh, S. L. *England in the Reign of Edward III.* Cambridge, UK: Cambridge UP, 2001.

Webber, N. *The Evolution of the Norman Identity, 911-1154.* Woodbridge, UK: The Boydell Press, 2005.

Weir, A. *Eleanor of Aquitaine: A Life.* New York, NY: Ballantine Books, 1999.

West, F.J. *The Justiciarship in England, 1066-1232.* Cambridge, UK: Cambridge UP, 1966.

White, Graeme J. *Restoration and Reform, 1153-1165: Recovery from Civil War in England.* Cambridge, UK: Cambridge UP, 2000.

White, S. D. 'Kinship and Lordship in Early Medieval England: The Story of Sigeberht, Cynewulf, and Cyneheard,' *Traditio* vol. 50 (1989): 1-18.

Whitelock, D. 'Archbishop Wulfstan, Homilist and Statesman,' *Transactions of the Royal Historical Society*, 4th Series, vol. 24 (1942): 25-45.

-----. 'Wulfstan and the Laws of Cnut,' *The English Historical Review*, vol. 63, no. 249 (Oct., 1948): 433-452.

-----. 'Wulfstan's authorship of Cnut's laws,' *The English Historical Review*, vol. 70, no. 274 (Jan., 1955): 72-85.

Williams, A. *The English and the Norman Conquest.* Woodbridge, UK: The Boydell Press, 1995.

-----. *Æthelred the Unready: The Ill-Counselled King.* London, UK: Hambledon and London, 2003.

Wormald, P. '*Inter cetera bona genti suae*: Law-making and peace-keeping in the earliest English kingdoms,' in *La Giustizia nell'alto Medioevo* (Secoli V-Viii), 7-13 Aprile 1994, tomo secondo (Spoleto: Presso la sede del centro, 1995): 963-993.

-----. *Legal Culture in the Early Medieval West: Law as Text, Image and Experience*. London, UK: The Hambledon Press, 1999.

-----. *The Making of English Law: King Alfred to the Twelfth Century, Volume 1, Legislation and its Limits.* Oxford, UK: Blackwell Publishers Ltd., 1999.

Wright, E.C. 'Common Law in the Thirteenth-Century English Royal Forest.' *Speculum*. vol. 3, no. 2 (April, 1928): 166-191.

Yorke, B. *Wessex in the Early Middle Ages*. London, UK: Cassell Publishers Ltd., 1995.

Young, C.R. 'English Royal Forests under the Angevin Kings' in *The Journal of British Studies* vol. 12, no. 1 (Nov., 1972): 1-14.

-----. 'The Forest Eyre in England during the Thirteenth Century.' *The American Journal of Legal History*. vol. 18, no. 4 (Oct., 1974): 321-331.

-----. *The Royal Forests of Medieval England.* Philadelphia, PA: University of Pennsylvania Press, 1979.

www.ingramcontent.com/pod-product-compliance
Ingram Content Group UK Ltd.
Pitfield, Milton Keynes, MK11 3LW, UK
UKHW020216290926
15470UKWH00001B/228

9 781433 123573